THE ANATOMY OF THE
COMMODORE 64

Authors:
Michael Angerhausen
Dr. Achim Becker
Lothar Englisch
Klaus Gerits
Translated by:
Detlev Kesten
Edited by:
Jeff Hanson
Kirby Hanson
Arnie Lee

Abacus Software

P.O. BOX 7211 GRAND RAPIDS, MICH. 49510

Third English Printing, June 1984

ISBN 0-916439-00-3

PREFACE

The Commodore 64 is a super machine. That became clear to us after working with the machine for only a short time. But even with the best computer you can't do much if you don't know much about its functioning and handling.

The only area which disappointed us about the Commodore 64 was the documentation. The user's guide was a good starting point, but lacked the detail which we sought. Further literature was not available. Therefore we decided to write the book ourselves.

The result is in front of you. It does not claim to be complete, nor to have literary qualities, but this book contains the results of months of long and intensive work. We hope that it will help you to take advantage of the superb qualities of the COMMODORE 64.

TABLE OF CONTENTS

CHAPTER 0: INTRODUCTION

The Commodore 64 sets a new standard in terms of price and performance in pesonal computing. At the price of a home computer, the Commodore 64 is a professional quality computer. As the owner of a Commodore 64, you have several computers in one. Let's look at these -

THE LEARNING AND INTRODUCTORY COMPUTER

At its low price, the Commodore 64 is an affordable introductory level computer. Add a cassette drive and the Commodore 64 is a very capable computer system. Yet as the beginner increases his computer proficiency, the Commodore 64 has enough capabilities so as not to limit his growth.

Since the Commodore 64 uses the familiar BASIC language, the beginner should have an easy time learning to program. Commodore 64 BASIC is very compatible to the BASIC interpreters of other Commodore computers. Adapting BASIC programs for the Commodore 64 is straightforward.

Although The Anatomy of the Commodore 64 is not written for the beginner, the first chapters should provide satisfactory reading for most of you. For those of you who want to start at a more advanced level, start with Chapter 4 (SYNTHESIZER) and Chapter 5 (GRAPHICS). For you VIC-20 owners converting to the Commodore 64, Chapter 7 gives you information on this subject.

THE BUSINESS COMPUTER

The Commodore 64 offers such high price-performance that many businesses find it extremely attractive in the office or industry setting. Whether it is used for maintaining mailing lists or accounts receivable, drawing graphs or charts, performing word processing or playing the "what-if" games, it can be a very productive member of the business team.

Without having to spend thousand of dollars, a business can sample the automated computer world with an inexpensive Commodore 64. We find that many Commodore 64 "home" computers are really being used for business purposes.

THE DEVELOPMENT COMPUTER

The advanced programmer will appreciate the large memory bank of the Commodore 64. With 64K RAM and 20K ROM, the Commodore 64 offers sufficient memory, even for the most sophisticated programs. The memory layout of the Commodore 64 is described in chapter 3.

This memory coupled with many of the advanced capabilities can be used to full advantage from machine language programs. In order to encourage BASIC programmers to use machine language programming, we present an introduction to machine and assembler language programming in Chapter 1. Machine language or assembler language programming can enhance working in BASIC and make you more aware of the Commodore 64's potential.

In chapter 6 we describe how to add new commands to the BASIC interpreter. After experimenting, you should be able to create your own new commands, similar to ones in our example program. An important help is the extensively documented ROM listing of Commodore BASIC and the operating system which is in APPENDIX A.

THE GRAPHICS COMPUTER

With many other computers you have to buy expensive hardware additions to create graphics. But the Commodore 64 offers these features as standard. The Commodore 64 gets its high resolution color graphics capabilities from a totally new computer chip whose qualities and capabilities we describe in Chapter 5.

We also describe the magic-like SPRITES. These super-large, user definable graphics symbols enable arcade and educational animation that, in the past, were possible only with a great amount of sophisticated programming.

THE SYNTHESIZER

There's music in the Commodore 64!

The Commodore 64 uses a high quality synthesizer which rivals some dedicated music machines. Here again, the reason for these capabilities is a newly developed integrated circuit whose capabilities and possibilities we examine closely for you.

All that's really missing is a piano keyboard to make a home organ out of the Commodore 64. With appropriate programming, this organ could outperform bigger and much more expensive ones. Some keyboards are beginning to appear on the market now.
Another interesting possibility is connecting the Commodore 64 to a stereo system. Music lovers will be delighted with the results. Their ears will be pleasantly surprised.

THE CONTROL COMPUTER

The Commodore 64 can be used for various kinds of control purposes provided it is appropriately interfaced. The electronic hobbyist and the industrial user can achieve an unusual amount of computer performance for their money. They will soon find a lot of areas where the Commodore 64 can be used. One of the areas described in this book is the use of the paddle port as an A/D converter. Further hints are given in the description of the input/output control, found in Chapter 8.

YOUR OWN COMPUTER

Whether you bought the Commodore 64 for composing music, maintaining a mailing list or learning how to program, The Anatomy of the Commodore 64 will help you as you encounter Commodore 64's fantastic capabilities.

You will find a range of applications for your computer which you never thought were possible.

CHAPTER 1: MACHINE LANGUAGE PROGRAMMING ON THE COMMODORE 64

1.1 Introductory Concepts

The main programming language of the Commodore 64 is BASIC. It's a language that is "spoken" by many computers and with which the user can solve most all of his problems. The BASIC language was originally developed for the beginner. In the course of time it became more and more common, and now it is being used on almost all microcomputers.

Today, most computer companies offer a version of BASIC written by the Microsoft Corporation. Since Microsoft BASIC is similar for most computers, it is not very difficult to rewrite programs for the Commodore 64.

Actually, the BASIC language is not directly understood by the computer. Though you write programs in BASIC, the computer must first interpret the BASIC language statements. The computer creates shorthand commands from the commands that we enter at the keyboard and converts them into machine language that the 6510 processor of the Commodore 64 understands.

Why not write all your programs in machine language? Quite simple. Programming in machine language is time-consuming and error prone, especially for the beginner. Most BASIC statements are equivalent to dozens of machine language instructions. Therefore machine language programs are more lengthy than an equivalent program written in BASIC. Here's a small example:

The 6510 CPU chip in the Commodore 64 can add numbers within the range of 0 thru 255. To add numbers outside of this range, then you must perform multiple additions. In BASIC you might program like this:

```
        PRINT 6 + 5
```

The whole operation can be entered as a single line.

In machine language you would do the following:

```
        CLC             ;clear carry flag
        LDA  #$06       ;load accumulator with 6
        ADC  #$05       ;add 5 to accumulator
        JSR  OUTPUT     ;print result
         .    .
         .    .         ;here are further commands
         .    .
OUTPUT  PHA             ;save the accumulator
        LSR  A          ;shift bits 7 thru 4
        LSR  A          ;  to bits 3 thru 0
        LSR  A          ;unoccupied bits become 0
```

```
        LSR  A
        JSR  HEXASC     ;transform numbers into characters
        PLA             ;get accumulator from stack
        AND  #$OF       ;mask bits 7 thru 4
HEXASC  CLC             ;clear carry flag
        ADC  #$F6       ;add 246
        BCC  $04        ;result <=255? yes-skip
        ADC  #$06       ;add 6 decimal
        ADC  #$3A       ;add 58 decimal
        JMP  $FFD2      ;output character
```

So the same process of adding to number and displaying the results requires more programming when written in machine language.

How does the computer understand these instructions.

You probably know that there are two electrical conditions in the field of electronics: **POWER ON** and **POWER OFF.**

We also find these conditions in computer technology. The smallest information unit in data processing is called a BIT (binary digit). Based on this idea, the binary number system was developed. The binary number system includes only two (binary) numbers: the 1 and the 0 (where 1 stands for POWER ON and 0 for POWER OFF). By combining strings of 1's and 0's you can create larger numbers.

The 6510 processor contained in the Commodore 64 works with groups of 8-bit at a time. Within a byte, each bit position has a corresponding decimal value. These values are:

bit position	b7	b6	b5	b4	b3	b2	b1	b0
corresponding value	128	64	32	16	8	4	2	1

Each bit position has a fixed value. Its value can be easily calculated by raising 2 to the power identical is position number:

```
The value of  b7 = 2**7 = 128
              b6 = 2**6 =  64
              b5 = 2**5 =  32
              b4 = 2**4 =  16
              b3 = 2**3 =   8
              b2 = 2**2 =   4
              b1 = 2**1 =   2
              b0 = 2**0 =   1
```

(2**x is pronounced as 2 to the x power)

Using this scheme, numbers up to 255 can be represented. For example, the number 14 is represented as 0001110 and is equivalent to 0*128 + 0*64 + 0*32 + 0*16 + 1*8 + 1*4 + 1*2 + 0*1. The number 117 is represented as 01110101 and is equivalent to 0*128 + 1*64 +1*32 + 1*16 +0*8 + 1*4 + 0*2 + 1*1.

The electronic circuitry of the 6510 processor is set to perform certain operation such as addition, subtraction, logical testing or branching in response to certain bit patterns. A set of bit patterns, carefully arranged to perform a desired set of operations is called a program. It is these programs which make the computer appear to understand.

So binary number system is fundamental to understanding machine language. If you are not yet acquainted with this system, we would recommend one of the books from our bibliography.

After this short introduction to the binary number system, we move onto actual machine language programming.

Comparing BASIC and machine language, you should recognize that using machine language requires a different approach than regular BASIC programming. It is certainly not easy for the beginner to understand this new kind of programming. But if you want to master the computer you need to deal with machine language.

For example, if you want to write a fast sort or search routine, you cannot do this with BASIC. For those who want to understand the operating system or to explore the underpinnings of BASIC, there is no other choice than using machine language.

If you find that this chapter is too difficult for you to understand, don't hesitate to skip it for now. Later you can come back to these chapters to review the material. We have tried to design all chapters, even those that deal with machine language and assembler language programming, in a way so that even beginners can understand them. Many things will become clearer after you read them; others may still be confusing. For those want who to know more things about machine and assembler language programming, consult the bibliography.

1.2 The MONITOR - and its uses

In order to program in machine language you need a **MONITOR.** A monitor is a program that allows you to inspect and change the computer's memory and registers. Additionally you can save and load programs with the monitor. Some monitors allow you to disassemble memory (display the machine mnemonics from raw code) and lets you test and correct machine language programs.

Here we show you how to work with a monitor. The commands illustrated are for the SUPERMON monitor included with the ASSEMBLER/MONITOR package from ABACUS Software. But most of these commands are identical to the commands used by other monitors.

After SUPERMON is loaded from diskette, you begin the monitor by typing **RUN**. The monitor identifies itself by printing **C*** and the contents of the 6510 registers on the screen.

The registers are special memory locations contained in the 6510 processor that allow a computer to perform arithmetic and logical operations, keep track of program locations, etc.

The purpose of the individual registers are:

Program counter: PC - keeps track of the address within the program that is to be processed next.

Interrupt vector: IRQ - is the address of the routine that gains control when a program interrupt occurs.

Status register: SR - contains indicators of conditions that have occured as the result of arithmetic or logical processing.

Accumulator: AC - contains the results of arithmetic or logical operations; used to transfer data during input or output operations.

The x-register: XR - index register used for differing ways to access memory

The y-register: YR - index register used for differing ways to access memory

The stack pointer: SP - contains the pointer to the top of the stack (work memory)

After **RUN**ning the monitor, the screen display looks like this:

```
C*
     PC   SR AC XR YR SP
  .; E145 31 40 E6 00 F6
```

All data is displayed or entered into the monitor in hexadecimal number format. For those of you unfamiliar with hexadecimal notation, see APPENDIX B.

If you want to change the contents of any of the registers,

position the cursor over the appropriate "old value", type in the "new value" and press the RETURN key.

The contents of memory can also be displayed and changed. To display the contents of a certain memory range, enter the command:

M XXXX YYYY <RETURN>

where M stands for MEMORY, XXXX for the 4-digit starting address and YYYY the 4-digit ending address.

Both addresses are entered as hexadecimal numbers. The contents of the memory locations XXXX thru YYYY are displayed. If the given memory range doesn't fit completely on the screen, the screen scrolls upward line by line. By pressing the STOP key, you get back in the command line.

As with the changing of the register contents, you can change individual memory locations. Simply place the cursor over the corresponding "old value", enter the desired "new value" and press the RETURN key.

To enter a machine language program into memory use the M command to display the contents of a particular area in memory. Then position the cursor over the area of memory to be overlayed with the desired machine langauge instructions in their hexadecimal equivalents.

The following is a display of a particular memory range:

```
.M C000 C010 <RETURN>
.: C000  A9 10 8D 16 03 A9 C0 8D
.: C008  17 03 A9 43 85 97 D0 16
.: C010  A9 42 85 97 D8 4A 68 8D
```

Memory can be displayed in another way by disassembling. Disassembling attempts to convert the hexadecimal contents of memory into the more easily understandable machine language instructions called mnemonics. Each 6510 machine language instruction is represented as a specific hexadecimal value. Disassembling converts these hexadecimal values into the corresponding mnemonics.

You can disassemble the contents of the above memory range by entering the command:

```
.D C000 C019 <RETURN>
```

When the above area of memory is disassembled it would look like this:

```
C000:  A9 10      LDA #$10
```

```
C002:  8D 16 03   STA $0316
C005:  A9 C0      LDA #$C0
C007:  8D 17 03   STA $0317
C00A:  A9 43      LDA #$43
C00C:  85 97      STA $97
C00E:  D0 16      BNE $C026
C010:  A9 42      LDA #$42
C012:  85 97      STA $97
C014:  D8         CLD
C015:  4A         LSR A
C016:  68         PLA
C017:  8D 18 03   STA $0318
```

Using the above as an example, the hexadecimal value A9 stands for the mnemonic instruction **L**oa**D** Accumulator and the value 8D stands for the mnemonic instruction **ST**ore **A**ccumulator.

The next step after entering or changing a program in memory is program testing. You test you program by given the monitor this command:

.G **XXXX** <RETURN>

Here G stands for GOTO and XXXX for the 4-digit hexadecimal starting address of the routine to be tested.

This command causes the monitor to jump to address XXXX and begin executing the the machine program that's written there. XXXX is any address within the Commodore 64's memory range.

If the machine language program contains a BRK (BREAK) instruction (hexadecimal value 00), the monitor stops, identifies itself with B* and displays the register contents.

Here the program counter PC contains the address after the BRK command. By inserting BRK instructions at various memory location of a machine language program, it is possible to test this program quickly and easily. After testing the program, you can replace the unneeded BRK instruction with the original instruction contained at that memory location.

You can also save or load machine langauge program to or from cassette or diskette.

To save a machine program on cassette or diskette, enter:

.S "NAME",XX,YYYY,ZZZZ <RETURN>

S indicates SAVE. For "NAME", you can enter any name for the program (the quotation marks are a must). XX is a two-digit device address (01-cassette, 08-diskette), YYYY is the starting address and ZZZZ the ending address of the program which must be hexadecimal.

After pressing the RETURN key, the machine language program starting at address YYYY and ending at address ZZZZ is saved on the selected device.

To LOAD program from cassette or diskette enter:

.L "NAME",XX <RETURN>

Here L means LOAD and XX the device address discussed above. The address of the program is not needed. The program is loaded into the area of memory from which it was originally saved.

When you are finished using the monitor you can exit to the BASIC interpreted by entering **X**.

A monitor is an invaluable aid to the machine langauge programmer. If you are going to do any significant amount of machine language or assembler language programming, you should become very familiar with the monitor.

1.3 How To Go About Programming in Machine Language

If you are familiar with the monitor to some degree, you can now start with the actual programming.

Programming can be divided into 5 parts:

1. Firstly you must clearly spell out exactly what the program is to accomplish. You must decide on an approach to take in building that program. Unfortunately this step is often given too little thought. The programmer is too anxious to get to the programming step that the program suffers. The author hasn't clearly thought out the method. This step is vital regardless of the programming langauge used. It must be addressed for a program written in BASIC or a machine language or assembly language program.

   For example, suppose you decide that you need to compute the logarithm in base 10 of various numbers. You could approach this program in several ways: a) creating a table of logarithms and looking them up as needed; b) finding the logarithm from scratch by using a complex series of formulas; c) using a derivative of a builtin function. By using one of the builtin functions of the Commodore 64, you can create a very simple solution. This eliminates the need for a complex program, thereby simplifying the overall task to be done, namely to compute the common logarithm for a given argument.

2. Secondly you have to decide where in memory to place the machine language program. Most machine language programs run alongside a BASIC program. So you must make sure that the machine language program is protected from accident destruction by BASIC .

   The simplest way is to tell BASIC that it has only a certain amount of memory at its disposal. Thus BASIC can run concurrent with the machine language program, but will not overwrite the machine langauge program.

   Another possibility is to place the machine program into memory where it can't be reached by BASIC. With the Commodore 64 this is no problem. Of the 64K RAM that Commodore 64 has, BASIC can address only 39K, while machine language has 52K at its disposal.

3. Thirdly you have to write the program itself. We recommend using an assembler Without using an assembler you will have to hand-assemble the assembler language source statements. We'll leave it to you to find a way of generating the resulting machine language code. We advise you to keep your routines as short as possible if you must resort to hand assembly techniques. Also take advantage of the builtin routines that are described elsewhere in this manual. They will save you much time and effort.

4. Forthly you have to decide how you will place the resultant machine language program into memory. One way is to POKE the resultant program into memory from a BASIC program. An alternative way is to use a machine language monitor as previously described. An assembler program lets you assemble code directly into the computers memory.

5. Lastly you have to decide how you will test your new program. It isn't too often that we write a program which runs correctly the first time that we try it. Once again, the machine language monitor offers some help in testing these programs. By inserting the BRK instructions into the program to be tested, you can cause the program to temporarily halt execution. At this time you may examine the contents of memory and registers and alter them if you desire. Then you can continue the execution of the program from this breakpoint. If you don't use a monitor, then you will have to test blindly. A single bad instruction in the program could hang up

the Commodore 64 forcing you to turn it off and back on to recover from the error.

By following these five steps, you are creating a careful plan and not a haphazard attempt at your problem solving. Use good programming sytle right from the start!

The following is an example planned program development.

First we state the objective of our program: To type a line of text in at the keyboard and then redisplay all of the text up to the <RETURN> key.

To simplify the program, we will use some builtin routines thar are part of the Commodore 64 ROMs.

Next we have to decide where this program is to be placed in memory.

One place for a machine program with a maximum length of 4K is a block of 4K RAM in the upper part of memory ($C000 upwards). In that location, the program can't be destroyed by BASIC.

Alternatively you locate a machine language program in memory that BASIC can access if you first protect this area. From BASIC this is done as follows:

```
POKE 55,XXX
POKE 56,YYY
CLR
```

where XXX and YYY are decimal numbers between 0 and 255. POKE 55,XXX sets the least significant byte and 56,YYY the most significant byte (b4,b5,b6,b7) of the new "memory limit".

When the Commodore 64 is first turned on, memory location 55 contains the value 0 and memory location 56 the value 160. Memory location 55 holds the least significant byte and memory location 56 the most significant byte of the memory limit of BASIC. If you convert these numbers into hexadecimal, you find the value $A000. This is the normal ending address of BASIC. By poking a different value into these two locations, you can make BASIC think that it has less memory to work with. For example, you can POKE 55,0: POKE 56,144 to set the new memory limit to $9000. BASIC will think that the top of its memory is $9000.

Let's say that we want our program to begin starting at address 49152 ($C000) in a place inaccessible to BASIC. The program will then look like this:

```
ADDR VALUE    LABEL  OPC OPERAND   REMARKS
0000                 ORG $C000
C000          BASIC  EQU $A474
C000          CLRSCR EQU $E544
C000          GET    EQU $FFE4
C000          STROUT EQU $AB1E
C000 20 44 E5 START  JSR CLRSCR    ;CLEAR SCREEN
C003 A2 00           LDX #$00      ;ZERO LENGTH
C005 8E 2F C0        STX SAVEX     ;SAVE IT
C008 20 E4 FF LOOP   JSR GET       ;READ KEYBOARD
C00B C9 00           CMP #$00      ;KEY PRESSED?
C00D F0 F9           BEQ LOOP      ;NO-BACK!
C00F AE 2F C0        LDX SAVEX     ;YES-RESTORE LENGTH
C012 C9 0D           CMP #$0D      ;RETURN KEY?
C014 F0 0A           BEQ OUT       ;YES OUTPUT!
C016 9D 30 C0        STA BUFF,X    ;NO-SAVE CHARACTER
C019 E8              INX           ;LENGTH TEXT +1
C01A 8E 2F C0        STX SAVEX     ;SAVE LENGTH
C01D 4C 08 C0        JMP LOOP      ;READ AGAIN
C020 A9 00    OUT    LDA #$00      ;PLACE $00 AT END
C022 9D 30 C0        STA BUFF,X    ;     OF TEXT
C025 A9 30           LDA #<BUFF    ;LSB OF TEXT START
C027 A0 C0           LDY #>BUFF    ;MSB OF TEXT START
C029 20 1E AB        JSR STROUT    ;PRINT STRING
C02C 4C 74 A4        JMP BASIC     ;RETURN TO BASIC
C02F 00       SAVEX  BYT 0         ;X-REG SAVE
C030 00       BUFF   DST 80        ;RESERVE 80-BYTES
```

The memory excerpt with the monitor looks like this:

```
>M C000 C028
>: C000 20 44 E5 A2 00 8E 2F C0
>: C008 20 E4 FF C9 00 F0 F9 AE
>: C010 2F C0 C9 0D F0 0A 9D 30
>: C018 C0 E8 8E 2F C0 4C 08 C0
>: C020 A9 00 9D 30 C0 A9 30 A0
.: C028 C0 20 1E AB 5C 74 A4 00
```

Our program is 48 bytes long. It uses only a few instructions of the total 6510 instructions available.

The program is being started from BASIC with the command:

SYS 49152

The purpose of this SYS command is to call a machine language program that begins at memory location 49152 ($C000). If the machine language program has errors in it, your computer program may "crash" and become inoperable. In this case, you have no alternative but to turn the computer off, and then back on again.

By the way, you can also use the SYS command to call routines in operating system (see Chapter 1.4). By using the builtin routines, you can save a lot of time and effort in your programming.

Now experiment with your own programs.

1.4 Useful addresses of the COMMODORE 64 ROMS

If you write your own programs in machine language, you can save a lot of time by taking advantage of the ROM routines that are built into the Commodore 64. Especially useful are the routines for accessing the peripheral devices such as the printer or floppy disk.

The most important routines of the Commodore 64 are summarized in a **jump table** located at the end of memory. This jump table contains the memory locations of commonly used routines of the operating system and is also called the KERNAL. Commodore has promised not to change these addresses as new Commodore computers appear on the market. Therefore it should be possible to transfer program to newer Commodore computers as they are introduced if these Kernal routines are used. The jump table of the Commodore 64 is for the most part identical with the VIC 20, so it is easy to convert VIC 20 programs to work with the Commodore 64 with the help of these routines.

Now we take a closer look at some of these routines:

ADDRESS	FUNCTION
$FF90	controls the output of kernal messages if bit 6 is set - control messages from kernal are displayed. if bit 7 is set - error messages from kernal are displayed.
$FF93	sends secondary address over the serial bus after LISTEN command
$FF96	sends secondary address over the serial bus after TALK command
$FF99	if carry flag set - returns the highest RAM address to X and Y registers; if carry flag is reset - sets the highest RAM address to that contained in X and Y registers;
$FF9C	if carry flag is set - returns the lowest RAM address to X and Y registers;

if carry flag is reset - sets the lowest RAM address to that contained in X and Y registers;

$FF9F	SCAN keyboard for pressed keys
$FFA2	sets the time-out flag for the serial bus
$FFA5	transfers data from the serial bus to the accumulator
$FFA8	transfers data from the accumulator to the serial bus
$FFAB	sends UNTALK command to the serial bus
$FFAE	sends UNLISTEN command to the serial bus
$FFB1	sends LISTEN command to the serial bus
$FFB4	sends TALK command to the serial bus
$FFB7	returns the I/O status word to the accumulator
$FFBA	sets the file parameters: accumulator = logical file number; X-reg = device number, Y-reg = secondary address
$FFBD	sets parameter for filename, accumulator = length of name, X-reg and Y-reg = address of the filename
$FFC0	OPEN logical file
$FFC3	CLOSE logical file, accumulator = logical file number
$FFC6	CHKIN prepares a logical file for input. The logical file has to first be OPENed.
$FFC9	CHKOUT prepares a logical file for ouput. The logical file has to first be OPENed
$FFCC	CLRCH resets input/output to the default devices (keyboard/screen).
$FFCF	BASIN transfers a character from input device to the accumulator.
$FFD2	BSOUT transfers a character from the accumulator to the output device.
$FFD5	LOAD program into memory
$FFD8	SAVE programs from memory

$FFDB	resets the system clock. A,X and Y registers contain the number of jiffies.
$FFDE	reads the system clock into A,X and Y registers.
$FFE1	checks to see if STOP key is depressed
$FFE4	GET, gets a character into the accumulator
$FFE7	CLALL closes all open files
$FFEA	updates the system clock
$FFED	returns the number of columns/rows on the screen in X and Y registers
$FFF0	if carry flag is set - returns cursor position in Y-reg (# of columns) and X-reg (# of rows) if carry flag is reset - sets cursor position to row in X-reg and column in Y-reg.
$FFF3	returns the starting address of the I/O component

There are other routines available for manipulating the screen.The more important routines are listed below:

ADDRESS	FUNCTION
$E518	completly reset the screen and the keyboard
$E544	CLR - clear the screen
$E566	HOME - position the cursor to the upper left corner of the screen
$E56C	calculates the cursor position and places its address at $D1-D2 (209-210 decimal).
$E5A0	loads the video controller with the standard values
$E5B4	gets a character from of the 10-byte keyboard buffer
$E5CA	waits for keyboard input
$E8EA	scrolls screen up one line
$E9FF	blank one screen line designed by X-reg.
$EA1C	sets a character in color on the screen at current cursor position (screen code in the accumulator and color in X-reg)

1.5 DATA INPUT/OUTPUT FROM MACHINE LANGUAGE PROGRAMS

There are two ways to perform data input or output from machine language programs on your Commodore 64. You can write the routines yourself or you can use the routines that are part of the builtin operating system.

This section describes how you can use the routines that are part of the operating system. The biggest advantage of using these builtin ROM routines is that they are already written and are proven to work correctly.

1.5.1 Input and Output of Single Characters

The two basic routines for inputting or outputting data are called:

BASIN which is located at $FFCF and inputs a character
and
BSOUT which is located at $FFD2 and outputs a character

The bytes to be input or output are transferred via the accumulator.

Example: Output 12-byte string of text to the screen.

```
OUTPUT    LDX    #0             ;zero index register
L1        LDA    TEXT,X         ;get one character text
          JSR    BSOUT          ;and display it on screen
          INX                   ;point to next character
          CPX    #12            ;all characters yet?
          BNE    L1             ;no-keep going
          RTS                   ;yes-we're done
TEXT      ASC 'EXAMPLE TEXT'
```

Input is performed similarly. For instance, if text is to be entered from the keyboard , the cursor flashes and each character is accepted until the RETURN key is pressed.

```
INPUT     LDX    #0             ;zero index register
L1        JSR    BASIN          ;get a character from keyboard
          STA    TEXT,X         ;and save it
          INX                   ;point to next character
          CMP    #13            ;RETURN key pressed?
          BNE    L1             ;no, get more characters
          RTS                   ;yes-we're done
TEXT      DST    80             ;space for saving the text
```

When writing onto the screen, you can take full advantage of the screen control characters. For instance, you can use the control character for clearing the screen or changing the character colors. The appropriate control code is loaded into the accumulator and sent to the output routine (BSOUT).

Example: clear screen

```
        LDA   #147          ;code for clearing the screen
        JSR   BSOUT         ;output
```

For the screen output there are some additional, helpful routines which can simplify your programming. The routine for clearing the screen can be called directly -

```
      JSR   CLRSCR          ;located at $E544
```

A routine for homing the cursor is:

```
      JSR   HOME            ;located at $E566
```

If you want to place the cursor at a specific screen position:

```
      LDX   #LINE         ;line number, 0 to 24
      LDY   #COL          ;column number, 0 to 39
      CLC                 ;set carry clear = cursor
      JSR   CURSOR        ;position cursor $FFF0
      LDA   #'A           ;character to be output
      JSR   BSOUT         ;output
```

The routine called CURSOR has two functions. When called with carry flag clear (as in the above example), it positions the cursor at the line and the column that are in the X and the Y register. If CURSOR is called with the carry flag set, the current cursor position is returned to you in the X and Y registers.

Once again here are the addresses of the routines used above:

```
      BASIN     $FFCF
      BASOUT    $FFD2
      CLRSCR    $E544
      CURSOR    $FFF0
      HOME      $E566
```

1.5.2 Input and Output Using Peripheral Devices

For input and output using peripheral devices the operating system contains the necessary routines.

The peripheral are assigned a device number from 0 to 15.

NUMBER	DEVICE
0	keyboard
1	datasette
2	RS 232 interface
3	screen
4-15	devices of the serial bus

In addition to this device number, there may be a secondary address which further specifies information required by the peripheral device and a file name. To establish a connection to the peripheral, you must OPEN a file.

The OPEN command specifies a logical file number, a device number and the optional secondary address. So as to avoid specifying the peripheral device number each time you want to transfer information, only the logical file number is used after the OPEN is complete. The logical file number then refers to the device number and secondary address with which it was OPENed.

Again, before any transfer of information can happen to or from peripheral devices, a file must be OPENed. You can OPEN a file from BASIC or from a machine language program.

To OPEN a file from a machine language program you must first set the file parameters. You must place the logical file number in memory location $B8 (184); the device number in $BA (186), secondary address in $B9 (185); length of file name in $B7 (183) (zero if no file name is given); and the address of the file name in $BB/$BC (187/188). Then the you may call the routine to OPEN a file at $FFC0.

The kernal contains several routines to set the file parameters. The routine SETLFS ($FFBA) sets the logical file number, device number and secondary address. The routine SETNAM ($FFBD) sets the filename for OPEN, LOAD and SAVE routines. The following example illustrates the use of these routines:

```
          LDA  #1      ;logical file number in accumulator
          LDX  #8      ;device number in X-register
          LDY  #4      ;secondary address in Y-register
          JSR  SETLFS  ;located at $FFBA
          LDA  #LNAME  ;length of filename
          LDX  #<NAME  ;low order address of filename
          LDY  #>NAME  ;high order address of filename
          JSR  SETNAM  ;located at $FFBD
          JSR  OPEN    ;located at $FFC0
           .
           .
NAME      ASC  'FILE1' ;this is the filename
LNAME     BYT  5       ;this is the length of filename
```

Before writing output to an OPEN file you must: call the routine CHKOUT ($FFC9) in order to ready the output path to the peripheral associated with the logical file number; place the data to be transferred into the accumulator; and call BSOUT ($FFD2) to output the data.

Here's a short program that does this:

```
        LDX  #LF         ;logical file number
        JSR  CHKOUT      ;$FFC9
        LDA  DATA        ;place data into accumulator
        JSR  BSOUT       ;write data to output file
```

All output is directed to this device until the routine CLRCH is called. CLRCH reset the standard ouput to the screen, so that subsequent calls to BSOUT results in the data being sent to the screen.

```
        JSR  CLRCH       ;$FFCC reset output to screen
```

If you want to input data from a file: call the routine CHKIN ($FFC6) in order to ready the input path to the peripheral associated with the logical file number; and call BASIN ($FFCF) to input the data. BASIN will return the data in the accumulator.

```
        LDX    #LF       ;file number of the input device
        JSR    CHKIN     ;located at $FFC6
        JSR    BASIN     ;located at $FFCF
        STA    DATA      ;save the data
```

All data is input from this device until the routine CLRCH is called. CLRCH reset the standard input to the keyboard, so that subsequent calls to BASIN results in data being input from the keyboard.

When CLRCH is called, all files remain open. CLRCH merely redirects input and output to or from the standard devices of the Commodore 64 (keyboard and screen respectively).

When you are finished using an input or output file, you must close each using the routine CLOSE ($FFC3).

```
        LDX   #LF      ;logical file number
        JSR   CLOSE    ;located at $FFC3
```

The alternative is to close all of the files by using the routine CLALL ($FFE7).

```
        JSR  CLALL     ;close all open files
```

1.5.3 Saving and Loading Data

For saving data and programs, the Commodore 64 offers you both tape and disk for secondary storage. Since both devices operate quite differently they are described separately.

1.5.3.1 Saving Data on Cassette

A cassette recorder allows sequential recording of data and reading it in that same order. You must read through all the data on a tape until you encounter the desired data. Likewise, you cannot change data written to a tape. You can only read the file completely through, change it in the computer's memory, and then rewrite the entire file onto the tape.

Since saving or loading programs requires only sequential writing or reading, a cassette recorder is a suitable medium for program storage. The major disadvantage or cassette is the slow speed of data transfer.

For reliability, data is written to the tape redundantly. Later, if errors are detected when reading the tape, the redundant data can be used to correct the errors.

Let's take a closer look at the technique of writing data to tape.

A file is written to tape in three parts. First a synchronizing sound is written to the tape. The enables the Commodore 64 to prepare itself for subsequent data transfer. Next a header is written to the tape. The header contains identifying information about the file that follows. Finally the data is written to the tape. This data is written redundantly.

Since various forms of data can be saved to tape, there must be a way to distinguish them from one another. This is the purpose of the header. The header contains the following information:

position within header	Value
1	type of header value: meaning: 1 BASIC program - it is loaded starting at the BASIC address 2 data block - bytes 2-192 contain the data 3 machine language program loaded at absolute addr 4 data header-data follows

	5	end-of-tape block - denotes end of tape
2-3		staring address (low,high)
4-5		ending address (low,high)
6-21		file name

For header types 1 (BASIC program) or 3 (machine language program), the header specifies the starting and ending addresses of the program and the program name. The program itself is contained in the next block. It is recorded redundantly (twice).

For header type 1, the starting address specified in the header is ignored, and the BASIC program contained on the tape is loaded beginning at the starting address of BASIC (normally $800). By using a secondary address of 1 during loading, you can override the starting address of BASIC and force the program to be loaded at the starting address indicated in the header. This is absolutely necessary when loading machine language programs, since such programs can only run in the memory area for which they were written.

```
SAVE "PRGM1",1          SAVE BASIC PROGRAM
SAVE "PRGM2",1,1        SAVE PROGRAM AS MACHINE LANG.
```

For header type 3, a program is loaded into the Commodore 64 beginning at the starting address specified in the header. For header type 2, data (not a program) is written to the cassette tape in blocks of 192 characters at a time. This avoids the time consuming process of starting and stopping the cassette drive each time a character is to be transferred. As each PRINT# command is performed, instead of writing single characters to the tape, the data is collected in a tape buffer until 192 such characters have been collected. When the tape buffer is full, the data in the buffer is written to the tape. The buffer is then emptied and readied for the next 192 characters. The tape buffer is located at the address 828 thru 1019 ($33C - $3FB).

When reading from a tape file using INPUT# or GET#, instead of reading single characters from the tape, a data block is read into the tape buffer. Each character read with INPUT# or GET# is retrieved from the data in the tape buffer. When all 192 characters of the block have been processed, the buffer is said to be empty and the next block of data is read from the tape and into the tape buffer.

Saving a program with a secondary address of 2 or 3 also writes an end-of-tape block after the program is recorded. An end-of-tape block will prevent the Commodore 64 from searching for any program on the tape that may have been recorded beyond the end-of-tape block.

Summarizing all the relations in a table again:

LOAD

```
LOAD "NAME",1       - loads BASIC program, at the start
                      of BASIC. Type 3 header is loaded
                      absolutely.
LOAD "NAME",1,1     - loads every program absolutely
```

SAVE

```
SAVE "NAME",1       - saves a BASIC program
SAVE "NAME",1,1     - saves a machine program
SAVE "NAME",1,2     - saves a BASIC program with an
                      additional EOT block
SAVE "NAME",1,3     - saves as machine program with an
                      additional EOT block
```

When opening a tape data file for processing the secondary address has the following meaning:

```
OPEN 1,1,0  "NAME" - opens file for reading
OPEN 1,1,1  "NAME" - opens file for writing
OPEN 1,1,2, "NAME" - opens file for writing with an
                          additional EOT block
```

The CLOSE command performs the necessary housekeeping for the file. If the file was open for writing, a zero byte is written into the tape buffer and the buffer is written onto the tape. Thus it is absolutely necessary to CLOSE a tape file. Otherwise, the final data is not written to the tape.

There are also restrictions concerning data transfer onto tape. Normally data is written onto the tape in ASCII format (letters, digits, and special symbols). If data is written with PRINT#1, CHR$(I), not all possible symbols can be written. In particular, CHR$(0) is filtered out, because it is used as an end symbol by the operation system.

1.5.3.2 Saving Data on Diskette

A diskette is divided into tracks and sectors which can be accessed individually. That makes it possible to have direct access to data without having to read thru all the other data.

Programs are saved as follows. The address of the program are transferred to the program file on diskette. The address is sent least significant byte first followed by the most significant byte. Then the program itself is transferred. On disk, there is no difference between saving a BASIC program or a machine language program. A distinction is only made when LOADing the program.

```
LOAD  "NAME",8      loads BASIC program at start of
                    BASIC address
LOAD  "NAME",8,1    loads BASIC program starting at the
                    saved starting address
```

If you want to find the starting address of a program that is contained on a diskette, you can use this little program:

```
10 OPEN 1,8,1,"NAME"          :REM program file for reading
20 GET#1, A$,  B$             :REM get start address
30 IF A$ = " " THEN A$ = CHR$(0)
40 IF B$ = " " THEN B$ = CHR$(0)
50 PRINT ASC(A$)+256*ASC(B$) :REM decimal address
60 CLOSE 1
```

The starting address of the program is printed out in decimal. The test for a null string in lines 30 and 40 is necessary, because the GET command does not accept a byte with a zero value.

If you want to write a machine language program to diskette, you can do it like this:

```
10 OPEN 1,8,0,"NAME,P,W"            :REM program file
20 PRINT#1, CHR$(AD-INT(AD/256)*256);:REM address low
30 PRINT#1, CHR$(AD/256);           :REM start address high
40 FOR I=0 TO N-1                   :REM save N bytes
50  PRINT#1, CHR$(PEEK(AD+I));      :REM this is your
60 NEXTI                            :REM    program data
60 CLOSE 1                          :REM close program file
```

The variable AD contains the starting address of the machine language program and the variable N contains the length of the program in bytes.

How do you save programs or areas of memory from within a machine language program?

Here again we have two operating system routines can be used:

LOAD $FFD5
SAVE $FFD8

The LOAD routine is used in the following way:

The name of the file and the appropriate device number must be set using the kernal routines SETFLS ($FFBA) and SETNAM ($FFBD). The accumulator is loaded with zero to indicate that a LOAD is to be performed. If LOAD is called with 1 in the accumulator, VERIFY is performed instead of LOAD.

The secondary address determines where in memory the loading is to take place. If the secondary address is 1 or 2, the program is loaded at the address from which the program was saved. If the secondary address is zero, the program is loaded at the address specified by the X and Y registers (low/high).

Example: Loading of a machine program from diskette to the original address.

```
           LDA  #8       ;logical file number
           LDX  #8       ;device number of the floppy
           LDY  #1       ;secondary address
           JSR  SETFLS   ;located at $FFBA-set file parms.
           LDA  #5       ;length of the file name
           LDX  #<NAME   ;address of the file name
           LDY  #>NAME   ;high byte of the address
           JSR  SETNAM   ;located at $FFBD-set file name
           LDA  #0       ;LOAD flag
           JSR  LOAD     ;load program
           STX  ADR      ;end address low
           STY  ADR+1    ;end address high
            .
            .
   NAME    ASC  'FILE1'
```

Note that the LOAD routine returns the ending address of the loaded program in the X and Y registers.

In the following example, a program is loaded from the tape, starting at address $6000. The saved address is ignored.

```
        LDA  #1      ;logical file number
        LDX  #1      ;device number cassette recorder
        LDY  #0      ;secondary address
        JSR  SETLFS  ;at $FFBA-set file parameters
        LDA  #5      ;length of the file name
        LDX  #<NAME  ;address of file name
        LDY  #>NAME  ;high byte of address
        JSR  SETNAM  ;at $FFBD-set parms for file name
        LDA  #0      ;LOAD-flag
        LDX  #$00    ;load address low
        LDY  #$60    ;load address high
        JSR LOAD     ;load program
        STX  ADR     ;end address low
        STY  ADR+1   ;end address high
         .
         .
NAME    ASC  'FILE2'
```

If a machine program is to be loaded with LOAD from a BASIC program, you will encounter a few difficulties.

You can load a program at an absolute address by using a secondary address of 0 during OPEN, but there still is a problem. After every LOAD, the ending address of the load is set equal to the ending address of the BASIC program and program execution starts at the beginning of the program. This makes sense for reloading of BASIC programs (overlay), but it creates problems when loading of machine language programs or the contents of a range or memory. In such a case, you can use a small machine language program (such as in the previous example) that you can call from the BASIC program by SYS.

Saving programs and any memory ranges with the SAVE routine happens similarly. In addition to the device number and file name information, the SAVE routine has to know the starting and the ending address of the program. The starting address kept in zero page in two consecutive memory locations (low and high byte). The address of this zero page location is transferred to the SAVE routine via the accumulator. The ending address is in the X-register (low byte) and the Y-register (high byte).

Suppose we now want to save the memory range from $C000 through $CFFF on a diskette under the name "PGRMB". The starting address of the program is in $FB/$FC.

```
         LDA    #1          ;logical file number
         LDX    #8          ;device number of the floppy
         LDY    #0          ;secondary address
         JSR    SETLFS      ;at $FFBA-set file parameter
         LDA    #5          ;length of file name
         LDX    #<NAME      ;address of file name
         LDY    #>NAME      ;high byte of address
         JSR    SETNAM      ;at $FFBD-set parms for file name
         LDA    #$C0        ;address high of the start
         STA    $FC         ;  of the program
         LDA    #$00        ;address low of the start
         STA    $FB         ;  of the program
         LDA    #$FB        ;pointer on start address
         LDX    #$00        ;end address +1 low
         LDY    #$D0        ;end address +1 high
         JSR    SAVE        ;save program
          .
          .
NAME     ASC    'PGRMB'  ;file name
```

In the above example, the ending address of the program is passed to the SAVE routine in the X and Y registers.

As a final example, here is how to save a BASIC program

without a file name but with EOT symbol on tape:

```
LDA   #1        ;logical file number
LDX   #1        ;device number of the recorder
LDY   #2        ;secondary address for EOT
JSR   SETLFS    ;at $FFBA-set file parameter
LDA   #0        ;no file names
JSR   SETNAM    ;at $FFBD-set parms for file names
LDA   #$2B      ;pointer to BASIC program start
LDX   #$2D      ;end address low of the program
LDY   #$2E      ;end address high
JSR   SAVE      ;save program
```

1.5.4 Programming the RS-232 Interface

The Commodore 64 has an RS-232 interface for connection to any peripheral device that follows the RS-232 protocol. There are hundreds of devices on the market that use RS-232. These include printers, modems, plotters and A/D controllers.

The RS-232 interface transfers data serially. What does serial transfer mean and when is it used? The Commodore 64 stores data in characters consisting of 8 bits. When a character is to be sent to or received from a peripheral device by a serial method, each of the 8 bits are transferred one bit at a time.

In contrast, a character can also be sent using a parallel method of transfer. Here, all 8 bits are sent or received from a peripheral device at one time. The advantage of parallel transfer is that it is faster than serial transfer. But parallel transfer is also more expensive as each bit must have its own line over which to transfer the information. Using serial transfer, fewer lines are required as each bit waits its turn to be sent to the peripheral device.

The kernal of the Commodore 64 contains software necessary to use the RS-232 interface. You can purchase a standard RS-232 connector as an add-on module, which can then be plugged into the USER port. With this RS-232 connector, the Commodore 64 is ready to communicate with any standard RS-232 device.

The RS-232 interface is assigned a device number of 2. When a logical file using device number 2 is OPENed, the kernal sets aside two buffers of 256 characters each for use by the RS-232 device. One buffer is used for data that is inputted from the peripheral and the second buffer is used for data that is outputted to the peripheral.

These buffers are normally set aside in memory at the end of

BASIC RAM. If the RS-232 interface is used from a BASIC program you should OPEN the RS-232 device before allocating any string variables. If not, when the RS-232 device is OPENed and the two buffers are allocated, then the string variables are overwritten and destroyed.

Also note that only one channel can be OPENed at one time for the RS-232 interface.

The characteristics of the RS-232 interface can adjusted when the channel is OPENed. This is done by setting both a control register and a command register.

The control register serves to define the baud rate, the number of data bits and the number of stop bits that are to be transferred. The baud rate determines the speed of the data transfer in bits per second. The number of data bits determines the length of each word (or character) that is to be transferred. The number stop bits are the number of bits to be sent after each word.

In the control register, the lower 4 bits determine the baud rate according to the following table:

BIT 3 2 1 0	DECIMAL	BAUD RATE
0 0 0 0	0	set by user (not implemented)
0 0 0 1	1	50
0 0 1 0	2	75
0 0 1 1	3	110
0 1 0 0	4	134.5
0 1 0 1	5	150
0 1 1 0	6	300
0 1 1 1	7	600
1 0 0 0	8	1200
1 0 0 1	9	1800
1 0 1 0	10	2400
1 0 1 1	11	3600 (not implemented)
1 1 0 0	12	4800 (not implemented)
1 1 0 1	13	7200 (not implemented)
1 1 1 0	14	9600 (not implemented)
1 1 1 1	15	19200 (not implemented)

You can program the RS-232 interface to use baud rates between 50 and 2400. The number of data bits are determined by bit 5 and 6.

BIT 6 5	DECIMAL	NUMBER OF DATA BITS
0 0	0	8 bits
0 1	32	7 bits
1 0	64	6 bits
1 1	96	5 bits

The number of stop bits is determined by bit 7.

BIT 7	DECIMAL	NUMBER OF STOP BITS
0	0	1
1	128	2

The command register determines the transfer mode, type of parity and mode of handshake.

The command register is organized as follows:

BIT 0	DECIMAL	HANDSHAKE
0	0	3-wire handshake
1	1	X-wire handshake

BIT 4	DECIMAL	TRANSFER MODE
0	0	full duplex
1	16	half duplex

BIT 7 6 5	DECIMAL	PARITY CHECK
X X 0	0	no parity check, no 8th data bit
0 0 1	32	odd parity
0 1 1	96	even parity
1 0 1	160	no parity check, 8th data bit always 1
1 1 1	224	no parity check, 8th data bit always 0

Let's try an example. Suppose you want to OPEN an RS-232 data channel, with the following parameters:

parameter	value in decimal
transfer rate 2400 baud	10
8 bit ASCII data	0
2 stop bits	128
no parity check	0
8th data bit always 0	224
full duplex	0
3-wire handshake	0

The OPEN directions would then look like this:

```
OPEN 1,2,0,CHR$(10+0+128)+CHR$(0+0+224)
```

Input and output are handled the same as with other peripheral devices. BASIN and BSOUT transfer data to or from the RS-232 device.

The only difference is the status register (ST). When using RS-232, the status register returns a different set of errors than when using other input or output devices.

Reading the status variable ST from BASIC clears the status each time it is read. Therefore you should always assign the status variable to another variable if you want to remember its value.
Reading the status variable from a machine language program does not clear the status.

ST gives you only the RS-232 status for data exchanged over the RS-232 interface. The meaning of the different bits of the RS-232 status is described below. If a particular bit is set (on), then that particular condition has occurred.

BIT	DESCRIPTION
0	parity mistake
1	frame mistake
2	receiver buffer full
3	unused
4	CTS (clear to send) signal missing
5	unused
6	DSR (data set ready) signal missing
7	break signal received

If you using the RS-232 interface from a machine language program, you can place the input and output buffers for data transmission anywhere in memory.
The pointers to these buffers are set during the OPEN command, but may be moved after the OPEN is complete. These pointers are located in zero page: $F7/$F8 points to the input buffer and $F9/$FA points to the output buffer. Programming the RS-232 is similar to programming for any other input or output device except that the device number is 2.
Other important addresses for RS-232 input/output are:

$0293	control word
$0294	command word
$0298	number of data bits, computed at OPEN
$0297	RS-232 status word

1.5.5 The Serial Bus

In order to communicate with peripheral devices, the Commodore 64 has a serial bus to which several devices can be connected at the same time. From a programming standpoint, the bus is similar to the IEEE-488 bus of earlier Commodore computers (PET, 8032, 4032, etc.). But the data is transmitted bit by bit over the serial bus. This is unlike the IEEE-488 which transmits data in parallel. The transmission speed of the serial bus is therefore considerably slower.

First we explain the concept of the serial bus.

Since several devices can be connected to the serial bus at the same time, there must to be a way of distinguishing one device from another. This is the purpose of the device number. The Commodore 64 assigns device numbers 4 thru 31 to the serial bus.

When a device is addressed, the Commodore 64 (called the bus controller) sends an attention signal (called ATN) over the bus. This alerts all connected devices that they should be aware that communication is being established with one of them. Next the Commodore 64 sends device number of the desired device over the bus. If the device is attached to the bus, then it responds to the ATN, otherwise we get a message DEVICE NOT PRESENT.

Next, the device is informed that it is to either receive data from or transmit data to the Commodore 64. If a device is to receive data, then the Commodore 64 sends a LISTEN command to the device. If a device is to send data, then the Commodore 64 sends a TALK command to the device.

A secondary address may also be sent to the device to perform any necessary setup. For example: OPEN 1,4,7 transmits secondary address 7 to the printer (device 4) which selects UPPER/LOWER case mode for printing.

Now the data can be sent to the device or received from the device. In order for the data transmission to function accurately, data is transmitted one character at a time. The receiver of the data informs the sender when the data has been successfully accepted. Only when the receiver acknowledges the receipt of the data may the sender transmit another character of data. This procedure is called **handshaking** and insures the integrity of the data as it transmitted.

When the data transmission is complete, the device is deaddressed: if the device was sending data, the Commodore 64 sends it an UNTALK command; if the device was receiving data, the Commodore 64 sends it an UNLISTEN command. At this point, the bus is free to handle the next transmission.

Now we move on to programming the serial bus from a machine language program!

The kernal of the Commodore 64 contains all of the routines necessary for communicating with devices over the serial bus.

Let's show you an example of the use of some of these builtin kernal routines. This short example reads the error channel from the disk drive. First we show you how to read the error channel using a BASIC program:

```
  10  OPEN 15,8,15:                       REM open error channel
  20  INPUT#15,A$,B$,C$,D$:               REM get error message
  30  PRINT A$;",";B$;",";C$;",";D$:REM and output
  40  CLOSE 15:                           REM close channel
```

You can do this only in program mode (not command mode) because the INPUT command is valid only in program mode. This machine program does the same thing:

```
                ACPTR  EQU  $FFA5
                CHROUT EQU  $FFD2
                FA     EQU  $BA
                SA     EQU  $B9
                TALK   EQU  $FFB4
                TKSA   EQU  $FF96
                UNTLK  EQU  $FFAB
C000 A9 08      START  LDA  #8         ;device number of disk
C002 85 BA             STA  FA         ;set device no.
C004 20 B4 FF          JSR  TALK       ;send talk
C007 A9 6F             LDA  #15+$60    ;sec. addr 15 + $60
C009 85 B9             STA  SA
C00B 20 96 FF          JSR  TKSA       ;sec. addr for talk
C00E 20 A5 FF   LOOP   JSR  ACPTR      ;read byte from device
C011 20 D2 FF          JSR  CHROUT     ;display on screen
C014 C9 OD             CMP  #13        ;is it carriage return?
C016 DO F6             BNE  LOOP       ;no-go back for more
C018 20 AB FF          JSR  UNTLK      ;yes-send untalk
C01B 60                RTS             ;return to caller
```

From BASIC you can call this routine by typing **SYS 12*4096.**

With the next machine language program, you can display the directory of a diskette. Using this routine, you do not have to LOAD"$",8 to view the directory and consequently lose your current BASIC program.

```
                        ACPTR  EQU   $FFA5
                        CHROUT EQU   $FFD2
                        CLSFIL EQU   $F642
                        FA     EQU   $BA
                        FNADR  EQU   $BB
                        FNLEN  EQU   $B7
                        LNPRT  EQU   $BDCD
                        SA     EQU   $B9
                        SENDNM EQU   $F3D5
                        STATUS EQU   $90
                        TALK   EQU   $FFB4
                        TKSA   EQU   $FF96
C000   A9 24                   LDA   #'$       ;$ char is file name
C002   85 FB                   STA   $FB       ;save
C004   A9 FB                   LDA   #$FB      ;addr of file name
C006   85 BB                   STA   FNADR
C008   A9 00                   LDA   #0        ;high byte
C00A   85 BC                   STA   FNADR+1
C00C   A9 01                   LDA   #1        ;length of file name
C00E   85 B7                   STA   FNLEN
C010   A9 08                   LDA   #8        ;dev.addr of floppy
C012   85 BA                   STA   FA
C014   A9 60                   LDA   #$60      ;sec. addr for LOAD
C016   85 B9                   STA   SA
C018   20 D5 F3                JSR   SENDNM    ;open file with name
C01B   A5 BA                   LDA   FA
C01D   20 B4 FF                JSR   TALK      ;send talk
C020   A5 B9                   LDA   SA
C022   20 96 FF                JSR   TKSA      ;send sec addr
C025   A9 00                   LDA   #0
C027   85 90                   STA   STATUS    ;clear status
C029   A0 03                   LDY   #3        ;skip first three bytes
C02B   84 FB          L1       STY   $FB       ;save as counter
C02D   20 A5 FF                JSR   ACPTR     ;get byte from floppy
C030   85 FC                   STA   $FC       ;and save it
C032   A4 90                   LDY   STATUS    ;status ok?
C034   D0 2F                   BNE   L4        ;no-get out
C036   20 A5 FF                JSR   ACPTR     ;get byte from floppy
C039   A4 90                   LDY   STATUS    ;test status
C03B   D0 28                   BNE   L4
C03D   A4 FB                   LDY   $FB       ;get counter
C03F   88                      DEY             ;  and decrement
C040   D0 E9                   BNE   L1
C042   A6 FC                   LDX   $FC
C044   20 CD BD                JSR   LNPRT     ;output no. blks used
C047   A9 20                   LDA   #'        ;space between
C049   20 D2 FF                JSR   CHROUT
C04C   20 A5 FF L3             JSR   ACPTR     ;get next byte
C04F   A6 90                   LDX   STATUS    ;test status
C051   D0 12                   BNE   L4
C053   AA                      TAX             ;zero?
C054   F0 06                   BEQ   L2        ;yes-then end of line
C056   20 D2 FF                JSR   CHROUT    ;no-output
C059   4C 4C C0                JMP   L3        ;and get next character
C05C   A9 0D          L2       LDA   #13       ;carriage return
```

```
C05E  20 D2 FF       JSR  CHROUT  ;output
C061  A0 02          LDY  #2      ;2 bytes addr
C063  D0 C6          BNE  L1      ;continue
C065  20 42 F6 L4    JSR  CLSFIL  ;close file
C068  60             RTS          ;all done
```

This routine is again called from BASIC with **SYS 12*4096.** The directory of the diskette is displayed on the screen without losing your BASIC program.

CHAPTER 2 : THE NEXT STEP - ASSEMBLER PROGRAMMING

2.1 Why Assembler Language?

What advantages does an assembler have compared to machine language programming? If you have ever used machine language, you know that you must figure out the opcode, translate decimal numbers into hexadecimal, keep track of absolute memory addresses, compute relative jumps, etc. These tasks are very tedious and error prone.

An assembler is a program that performs all of the these tasks very quickly and accurately. An assembler allows you to use symbols to represent memory location and data. With an assembler you use LABELS to represent actual memory addresses. For example:

Machine language			Assembler		
C000	JSR	$E544	BEGIN	JSR	CLRSCR
	"			"	
C056	JMP	$C129		JMP	TEST
	"			"	
C129	JSR	$A474	TEST	JMP	BASIC
				"	
			CLRSCR	EQU	$E544
			BASIC	EQU	$A474

The label CLRSCR stands for "clear screen". When an assembler language programmer want to clear the screen he can code JSR CLRSCR to perform this task. This is certainly much easier to remember than JSR $E544. Yet this is not the only advantage of assembler language programming.

Imagine you have just written a very long machine language program, and now you want to change some code. Consider how bothersome this procedure is: you must recalculate all the addresses of relative branch instruction that may have changed; you must recalculate all absolute addresses for JSR or JMP instructions that may have changed; you must respecify the addresses of any data or tables that may have changed, etc.

But if you were writing in assembler language, the assembler program recalculates all these addresses for you. After making the change to the assembler source program, it is assembled again and saved onto cassette or diskette as a new machine language program. All this takes place quickly and accurately.

Just as a monitor is a necessary prerequisite for machine language programming, an assembler is necessary if you are to write long or numerous machine language programs.

2.2 Table of 6510 Instructions

The following table lists all of the 6510 instructions.

You should note that the binary equivalents of many of the 6510 instructions are not complete. They may contain several small letter **b**'s. The value of the binary equivalent of the instruction varies according to the addressing mode of the instruction.

Command	Function	Binary
ADC	add with carry	011bbb01
AND	logical AND	001bbb01
ASL	shift left one bit	000bbb10
BCC	branch on carry clear	10010000
BCS	branch on carry set	10110000
BEQ	branch on result zero	11110000
BIT	tests bit	0010b100
BMI	branch on result minus	00110000
BNE	branch on result not zero	11010000
BPL	branch on result plus	00010000
BRK	software break	00000000
BVC	branch on overflow clear	01010000
BVS	branch on overflow set	01110000
CLC	clear carry flag	00011000
CLD	clear decimal flag	11011000
CLI	clear interrupt disable bit	01011000
CLV	clear overflow flag	10111000
CMP	compare memory and accumulator	110bbb01
CPX	compare memory and X-register	1110bb00
CPI	compare memory and Y-register	1100bb00
DEC	decrement memory	110bb110
DEX	decrement X-register	10101010
DEY	decrement Y-register	10001000
EOR	"exclusive-OR"	010bbb01
INC	increment memory	111bb110
INX	increment X-register	11101000
INY	increment Y-register	11001000
JMP	jump to new location	01b01100
JSR	jump to new location in sub program	00100000
LDA	load accumulator	101bbb01
LDX	load X-register	101bbb10
LDY	load Y-register	101bbb00
LSR	logical right shift	010bbb10
NOP	no operation	11101010
ORA	logical "OR"	000bbb01
PHA	put accumulator on stock	01001000
PHP	put status register on stack	00001000
PLA	get accumulator from stack	01101000

PLP	get status register from stack	00101000
ROL	rotate one bit left	001bbb10
ROR	rotate one bit right	011bbb10
RTI	return from interrupt	01000000
RTS	return from subprogram	01100000
SBC	subtract with carry	111bbb01
SEC	set carry flag	00111000
SED	set decimal	00111000
SEI	set interrupt disable status	01111000
STA	store accumulator	100bbb01
STX	store X-register	100bb110
STY	store Y-register	100bb100
TAX	transfer accumulator to X-register	10101010
TAY	transfer accumulator to Y-register	10101000
TSX	transfer stack pointer to X-register	10111010
TXA	transfer X-register to accumulator	10001010
TXS	transfer X-register to stack pointer	10011010
TYA	transfer Y-register to accumulator	10011000

For a more detailed index of the commands and their usage, consult one of the books listed in Appendix D.

2.3 A Typical Assembler Program

An assembler is a program that translates a symbolic source program into its binary equivalent. Each symbolic instruction is translated into a machine language instruction that is 1, 2, or 3 bytes in length. The resulting machine language program is called object code.

A line of a typical assembly language source program consists of several elements:

1. the line number - comparable to BASIC line number
2. the address - the memory location of this line
3. the code - the hexadecimal representation of the instructions and data (object code)
4. the label - a symbolic name for the beginning of this instruction
5. the opcode - the symbolic name for a 6502 instruction
6. the operand - symbolic names for any parameters of the instructions
7. the remark - commentary to describe the machine language code

Elements 4 thru 7 are optional. They are not necessary in each line of the assembly language source program.

In addition to the 6510 instructions, most assemblers

understand some special instructions called pseudo opcodes. For instance some assemblers have a pseudo opcode called BYT. This pseudo opcode allows you to insert data into the program. You can specify the data in decimal format or hexadecimal format.

More sophisticated assemblers allow you to peform conditional assembly. Using conditional assembly, you can choose to translate parts of source programs into object code if certain conditions are satisfied.

Here is a typical printout of an assembler listing:

```
line addr code       label  oper operand  comment

 10  0000            BUFFER  EQU  $C000   ;variable BUFFER
                                           is stored at $C000
 20  0000                    ORG  $0000   ;start code at $0000
 30  0000 A9 00      TEST    LDA  #$00    ;zero accumulator
 40  0003 8D 00 C0           STA  BUFFER  ;store into BUFFER
 50  0006 4C 23 01           JMP  JUMP    ;at JUMP it goes on
                             ...
                             ...
180  0123 38         JUMP    SEC          ;carry flag set
190  0124 E9 0A              SBC  #$0A    ;subtract 10
                             ...
                             ...
```

You can clearly see the difference between machine language programming and assembler language programming: you don't have to calculate addresses and memory locations anymore. These calulation are taken care of by the assembler. At the same time the assembler can identify possible mistakes and notify the user. Assembler language programming is not only faster, but considerably more accurate than machine language programming.

Let's now turn to another assembler language program. This routine is much more accurate and faster than the SQR routine in BASIC. The algorithm for this function is:

```
X (N+1) = X (N) - F (X(N)) / F (X(N))
X = F (A)
X (N+1) = (X(N) + A / X (N)) / 2
```

The running time of this function is only about 14 ms.

The program is as follows:

```
;
;FAST SQR ROUTINE, ABOUT 14MS
```

```
                    ;ALGORITHM X(N+1)=X(N)-F(X(N))/F(X(N)
                    ;X=F(A),    X(N+1)=(X(N)+A/X(N))/2
                    ;
                    ;
033C                SIGN     EQU $BC2B
033C                ILLEGAL  EQU $B248
033C                EXP      EQU $61
033C                ACCU3    EQU $57
033C                ACCU4    EQU $5C
033C                COUNT    EQU $67
033C                AlTOA3   EQU $BBCA
033C                AlTOA4   EQU $BBC7
033C                MEMDIV   EQU $BB0F
033C                MEMPLUS  EQU $B867
033C                         ORG $33C      ;PGM IN TAPE BUFFER
033C 20 2B BC                JSR SIGN      ;GET SIGN
033F F0 34                   BEQ END       ;0? YES->OK
0341 10 03                   BPL OK        ;+? YES->OK
0343 4C 48 B2                JMP ILLEGAL   ;ILL. QUAN. ERR.
0346 20 C7 BB       OK       JSR AlTOA4    ;ACCU#1->ACCU#4
0349 A5 61                   LDA EXP       ;EXP.->ACCU
034B 38                      SEC
034C E9 81                   SBC #$81      ;NORMALIZE EXPONENT
034E 08                      PHP           ;STAT.REG. ON STACK
034F 4A                      LSR           ;HALVE EXPONENT
0350 18                      CLC           ;CLEAR CARRY FLAG
0351 69 01                   ADC #$01      ;ADD 1
0353 28                      PLP           ;STAT.REG.FROM STACK
0354 90 02                   BCC S1        ;CARRY?NO->S1
0356 69 7F                   ADC #$7F      ;ADD 127
0358 85 61          S1       STA EXP       ;MEMORY AS EXPONENT
035A A9 04                   LDA #$04      ;FOUR ITERATIONS
035C 85 67                   STA COUNT     ;MEMORY IN VARIABLE
035E 20 CA BB       ITER     JSR AlTOA3    ;ACCU#1->ACCU#3
0361 A9 5C                   LDA #<ACCU4   ;LOAD LSB FROM AC.4
0363 A0 00                   LDY #>ACCU4   ;LOAD MSB FROM AC.4
0365 20 OF BB                JSR MEMDIV    ;DIVIDE BY ACCU#1
0368 A9 57                   LDA #<ACCU3   ;LOAD LSB FROM AC.3
036A A0 00                   LDY #>ACCU3   ;LOAD MSB FROM AC.3
036C 20 67 BB                JSR MEMPLUS   ;ADD TO ACCU#1
036F C6 61                   DEC EXP       ;ACCU#1/2(EXP.-1)
0371 C6 67                   DEC COUNT     ;ONE ITERAT. LESS
0373 DO E9                   BNE ITER      ;MORE ITER.? YES
0375 60              END     RTS           ;BACK TO PROGRAM
```

(LSB=least significant byte
MST=most significant byte)

You can enter this program using either a monitor or an assembler. To use it, you can call it from BASIC. You can do this by using the BASIC USR command. The USR command passes control to the routine whose address is placed in memory locations $311/$312. The parameter passed via the USR routine is automatically made available to this routine.

Here is an example:

```
10  POKE 785,60: REM LSB - 60 DECIMAL = 3C HEX
20  POKE 786,03: REM MSB - 03 DECIMAL = 03 HEX
30  A=10
40  B=USR(A)
50  PRINT "SQR OF ";A;" IS ";B
60  END
RUN

SQR OF 10 IS 3.16227766
```

If you are interested in further mathematical functions, please read Chapter 6.3.3. There you will find more information.

In Chapter 6.3, you will find more about communicating between BASIC and machine language programs.

2.4 Still More Programs

Next are several more examples of assembler language programming. The routines are useful as well as illustrative.

These programs are intended to serve as models for developing programs of your own.

First, is a routine which prints the contents ofthe accumulator in hexadecimal format to the currently assigned output device. If the current output device is the screen (default), then the contents of the accumulator are printed onto the screen. If you OPENed a printer as the output device (OPEN 4,4), then the contents of the accumulator are sent to the printer.

This program is placed in the Commodore 64 cassette buffer. This location is suitable for such small routines because it is not affected by BASIC unless input from or output to the cassette drive is attempted.

```
033C                    ORG  $033C    ;starting addr of pgm.
033C           BSOUT    EQU  $FFD2    ;declare addr of the
                                      ; kernal o/p routine
033C 48        START    PHA           ;save value of accum
033D 4A                 LSR           ;shift bits 4
033E 4A                 LSR           ; thru 7 to positions
033F 4A                 LSR           ; of bits 0
0340 4A                 LSR           ; thru 3
0341 20 47 03           JSR   HEXASC  ;convert digit to ASCII
0344 68                 PLA           ;restore accumulator
0345 29 OF              AND   #$OF    ;mask out bits 4-7
```

```
0347 18       HEXASC   CLC             ;clear carry flag
0348 69 F6             ADC    #$F6     ;prepare for conversion
034A 90 02             BCC    * + 4    ;branch is <=255
034C 69 06             ADC    #$06     ;normalize for A-F
034E 69 3A             ADC    #$3A     ;make ASCII value
0350 4C D2 FF          JMP    BSOUT    ;write result
```

Here's an explanation. Suppose the accumulator contains the value $FE (254 in decimal). Keep in mind that the hexadecimal number $FE is represented as a single character (8 bits) inside the computer. To display this value however, you must change it two two individual ASCII characters.

To display the value, first divide the hexadecimal number into two separate numbers. To do this, "split" the 8- bit byte into two four bit nibbles. You do this by shifting the left four bits of this number to the right which at the same time fills the vacated bits with zeros. As a result you have a one-digit number between 0 and F. Shifting is done with the 6510 **LSR** instruction. Since we must shift four bits, we execute the **LSR** instruction 4 times.

Shifting causes us to lose the right four bits of the number. This is why we saved the original number with a **PHA** instruction. The accumulator is saved on the STACK.

Before outputting the each hexadecimal digits, convert them to ASCII characters. The routine called HEXASC does exactly this. Hexadecimal numbers have this order: 0, 1, 2, 3, 4, 5, 6, 7, 8, 9, A, B, C, D, E, F. However the ASCII equivalent of these numbers are not in this sequence. Adding $F6 to the digit makes the next step easier.

If the digit is between 0 and 9, the result of this addition is either less than or equal to 255 and the carry flag will remain clear. Therefore adding $3A to the digit, creates a value between $30 (ASCII 0) and $39 (ASCII 9) and the digit is ready for display.

If the digit is between A and F, the result of adding $F6 is greater than 255 and the carry flag will be set. The BCC *+4 instruction tests this condition and the next instruction normalizes the digit for the correct ASCII values of A-F by adding an $06 to the digit to arrive at a value between $41 (ASCII A) and $46 (ASCII F).

After outputting the first digit (in our example F) we can output the second digit. For this purpose, we have to mask out left four bits of the original number. We can do this by using an **AND** instruction using a mask of $0F. The value $0F looks like this:

0 0 0 0 1 1 1 1

When ANDing two values, each bit is only set on only if both corresponding bits are set. In this example:

```
original        FE: 1 1 1 1 1 1 1 0
mask            0F: 0 0 0 0 1 1 1 1
result of AND   0E: 0 0 0 0 1 1 1 0
```

The number is now correctly formatted to be output.

Finally, we present a program that aids you in inputting your machine language programs. You can enter the instructions in hexadecimal.

```
100    AD=828: REM AD-> START ADDR OF MACHINE PGM (DECIMAL)
110     READ OP$
120     GOSUB 65000
130     POKE AD,OP
140     AD=AD+1
150     IF X<>96 THEN GOTO 110
160     END
170    REM  FOLLOWING DATA LINES CONTAIN THE OPCODES OF YOUR
175     REM  MACHINE LANGUAGE PROGRAM. THIS EXAMPLE IS THE
180     REM  ROUTINE PREVIOUSLY EXPLAINED THAT PRINTS THE
190     REM  CONTENTS OF THE ACCUMULATOR IN HEX FORMAT
200     DATA 48,4A,4A,4A,4A,20 47 03
210     DATA 68,29,0F,18,69,F6,90,02
220     DATA 69,06,69,3A,4C,D2,FF,96
65000   REM  THIS ROUTINE CONVERTS HEX NUMBERS INTO DECIMALS
65010   OL$=LEFT$(OP$,1): OR$=RIGHT$(OP$,1)
65020   OL=VAL(OL$): IF OL=0 AND OL$<>"0" THEN OL=ASC(OL$)-55
65030   OR=VAL(OR$): IF OR=0 AND OR$<>"0" THEN OR=ASC(OR$)-55
65040   OP=OL*16+OR
65050   RETURN
```

Using this program you can input a machine language routine byte by byte. Even though this method of placing machine language routines is convenient, it still does not match a monitor or assembler for convenience.
We hope that this chapter better aquainted you with machine and assembler language programming. The best advice we can give to the reader is to try writing his own program.

PRACTICE MAKES PERFECT!

After a short while, you will become more accomplished. In any event, you will discover that programming in machine language is just as much fun as programming in BASIC.

3.1 What you should know about the Commodore 64

The Commodore 64 is an outstanding achievement, considering its remarkably affordable price.

When working with the Commodore 64, you will soon notice that, as far as hardware is concerned, very little is missing. If you also own a VIC-20, you might want to take a time to look at the insides of both devices.

You will notice that the Commodore 64 contains fewer integrated circuits (ICs) than the VIC-20, even though it contains far more power than the VIC-20. This is made possible by extremely high density of the ICs.

There are a several newly developed, ICs inside the Commodore 64.
The Commodore succeeded in putting the following things into 64K address space:

* 64K dynamic RAM
* 1K color RAM
* 4K character generator
* Color video-controller with hires graphics
* Synthesizer with three independent voices
* 8K BASIC interpreter
* 8K operating system
* 2 parallel I/O ports
* RS-232 interface

3.2 An Overview of the Hardware

The Commodore 64 contains 64K of RAM, 20K of ROM and a bank of memory for accessing the input and output devices. Since the 6510 processor can only address a 64K memory space, a method is required to allow access to this larger array of memory space.

The method used is called multiplexing. Multiplexing allows several system components to share the same bus (communication) lines by using them at different times. This complex function is coordinated by a special IC which we will simply call address-space manager, since we don't have a name for it. More about this in section 3.4.

The character generator and I/O bank are located in the same address range. But this apparent conflict presents no problems, since the video interface chip takes advantage of the 6510's unused cycles when accessing the character generator.

The complete ROM and parts of the RAM overlap over a range of 20K. A description of this overlap is presented in section 3.4.

Besides handling the screen display, the video interface chip (VIC) also performs an additional function of refreshing the RAM. All of these procedures are taken care of by the video controller which must also provide generate the text and graphics.

3.3 Special features of the 6510 processor

The Commodore 64 contains a 6510 CPU. It is an 8-bit processor which is run at a frequency of about 980 Khz. The 6510 is the newest member of the 65xx family of microprocessors.

The most significant difference from the well-known 6502 is that the chip has 6 I/O lines available. Compared to the 6502 which has no I/O lines available, the 6510 can communicate over these six I/O lines without requiring additional ICs to perform the I/O.

These lines support the cassette operation and memory management.

Here is a list of the 6510 pinouts. These pinouts were derived from an empirical testing approach. lines actually go. Here is the result:

1	$\emptyset_1$IN input clock cycle time; 980 KHz
2	RDY ready; 0 = processor stops at the next reading cycle until RDY=1;
3	-IRQ interrupt request; 0=processor gets next command from vector $FFFE and continues there. Permitted if status register bit 2=0
4	-NMI non-maskable interrupt; 0=processor gets next command from vector $FFFA and continues there.
5	AEC address enable control; 0=processor brings data address and operation bus into tri-state. The bus can now be used by other units, i.e. a second processor.
6	operating voltage +5V
7-20	AO-A13; address bus
21	GND
22-23	A14-A15; address bus
24-29	P5-P0; I/O port
30-37	D7-D0; data bus

38 R/-W;
0=write access
1=read access
39 $\emptyset_2$IN clock cycle
40 RES reset;
0=processor goes into non-operating state. After transition from 0 to 1, the processor gets vector from $FFFC and begins execution there.

3.4 Memory Configurations

As mentioned before, the Commodore 64 has 64K of RAM, 20K of ROM, 4K of I/O RAM and 8K character generator ROM. The 6510 processor can access all of this memory with the help of an IC which we call the address manager.

By programming memory locations 0 and 1, you can affect the address manager to make different combinations of RAM, ROM and I/O available to the Commodore 64.

Memory location 1 is called the input/output. Memory location 0 is the control port for the input/output port and in part determines the memory configurations.

Three bits of the control port are of note:

Bit 0	called LORAM	0=selects RAM at $A000-$BFFF
		1=selects ROM at $A000-$BFFF
Bit 1	called HIRAM	0=selects RAM at $E000-$FFFF
		1=selects ROM at $E000-$FFFF
Bit 2	called CHAREN	0=selects ROM at $D000-$DFFF
		1=selects I/O at $D000-$DFFF

An example shows you how you can program the control port. Suppose you want to disable the ROMS that contain the BASIC interpreter at $A000-$BFFF. To do this you would have to set the bit LORAM to zero. The following statement could do this for you:

```
POKE 0,PEEK(0)AND254
```

It is necessary to use the **AND** the original contents of the control port (**PEEK(0)**) since the other bits control port must not be disturbed.

There are also two lines which are connected to the address manager. One line is called EXROM and is set when a ROM cartridge is found is the expansion slot. The other line is called GAME and is also set when a ROM cartridge is found in the expansion slot.

Thus using these five variables, we can describe the eight major memory configurations that are possible with the

Commodore 64. The following pages pictorally describe these different memory configurations.

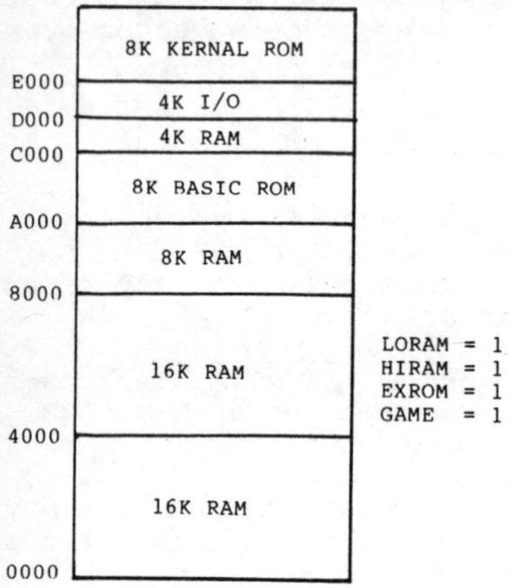

THIS CONFIGURATION APPEARS WHEN THE COMMODORE 64 IS TURNED ON.

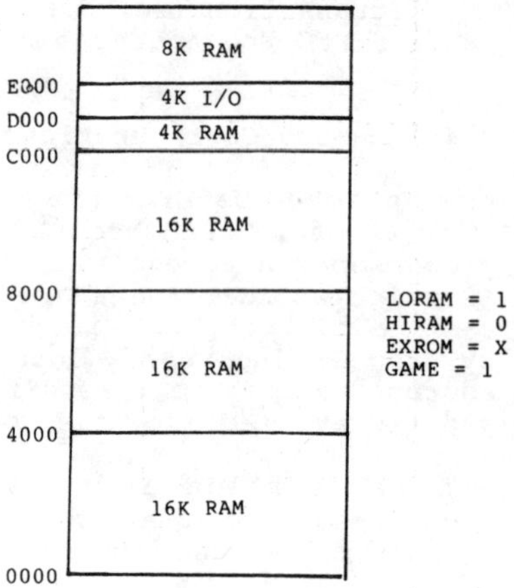

THIS CONFIGURATION GIVES YOU 60K OF RAM, BUT YOU MUST PROVIDE YOUR OWN DRIVER TO HANDLE I/O TO DEVICES.

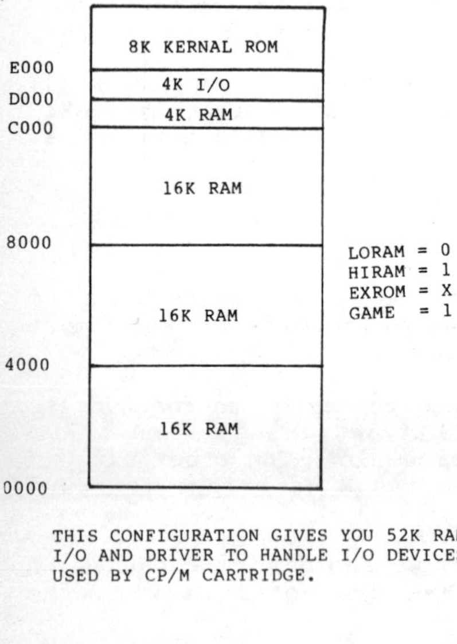

THIS CONFIGURATION GIVES YOU 52K RAM, I/O AND DRIVER TO HANDLE I/O DEVICES. USED BY CP/M CARTRIDGE.

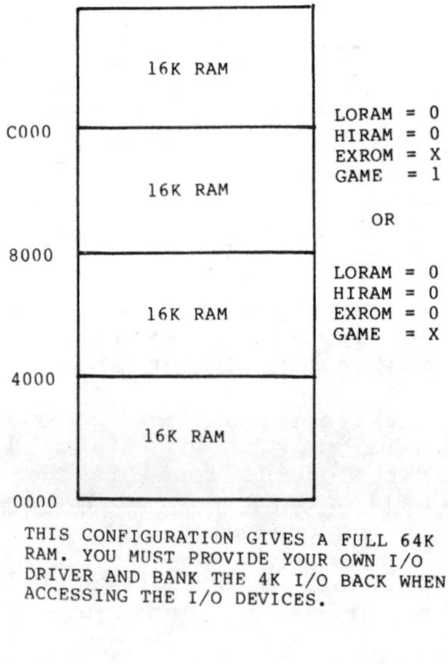

THIS CONFIGURATION GIVES A FULL 64K RAM. YOU MUST PROVIDE YOUR OWN I/O DRIVER AND BANK THE 4K I/O BACK WHEN ACCESSING THE I/O DEVICES.

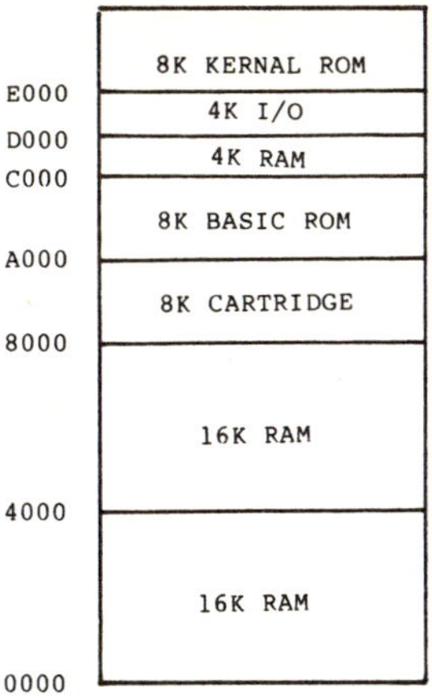

LORAM = 1
HIRAM = 1
EXROM = 0
GAME = 0

THIS CONFIGURATION SHOWS A STANDARD BASIC SYSTEM USING AN EXPANSION CARTRIDGE.

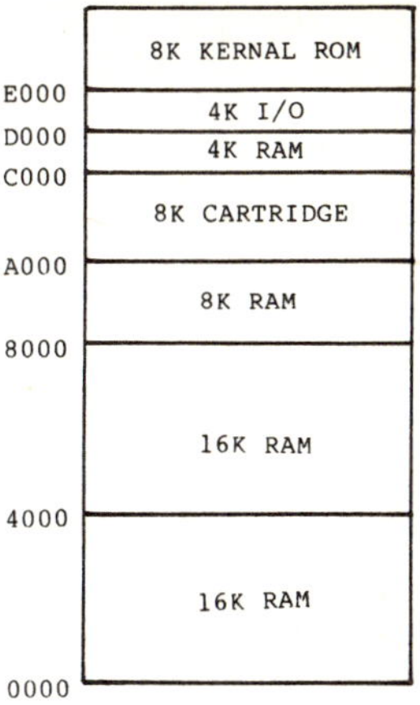

LORAM = 0
HIRAM = 1
EXROM = 0
GAME = 0

THIS CONFIGURATION GIVES YOU 40K RAM AND LETS YOU REPLACE THE BUILT IN BASIC WITH AN 8K ROM CARTRIDGE.

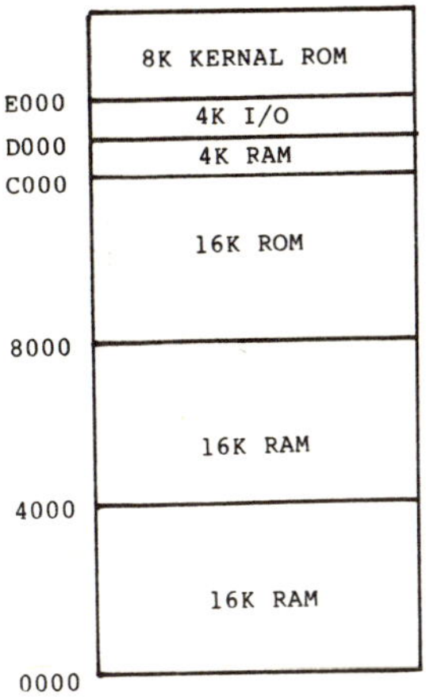

LORAM = 1
HIRAM = 1
EXROM = 0
GAME = 0

THIS CONFIGURATION GIVES YOU 32K RAM AND LETS YOU REPLACE THE BUILT IN BASIC WITH A 16K CARTRIDGE.

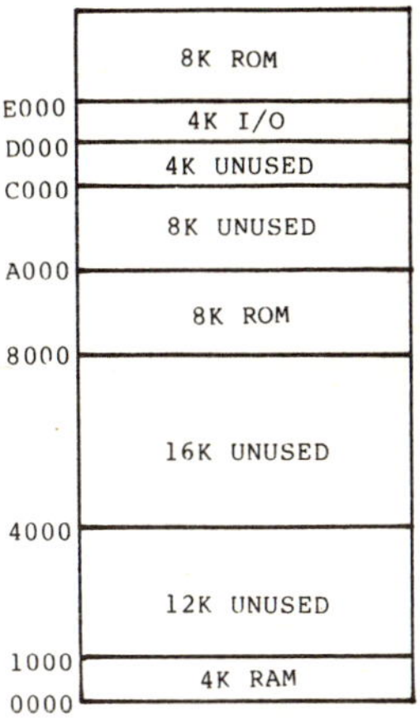

LORAM = X
HIRAM = X
EXROM = 1
GAME = 0

THIS CONFIGURATION GIVES YOU THE IMAGE OF THE ULTIMAX COMPUTER WHICH IS STILL YET TO BE RELEASED BY COMMODORE.

3.5 The Expansion Port

At the back of the Commodore 64 is a 44-pin connector. This is called an expansion slot. This slot contains connections for the complete system bus and the accompanying control channel.

Among the things that are connected at this port are BASIC and operating system expansions and game and input/output expansion (serial bus).

Since many signals are not self-explanatory, we explain the pin overlay here:

1	GND
2-3	+5V
4	-IRQ; connected with the IRQ of the processor
5	R/-W; connected with the R/-W of the processor
6	DOT CLOCK;dot scanning cycle for the VIC chip, 8.18 MHz
7	-I/O_1; usually =0 in the address range $DEOO to $DEFF
8	-GAME; input to the address manager
9	-EXROM; input to the address manager
10	-I/O_2; usually =0 in the range $DFOO to $DFFF
11	-ROML; output from AM; see ch.3.4.
12	BA; signal from VIC, which indicates the validity of reading data.
13	-DMA; input. 0=reserve bus system for external access
14-21	CD7-CDO; data bus
22	GND
A	GND
B	-ROMH; output from address manager at $E000
C	-RESET
D	-NMI
E	$Ø_2$; system cycle output
F-Y	A15-AO; address bus
Z	GND

3.6 The User Port

With the user port, the Commodore 64 offers an versatile interface. It is possible to connect analog to digital controllers or parallel interfaces (Centronics-type) for example.

Basically, the user port consists of an 8-bit port and several control channels explained as follows:

1	GND
2	+5V;
3	-RESET; connected with the processor of the same name

4	CNT1; connected with CNT from CIA1
5	SP1; connected with SP from CIA 1
6	CNT2; connected with CNT from CIA 2
7	SP2; connected with SP from CIA 2
8	-PC2; handshake output from CIA 2
9	SERIAL ATN; control channel of the serial bus
10	9V AC; + phase
11	9V AC; - phase
12	GND
A	GND
B	-FLAG2; handshake input from CIA 2
C-L	PB0-PB7; I/O lines from CIA 2
M	PA2; I/O line from CIA 2; This line substitutes for the CB2 which is known from other CBMs of the VIA 6522.
N	GND

Some of the lines mentioned before already have definitely pre-assigned functions. For more information on using the CIAs please refer to chapter 8.

4.1 The Sound Controller 6581

4.1.1 General notes about the SID 6581

The sound synthesizer included in the Commodore 64 gives you the opportunity to produce all kinds of sounds, ranging from a flute to a big steam engine. Most computer synthesizers have only one voice, the Commodore 64 offers a three-voice synthesizer.

All the elements necessary to produce quality sound are found on a single IC. This IC is called the sound interface device (SID) 6581. It is a new component of the 65xx family. It is provided with:

* 3 seperately programmable, independent oscillators (voices)
* 4 mixable waveforms for every voice
* 3 mixable filters (high-low tape pass)
* Attack/decay/sustain/release control (ADSR-control) for every voice
* 2 ring modulators
* alternation possibility for external signal source
* 2 8-bit A/D transformer

Pin layout of the 6581 are:

1-2 CAP1A,CAP1B; condenser connector for the programmable filters. Recommended capacity: 2200 pF.
3-4 CAP2A,CAP2B; as 1-2
5 -RES (reset); =0 brings SID into basic state
6 $\emptyset_2$(system frequency 2); all data-bus actions only take place during $\emptyset_2$=1.
7 R/W: 0=write access, 1=read access
8 -CS (chip select);0=data valid, 1=data invalid
9-13 A0-A4 (address bits 0-4); select one of the 29 registers of the SID.
14 GND(ground); The SID should have its own ground so as to avoid interferences from other system components.
15-22 D0-D7; data lines to/from the 6510 processor
23 A2IN analog input 2
24 A1IN analog input 1
25 VCC; supply voltage +5V
26 EXT IN (external input); input for external audio signals for mixing with SID.
27 AUDIO OUT; output for signals that were produced by SID.
28 VDD; supply voltage +12V

The SID 6581 can produce three synthesized voices that can

be controlled independently of each other. This is an unusually powerul capability for a single integrated circuit. Additionally, the voices can be used in combination to produce some extremely complex sounds.

Each voice consists of an oscillator, a waveform generator capable of producing four different timbres, an envelope generator, and an amplitude modulator.

The oscillator produces the basic frequency in the range from 0-8200 Hz with a reslolution of 16 bits.

The SID can produce four different waveforms: triangular, sawtooth, pulse and white noise. The choice of waveforms influences the sound quality.

A triangular waveform has a very soft sound, like a recorder. The sawtooth waveform produces a full spectrum sound. Consequently, it has a more harsh sound, like a trumpet. The pulse waveform is missing some some harmonic ranges. It sounds a little hollow, somewhat like a clarinet. The white noise consists of a random sequence of different frequencies within defined limits.

The volume of a tone is influenced by an amplitude modulator which is controlled by the envelope generator. When the envelope generator is triggered, the amplitude (volume) of the sound is controlled by the ADSR parameters that define the envelope.

Additionally, the outputs of each voice can be sent through adjustable filters which further define the sound.

The SID also lets you use voices 1 or 2 in combination with voice 3 to produce a ring modulated sound much like a bell sound.
The SID also contains two 8-bit analog to digital converters. These A/D converters can be used to connect game paddles, electrical controllers, etc.

4.1.2 Explaination of the Registers

The SID is located at address $D400 (54272). The registers that control the SID are:

REG 0   oscillator frequency low byte for voice 1

REG 1   oscillator frequency high byte for voice 1

REG 2   pulse width low byte for voice 1
REG 3   pulse width high byte for voice 1
Registers 2 and 3 determine the pulse width relation of the pulse waveform output of voice 1. Only the bits 0-3 are used by register 3.

REG 4 control register for voice 1

bit 0 GATE: gate bit for the envelope generator. When this bit is set to one, the ATTACK/DECAY/SUSTAIN cycle begins. The volume of voice 1 increases from zero to the maximum according to the attack time set in REG 5 and then decreases according to the decay time in also set in REG 5 to the sustain level set in REG 6.

When this bit is set to zero, the RELEASE cycle begins. The volume decreases to zero according to the release time set in REG 6.

Bit 1 SYNC: When set to 1, the frequency of voice 1 is synchronized with that of voice 3.

Bit 2 RING: When set to 1, the triangular waveform output of voice 1 is replaced by a ring modulated combination of voices 1 and 3.

Bit 3 TEST: When set to 1, voice 1 is locked until the TEST bit is reset to 0.

Bit 4 TRI: When set to 1, a triangular waveform selected

Bit 5 SAW: When set to 1, a sawtooth waveform selected

Bit 6 PUL: When set to 1, a pulse waveform selected.

Bit 7 NSE: When set to 1, a noise generator selected.

* It is possible to select several waveforms simultaneously. The result is a logical ANDing of the waveworms.

REG 5 ATTACK/DECAY (see TABLES 4.1 and 4.2)

Bits 0-3 DECAY: Sets the time in which the volume falls from maximum to the sustain level. The range is variable from 6msec to 24sec.

Bits 4-7 ATTACK: Sets the time in which the volume increases from zero to maximum volume after gating the voice. The range is variable from 2msec to 8 sec.

REG 6 SUSTAIN/RELEASE (see TABLE 4.2)

Bits 0-3 RELEASE: Sets the time in which the volume falls from the sustain level to zero volume after resetting the GATE bit to zero. The range is variable from 6msec to 24 sec.

Bits 4-7 SUSTAIN: The proportion of the peak volume that constitutes the sustain level. A zero value indicates a zero volume, a value of 8 is a sustain level equal to one-half of the peak volume and a value of 15 is a sustain level equal to the peak volume.

REG 7-
REG 13 These registers control voice 2 analogously to registers 0-6 with the following exceptions:
SYNC synchronizes voice 2 with voice 1
RING replaces the triangular output of voice 2 with the ring-modulated combination of the voices 1 and 2.

REG 14-
REG 20 These registers control voice 3 analogously to registers 0-6 with the following exceptions:
SYNC synchronizes voice 3 with voice 2.
RING substitutes the triangular output of voice 3 with the ring-modulated combination of voice 3 and 2.

REG 21 filter frequency low. Only bits 0-2 are used.

REG 22 filter frequency high.
The 11-bit number of registers 21 and 22 determine the cutoff frequency of the filters. This frequency is computed as follows:
F=(30+W*5.8)Hz, W is this 11-bit number.

REG 23 Filter resonance and switch.
Bit 0 1=output voice 1 through the filter.
Bit 1 1=output voice 2 through the filter.
Bit 2 1=output voice 3 through the filter.
Bit 3 1=input external signal source through filter
Bits 4-7 Resonance frequency of filter.
The resonance frequency is variable from zero (no resonance) to 15 (maximum resonance) which emphasizes the frequencies at the cutoff frequency.

REG 24 This register has the following functions:
Bits 0-3: overall volume
Bit 4 : LP sets the low-pass output of the filter.
Bit 5 : BP sets the band-pass output of the filter.
Bit 6 : HP sets the high-pass ouput of the filter.
Bit 7 : 3OFF 1=disconnect voice 3 output. Use this to modulate the other voices without audible results from voice 3.

You may only write to the registers listed above. You may only read the registers listed below:

REG 25 POTX : reads the position of the potentiometer (A/D converter) at pin 24.

REG 26 POTY: reads the position of the potentiometer (A/D converter) at pin 23.

REG 27 Noise generator 3
This register allows you to read the output of

voice 3. This allows you to modulate the other voices to produce interesting sounds.

REG 28 Envelope generator 3
This registers allows you to read the output of voice 3 envelope generator. This allows you to produce harmonic envelopes by adding this register to the filter frequency.

VALUE	ATTACK RATE
0	2 ms
1	8 ms
2	16 ms
3	24 ms
4	38 ms
5	56 ms
6	68 ms
7	80 ms
8	100 ms
9	250 ms
10	500 ms
11	800 ms
12	1 sec
13	3 sec
14	5 sec
15	8 sec

TABLE 4-1

VALUE	DECAY/RELEASE RATE
0	6ms
1	24ms
2	48ms
3	72ms
4	114ms
5	168ms
6	204ms
7	240ms
8	300ms
9	750ms
10	1.5sec
11	2.4sec
12	3sec
13	9sec
14	15sec
15	24sec

TABLE 4-2

4.1.3 The Analog/Digital Converter (Potentiometers)

The A/D converter, also called a potentiometer is a device that changes an analog signal (i.e. voltage) into a digital value. The critical problem with such a transformation is to change an analog value with an infinite gradation into a digital value with a finite gradation (fixed intervals). Inevitably, a maximum error of +/- of the smallest digital step occurs.

The SID 6581 contains two A/D converters named POTX and POTY. They each use a fixed reference voltage of 5V. They produce a reading as follows: a capacitor is discharged and its is value is read into register 25 or 26. This value is porportional to the time required for a recharging of the capacitor using the reference voltage. This procedure is repeated cyclically.

4.1.3.1 Handling the A/D Converter

It becomes clear from the points made above that only potentiometrical switching is possible. If currents have to be measured, they must to be put into a suitable form first. This can be achieved by using a unijunction transistor.

The measuring arrangements are such that the one end of the measuring resistance is connected to +5V (available at the control port of the Commodore 64) and the other end is connected to the analog input of the SID (also available at the control ports, marked as POTX and POTY). The value read from registers 25 and 26 is a measurement of the resistance.

In order to take advantage of the entire 8-bit range, the resistance must operate in range from 0 to 500 megaohm.

4.1.3.2 Using the Game Paddles

You can connect regular game paddles to the Commodore 64. Two sets of game paddles (four in all) may be connected at one time. They are simply plugged into the control ports on the right side of the device. A game paddle is nothing more than a potentiometer (which is connected to the SID as was explained in the preceding section), and a key which has an effect on joystick position LEFT for the one paddle and RIGHT for the other paddle.

The procedure of reading the game paddle values from program presents a little problem. The game paddles and the keyboard share some of the lines of CIA 1 and CIA 2. Because two sets of the paddles (four paddles in all) may be connected at on time and because there are only two analog converters in the Commodore 64, a way of sharing the converters is required. So as to avoid inteference of the game paddles with the keyboard, we have to write a small machine language routine to read the game paddle values without disturbing the keyboard functions.

The solution is the following program which allows us to access all four paddles. The program is located in a memory range that is not normally used by the operating system.

```
CFBE  SEI          ;prevent keyboard interruptions
CFBF  LDA #$80     ;parameter for paddle-set A
CFC1  JSR $CFEC    ;get A/D values A1 and A2
CFC4  STX $033C    ;save POTX
CFC7  STY $033D    ;    and save POTY
CFCA  LDA $DC00    ;get key A from CIA 1
CFCD  AND #$0C     ;filter required bits
CFCF  STA $029F    ;and save
CFD2  LDA #$40     ;parameter for paddle -set B
CFD4  JSR $CFEC    ;get A/D values B1 and B2
CFD7  STX $033E    ;and save
CFDA  STY $033F
CFDD  LDA $DC01    ;get keys B from CIA 2
CFE0  AND #$0C     ;filter required bits
CFE2  STA $02A0    ;and save
CFE5  LDA #$FF     ;all bits output in CIA 1
CFE7  STA $DC02    ;in order to enable
CFEA  CLI          ;keyboard inquiry
CFEB  RTS          ;back to basic program
CFEC  STA $DC00    ;select paddle set
CFEF  ORA #$C0     ;and set appropirate bits
CFF2  STA $DC02    ;on output
CFF4  LDX #$0      ;time delay to
CFF6  DEX          ;  stabilize input
CFF7  BNE $CFF6    ;A/D input
CFF9  LDX $D419    ;get A/D 1 (POTX)
CFFC  LDY $D41A    ;get A/D 2 (POTY)
CFFF  RTS          ;return to main program
```

Here is A BASIC program which POKEs the above program into memory. Connect the paddles, load and start the program and see what happens.

```
10  DATA 120,169,128,32,236,207,142,60,3,140,61,3,173
20  DATA 0,220,41,12,141,159,2,169,64,32,236,207,142
30  DATA 62,3,140,63,3,173,1,220,41,12,141,160,2,169
40  DATA 255,141,2,220,88,96,141,0,220,9,192,141,2
50  DATA 220,162,0,202,208,253,174,25,212,172,26,212,96
60  FOR M=53182 TO 53247
70  READ A: POKE M,A: NEXT: read in REM machine program
80  AX=830: REM paddle 1 at control port 1
90  AY=831: REM paddle 2 at control port 1
100 BA=672: REM keys from paddle pair A
110 BX=828: REM paddle 1 at control port 2
120 BY=829: REM paddle 2 at control port 2
130 BB=830: REM keys from paddle pair B
140 SYS 53182: REM get all values
150 PRINT PEEK(AX)" "PEEK(AY)" "PEEK(BA)" ";
```

```
160 PRINT PEEK(BX)" "PEEK(BY)" "PEEK(BB)" ";
170 GOTO 140
```

4.2 Programming the SID 6581

This section describes the programming the synthesizer. For the simple production of a tone you should: 1) load register 24; 2) set the appropriate ADSR registers (5,6,12,13,19,20); 3) set the remaining registers, preferably in the order of their voice range with the exception of the registers 4, 11 and 18; 4) load registers 4,11 and 18 at the end (don't forget bit 0!) and then you'll hear the tone.

The following brief program will acquaint you with the waveforms and the tone range of the synthesizer:

```
10   S1=54272: REM voice 1
20   S2=54279: REM voice 2
30   S3=54286: REM voice 3
40   FL=54293: REM filter lo-byte
50   FH=54294: REM filter hi-byte
60   RS=54295: REM resonance+switch
70   PL=54296: REM pass kind+volume
80   POKE S1+4,0: POKE S2+4,0: POKE S3+4,0
100  POKE S1+2,0: POKE S1+3,8
110  POKE S1+5,0: POKE S1+6,240
120  POKE RS,0: POKE PL,15
130  PRINT "TRIANGLE"
140  T=16: GOSUB 300
150  PRINT "SAWTOOTH"
160  T=32: GOSUB 300
170  PRINT "RECTANGLE"
180  T=64: GOSUB 300
190  PRINT "NOISE"
200  T=128: GOSUB 300
210  END
300  POKE S1,0: POKE S1+1,0
310  POKE S1+4,T+1: REM switch on tone
320  FOR I=0 TO 255: FOR J=0 TO 255 STEP 50
330  POKE S1,J: POKE S1+1,I
340  NEXT J,I
350  POKE S1+4,T: REM switch off tone
360  RETURN
```

Lines 10 thru 80 shuld be written before each of your sound programs. It makes the program a lot easier to handle.

The next program makes the function of the envelope generator clearer. For reasons of simplicity, just copy lines 10 to 80 from the preceding program, and add lines 100 through 160 as found below.

```
100  A=9: D=9: S=8: R=9: H=400
110  POKE S1+5,16*A+D: POKE S1+6,16*S+R
120  POKE RS,0: POKE PL,15
130  POKE S1,37: POKE S1+1,17
140  POKE S1+4,33
150  FOR I=0 TO H: NEXT
160  POKE S1+4,32
```

Now try changing the data in line 100 in order to get a feeling for the parameters and what influence they have on the tone. The values A,D,S, and R may only be in a range from 0 to 15, otherwise you will get an **ILLEGAL QUANTITY ERROR.**

As you probably found out by now, variable A determines the increment time and variable D the decrement time of the volume level; variable H determines the time to hold the tone at the sustain level and variable R the release time to zero volume after resetting the GATE bit.

Here is a program to play a three voice chord on the harpsichord. Again, keep lines 10 to 80 from the first program!

```
100  A=0: D=1: S=13: R=10: H=100
110  POKE S1+5,16*A+D: POKE S1+6,16*S+R
120  POKE S2+5,16*A+D: POKE S2+6,16*S+R
130  POKE S3+5,16*A+D: POKE S3+6,16*S+R
140  POKE RS,0: POKE PL,15
150  POKE S1,37: POKE S1+1,17
160  POKE S2,154: POKE S2+1,21
170  POKE S3,177: POKE S3+1,25
180  POKE S1+4,33: POKE S2+4,33: POKE S3+4,33
190  FOR I=0 TO H: NEXT
200  POKE S1+4,32: POKE S2+4,32: POKE S3+4,32
```

In the next example, the frequency of the tone is changed by reading the envelope generator of voice 3 (54300). Try experimenting with the data in line 100 again.

```
100  A=9: D=9: S=9: R=9: H=30
110  POKE RS,0: POKE PL,15
120  POKE S3+5,16*A+D: POKE S3+6,16*S+R
130  POKE S3+4,33
140  FOR I=0 TO H: POKE S3+1,PEEK(54300): NEXT
150  POKE S3+4,32
160  FOR I=0 TO R*4: POKE S3+1,PEEK(54300): NEXT
```

Finally, let the "STARSHIP ENTERPRISE" pass by acousticly:

```
100  A=15: D=0: S=8: R=13: H=8000
110  POKE RS,0: POKE PL,15
120  POKE S1,0: POKE S1+1,30
130  POKE S2,0: POKE S2+1,1
140  POKE S3,0: POKE S3+1,100
150  POKE S1+5,16*A+D: POKE S1+6,16*S+R
160  POKE S1+4,129: POKE S3+4,23
170  FOR I=0 TO H: NEXT
180  POKE S1+4,128: POKE S3+4,16
```

We are sure that all these examples provide you enough incentive to try your own programs on the synthesizer. Have fun!

4.3 SYNTHY-64 - Full-fledged Synthesizer software

When people heard about the Commodore 64 and its tremendous capabilities in graphics and sound, they became excited. But after reading the user's guide, some people started to wonder whether some pages in this book were missing. Very little was said about programming color, sound, or graphics.

You have to admit that programming color, sound, and graphics is not necessarily easy. You must set every register and memorize addresses to create the different sound.

For example you need three POKE commands for the note "C":

```
POKE 54272,37: POKE 54273,17: POKE 54276,65
```

This is, of course, not very suitable for writing long compositions. You have to control the production of quarter or eighth notes, etc. All this may dim your joy in the Commodore 64 slightly. Fortunately, there is software that save you from the bothersome procedures of POKEs and PEEKs and machine language programming.

One such software packages is **SYNTHY 64.** It allows you to take advantage of the fantastic sound capabilities of the Commodore 64, without having to resort to machine language programming. Using the SYNTHY 64 as an example, we will show you how easy and relaxing the composition of music can be. This program allows you to play several voices, indicate the presently played tone, save and load the different songs and much more. **SYNTHY-64** is a product of ABACUS Software.

With SYNTHY-64, the composition of music is similar to the process used in writing regular sheet music - and using a structure similar to BASIC. You put in a line number and afterwards the commands or the notes.

Notes are entered according to their names: the note "C" is entered simply as **C.**

For the first note of each voice you may add the following information:

VOICE NOTE VALUE OCTAVE / NOTE DURATION

Example: +G5/4. + stands for voice 1, "G" note is played in the fifth octave as a quarter note. If you don't change the voice, octave or note duration you need only indicate the note value on subsequent commands.

When used to write music, SYNTHY-64 gives you a BASIC shell in the editor. If you LIST the SYNTHY-64 shell, it looks like this:

```
1     RUN"<clr>"          <clr> appears as a reversed heart
63000 REM
63005 REM*******
63010 @WP @P8 @A0 @D9 @S0 @R0 @F0 RETURN PIANO
63020 @WT @A4 @D2 @S10 @R5 @F0 RETURN FLUTE
63030 @WS @A6 @D0 @S10 @R1 CB X10 Y12 @F1
      RETURN TRUMPET
63040 @WP @P1 @A0 @D9 @S0 @R0 @F0 RETURN BANJO
63050 @WS @A6 @D5 @S2 @R2 ZH X8 Y12 @F1 RETURN
      ACCORDION
```

The RUN command in line 1 must be the first command in every music program which you compose. Lines 63010 to 63050 are five independent routines that can be used to set up a voice to sound like a particular instrument. You set a voice from anywhere within the program to GOSUB to the proper subroutine. In our example, we would GOSUB the subroutine in line 63050 (accordion).

+GOSUB 63050
where + stands for voice 1

The commands that you see in lines 63010 to 63050 are special features of SYNTHY-64. With these commands the proper registers in the Commodore 64 are set by SYNTHY-64. For example:

@WP sets a voice to a pulse waveform
@P8 sets the pulse width to 8
@A0 sets the attack speed to 0

You can use SYNTHY-64 to easily control the envelope generator, filters, ring modulator, and dozens of other variations allowed by the SID chip.

Below, is an example of using SYNTHY-64 to play a familiar piece of music - "Swing Low, Sweet Chariot".

```
1  RUN"<clr>"
10 +GOSUB63050  -GOSUB63020
50 T130
100 +B5/4  G4/1 +G4/2 B5/4 G4/4.  G +G/8 E/8  D/4.
150 G/A  G +G G G B5 B B/4   D +D/1
200 E/8  G + D B/2 D/4 G4/4.  C/2 +G/8 E  G + D/4.
250 G/8  G +G G G B5  D +B A/4 G4/2.  G/1 +B5/4
300 D  G +G4/8 E G G/4 G/8 G  C/2 +G G/4 E/8  G + D/4.
350 G/8  G/1 +G G G B5 B D/4 D/2.  D +D/4
400 E/8  G + D B/4 B G4 G/8   C/2 +G G G E  G/2 + D/4.
450 A/8  G +G G G B5   D +B A/4 G4/1   G
999 END
63000 REM
63005 REM*******
63010 @WP @P8 @A0 @D9 @S0 @R0 @F0 RETURN           PIANO
63020 @WT @A4 @D2 @S10 @R5 @F0 RETURN              FLUTE
63030 @WS @A6 @D0 @S10 @R1 ZB X10 Y12 @F1 RETURN  TRUMPET
63040 @WP @P1 @A0 @D9 @S0 @R0 @F0 RETURN           BANJO
63050 @WS @A6 @D5 @S2 @R2 ZH X8 Y12 @F1 RETURN    ACCORDION
```

You can see in lines 10 through 450 that it is much easier to enter music using a note-oriented language as opposed to a POKE-oriented language. After entering the above music and listen to your song. Have fun composing!

Of course, you can use **SYNTHY-64** to create your own sounds and instruments. The Commodore 64 has a remarkable ability to make music and sound effects.

Chapter 5 GRAPHICS PROGRAMMING

5.1 The Video Interface Chip 6567

5.1.1 CHIP Description

The VIC chip is a very sophisticated integrated of the 65xx family. Not only is it responsible for producing the pictures on the screen, but it also handles refreshing of the Commodore's 64K of dynamic memory. Here are the most important features:

* ability to display 16 colors
* produces a 40 characters X 25 lines picture
* has high resolution graphics with 320 x 200 pixels
* 5 types of bit mapping operations
* handles 8 sprites with 24x21 dots each simultaneously
* independent refreshing of 64K dynamic ram
* movable character generator
* movable video RAM

Pin description of the VIC 6567 follow:

1-7	D6-D0; processor data bus
8	-IRQ; 0 if a bit of the IMR and the IRR coincide
9	-LP; input, light-pen strobe
10	-CS; processor-bus action only take place if CS=0.
11	R/W; 0=taking over data from bus
12	BA; 0= data not ready at reading access
13	VDD; +12V
14	COLOR; color information output
15	SYNC; Impulses to synchronize lines and screen
16	AEC; 0=VIC uses system bus, 1= bus free
17	Ø$_0$OUT; clock output
18	-RAS; Dynamic ram control-signal
19	-CAS; as above
20	GND
21	ØCOLOR; Input color frequency
22	ØIN; Input dot frequency
23	A11; processor address-bus
24-29	A0/A8-A5/A13; multiplexed (video-) ram address-bus
30-31	A6-A7; (video-) ram address bus
32-34	A8-A10; processor address bus
35-38	D11-8; data from color ram
39	D7; processor data-bus
40	VCC; +5V

5.1.2 Register Descriptions

The VIC has 47 registers that are explained here.

REG 0 sprite 0 X-coordinate
This is the low-order 8 bits of the X-coordinate of sprite 0 position. The ninth bit is found in REG 16.

REG 1 sprite 0 Y-coordinate
This is the Y-coordinate of sprite 0 position.

REG 2-15 same as above for sprites 1 thru 7
The register pair 2/3 is for sprite 1, pair 4/5 for sprite 2 etc.

REG 16 sprite 0 X-coordinate MSB
These are the high order bits of the sprite X-registers, bit 0 for sprite 0, bit 1 for sprite 1 etc.

REG 17 Control register 1
Bit 0-2 number of dots to smooth scroll y-direction
Bit 3 0=display 24 rows; 1=display 25 rows
Bit 4 0=blank screen
Bit 5 1=standard bitmap mode

Bit 6 1=extended color mode
Bit 7 raster compare high order bit REG 18

REG 18 When read, contains current raster position (8 bits plus bit 7, REG 17).
When written to, contains the raster compare value. In this case, a raster interrupt is triggered when the current raster matches this value

REG 19 Contains the X-position of the light pen input after the light pen is triggered.

REG 20 Contains the Y-position of the light pen input after the light pen is triggered.

REG 21 Sprite enable
Each spirte 0 thru 7 is enabled (turned on) when its corresponding bit is set to 1.

REG 22 Control register 2
Bit 0-2 number of dots to smooth scroll x-direction
Bit 3 0=38 column display; 1=40 column display
Bit 4 1=multicolor mode
Bit 5 1=reset VIC chip

REG 23 Sprite expand X
Each sprite 0 thru 7 is expanded to twice normal width in the x-direction when its corresponding bit is set to 1.

REG 24 Base address of character generator and video ram
Bit 1-3 address bits 11-13 for the character base
Bit 4-7 address bits 10-13 for the video-ram base

REG 25 IRR interrupt request register
Bit 0 raster interrupt (REG 18)
Bit 1 sprite-background interupt (REG 31)
Bit 2 sprite-sprite interrupt (REG 30)
Bit 3 light pen interrupt (pin LP)
Bit 7 set if zero if of the above bits is set to 1

REG 26 IMR interrupt mask register
Bit 0 raster interrupt enable
Bit 1 sprite-background interrupt enable
Bit 2 spite-sprite interrupt enable
Bit 3 light pen interrupt

REG 27 Sprite-background priority
Each sprite 0 thru 7 has a priority higher than the background if the corresponding bit is zero. Background has higher priority if corresponding bit is one.

REG 28 Sprite multicolor mode
Each sprite 0 thru 7 is displayed in multicolor mode if the corresponding bit is one.

REG 29 Sprite expand Y
Each sprite 0 thru 7 is expanded to twice the normal height in the Y-direction if the corresponding bit is one.

REG 30 Sprite-sprite collision
For each sprite 0 thru 7 that has collided (non-transparent areas are coincident) the corresponding bit is set to one and IRR bit 2 is also set to one. The bits in this register remain set until the register is read.

REG 31 Sprite-background collision
For each sprite 0 thru 7 that has collided (non-transparent area are coincident with non-background color characters) the corresponding bit it set to one and the IRR bit 1 is set to one. The bits in this register remain set until the register is read.

REG 32 Border color
Bits 0 thru 3.

REG 33 Background color #0
Bits 0 thru 3.

REG 34 Background color #1
Bits 0 thru 3.

REG 35 Background color #2

Bits 0 thru 3.

REG 36 Background color #3
Bits 0 thru 3.

REG 37 Sprite multicolor #0
Bits 0 thru 3.

REG 38 Sprite multicolor #fl
Bits 0 thru 3.

REG 39- Sprite color
46 Color of sprites 0 thru 7.

5.1.3 Display Techniques

The VIC chip can produce different types of displays:

a) standard characters displayed by the character generator; b) multicolor characters; c) extended color mode; d) high resolution bit mode; e) multicolor bit mode; f) sprite graphics. Each is described below:

a) standard character generation:
Each character on the keyboard is assigned a screen code. The letter A is given a screen code of 1, B a screen code of 2, etc. The list of screen codes appears in Appendix E of the Commodore 64 User's Guide.

Screen memory holds the screen codes of the characters to be displayed. Since the Commodore 64 can display 25 lines of 40 characters each, there are 1000 screen memory locations. Screen memory is normally located beginning at $400 (1024 decimal) thru $7E7 (2023 decimal) but can be moved if desired. When a character is to be displayed, the character's corresponding screen code is written to the appropriate screen memory location.

For each of the 1000 screen memory locations, there is a corresponding **color memory** location. Color memory is located beginning at $D800 (55296 decimal) thru $DBE7 (56295) decimal. There is a one-to-one correspondence with screen memory. Each position in color meory contains a value of the color of the corresponding screen memory character to be displayed. The Commodore 64 can display 16 colors, so only four bits of each color memory location are used.

The **character generator** contains a set of patterns that make up the letters, numbers and graphics symbols that are to be displayed. The character generator is located beginning at $D000 (53248 decimal) thru $D7FF (55295 decimal). Each pattern is 8 bytes long amd corresponds to the 8 rows of dots which make up a display character. For example, the pattern in the character generator for the symbol @ looks like this:

```
 <lbyte >
  BITS                          Memory
 76543210                     location:    Value
    ***        Row 1            $D000       $1C
   *   *       Row 2            $D001       $22
  *  * *       Row 3            $D002       $4A
  * * **       Row 4            $D003       $56
  *  **        Row 5            $D004       $4C
   *           Row 6            $D005       $20
   *****       Row 7            $D006       $3E
               Row 8            $D007       $00
```

The screen code for @ is 0; the screen code for A is 1; the screen code for B is 2, etc. The patterns in the character generator are ordered by this same screen code. Thus the pattern for the letter A would follow the pattern for the symbol @ and the pattern for the letter B would follow pattern for the letter **A**, etc.

Now to display characters on the screen. As each raster line (TV scan) is displayed, the VIC chip gets the value of the screen code from screen memory. The screen code is multiplied by 8 and added to the address of beginning of the character generator ($D800). The resulting address is the location of the pattern to be used for this character. The corresponding color memory location is also read to determine the color in which the character is to be displayed. The pattern is read out bit by bit, row by row to create the character in the correct color on the screen. Using this method, up to 256 different characters can be depicted.

Diagram 5-1 shows this in pictorial form.

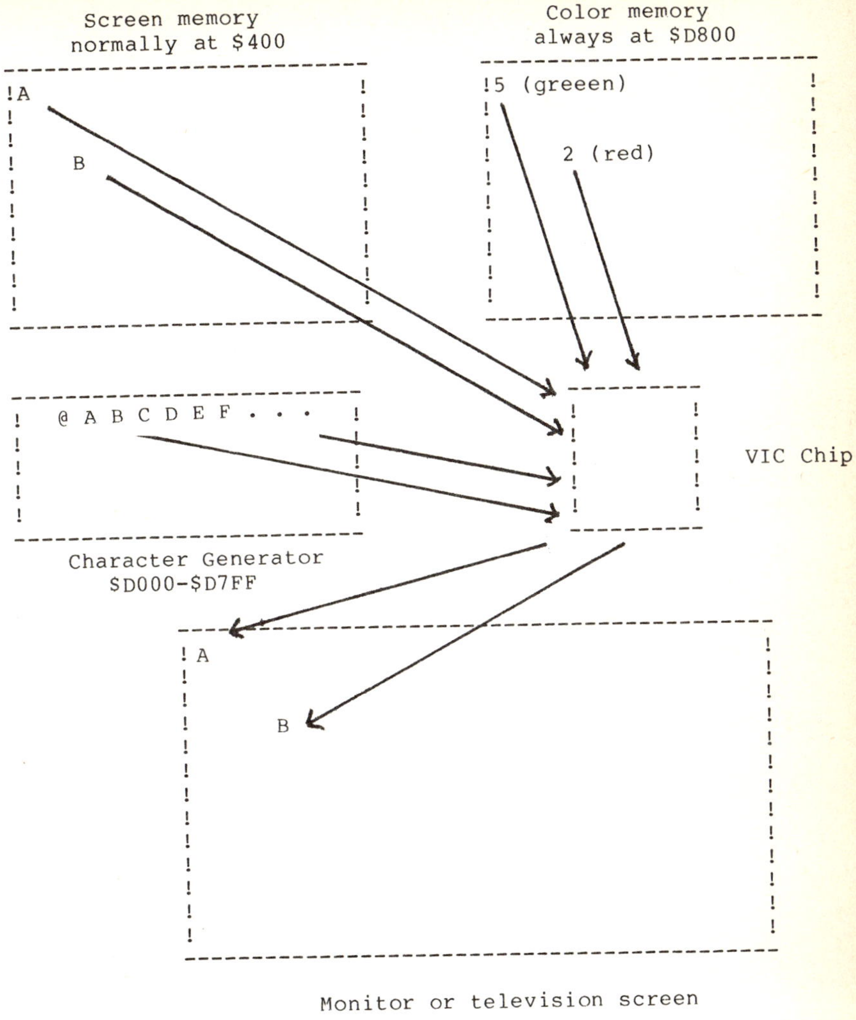

DIAGRAM 5-1

b) Multicolor character generation:
Using the standard character method of display, a character is displayed in a single color only. This is because each bit from the character generator is translated as either on or off. A bit which is on takes on the foreground color (as determined by the corresponding color memory location), while a bit which

is off takes on the background color.

You tell the VIC chip that you want to use the multicolor character mode by setting set 4 of REG 22. Using the multicolor character mode, the Commodore 64 can display characters in one of four different colors. In the multicolor character mode, VIC chip translates the color and character generator information diffently than the standard character method.

Here the color memory location for each screen code is examined. If bit 3 of a color memory location is 0 (making the color value 0 thru 7), then the character is displayed in the standard character mode as described in a) above. However if bit 3 of a color memory location is 1 (making the color value 8 thru 15), then the character is displayed in the multicolor mode.

During multicolor display, the VIC chip interprets the character generator differently. Instead of the bits of a pattern being interpreted as either on or off, multicolor character mode uses consecutive pairs of bits to construct a display character. The pairs of bits are interpreted as follows:

BIT PAIR	COLOR DISPLAYED	COLOR TAKEN FROM
00	Background color 0	$D021 (53281)
01	Background color 1	$D022 (53282)
10	Background color 2	$D023 (53283)
11	Color from low 3-bits of color memory	color memory

This makes it possible to display a character made up of four different color within any 8X8 cell on the screen. Of course the character is now depicted as a 4X8 pattern, but with pixels twice as wide as with standard character mode. Again, up to 256 different characters can be displayed in multicolor character mode.

c) **Extended color mode:**
In the extended color mode, you can control the color of the background for each individual character. Using the extended color mode, the VIC chip can display a character in one color, having a second color as a background, on a screen of a third color. Thus, every character can be made up of two colors, but the background color is not necessarily the same for each character.

To get into the extended color mode, you set bit 6 of REG

17. In the extended color mode, color memory is used the same way as in the standard character mode. However screen memory is interpreted differently. The two high-order bits (bits 7 and 6) are used to select the register from which to get the color value for the background. The following tables describes this:

Screen code value of bits 7	6	Use Background Register #	Taken from
0	0	0	$D021 (53281)
0	1	1	$D022 (53282)
1	0	2	$D023 (53283)
1	1	3	$D024 (53284)

Since two bits of the screen code are used to select the background color of the character, only six bits of the screen code are left to select the character pattern. Thus only 64 different patterns can be displayed.

d) High resolution bit mode:
Using high resolution bit mode of display, the VIC chip can display 320 X 200 pixels in a choice of two colors within each 8 X 8 screen cell. Thus the 64,000 (320 X 200) individual pixels require 8K of memory to represent an image on the high resolution screen. We call this 8K, bit-mapped memory. Each bit of the bit-mapped memory represents a pixel on the high resolution screen.

To enable high resolution bit mode, bit 5 of REG 17 is set and REG 24 must be primed with the address of the bit-mapped memory. Color memory is ignored in the high resolution bit mode. Instead, the normal screen memory is utilized as a sort of color memory.

Each byte of the normal screen memory supplies the color information for each 8 X 8 cell. Here normal screen memory is divided into two four-bit nibbles. If a bit in the bit-mapped memory is set to 1, then the high order nybble (bits 4-7) of normal screen memory specifies the color of these bits within that 8 X 8 cell. If a bit in the bit-mapped meory is set to 0, then the low order four bits (bits 0-3) specifies the color of these bits in that same cell.

e) Multicolor bit mode:
The multicolor bit mode allows each 8 X 8 cell to display up to four different colors. In the multicolor bit mode there are 160 X 200 pixels. The pixels are displayed

twice as wide on the screen in multicolor bit mode as in the high resolution bit mode.

Multicolor bit mode is enabled by setting bit 5 or REG 17 and bit 4 of REG 22 and REG 24 must be primed with the address of the bit-mapped memory.

There is a one-to-one correspondence between the bit-mapped memory and screen display except that here the 8K bit-mapped memory is interpreted in pairs of two bits. The pairs of bits cause the double wide pixels to appear in color as follows:

Bit pair	Color from
00	background register #0
01	screen memory low nybble
10	screen memory high nybble
11	color memory

f) Sprites:
Sprites are large user definable characters that can be displayed anywhere on the screen. They can be displayed independently of the other types of displays on the screen. Sprites also have other properties:

1) Up to 8 sprites can be defined and maintained by the VIC chip. The sprites are numbered 0 thru 7 and each sprite is 24 X 21 pixels large.
2) Each sprite can be expanded in the horizontal direction and/or the vertical direction immediately.
3) Each sprite can be positioned on the screen independently of other sprites.
4) A sprite can be defined as high resolution cr multicolor.
5) Sprites have priorities with respect to each other. Sprite 0 has priority over sprite 1. This means that if sprite 0 and sprite 1 are positioned so as to overlap, sprite 0 would appear in front of spirte 1.
6) Sprites have priorities with respect to background objects. A backgroud object is defined as any character or graphics on the screen that has other than the background color. Each sprite can be made to have a higher or lower priority than a background object.
7) Collisions between sprites occur when they are positioned so as to overlap. Sprite to sprite collisions can be set to notify the Commodore 64 automatically.
8) Collisions between sprites and the background occur when a sprite is positioned to overlap a background object. Sprite to background collisions can be set to

notify the Commodore 64 automatically.

A high resolution sprite is defined as a 24 X 21 pixel character. This means that 504 bits or 63 bytes are needed to define a high resolution sprite. In defining a high resolution sprite, each bit that is set to 1 appears in that sprites foreground color (REG 39 thru 46). Each bit that is set to 0 is transparent and whatever color is behind it appears.

A multicolor sprite is defined as a 12 X 21 pixel character with the horizontal pixels being double wide. Still 504 bits define a multicolor sprite, but the bits are interpreted in pairs. This allows a sprite to take on up to four colors. To set a sprite to multicolor mode, you must set the corresponding bit (0 thru 7) to one in REG 28.

The sprite colors are defined by the bit pairs as follows:

BIT Pair	Color	FROM
00	Transparent	Screen color
01	Sprite MC REG 0	$D025 (53285)
10	Sprite color reg	$D027-$D02E
11	Sprite MC REG 1	$D026 (53286)

The VIC chip must be told where to find the definition of the sprites. You pass this information to the VIC chip in the last 8 bytes of screen memory. Thus if you were using the normal screen memory location $400-$7FF, the memory locations $7F8 (2040) thru $7FF (2047) contain the pointers to the sprite definitions. The pointer for sprite 0 is found at $7F8 (2040); the pointer for sprite 1 is found at $7f9 (2041), etc.

This pointer is actually the number of the 64-byte chunk of memory in which the sprite definition is found. For example the pointer, to a sprite located at $340 (832) is 13 (832/64). This pointer would have to be placed in the appropriate screen memory pointer location for that sprite. For example, if we were using sprite 0, then we would place the value of the pointer (13) into the screen memory location for that pointer $7F8 (2040). Sprites do not appear on the screen until they have been enabled. This is done by setting the appropriate bit (0 thru 7) in REG 21 to on. To turn off that same sprite, the same bit in REG 21 must be turned off.

A sprite may be positioned at one of 512 horizontal locations or 256 vertical locations on the screen. These are more than the 320 horizontal and 200 vertical screen locations that appear on the screen. But since a sprite is so large, these extra locations allow a sprite to be moved smoothly into the viewing area of the screen.

When using sprites, the viewing area can be thought of as the 320 horizontal and 200 vertical pixels on the screen as depicted below:

```
0,0                                                    511,0
   +-----------------------------------------------------+
   ! 24,30                                   343,30      !
   !     +----------------------------------------+      !
   !     ! ^                                      !      !
   !     ! |                                      !      !
   !     ! |                                      !      !
   !     ! |                                      !      !
   !     ! |                                      !      !
   !     ! |                                      !      !
   !     !200          VIEWING AREA               !      !
   !     ! |                                      !      !
   !     ! |                                      !      !
   !     ! |                                      !      !
   !     ! |                                      !      !
   !     ! |                                      !      !
   !     ! v  <--------- 320 pixels ----------->  !      !
   !     +----------------------------------------+      !
   ! 24,250                                  343,250     !
   +-----------------------------------------------------+
0,255                                                  511,255
```

Note that the above diagram shows this 320 X 200 pixel viewing area. A sprite's position is figured from its upper left corner.

To position a sprite, the desired X-position is placed into the corresponding REG 0 thru 14 (even registers) and its Y-position is placed into the corresponding REG 1 thru REG 15 (odd registers). Since the register can hold only 256 positions, the extra bit (which makes possible the 512 positions) is located in REG 16. REG 16 contains the most significant bit for the X-position of each sprite.

Anytime the non-transparent area of one sprite overlaps that of another sprite, the two are said to be coincident. When they are coincident, the sprite with the lower sprite number will appear in front of the other. This is called sprite-sprite priority and is strictly a function of the sprite number. So sprite 0 has the highest priority of any sprite and always appears to pass in front of a higher numbered sprite.

A sprite may also be coincident with background area. The background area is any data on the screen that has a color different from the background color. When the sprite and the background area are coincident, either the sprite or the background can be made to appear in front of the other. This is controlled by the sprite-background priority register, REG 27. If the corresponding bit (0 thru 7) in REG 27 is set to one, then the sprite has a lower priority than the background area and appears to pass behind the background area. If the corresponding bit (0 thru 7) in REG 27 is set to zero, then the sprite has a higher priority than the background area and appears to pass in front of the background area.

The Commodore 64 also has the ability to detect when two sprites are coincident. This is called sprite-sprite collision detection. To enable this feature, bit 2 of REG 26 must be set to one. When at least two sprites have collided, the Commodore 64 jumps to the IRQ vector (interrupt handling routine) and sets bit 2 of REG 25 to indicate the sprite-sprite collision. At the same time, the corresponding bit (0 thru 7) in REG 30 for each sprite that is coincident is set to one.

Similarly, the Commodore 64 has the ability to detect when a sprite and background area are coincident. This is called sprite-background collision detection. To enable this feature, bit 1 of REG 26 must be set to one. When a sprite and a background area have collided, the Commodore jumps to the IRQ vector (interrupt handling routine) and sets bit 1 of REG 25 to indicate the sprite-background collision. At the same time, the corresponding bit (0 thru 7) in REG 31 for each sprite that has collided with a background area is set to one.

Sprites can also be expanded. You can double the height, the width or both to produce larger objects on the screen. To expand a sprite in width, the corresponding bit (0 thru 7) in REG 29 is set to one. To expand a sprite in height, the corresponding bit in REG 23 is set to one. You can expand a sprite in either the hires or multicolor modes.

5.2 Programming color and graphics

The outstanding features of the Commodore 64 are certainly its color and its builtin synthesizer. But how can you appreciate these features if you aren't told how to program graphics and sprites? On the following pages we will explain to you how to go about programming these Commodore 64 specialties.

The graphic possibilities of the Commodore 64 are better than those of many other computers in the same or higher price category.

The most important feature is the ability of the Commodore 64 to control up to eight user definable objects on the screen called **sprites.** Each sprite can be made to appear in any of the 16 different colors. In addition, you can define and display multicolor sprites which can take on up to four different colors. A sprite is a 24 X 21 pixel character - comparable to a block of 3 X 3 normal size characters. And sprites can be made to move independently of one another with ease.

The Commodore 64 allows you to display in up to 16 colors. The color of the background, foreground and the character can be changed. In order to change the character color from the keyboard, you hold the CTRL key or C= key while pressing a number key between 1 and 8. Table 5-1 lists the color that are possible:

KEY	COLOR	COLOR VALUE
CTRL - 1	BLACK	0
CTRL - 2	WHITE	1
CTRL - 3	RED	2
CTRL - 4	TURQUOISE	3
CTRL - 5	PURPLE	4
CTRL - 6	GREEN	5
CTRL - 7	BLUE	6
CTRL - 8	YELLOW	7
C= - 1	ORANGE	8
C= - 2	BROWN	9
C= - 3	LIGHT RED	10
C= - 4	GRAY 1	11
C= - 5	GRAY 2	12
C= - 6	LIGHT GREEN	13
C= - 7	LIGHT BLUE	14
C= - 8	GRAY 3	15

TABLE 5-1

Note **C=** is the Commodore key

You can change the border and background colors by POKEing the color values into the corresponding registers. The border color is in REG 32 and the background color is in REG 33. To change the border color, POKE 53280 with the desired color value. To change the background color, POKE 53281 with the desired color value. For instance:

POKE 53280,0: POKE 53281,0

makes a totally black screen. In order to change the color of just one screen character, all you need is:

POKE 55296,1

This POKE changes the color of the character in the upper left corner of the screen to white. The color of any other characters on the screen would remain unchanged. Location 55296 is the beginning of an area called color memory and continues to location 56295. Location 55296 contains the color of the character in line 1, column 1; location 55297 the color of the character in line 1, column 2; location 56295 the color of the character in line 25, column 40, etc.

In order to get the screen full of A's, you could write the following brief program:

```
10 PRINT CHR$(147):REM CLR SCREEN
20 FOR I=1024 TO 2023:REM SCREEN MEMORY
30 POKE I,ASC("A")
40 NEXT I
50 END
```

You will see how the screen fills up with A's from the upper left to the lower right.

In order to add color to the display, you would add the following line to the program:

```
35 POKE 55296+I-1024,INT(RND(1)*15):REM ADD COLOR RANDOMLY
```

The program runs almost the same. with the difference that after POKEing the letter "A" into screen memory, the corresponding color memory location was set to a random color.

Now lets investigate high resolution graphics. One use of high resolution color graphics is for plotting mathematical function. The following program illustrates the calculation of the bit mapped memory locations needed for X and Y coordinates.

Commodore BASIC does not have builtin graphics commands. So drawing lines or circles is not very convenient from BASIC. But the fact that these builtin commands don't exist does not mean that the Commodore 64 is not capable of spectacular graphics. All that is needed are some programming tools.

Towards the end of this section, we introduce you to such a

tool which we call HIRES GRAPHIC AID. Using this program, you can conveniently make draw graphics. This program even enables you to save complete graphics on cassette or diskette for later loading them from there. This program is written in a way that should enable you to use it practically and even extend it.

Now back to the sample plotting program. The objective of this program is to draw a sine-wave on the screen. It is a very common example of the application of graphics.

```
10  REM SINE - PLOT PROGRAM
20  V=53248: REM START ADDR OF THE GRAPHIC PROCESSOR
30  AD=8192: REM START ADDR OF THE HIRES BIT MAP
40  POKE V+17,59: REM SET HIRES MODE
50  POKE V+24,24: REM POINT TO SCREEN MEMORY
60  FOR I=1024 TO 2023: REM SET COLOR RAM
70  : POKE I,16
80  NEXT I
90  FOR I=8192 TO 16383: REM CLEAR SCREEN MEMORY
100 : POKE I,0
110 NEXT I
120 FOR X=0 TO 319: REM DRAW THE X-AXIS
130 : Y=100: REM POSITION OF THE X-AXIS
140 : GOSUB 1000: REM CALL DRAWING ROUTINE
150 NEXT X
160 FOR Y=0 TO 199: REM DRAWING OF THE Y-AXIS
170 : X=160: REM POSITION OF THE Y-AXIS
180 : GOSUB 1000: REM CALL DRAWING ROUTINE
190 NEXT Y
200 X=0
210 FOR I=-3.14159265 TO 3.14159265 STEP 0.0196349541
220 : REM INTERVAL LIMITS
230 : Y=100+99*SIN(I): REM FUNCTION
240 : GOSUB 1000
250 : X=X+1
260 NEXT I
270 GOTO 270
1000 OY=320*INT(Y/8)+(Y AND 7): REM CALCULATE DOT POSITION
1010 OX=8*INT(X/8)
1020 MA=2^((7-X) AND 7)
1030 AV=AD+OY+OX
1040 POKE AV,PEEK(AV) OR MA: REM PLOT DOT
1050 RETURN
```

The SINE PLOT PROGRAM assumes that the hires screen is arranged such that the origin (0,0) is located in the upper left corner. The subroutine beginning at line 1000, calculates the position of the individual dot to be plotted and then proceeds to plot that dot.

What all happens now in our plot-program? First, the two starting addresses of the VIC chip registers and hires screen memory are defined in lines 20 and 30. The next two POKE commands:

POKE V+17,27+32 and POKE V+24,16+8

switch to graphics mode by changing the VIC chip registers. POKE V+17,27+32 changes the Commodore 64 from the standard character display (text mode) to the graphics mode of display. POKE V+24,16+8 point sets the VIC chip to use the bit map screen memory starting at 8192.

If you want to switch back to the text page later on, you have to save their old values old values before changing the addresses in the VIC chip. You should save the values in two variables, since you will need these values later on. This could look like this:

A1=PEEK(V+17) and A2=PEEK(V+24)

To get back into text mode later, after having worked with graphics, you can just restore the VIC registers with these saved values:

POKE V+17,A1 and POKE V+24,A2

Then you are back into the text page and can proceed normally.

In lines 60 thru 80, you have to change the color of the graphics display. You do this by changing each byte of color memory. Lines 90 thru 110 clear the bit-mapped area to off so that nothing is displayed on the screen.

Each bit in the bit-mapped screen area represents one screen pixel. Each bit has a value of either 0 or 1 and if the bit is set to one, then the pixel is to be displayed; if the bit is set to zero, then the pixel is not to be displayed. Eight bits constitute a byte. One line of is represented as 8 bits/byte X 40 bytes/line = 320 bits / line. One column is represented as 8 bits/byte X 25 bytes/column = 200 bits/column. Altogether there are 64,000 bits in hires bit-mapped memory.

Let's continue by looking at a character. A character is composed of 8 X 8 dots giving us 64 dots in a character. Each of these dots can be set or cleared independently of the others. A character arranged as such:

```
. . . . . . . . .
. . . . . . . . .
. . . . . . . . .
. . . . . . . . .
. . . . . . . . .
. . . . . . . . .
. . . . . . . . .
. . . . . . . . .   64 dots
```

To enable each of the 64,000 bits to be displayed in 16 (2^4) colors, we would need 4 X 64,000 bits or color memory. This is not practical since 16K of memory would be required just for this. So the 64 dots within this this 8 X 8 matrix must have the same color. This is not too serious a problem, since most television sets do not permit much higher resolution without the colors bleeding into each other.

By using the bit mapped technique to draw graphics, we seem to lose the capability to write text to the graphics screen. But by duplicating the pixels that form a text character on the graphics screen, you can add text to graphics.

On the following pages you will find the program **HIRES GRAPHIC AID** that will simplify graphics programming.

If you are interested in programming graphics without the hassle of POKEs and PEEKs, then we recommend either **SCREEN GRAPHICS 64** or **ULTRABASIC 64** from ABACUS Software. Each provide graphics extensions to BASIC which make graphics programming a cinch. Contact your dealer or ABACUS Software for details.

The assembler listing for HIRES GRAPHIC AID follows:

```
                        ;        HIRES GRAPHIC AID
180:                             ORG   $C000
190:   C000             CR       EQU   13
200:   C000             XCOORD   EQU   $14
210:   C000             FLAG     EQU   $97
240:   C000             LF       EQU   $B8      ;LOGICAL FILENUMBE
250:   C000             SA       EQU   $B9      ;SECONDARY ADDRESS
260:   C000             FA       EQU   $BA      ;DEVICE NUMBER
270:   C000             TMP      EQU   $FD
280:   C000             ADR      EQU   TMP
290:   C000             AV       EQU   TMP
300:   C000             COLLOW   EQU   $400    ;START HIRES COLOR RAM
310:   C000             COLHI    EQU   $80     ;END HIRES COLOR RAM
320:   C000             GRALOW   EQU   $2000   ;START HIRES BIT MAP
330:   C000             GRAHI    EQU   $4000   ;END
340:   C000             GETCOR   EQU   $B7EB   ;GETS X-AND Y COORD.
350:   C000             CHKCOM   EQU   $AEFD   ;CHECKS ON COMMA
360:   C000             GETBYT   EQU   $B79E   ;GETS BYTE VALUE
```

```
370:  C000              VIDEO    EQU  $D000   ;VIDEO CONTROLLER
380:  C000              GETPAR   EQU  $E1D4   ;GET FILE- AND DEVICE #
390:  C000              CLSCRN   EQU  $E544   ;CLEAR SCREEN
400:  C000              CHKOUT   EQU  $FFC9   ;SET OUTPUT DEVICE
410:  C000              PRINT    EQU  $FFD2   ;OUTPUT ROUTINE
420:  C000              CLRCH    EQU  $FFCC   ;OUTPUT ON DEFAULT
430:  C000              LOAD     EQU  $FFD5   ;LOAD ROUTINE
440:  C000              SAVE     EQU  $FFD8   ;SAVE ROUTINE
450:                 ;        JUMP TABLE FOR FUNCTIONS
460:  C000 4C 1E C0              JMP  INIT    ;SWITCH ON GR. MODE
470:  C003 4C 3D C0              JMP  CLEAR   ;CLEAR GRAPHIC
480:  C006 4C 54 C0              JMP  COLOR   ;SET COLOR
490:  C009 4C 71 C0              JMP  REVERS  ;INVERT GRAPHIC
500:  C00C 4C 8B C0              JMP  SET     ;SET POINT
510:  C00F 4C 8E C0              JMP  RESET   ;RESET POINT
520:  C012 4C 52 C1              JMP  GLOAD   ;LOAD GRAPHICS
530:  C015 4C 3A C1              JMP  GSAVE   ;SAVE GRAPHICS
540:  C018 4C 18 C0 SELF         JMP  SELF    ;NOT USED
550:  C01B 4C 62 C1              JMP  GOFF    ;SWITCH OFF GR. MODE
560:  C01E AD 11 D0 INIT         LDA  VIDEO+17
570:  C021 8D 72 C1              STA  STORE1
580:  C024 AD 18 D0              LDA  VIDEO+24
590:  C027 8D 73 C1              STA  STORE2
600:  C02A A9 3B                 LDA  #27+32   ;SET GR. MODE
610:  C02C 8D 11 D0              STA  VIDEO+17
620:  C02F A9 18                 LDA  #16+8
630:  C031 8D 18 D0              STA  VIDEO+24
640:  C034 20 3D C0              JSR  CLEAR
650:  C037 A2 10                 LDX  #16
660:  C039 20 5A C0              JSR  COL
670:  C03C 60                    RTS
680:  C03D A0 00    CLEAR        LDY  #0       ;CLEAR GR. MEMORY
690:  C03F A9 20                 LDA  #>GRALOW
700:  C041 84 FD                 STY  TMP
710:  C043 85 FE                 STA  TMP+1
720:  C045 98       CLR1         TYA
730:  C046 91 FD    CLR2         STA  (TMP),Y
740:  C048 C8                    INY
750:  C049 D0 FB                 BNE  CLR2
760:  C04B E6 FE                 INC  TMP+1
770:  C04D A5 FE                 LDA  TMP+1
780:  C04F C9 40                 CMP  #>GRAHI
790:  C051 DO F2                 BNE  CLR1
800:  C053 60                    RTS
810:  C054 20 FD AE COLOR        JSR  CHKCOM    ;SET COLOR
820:  C057 20 9E B7              JSR  GETBYT    ;GET COLOR CODE
830:  C05A A0 00    COL          LDY  #0
840:  C05C A9 04                 LDA  #>COLLOW
850:  C05E 84 FD                 STY  TMP
860:  C060 85 FE                 STA  TMP+1
870:  C062 8A       COL1         TXA            ;COLOR CODE IN ACC.
880:  C063 91 FD    COL2         STA  (TMP),Y
890:  C065 C8                    INY
900:  C066 DO FB                 BNE  COL2
910:  CO68 E6 FE                 INC  TMP+1
```

```
920:  C06A A5 FE             LDA  TMP+1
930:  C06C C9 08             CMP #>COLHI
940:  C06E D0 F2             BNE  COL1
950:  C070 60                RTS
960:  C071 A0 00    REVERS   LDY  #0        ;INVERT GRAPHICS
970:  C073 A9 20             LDA  #>GRALOW
980:  C075 84 FD             STY  TMP
990:  C077 85 FE             STA  TMP+1
1000: C079 B1 FD    REV1     LDA  (TMP),Y
1010: C07B 49 FF             EOR  #%11111111 ;INVERT BITS
1020: C07D 91 FD             STA  (TMP),Y
1030: C07F C8                INY
1040: C080 D0 F7             BNE  REV1
1050: C082 E6 FE             INC  TMP+1
1060: C084 A5 FE             LDA  TMP+1
1070: C086 C9 40             CMP  #>GRAHI
1080: C088 D0 EF             BNE  REV1
1090: C08A 60       ILL      RTS  ;RETURN IF INVALID COORD.
1100: C08B A9 00    SET      LDA  #0      ;SET POINT
1110: C08D 2C                .BYT $2C  ;SKIP INSTRUCTION
1120: C08E A9 80    RESET    LDA  #$80    ;RESET POINT
1130: C090 85 97             STA  FLAG
1140: C092 20 FD AE          JSR  CHKCOM
1150: C095 20 EB B7          JSR  GETCOR ;X TO XCOOR,Y TO X-REG
1160: C098 E0 C8             CPX  #200
1170: C09A B0 EE             BCS  ILL     ;Y COORDINATE > 199
1180: C09C A5 15             LDA  XCOORD+1
1190: C09E C9 01             CMP  #>320
1200: C0A0 90 08             BCC  OK
1210: C082 D0 E6             BNE  ILL
1220: C0A4 A5 14             LDA  XCOORD
1230: C0A6 C9 40             CMP  #<320   ;X COORDINATE > 319
1240: C0A8 B0 E0             BCS  ILL
1250: C0AA 8A       OK       TXA          ;Y COORDINATE TO ACC.
1260: C0AB 4A                LSR
1260: C0AC 4A                LSR
1260: C0AD 4A                LSR          ;DIVIDED BY 8
1270: C0AE A8                TAY  ;OFFY=320*INT(Y/8)+(YAND7)
1290: C0AF E9 21 C1          LDA  MULTLO,Y
1300: C0B2 8D 75 C1          STA  OFFY
1310: C0B5 B9 08 C1          LDA  MULTHI,Y   ;TIMES 320
1320: C0B8 8D 76 C1          STA  OFFY+1
1330: C0BB 8A                TXA             ;Y COORDINATE
1340: C0BC 29 07             AND  #%111
1350: C0BE 18                CLC             ;PLUS Y AND 7
1360: C0BF 6D 75 C1          ADC  OFFY
1370: C0C2 8D 75 C1          STA  OFFY
                    ;OFFX=8 * INT(X/8)
1390: C0C5 A5 14             LDA  XCOORD
1400: C0C7 29 F8             AND  #%11111000
1410: C0C9 8D 74 C1          STA  OFFX
1420: C0CC 18                CLC          ;AV=GRALOW+OFFY+OFFX
1430: C0CD A9 00             LDA  #<GRALOW
1440: C0CF 6D 75 C1          ADC  OFFY
1450: C0D2 85 FD             STA  AV
```

```
1460: C0D4 A9 20                LDA  #>GRALOW
1470: C0D6 6D 76 C1             ADC  OFFY+1
1480: C0D9 85 FE                STA  AV+1
1490: C0DB 18                   CLC
1500: C0DC A5 FD                LDA  AV
1510: C0DE 6D 74 C1             ADC  OFFX
1520: C0E1 85 FD                STA  AV
1530: C0E3 A5 FE                LDA  AV+1
1540: C0E5 65 15                ADC  XCOORD+1
1550: C0E7 85 FE                STA  AV+1   ;MA = 2↑((7-X)AND 7)
1570: C0E9 A5 14                LDA  XCOORD
1580: C0EB 29 07                AND  #7
1590: C0ED 49 07                EOR  #7
1600: C0EF AA                   TAX         ;MA
1610: C0F0 A9 01                LDA  #1
1620: C0F2 CA         SET4      DEX         ;
1630: C0F3 30 03                BMI  SET3
1640: C0F5 0A                   ASL          ;SHIFT BIT LEFT
1650: C0F6 D0 FA                BNE  SET4    ;ABSOLUTE JUMP
1660: C0F8 A0 00      SET3      LDY  #0      ;ACC. CONTAINS MASK
1670: C0FA 24 97                BIT  FLAG
1680: C0FC 10 05                BPL  SET5
1690: C0FE 49 FF                EOR  #$FF
1700: C100 31 FD                AND  (AV),Y ;CLEAR BIT
1710: C102 2C                   .BYT  $2C
1720: C103 11 FD      SET5      ORA  (AV),Y ;SET BIT
1730: C105 91 FD                STA  (AV),Y
1740: C107 60         END       RTS
1750: C108            MULTHI    EQU  END+1
                      ;TABLE HIBYTES N*320
      C108 00 00 01 02 03 05 06 07
      C110 08 0A 0B 0C 0D 0F 10 11
      C118 12 14 15 16 17 19 1B 1C
      C120 1D
1760: C121            MULTLO    EQU  MULTHI+25
                      ;TABLE LOBYTES N*320
      C121 00 40 80 C0 00 40 80 C0
      C129 00 40 80 C0 00 40 80 C0
      C131 00 40 80 C0 00 40 80 C0
      C139 00
1870: C13A 20 FD AE   GSAVE     JSR  CHKCOM      ;SAVE GRAPHIC
1880: C13D 20 D4 E1             JSR  GETPAR      ;GET FILENAME
                                                 & DEVICE ADDR
1890: C140 A2 00                LDX  #<GRAHI
1900: C142 A0 40                LDY  #>GRAHI
1910: C144 A9 00                LDA  #<GRALOW
1920: C146 85 FD                STA  TMP
1930: C148 A9 20                LDA  #>GRALOW
1940: C14A 85 FE                STA  TMP+1
1950: C14C A9 FD                LDA  #TMP
1960: C14E 20 D8 FF             JSR  SAVE
1970: C151 60                   RTS
1980: C152 20 FD AE   GLOAD     JSR  CHKCOM      ;LOAD GRAPHIC
1990: C155 20 D4 E1             JSR GETPAR       ;GET FILENAME
                                                 & DEVICE ADDR
```

```
2000: C158 A9 61            LDA  #$61         ;SEC ADDR 1
2010: C15A 85 B9            STA  SA
2020: C15C A9 00            LDA  #0           ;LOAD FLAG
2030: C15E 20 D5 FF         JSR  LOAD
2040: C161 60               RTS
2050: C162 AD 72 C1  GOFF   LDA  STORE1
2060: C165 8D 11 D0         STA  VIDEO+17
2070: C168 AD 73 C1         LDA  STORE2
2080: C16B 8D 18 D0         STA  VIDEO+24
2090: C16E 20 44 E5         JSR  CLSCRN       :CLEAR SCREEN
2100: C171 60               RTS
2110: C173           STORE1 BYT  *+1
2120: C174           STORE2 BYT  *+1
2130: C175           OFFX   BYT  *+1
2140: C177           OFFY   BYT  *+2
```

To use this machine language routine, you can use the following calls from BASIC:

SYS49152	INIT	turn graphics mode on
SYS49555	CLEAR	clear the screen
SYS49158,c	COLOR	set plotting color to c
SYS49161	REVERSE	reverse each point on screen
SYS49164,x,y	SET	set point at coord. x,y
SYS49167,x,y	RESET	reset point at coord. x,y
SYS49570,"f",d	GLOAD	load graphics picture with name "f" from device d
SYS49573,"f",d	GSAVE	save graphics picture with name "f" to device d
SYS49579	GOFF	turn graphics mode off

5.3 SPRITES - Some graphics magic on the Commodore 64

5.3.1 Introduction to Sprites

Aside from its superb sound synthesis capabilities, the ability to create and manipulate sprites is certainly the outstanding feature of the Commodore 64. Sprites are large graphics designs that can be controlled independently of the other graphics or text on the screen.

5.3.2 Sprite Capabilities

For a moment, let's imagine that there are no such thing as sprites. You are creating an arcade game and want to draw a finely detailed character (we'll call it a blob) on the screen and and animate it. The fine detail requires that you use the high resolution screen. As previously discussed, you have to draw the blob on the screen by using bit mapped techniques to place the character at the desired position on the screen. This involves setting each pixel that comprises the blob to on. If a blob is made up of 60 pixels, then all 60 pixels must be turned on. Additionally, you have to coordinate the color of the pixels, by manipulating the screen memory (which control the bit mapped graphics colors).

In order to move the blob, you have to calculate a new position for each pixel that makes up the blob. But befoie you redraw the blob at its new position, you must first make the earlier blob disappear from its old position. You do this by resetting (turning off) each pixel that was on. Then you can proceed to redraw the blob at its new position. Repeating this technique, you can make the blob move across the bit mapped graphics screen.
Now let's say that there are some other stationary objects on the screen, maybe a house. In order to make it appear that the blob is entering the house, we must make the blob gradually disappear as its pixels meet the pixels that make up the house. To do this, you must know the position of the house's pixels on the screen. As the blob's new pixel positions are calculated, they are compared to the pixel positions of the stationary house. If these pixel position coincide, then the blob's new pixel at that position is not set on. Instead, that position is left to display the house. If you continue along these same lines, you can make the blob disappear into the house.

In a like manner, you can make the blob pass in front of the stationary house. When the blob's new pixel position coincides with the pixel position of the house, the blob's pixel is displayed instead of the house's pixel. The same technique is applicable to collisions that might occur with other blobs.

You can see that all of these calculations and logic to determine which pixels need to be turned on or off is not only complicated, but very time consuming. If done from a BASIC program, the blob might be able to move about as fast as molases. If done from a machine language program, the blob can be made to move fast, but only at the expense of a lot of program coding and testing.

The idea behind sprites is that most of the tedious and time-consuming calculations to determine the blob's new position are handled by the VIC chip. A sprite, once defined, can be moved and manipulated very easily from within a program.

After you define a sprite, you do not have to turn on or off individual pixels when drawing the sprite. When you move the sprite from one position on the screen to another, you do not have to erase the previous positon of the sprite. You can make a sprite pass in front of or behind stationary objects automatically. In fact, you can make one sprite pass in front of or behind another sprite. Or make it disappear altogether. Eight such sprites can be handled by the Commodore 64 at one time.

If you want, you can have the Commodore 64 notify you when a sprite and a stationary object or two different sprites have collided. And changing the color of the sprite is also very simple. These sprite capabilties makes the Commodore 64 a very powerful computer.

5.3.3 Sprite Structure

When using sprites, it is good idea to be familiar with binary arithmetic. Sections 1.1 and 5.1 will acquaint you with the registers of the VIC chip.
When using sprites, the majority of the work involves setting up the registers of the VIC chip that control movement, color, and the other features of the sprites. Each register consists of 8 bits which the user can set or reset according to the desired effect.

When using sprites, we refer to the numbers which define hcw the sprite looks as the **sprite pattern.** An important point in using sprites is the location in memory of the sprite pattern. As you know, one sprite consists of 24x21 points (pixels). Horizontally a sprite has 24 pixels and vertically it has 21 pixels.

SPRITE LAYOUT

```
                1                  2                  3

ROW 1   . . . . . . . .   . . . . . . . .   . . . . . . . .
ROW 2   . . . . . . . .   . . . . . . . .   . . . . . . . .
ROW 3   . . . . . . . .   . . . . . . . .   . . . . . . . .
ROW 4   . . . . . . . .   . . . . . . . .   . . . . . . . .
ROW 5   . . . . . . . .   . . . . . . . .   . . . . . . . .
ROW 6   . . . . . . . .   . . . . . . . .   . . . . . . . .
ROW 7   . . . . . . . .   . . . . . . . .   . . . . . . . .
ROW 8   . . . . . . . .   . . . . . . . .   . . . . . . . .
ROW 9   . . . . . . . .   . . . . . . . .   . . . . . . . .
ROW 10  . . . . . . . .   . . . . . . . .   . . . . . . . .
ROW 11  . . . . . . . .   . . . . . . . .   . . . . . . . .
ROW 12  . . . . . . . .   . . . . . . . .   . . . . . . . .
ROW 13  . . . . . . . .   . . . . . . . .   . . . . . . . .
ROW 14  . . . . . . . .   . . . . . . . .   . . . . . . . .
ROW 15  . . . . . . . .   . . . . . . . .   . . . . . . . .
ROW 16  . . . . . . . .   . . . . . . . .   . . . . . . . .
ROW 17  . . . . . . . .   . . . . . . . .   . . . . . . . .
ROW 18  . . . . . . . .   . . . . . . . .   . . . . . . . .
ROW 19  . . . . . . . .   . . . . . . . .   . . . . . . . .
ROW 20  . . . . . . . .   . . . . . . . .   . . . . . . . .
ROW 21  . . . . . . . .   . . . . . . . .   . . . . . . . .
```

Each "row" consists of 3-bytes each with 8 pixels or bits each. The color of a sprite can be specified in either of two ways:

1. HIRES SPRITE
   When using hires sprites, one bit in the sprite pattern produces one point on the screen. This point has either the background color if the bit is zero, or the color specified by its corresponding register (REG 39 thru 46) if the bit is one.

2. MULTICOLOR SPRITE
   When using multicolor sprites, two bits in the sprite pattern produces one point on the screen. The point is actually two pixels wide on the screen. The point is either: the color of the background if the bits are 00; the color specified by REG 37 if the bits are 01; the color specified by its corresponding register (REG 39 thru 46) if the bits are 10; or the color specified by REG 38 if the bits are 11.

In the following section, we deal with the programming of these sprites.

5.3.4 Programming sprites

5.3.4.1 Sprite Patterns

When programming sprites, you must first set up the sprite pattern which is to represent the sprite.

In order to help you in developing sprites, Diagram 5-1 is a a design sheet. You may either copy this design sheet or use it as a sample for your own design sheet.

First draw a rough sketch of the sprite on a separate piece of paper. Decide whether the sprite is to be one color or multicolor. Next transfer this rough sketch to the sprite design sheet.

If using one color sprites, fill in each box on the sprite design sheet that corresponds to the rough sketch. Treat one box on the sheet as one pixel on the screen. If you fill the squares that make the pattern completely and then stand back from the sprite design sheet, it is quite easy to recognize the pattern and determine if any changes are required to give the sprite the final touches.

If using multicolor sprites, fill in each box with the desired color (color pencils work nicely) that corresponds to the rough sketch. Keep in mind that two horizontally adjacent boxes on the sprite design sheet correspond to one pixel (each pixel is twice as wide) on the screen. Only four different colors may be used. One color is common and is the background color; one color is unique for each sprite; and two colors are common to all sprites that are used. The background color is always given a value of 00, so the values for the two horizontally adjacent boxes is also 00. The unique color is always given a value of 10, so the values for the two horizontally adjacent boxes is also 10. The color specified by multicolor register 0 is given a value of 01, while the color specified by multicolor register 1 is given a value of 11 and these are the values for the two horizontally adjacent boxes if these colors are chosen on the sprite design sheet.

With either one color or multicolor sprites, the next step is to determine the numeric values that make up the sprite as drawn on the sprite design sheet. To do this, you treat each group of eight horizontal boxes as a unit. Add the number that corresponds to that column for all boxes. Keep in mind that the multicolor sprites may have a value or 00, 01, 10, or 11 according to the color that is represented by the pair of horizontally adjacent boxes.

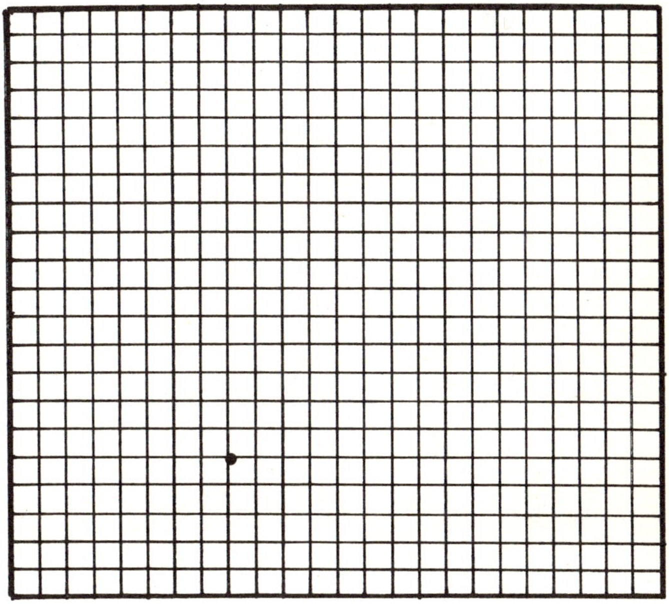

5-2 SPRITE DESIGN SHEET

For each unit of eight boxes, the sum of these eight values are used in subsequent POKE commands. The most convenient way to define the points of a spirte pattern is by entering them into BASIC DATA statements. Then you can READ them from within a FOR-NEXT loop and POKE them into a memory area that you've set aside for the pattern. The sprite is now in memory and ready for use. In order to get the programming a little more organized, you may want to arrange your DATA statements to look like this:

```
1000 DATA 000,000,000
1010 DATA 000,000,000
1020 DATA 000,000,000
1030 DATA 000,000,000
1040 DATA 000,000,000
1050 DATA 000,000,000
1060 DATA 000,000,000
1070 DATA 003,255,255
1080 DATA 000,002,000
1090 DATA 192,170,128
1100 DATA 194,150,080
1110 DATA 234,150,080
1120 DATA 194,170,168
1130 DATA 192,170,168
1140 DATA 000,032,128
1150 DATA 000,170,160
1160 DATA 000,000,000
1170 DATA 000,000,000
1180 DATA 000,000,000
1190 DATA 000,000,000
1200 DATA 000,000,000
```

This structure represents the 3 bytes (24 bits) X 21 bit of a sprite. Each number between 0 and 255 represents the pixel pattern that makes up the sprite. Thus it is possible to program any figure - from a single point to a full 24 X 21 block or any other combination in between.

5.3.4.2 The Program

Now let's move on to programming the sprites. Back to our example. What do these DATA statement represent? For this we have to present the decimal numbers in binary again:

SPRITE PATTERN

	1	2	3
LINE 1	0 0 0 0 0 0 0 0	0 0 0 0 0 0 0 0	0 0 0 0 0 0 0 0
LINE 2	0 0 0 0 0 0 0 0	0 0 0 0 0 0 0 0	0 0 0 0 0 0 0 0
LINE 3	0 0 0 0 0 0 0 0	0 0 0 0 0 0 0 0	0 0 0 0 0 0 0 0
LINE 4	0 0 0 0 0 0 0 0	0 0 0 0 0 0 0 0	0 0 0 0 0 0 0 0
LINE 5	0 0 0 0 0 0 0 0	0 0 0 0 0 0 0 0	0 0 0 0 0 0 0 0
LINE 6	0 0 0 0 0 0 0 0	0 0 0 0 0 0 0 0	0 0 0 0 0 0 0 0
LINE 7	0 0 0 0 0 0 0 0	0 0 0 0 0 0 0 0	0 0 0 0 0 0 0 0
LINE 8	0 0 0 0 0 0 1 1	1 1 1 1 1 1 1 1	1 1 1 1 1 1 1 1
LINE 9	0 0 0 0 0 0 0 0	0 0 0 0 0 0 0 0	0 0 0 0 0 0 0 0
LINE 10	1 1 0 0 0 0 0 0	1 0 1 0 1 0 1 0	1 0 0 0 0 0 0 0
LINE 11	1 1 0 0 0 0 1 0	1 0 0 1 0 1 1 0	0 1 0 1 0 0 0 0
LINE 12	1 1 1 0 1 0 1 0	1 0 0 1 0 1 1 0	0 1 0 1 0 0 0 0
LINE 13	1 1 0 0 0 0 1 0	1 0 1 0 1 0 1 0	1 0 1 0 1 0 0 0
LINE 14	1 1 0 0 0 0 0 0	1 0 1 0 1 0 1 0	1 0 1 0 1 0 0 0
LINE 15	0 0 0 0 0 0 0 0	0 0 1 0 0 0 0 0	1 0 0 0 0 0 0 0
LINE 16	0 0 0 0 0 0 0 0	1 0 1 0 1 0 1 0	1 0 1 0 0 0 0 0
LINE 17	0 0 0 0 0 0 0 0	0 0 0 0 0 0 0 0	0 0 0 0 0 0 0 0
LINE 18	0 0 0 0 0 0 0 0	0 0 0 0 0 0 0 0	0 0 0 0 0 0 0 0
LINE 19	0 0 0 0 0 0 0 0	0 0 0 0 0 0 0 0	0 0 0 0 0 0 0 0
LINE 20	0 0 0 0 0 0 0 0	0 0 0 0 0 0 0 0	0 0 0 0 0 0 0 0
LINE 21	0 0 0 0 0 0 0 0	0 0 0 0 0 0 0 0	0 0 0 0 0 0 0 0

Here we have a pattern of a helicopter. If you don't recognize it on paper, you will when it appears on the screen.

5.3.4.3 Turning the Sprite On

After having defined the sprite pattern, you have to turn it on. The sprite number determines how to turn that sprite on. The corresponding bit (bit 0 thru 7) in REG 21 is set to one for the sprite number that is to be displayed.

Sprite:	7	6	5	4	3	2	1	0
Bit :	b7	b6	b5	b4	b3	b2	b1	b0
Value :	128	64	32	16	8	4	2	1

POKE V+21,1 makes sprite 0 visible; POKE 21,3 (values of 1 + 2) makes sprites 0 and 1 visible; and POKE V+21,255 (values of 1 + 2 + 4 + 8 + 16 + 32 + 64 + 128) makes spirtes 0 thru 7 visible.

5.3.4.4 Memory Areas for Sprites

Next the addresses of the sprite patterns must be specified. The addresses of the sprite patterns are placed in the last eight locations of screen memory and are called pointers. If screen memory in its default location ($400), then these pointers are located at 2040 thru 2047. Each sprite pattern is 63 bytes in length (24 bits X 21 rows) = 63 bytes. An extra byte is added to the sprite pattern as a separator and is set to zero. Thus we should speak of each sprite pattern as being 64 bytes in length.

Within a 16K memory bank, there are 256 64-byte blocks. The value in a sprite pointer is actually the number of the block within that 16K block where the sprite's pattern is located.

For example, if a sprite is defined beginning at memory location 832, then the pointer for that sprite is 13 (832 / 64 =13). If this pattern is to be used for sprite 0, then we would POKE 2040,13 to set the correct sprite pointer. Location 2040 is the pointer for sprite 0. The value of 13 is the 13th 64-byte block in the 16K memory bank that the VIC chip can address.

From the above, it is clear that a sprite pattern must start on a 64-byte boundary. When screen memory is at its default location ($400 = 2048 decimal), the following addresses and pointer values may be used for sprite definitions:

Address	Pointer
640	10
704	11
768	12
832	13
896	14
960	15
1024	16
1088	17
1152	18
1216	19
1280	20

The following table gives you the pointer location of each sprite for the default screen memory:

POINTER :	2040	2041	2042	2043	2044	2045	2046	2047
Sprite :	0	1	2	3	4	5	6	7

If you place the value 13 in memory 2040 it means that the sprite pattern begins at memory location 832. You can also write 13 in memory location 2041. This means that sprite 1 is has the same pattern as sprite 0. In this case, all of the other information, such as color, position, expansion etc., may be different for these two sprites, but the basic shapes are identical.

This feature of sprites can potentially reduce the programming effort tremendously. In games, for example, you may have several alien creatures that are clones of each other, except for position. One sprite pattern can serve as the model for all of these aliens. By setting the appropriate sprite pointer to refer to the same pattern, you can clone seven more of these creatures while the computer takes care of the display. Each of the creatures can have its own color. Furthermore, each creatures can be positioned independently of each other.

By using a FOR-NEXT loop from BASIC, the values of sprite pattern may be transferred to the memory area, starting at 832.

```
FOR I=0 TO 62: REM 63 BYTES OF A SPRITE
READ X       : REM READING OF THE BYTE
POKE 832+I,X : REM WRITING OF THE BYTE INTO THE BLOCK
NEXT I       : REM END OF LOOP
```

5.3.4.5 Sprite Positioning

Next we want to specify the position of the sprite on the screen. A sprites's position is set by priming two registers: one that specifies the sprite's X-position and one that specifies the sprites's Y-position.

From now on we'll use variable **V** in or examples to stand for the beginning address of the video controller registers. We set **V = 53248**, the address is the start address of the video controller. So one of the first line number of every program that uses graphic or sprites should read like this:

```
10 V=53248: REM START OF VIDEO CONTROLLER
```

To position a sprite on the screen you need two POKE commands:

```
POKE V+0,COLUMN: REM   SPRITE 0 - X position
POKE V+1,LINE  : REM   SPRITE 0 - Y position
```

So if you want to position the helicopter near the middle of the screen, all you need is

```
POKE V+0,184
POKE V+1,125
```

5.3.4.6 Shifting Sprites

We can also move the sprites quite easily. In order to achieve smooth movement, we should change the location of the sprite by one screen point at a time. We can do this by using a FOR-NEXT loop:

```
100  FOR I=159 TO 100 STEP -1
110  :      POKE V+0,I
120  NEXT I
```

The above routine moves the helicopter to the left, yet it remains in the same vertical position. If you want to watch the movement more slowly, you have to insert another loop before the NEXT I:

```
115  FOR II=1 TO 100: NEXT
```

Now the sprite moves much slower and you can watch it.

You might have recognized one problem: there are 320 horizontal positions. But the highest value of a POKE into the X-register can only be 255. How can you move the sprite to the right side of the screen?

For this, there is another register. Register 16 holds one high order bit for each sprite. If the X-coordinate of a sprite is higher than 255, then the bit for the corresponding sprite is set to one. For sprite 1, we would do the following for an X-coordinate greater than 255:

POKE V+16,1

After this POKE, 255 is added to our addressing. Now POKE V+0,1 would mean a positioning on dot 256. In order to get to dots smaller than 256, this bit has to be set back again:

POKE V+16,0

5.3.4.7 Sprite Color

We can also change the color of a one color sprite. Each sprite has its own color register. These registers are located at V+39 to V+46:

Register:	39	40	41	42	43	44	45	46
Sprite :	0	1	2	3	4	5	6	7

Below is the numbers which correspond to the specific colors:

	COLOR
0	BLACK
1	WHITE
2	RED
3	TURQUOISE
4	PURPLE
5	GREEN
6	BLUE
7	YELLOW
8	ORANGE
9	BROWN
10	LIGHT RED
11	GRAY 1
12	GRAY 2
13	LIGHT GREEN
14	LIGHT BLUE
15	GRAY 3

For example, by using POKE V+39,14 a sprite becomes light blue in color.

5.3.4.8 Enlarging Sprites

You can magnify or enlarge a sprite in the horizontal and/or a vertical direction. Two registers perform this enlargement. One register is for enlargement in the X direction, and the other for enlargement in the Y direction. Thus every sprite control-register is constructed as follows:

Bit	: 7	6	5	4	3	2	1	0
Sprite	: 7	6	5	4	3	2	1	0
Value	:128	64	32	16	8	4	2	1

If sprite 0 is to be enlarged in X as well as in Y direction, the following POKE commands are necessary:

```
POKE V+23,1: REM ENLARGES SPRITE 0 IN Y-DIRECTION
POKE V+29,1: REM ENLARGES SPRITE 0 IN X-DIRECTION
```

In order to enlarge sprites 0 and 1 in Y direction, POKE V+23,3 (value of 1 + 2) will handle the job.

Every sprite can be doubled in the X and Y directions. This means that one character can be enlarged to 4 times its original size.

5.3.4.9 Background

The next example shows another feature of the Commodore 64. You can choose whether the sprite is placed in front of or behind the background. Some nice effects result. When you have the helicopter on the screen, type:

```
POKE V+27,1
```

With this poke, you can direct the sprite to appear in front of or behind the background. In order to see the effect, bring the cursor to the same line as the sprite. Then you simply enter a few characters, just enough to cover the sprite with the letters. The letters are considered to be background. Try different colors to see the best contrast to the sprite. You'll see that the writing appears in front of the sprite. Actually you moved the sprite into another "level" - namely under the background. Now go to another line and type:

```
POKE V+27,0
```

The sprite will move in front of the text again. The register for the background-sprite priority then looks like this:

Bit	: b7	b6	b5	b4	b3	b2	b1	b0
Sprite-Priority	: 7	6	5	4	3	2	1	0

With this register you can change the priority of every sprite at will. If the bit is set to 0, it means that the sprite appears is in front of the background; set to 1, the sprite appears behind the background. By setting and clearing of the bits there is the possibility of setting several sprites on top of each other and still be able to differentiate between foreground and background. As already mentioned, this enables the Commodore 64 to create three-dimensional pictures.

5.3.4.10 Sprite-sprite Collisions

There is more to say about the overlapping of sprites. There is a register in which a collision of different sprites is recorded. The contents of this register remains set to zero until two or more sprites collide, or until you reset this register. Once the sprites have overlapped (collided), have collided.

The value of this register tells us what sprites have collided. For example, if we have the following statement:

```
CO=PEEK (V+30)
```

and the value of CO = 3, then we know that sprites 1 and 2 have collided. The bit structure of the register is the same as the other registers.
After this PEEK, the register has to be reset by:

```
POKE V+30,0
```

If you did not clear REG 30, then the registers would stay set even if a collision was not taking place.

5.3.4.11 Sprite-background Collisions

A collision between a sprite and the background can be recorded too. Register 31 serves this purpose. This register is treated similar to register 30. The only difference is the result of the PEEK. The value informs us which sprite(s) has collided with a character. It does not tell us which background character it was not its location. In order to get this information you have to determine that yourself from the other registers and memory locations.

```
CO=PEEK (V+31)
```

This register has to be cleared after a collision, too.

5.3.4.12 Multicolor Sprites

Multicolor sprites add much flavor to the Commodore 64 graphics capabilities. A multicolor sprite can be made up of three colors. The expense for the extra two colors less resolution since two bits of the sprite pattern appear as one double-wide pixel on the screen. Therefore we have a 4 x 8 matrix instead of an 8 x 8 one. These two bits contain the information about the color.
We already know that we can transfer 4 pieces of information with 2 bits: 00, 01, 10, and 11. When using multicolor these 2 bits have the following effects:

00 - The dot has the background color
(you don't see a dot)
01 - The color displayed is in register 37
10 - The color displayed is in corresponding
register 38-46
11 - The color displayed is in register 38

This means that a sprite can have its own color and two colors that are common to all sprites.

Maybe you asked yourself why our helicopter looks a little strange. We can answer this question now: it was designed as a multicolor sprite. Since a multicolor sprite consists of fewer dots, you can't get a decent picture in the normal sprite mode. To finish this chapter, we want to show you the complete program with the multicolor helicopter. It is advisable to experiment with the programming of sprites, using this program as an example. That way you become readily acquainted with the programming technique.

```
5 REM
10 REM SPRITE DEMONSTRATION - HELICOPTER
15 REM
20 V=53248: REM START VIDEO CONTROLLER
30 POKE V+32,15: POKE V+33,14: REM BACKGROUND COLORS
40 PRINT "<CTRL>-7": REM PRINTING CONTROL AND 7
50 POKE V+21,3: REM TURN ON SPRITE 1 AND 2
60 POKE V+28,3: REM SPRITE 1 AND 2 ARE MULTICOLOR
70 POKE V+39,6: REM COLOR OF SPRITE 1 - BLUE
80 POKE V+40,2: REM COLOR OF SPRITE 2 - RED
90 POKE V+37,14:REM MULTICOLOR COLOR 1 - LIGHT BLUE
100 POKE V+38,0: REM MULTICOLOR COLOR 2 - BLACK
110 POKE 2040,13: REM SPRITE 1 FROM MEMORY RANGE 832-895
120 POKE 2041,13: REM SPRITE 2 FROM MEMORY RANGE 832-895
125 REM THAT MEANS SPRITE 1 AND 2 HAVE THE SAME FORM
130 FOR I=0 TO 62: REM LOOP TO READ IN THE DATA
140 : READ X: REM READING OF THE DOT COMBINATION
150 : POKE 832+I,X: REM SAVING OF THE DOT COMBINATION
160 NEXT I: REM END OF LOOP
170 POKE V+0,24: POKE V+1,50: REM POSITION OF SPRITE 1
180 POKE V+2,60: POKE V+3,50: REM POSITION OF SPRITE 2
190 END
997 REM
998 REM  SPRITE PATTERN FOLLOWS
999 REM
1000 DATA 000,000,000
1010 DATA 000,000,000
1020 DATA 000,000,000
1030 DATA 000,000,000
1040 DATA 000,000,000
1050 DATA 000,000,000
1060 DATA 000,000,000
1070 DATA 003,255,255
1080 DATA 000,002,000
1090 DATA 192,170,128
1100 DATA 194,150,080
1110 DATA 234,150,080
1120 DATA 194,170,168
1130 DATA 192,170,168
1140 DATA 000,032,128
```

```
1150 DATA 000,170,160
1160 DATA 000,000,000
1170 DATA 000,000,000
1180 DATA 000,000,000
1190 DATA 000,000,000
1200 DATA 000,000,000
```

We hope that you use this program as a guide to writing your own sprite programs.

CHAPTER 6 : Basic From a Different Viewpoint

6.1 How the BASIC Interpreter Works

Let's see how the BASIC interpreter works. As you enter text into the Commodore 64, the interpreter first checks to see if there is a number at the beginning of the text. When it sees a number there, it assumes that the text is a program line. The interpreter uses this number as a line number and assumes that the text following are part of the program statements. If the line number does not already exist, then the program line is new and is placed into memory in program line sequence. If the line number already exists, then this program line replaces the previously entered program line. A program line number without any text following it merely deletes any previously entered program line.

As the program lines are entered, the interpreter also searches for any keywords that are imbedded within the text. Keywords are the special reserved words such as: IF, GOTO, OPEN, REM, SIN, etc. When it recognized a keyword, the interpreter replaces the keyword with a one-byte **token.** The value of the token is a hexadecimal number between $80 and $FE. Therefore any character with its high bit set (bit 7) is a token for a BASIC keyword.

As a BASIC program is executed, the interpreter can easily find tokens within the text since their high bit is set. Using the token, it finds the appropriate BASIC routines in ROM which handle the particular function or action. The addresses of the routines are found in Chapter 6.4; the routines themselves are described in Appendix A.

In order to take the most advantage of the built in ROM routines, you should understand something about the number representation of the interpreter. BASIC differentiates between three data types: real numbers, integer numbers, and strings. Real numbers are in a range from +/- 1E-39 to +/- 1E38. Integer numbers can only take whole-number values from -32768 to 32767. Strings are character strings with a length from 0 to 255 characters.

Variables are used to store values. Each variable occupies seven bytes of memory. Here we discuss only **simple** variables (non-array variables).

The first two bytes of each variable contain the variable name. The next five bytes contain the value of the variable. If the variable represents a floating point number, the first byte is the exponent and the next 4 bytes represent the mantissa. If the variable represents an integer number, only two bytes are used - the high and the low byte of a 16-bit binary number. If the variable represents a string, the first byte contains the length of the string (0 to 255), and the next two bytes contain the address of the strings.

The BASIC interpreter differentiates the the different variable types by encoding the variable name. or floating point variables, the variable name is the first two characters of the name. For integer variables, the high order bit (bit 7) of both the first and second characters of the name are set. For string variables, the high order bit of the second character is set.

For example:

Variable name :	AB	AB%	AB$
Stored as (hex):	41 42	C1 C2	41 C2

The variable table is the place in memory where all simple variables are stored. The variable table starts immediately following the BASIC program. A pointer located at $2D/2E (45/46 in decimal) indicates the start of the variable table.

For example, if you make the following assignments, the variable table looks like this:

```
A  = 10.3
B% = -23
C$ = "Commodore 64"
```

With the monitor you can now look at the memory content:

```
002D  03 08                    variable table starts at $0803
0803  41 00 84 24 CC CC CD var. A, floating point value 10.3
080A  C2 80 FF E9 00 00 00 var. B%,integer value -23
0810  43 80 0C F4 9F 00 00 var. C$,length 12, address $9FF4
```

6.2 Using Variables in your Program

How can the variables or terms be passed from BASIC to a machine language program? There is a convenient routine in the BASIC interpreter that lets you do this. It evaluates any term in a BASIC expression.

The routine called **FRMEVL** (formula evaluation) and is located at $AD9E. Routine FRMEVL evaluates numeric as well as string parameters.

When FRMEVL is called, it sets the type flag (located at $0E, decimal 14). If the type flag is $00 then the expression that was evaluated was numeric. If the type flag is $FF, then the expression that was evaluated was a string.

If the expression is numeric, then the result of the evalution is stored in the floating point accumulator 1 (FAC). The FAC is located at memory location $61-$65 (decimal 97-101). There is also a second floating point accumulator called ARG, that is used for for arithmetic operations such as additions. ARG is located in memory at $69-$6D (decimal 105-109). The result after calling routines such as addition is always found in FAC. Also when calling functions, the argument is transferred to FAC and the result placed there.

If the expression is a string, then a pointer at $64-$65 (decimal 100-101) to a string descriptor is set. The string descriptor contains the length and the address of the evaluated string. By calling the routine at $B475 you can transfer the string length into the accumulator and the address into the X-(low byte) and into the Y-(high byte) register.

You might want to keep in mind that all arithmetic takes place using floating point numbers. If any operands are integer numbers, these are first changed into the floating point format, the operations are carried out in floating point format, and finally the results are converted back to integer format.

Now let's look at some useful routines of the BASIC interpreter that execute arithmetic tasks.

ADDRESS	FUNCTION	
$B853	minus	FAC = ARG - FAC
$B86A	plus	FAC = ARG + FAC
$BA28	multiplication	FAC = ARG * FAC
$BB12	division	FAC = ARG / FAC
$BF7B	exponentiation	FAC = ARG to the power of FAC

The addresses of further routines as well as the memory map of zero-page and the operating system are found at the end of this chapter.

6.3 GET more out of your BASIC

6.3.1 How to Extend BASIC?

Let's say that you want to tie a machine language routine into BASIC. First find the part of the interpreter that examines a BASIC statement and then executes it. Here is that excerpt from the ROM listing:

```
A7E1 6C 08 03 JMP ($0308) ; normally points on $A7E4
A7E4 20 73 00 JSR $0073   ; get next char. from BASIC-text
A7E7 20 A7 ED JSR $A7ED   ; executes statement
A7EA 4C AE A7 JMP $A7AE   ; back to interpreter loop
```

We can easily insert our own routine by changing the vector that normally resides at $308/$309. This vector normally points to $A7E4, but we can chnage it to point to our own machine language routine.

One common way of extending BASIC is to prefix the new commands with a special character, such as an exclamation mark. So we can extend BASIC with our own version of a PRINT command like this:

```
100 !PRINT
```

Our routine first checks for an exclaimation point. If found, you can branch to your own routine to handle a new PRINT command; otherwise the normal PRINT command is performed. A program excerpt could look like this:

```
DECODE  JSR  $0073    ; CHRGET, next character
        CMP  #"!"     ; is it our special character?
        BEQ  FOUND    ; yes-we handle it
        JMP  $A7E7    ; no-BASIC handles it
FOUND   JSR  COMMAND  ; execute our own command
        JMP  $A7AE    ; back to interpreter loop
```

The pointer in $0308/$0309 has to be set to point to the address of DECODE in the above example when the initializirg the BASIC extensions. If you want to implement several commands, you can build in a routine to differentiate the command words that select the various new commands. In the following sections, you will find some suggestions for the implementation of your own routines.

6.3.2 HARDCOPY - RENEW - PRINT USING

Example 1 - Hardcopy Function to 1515 or 1525E printer

This hardcopy command copies the BASIC text screen content to a printer (device number 4) and can be called directly with SYS 9*4096.

```
                              ; HARDCOPY FUNCTION
9000 A9 04        LDA #4
9002 85 BA        STA FA      ; device number of printer
9004 A9 7E        LDA #126
9006 85 B8        STA LF      ; logical file number
9008 A9 00        LDA #0      ; address low of screen
900A A0 04        LDY #4      ; address high of screen
900C 85 71        STA TEMP    ; remeber as pointer
900E 84 72        STY TEMP+1
9010 85 B7        STA FNLEN   ; no file name
9012 85 B9        STA SA      ; secondary address zero
```

```
9014 20 C0 FF       JSR OPEN   ; open printer file
9017 A6 B8          LDX LF     ; logical file number of printer
9019 20 C9 FF       JSR CKOUT  ; printer as output device
901C A2 19          LDX #25    ; number of screen lines
901E A9 0D LOOP     LDA #13    ; new line
9020 20 D2 FF       JSR BSOUT  ; to printer
9023 20 E1 FF       JSR STOP   ; ask stop key
9026 F0 2E          BEQ EXIT   ; pressed, the end
9028 A0 00          LDY #0
902A B1 71 LOOP 2   LDA (TEMP),Y;get character from screen
902C 85 67          STA STORE
902E 29 3F          AND #$3F
9030 06 67          ASL STORE
9032 24 67          BIT STORE  ; screen code
9034 10 02          BPL *+4    ; change to ASCII code
9036 09 80          ORA #$80
9038 70 02          BVS *+4
903A 09 40          ORA #$40
903C 20 D2 FF       JSR BSOUT  ; and send to printer
903F C8             INY
9040 C0 28          CPY #40    ; line finished?
9042 D0 E6          BNE LOOP 2
9044 98             TYA
9045 18             CLC        ; yes, set pointer
9046 65 71          ADC TEMP   ; on next line
9048 85 71          STA TEMP
904A 90 02          BCC *+4
904C E6 72          INC TEMP+1
904E CA             DEX        ; all lines put out yet?
904F D0 CD          BNE LOOP
9051 A9 0D          LDA #13
9053 20 D2 FF       JSR BSOUT  ; new line
9056 20 CC FF EXIT  JSR CLRCH  ; output back on screen
9059 A2 7E          LDX #126
905B 4C C3 FF       JMP CLOSE  ; close print-data and done
```

Example 2 - RE-NEW

The following program can be very useful if you accidentally typed **NEW.** The program finds the end of the program ard sets the BASIC-pointers back on the previous value. It will work only if no new program lines have been entered and if nor new variables have been used. The start address here is 12*4096+15*256.

```
                   ; RE-NEW FUNCTION
                   ; GETS BACK CLEARED PROGRAM
CF00 A5 2B         LDA PRGSTRT    ; BASIC program-start
CF02 A4 2C         LDY PRGSTRT +1
CF04 85 22         STA TEMP       ; save as pointer
CF06 84 23         STY TEMP +1
```

```
CF08 A0 03          LDY #3
CF0A C8     ZERO    INY
CF0B B1 22          LDA (TEMP),Y   ; Looks for end of first line
CF0D D0 FB          BNE ZERO       ; (zero byte)
CF0F C8             INY
CF10 98             TYA
CF11 18             CLC
CF12 65 22          ADC TEMP       ; add offset
CF14 A0 00          LDY #0
CF16 91 2B          STA (PRGSTRT),Y; save as pointer
CF18 A5 23          LDA TEMP+1
CF1A 69 00          ADC #0          ; on next line
CF1C C8             INY
CF1D 91 2B          STA (PRGSTRT),Y
CF1F 88             DEY             ; now contains zero
CF20 A2 03 AGAIN    LDX #3
CF22 E6 22 TDREIO   INC TEMP
CF24 D0 02          BNE *+4         ; program end equal
CF26 E6 23          INC TEMP+1      ; look for three zero-bytes
CF28 B1 22          LDA (TEMP),Y
CF2A D0 F4          BNE AGAIN
CF2C CA             DEX
CF2D D0 F3          BNE TDREIO
CF2F A5 22          LDA TEMP
CF31 69 02          ADC #2
CF33 85 2D          STA PRGEND
CF35 A5 23          LDA TEMP+1      ; set pointer on program-end
CF37 69 00          ADC #0
CF39 85 2E          STA PRGEND+1
CF3B 4C 63 A6       JMP CLR         ; CLR and ready.
```

Example 3 - **PRINT USING**

A very useful routine is the formatted output of numbers, often called **PRINT USING.** This routine works as follows: (see address $C900-$C90C): first a numeric term is placed into the floating point accumulator; then it is changed into its ASCII string representation; next the formatting is carried out using the ASCII string; and finally the formatted string is output.

To use the routine, you use the following call:

SYS (AD),X

Here AD is the start address of the print using routine and X the variable or numeric term to be printed. The parameters for the term are set with POKEs:

```
POKE 51612, X   0 = whole number, 1 = number with decimal-point
POKE 51613, L   0 - 10, complete length - 1
POKE 51614, N   number of digits after the decimal point
POKE 51615, ASC(" ") fill-character before the number
```

POKE 51549, ASC(" ") leading character before the number

The default values are: decimal number, length 10 (9+1), 2 decimal digits, blank character as leading character and filler.

SYS(51456),100 leads to the following printout:

100.00

With POKE 51613,3 : POKE 51615,ASC("*") : POKE 51549ASC("$") the output of the example above looks like this:

**$100.000

```
                                 ; PRINT USING
C900 20 8A AD               JSR FRMNUM   ; get numeric term
C903 20 BB BD               JSR ASCII    ; change to ASCII
                                         ;   beginning at $100
C905 20 0D C9               JSR USING    ; out new routine
C909 20 1E AB               JSR OUT      ; string output
C90C 60                     RTS          ; return to caller
C90D A9 45      USING       LDA #'E
C90F 20 8E C9               JSR CHECK    ; checks on exp.format
C912 B0 59                  BCS SETPTR
C914 AD 9C C9               LDA DECINT ; flag for dec/integer
C917 F0 59                  BEQ INTEGER
C919 AD 02 01               LDA $102
C91C D0 0B                  BNE L1
C91E AC 9D C9               LDY LENGTH   ; complete length - 1
C921 A9 30                  LDA #'0
C923 99 02 01 L2            STA $102,Y   ; fill buffer w/ zeros
C926 88                     DEY
C927 D0 FA                  BNE L2
C929 A9 2E    L1            LDA #'.
C92B 20 8E C9               JSR CHECK
C92E A8                     TAY
C92F 90 02                  BCC *+4
C931 A0 30                  LDY #'0
C933 A9 00                  LDA #0
C935 20 8E C9               JSR CHECK
C938 98                     TYA
C939 9D 00 01               STA $100,X
C93C A9 2E                  LDA #'.
C93E 20 8E C9               JSR CHECK
C941 AC 9E C9               LDY DECLEN   ; # of decimal digits
C944 E8       L3            INX
C945 88                     DEY
C946 D0 FC                  BNE L3
C948 EC 9D C9 L8            CPX LENGTH
C94B B0 20                  BCS SETPTR
C94D AC 9D C9               LDY LENGTH
C950 A9 00                  LDA #0
C952 99 01 01               STA $101,Y
```

```
C955 BD 00 01 L6        LDA $100,X
C958 C9 20              CMP #'       ; leading char. blank
C95A D0 02              BNE L5
C95C A9 20              LDA #'
C95E 99 00 01 L5        STA $100,Y
C961 CA                 DEX
C962 10 06              BPL L4
C964 AD 9F C9           LDA FILLER
C967 88                 DEY
C968 10 F4              BPL L5
C96A 88       L4        DEY
C96B 10 E8              BPL L6
C96D A9 00    SETPTR    LDA #0       ; set pointer on buffer
C96F A0 01              LDY #1
C971 60                 RTS
C972 A9 00    INTEGER   LDA #0
C974 20 8E C9           JSR CHECK
C977 90 F4              BCC SETPTR
C979 8A                 TXA
C97A A8                 TAY
C97B AD 02 01           LDA $102
C97E F0 09              BEQ L7
C980 A9 2E              LDA #'.
C982 20 8E C9           JSR CHECK
C985 90 02              BCC L7
C987 8A                 TXA
C988 A8                 TAY
C989 98       L7        TYA
C98A AA                 TAX
C98B CA                 DEX
C98C 10 BA              BPL L8
C98E A2 00    CHECK     LDX #0
C990 DD 00 01 L9        CMP $100,X
C993 F0 06              BEQ L10
C995 E8                 INX
C996 E0 0C              CPX #12
C998 D0 F6              BNE L9
C99A 18                 CLC
C99B 60       L10       RTS
C99C 01       DECINT    BYT 1       ;decimal
C99D 09       LENGTH    BYT 9       ;length 9
C99E 02       DECLEN    BYT 2       ;# of decimal digits
C99F 20       FILLER    BYT ' '     ; fill character
C9A0          LEADING   EQU L5-1    ;leading character
```

6.3.3 Self-developed mathematical routines

If we have the need for mathematical routines, ones that the interpreter doesn't offer, quite often it is worthwhile to write a subprogram in machine language yourself. For functions with one argument, the USR function would be best.

How does the USR function work? The USR function, just like all other function-calls of the interpreter, can serve like the SIN function in terms for the calculation of variables or it can be in a PRINT statement. When calling the USR function, you must place the starting address of the routine in memory locations $311-$312 (decimal 785-786). You can POKE these locations with the address of your routine.
When calling the USR function, the value of the argument (it can be any complicated term) is passed in floating point accumulator 1. Now the function can be calculated in your machine language routine. You place the result of the function back into the FAC issue an RTS instruction to transfer control and the value back to BASIC.

Now let's look at some examples of how to write your own functions.

6.3.4 SQR, SUM, and PROD Functions

First is a routine for calculating a square root. Though the BASIC interpreter already provides such a routine, this one is faster and more precise. As a starting point, we take the argument and halve the exponent which already constitutes a good estimation of the square root value. The algorithm is **x(n+1) = (x(n)+a/x(n)) / 2**, with 'a' being the argument and 'x(n)' and 'x(n+1)' being the old and new estimate-value. Through experimenting it becomes clear that after 4 iterations the result doesn't change anymore.

```
C800 20 2B BC        JSR SIGN   ;check signs
C803 F0 34           BEQ END    ;value=0, ready
C805 10 03           BPL OK     ;positive, then ok
C807 4C 48 B2        JMP ILL    ;negative, 'illegal quantity'
C80A 20 C7 BB   OK   JSR FACA4  ;transfer FAC to accu#4
C80D A5 61           LDA EXP
C80F 38              SEC
C810 E9 81           SBC #$81   ;normalize exponent
C812 08              PHP
C813 4A              LSR A      ;halve exponent
C814 18              CLC
C915 69 01           ADC #1
C817 28              PLP
C818 90 02           BCC S1
C81A 69 7F           ADC #$7F   ;restore exponent
C81C 85 61      S1   STA EXP
C81E A9 04           LDA #4     ;4 iterations
C820 85 67           STA COUNT
C822 20 CA BB   ITER JSR FACA3  ;FAC to accu#3
C825 A9 5C           LDA #$5C
C827 A0 00           LDY #$00   ;pointer on accu#4
C829 20 0F BB        JSR DIV    ;divide by FAC
C82C A9 57           LDA #$57
C82E A0 00           LDY #$00   ;pointer on accu#3
```

```
C830 20 67 B8         JSR PLUS  ;add to FAC
C833 C6 61            DEC EXP   ;FAC/2(exponent - 1)
C835 C6 67            DEC COUNT ;lower counter
C837 D0 E9            BNE ITER  ;another iteration
C839 60          END  RTS       ;ready
```

Before calling this USR function we have to tell the interpreter first where our USR function starts. For this, the low-byte of the address is poked to $311 (decimal 785) and the high-byte is poked to $312 (786). For our function this would look like this:

```
POKE 785,0 : POKE 786, 12*16+8
```

Now to call the routine you can use a statement such as: **PRINT USR(A).** If you compare the execution time this routine with built in the SQR routine of the interpreter, it takes just 12 milliseconds which is about 4 times as fast as SQR which take about 52 milliseconds.

Now let's look at a little more complicated example. Often you're confronted with the task of adding up arrays of numbers, for example if you have to determine the mean or any statistical calculations. Let's assume that the data is available in an array (dimensioned variable).

```
10 DIM A(100)
100 S = 0:REM CALCULATION OR READ IN OF DATA
110 FOR I = 0 TO 1000 : S = S + A(I) : NEXT
120 PRINT S
```

If we substitute a USR function for BASIC lines 100 and 110. we get the statement:

```
  100 S = USR(A)
```

Here parameter A stands for the array name. As we will see later on, the product of the array elements can be calculated by changing two machine commands.

```
033C 20 8D AD         JSR NUMTEST    ;variable numeric?
033F A6 2F            LDX ARRTAB
0341 A5 30            LDA ARRTAB+1   ;ptr to array-list.
0343 86 5F      S3    STX TEMP
0345 85 60            STA TEMP+1     ;running pointer
0347 C5 32            CMP ARREND+1
0349 D0 04            BNE S1
034B E4 31            CPX ARREND     ;end of array listing?
034D F0 1D            BEQ NOTFOUND
034F A0 00      S1    LDY #0
0351 B1 5F            LDA (TEMP),Y   ;first letter of name
0353 C8               INY
0354 C5 45            CMP VARNAM  ;comp. w/searched name
0356 D0 06            BNE S2      ;no, check next array
```

```
0358 A5 46                  LDA VARNAM+1 ;second letter
035A D1 5F                  CMP (TEMP),Y ;compare
035C F0 17                  BEQ FOUND    ;found
035E C8        S2           INY
035F B1 5F                  LDA (TEMP),Y
0361 18                     CLC
0362 65 5F                  ADC TEMP  ;+ offset of next array
0364 AA                     TAX
0365 C8                     INY
0366 B1 5F                  LDA (TEMP),Y
0368 65 60                  ADC TEMP+1
036A 90 D7                  BCC S3
036C A2 E2   NOTFOUND       LDX #<TAB
036E 86 22                  STX $22      ;ptr. to error message
0370 A9 03                  LDA #>TAB
0372 4C 45 A4               JMP ERROUT   ;output of error message
0375 C8      FOUND          INY
0376 B1 5F                  LDA (TEMP),Y
0378 18                     CLC
0379 65 5F                  ADC TEMP
037B 85 24                  STA STORE
037D C8                     INY
037E B1 5F                  LDA (TEMP),Y
0380 65 60                  ADC TEMP+1
0382 85 25                  STA STORE+1
0384 C8                     INY
0385 B1 5F                  LDA (TEMP),Y  ;number of elements
0387 20 96 B1               JSR SETARR    ;ptr. 1st array elem.
038A 85 5F                  STA TEMP
038C 84 60                  STY TEMP+1    ;pointer to temp
038E 24 0E                  BIT INTFLG    ;check integer flag
0390 30 1F                  BMI INTEGER
0392 20 A2 BB               JSR MEMAC1    ;element in FAC
0395 18                     CLC
0396 90 04                  BCC LOOP      ;jump in loop
0398 20 67 B8 S5            JSR MEMPLUS   ;variable plus FAC
039B 18                     CLC
039C A5 5F     LOOP         LDA TEMP
039E 69 05                  ADC #5       ;ptr to next element
03A0 85 5F                  STA TEMP
03A2 90 02                  BCC S4
03A4 E6 60                  INC TEMP+1
03A6 A4 60     S4           LDY TEMP+1
03A8 C5 24                  CMP STORE    ;end of array?
03AE 90 E8                  BCC S5
03B0 60        READY        RTS          ;yes, ready
03B1 20 D5 03 INTEGER       JSR INTAKK   ;integer variable to FAC
03B4 20 0C BC S6            JSR A1TOA2   ;FAC to ARG
03B7 18                     CLC
03B8 A5 5F                  LDA TEMP
03BA 69 02                  ADC #2   ;ptr to next array elem.
03BC 85 5F                  STA TEMP
03BE 90 02                  BCC S7
03C0 E6 60                  INC TEMP+1
03C2 C5 24     S7           CMP STORE    ;end of array range?
```

```
03C4 90 06              BCC S8
03C6 A5 60              LDA TEMP+1
03C8 C5 25              CMP STORE+1
03CA B0 E4              BCS READY
03CC 20 D5 03 S8        JSR INTAKK   ;integer var to FAC
03CF 20 6F B8           JSR ACPLUS   ;FAC +ARG
03D2 4C B4 03           JMP S6
03D5 A0 00    INTAKK    LDY #0
03D7 B1 5F              LDA (TEMP),Y
03D9 AA                 TAX
03DA C8                 INY
03DB B1 5F              LDA (TEMP),Y
03DD A8                 TAY
03DE 8A                 TXA
03DF 4C 91 B3           JMP INTFLOAT  ;to floating comma
03E2 41 52 52 TAB       ASC 'ARRAY NOT FOUN'
03E5 41 59 20 4F 54 20 46 50 55 4F
03F0 C4                 BYT 'D'+$80
```

The program can process arrays with real numbers as well as integer arrays. If an array can't be found, the message **ARRAY NOT FOUND** is output.

Since the logic for calculating the array elements is the same, you can obtain a product function by substituting the calls for addition with the multiplication routine. For this at $0398 substitute 20 28 BA and at $03CF substitute 20 2B BA.

In order to use our routine, which is in the tape buffer this time, we have to poke the start address again:

```
POKE 785,3*16+12 : POKE 786,3
```

For a comparison, calculate the sum with the BASIC loop once and then with our routine - the time difference is immense!

6.3.5 Changing to Different Data Formats

If more than one parameter is to be transferred, the USR function is not suitable anymore. Here an extended variant of the SYS command is most suitable. Normally the SYS command only carries out the machine program starting from this address and transfers no further parameters. The above routine FRMEVL evaluates the parameter following the SYSxxx and transfers the value to the floating point accumulator.

If separated by a comma or parenthesis, any number of parameters can be transferred. For the formula evaluation routine there are several more routine addresses and sub routines available which check, for instance, for a comma or evaluate parameters in parenthesis. The type of variable or numeric string can be checked, too. For numeric variables, there is an additional range-check possible. The most important routines are summarized below. For further details, please check chapter 6.4 for the ROM listings.

ADDRESS	DESCRIPTION
AD8A	evaluate argument and check on numeric
AD8D	check on numeric
AD8F	check on string
AD9E	argument evaluation, any term
AEF1	evaluate argument in parenthesis
AEF7	checks on parenthesis closed
AEFA	checks on parenthesis open
B79E	checks on comma
0073	gets next character from BASIC text

In using these routines, if a value is out of range an error message **ILLEGAL QUANTITY** is issued. If a variable type does not coincide with the intended type an error message **TYPE MISMATCH** is issued.

You can convert to different formats using the following routines:

ADDRESS	DESCRIPTION
B1BF	changes FAC to integer
B395	changes 16-bit integer-number in A/X to running-comma
B3A2	changes byte in Y to floating comma
BC9B	changes FAC to 16-bit number
BCF3	changes digit string to floating-comma
BDDD	changes FAC in digit-string

Now let's look at an example of a SYS routine with parameter passing. Say you want to output from BASIC to a certain position on the screen. Here's an easier way of doing this with a short machine language routine.

The call has the following syntax:

```
  SYS PR, column,line, printlist
```

Here PR is the starting address of the routine, line and column are the cursor positions at which the variables or terms of the printlist are to be output.

```
C000 20 FD AE     JSR CKCOM    ; checks comma
C003 20 9E B7     JSR GETBYT   ; gets column value to X
C006 8A           TXA
C007 48           PHA          ; remember column-number
```

```
C008 20 FD AE      JSR CKCOM    ; checks on comma
C00B 20 9E B7      JSR GETBYT   ; gets line value
C00E 68            PLA
C00F A8            TAY          ; column value to Y
C010 18            CLC
C011 20 F0 FF      JSR CURSOR   ; sets cursor
C014 20 FD AE      JSR CKCOM    ; checks on comma
C017 4C A4 AA      JMP PRINT    ; continue with PRINT command
```

If you assign start address $C000 of the routine to the variable PR at the beginning of the program, you can output the text "example" with the following command, starting with the 24th column in line 20:

```
10  PR = 12*4096
100  SYS PR,24,20,"EXAMPLE"
```

6.4 Routines Of The BASIC Interpreter

The BASIC interpreter of the Commodore 64 is almost identical to VIC-20 interpreter. The major difference is in their positions in memory. The conversion of an address for the Commodore 64 into the corresponding address for the VIC-20 happens as follows:

At addresses from $A000 to $BFFF you simply add $2000, $A860 becomes the address $C860 in the VIC-20. At addresses from $E000 to $E73A, 3 is subtracted from the Commodore 64 address. $E30E becomes address $E30B at the VIC-20.

Appendix A contains the full disassembled listing of the Commodore 64 BASIC and kernal routines.

ADDRESS	DESCRIPTION
A000	start vector
A002	NMI vector
A004	'cbmbasic'
A00C	addresses of the BASIC commands minus 1
A052	addresses of the BASIC functions
A080	hierarchy-codes and addresses of the BASIC operators
A09E	list of BASIC command words
A19E	BASIC error-messages
A364	messages of the BASIC interpreter
A38A	stack search-routine for FOR-NEXT and GOSUB
A3B8	block-shifting routine
A3FB	checks on space in stack
A408	makes space in memory
A435	output of 'out of memory'
A437	output of error message
A469	break vector

A474	ready vector
A480	input waiting-loop
A49C	clear and inserting program lines
A533	tie BASIC program-lines anew
A560	gets a line into input-buffer
A571	output of 'string too long'
A579	change of a line into interpreter-code
A613	look for start address of a BASIC line
A642	BASIC-command NEW
A65E	BASIC-command CLR
A68E	set program-pointer to BASIC start
A69C	BASIC-command LIST
A717	change interpreter-code to command word
A742	BASIC-command FOR
A7AE	interpreter loop, carries out BASIC commands
A7ED	carries out BASIC-command
A81D	BASIC-command RESTORE
A82C	interrupts program at pressed stop-key
A82F	BASIC-command STOP
A831	BASIC-command END
A857	BASIC-command CONTINUED
A871	BASIC-command RUN
A883	BASIC-command GOSUB
A8A0	BASIC-command GOTO
A8F8	BASIC-command RETURN
A8F8	BASIC-command DATA
A906	looks for next statement
A909	looks for next line
A928	BASIC-command IF
A93B	BASIC-command REM
A94B	BASIC-command ON
A96B	looks for address of a BASIC line
A9A5	BASIC-command LET
AA80	BASIC-command PRINT#
AA86	BASIC-command CMD
AAA0	BASIC-command PRINT
AB1E	output string
AB3E	output empty-character(or cursor right)
AB4D	error handling for INPUT
AB7B	BASIC-command GET
ABA5	BASIC-command INPUT#
ABBF	BASIC-command INPUT
AC06	BASIC-command READ
ACFC	'?extra ignored' and '?redo from start'
AD1D	BASIC-command NEXT
AD8A	FRMNUM gets term and checks on numeric
AD8D	checks on numeric
AD8F	checks on string
AD99	output of 'type mismatch'
AD9E	FRMEVL gets and evaluates any term
AE83	get arithmetic term
AEA8	floating-point constant for pi
AED4	BASIC-command NOT
AEF1	gets term in parenthesis
AEF7	checks on 'parenthesis closed'

AEFA	checks on 'parenthesis open'
AEFD	checks on 'comma'
AEFF	checks on characters in accumulator
AF08	output of 'syntax error'
AF28	gets variable
AFE6	BASIC-command OR
AFE9	BASIC-command AND
B016	comparison-operations
B081	BASIC-command DIM
B113	checks for letter
B194	calculates pointer to first array-element
B1A5	floating-point constant -32768
B1AA	change FAC to integer
B245	output of 'bad subscript'
B248	output of 'illegal quantity'
B34C	calculates array-size
B37D	BASIC-function FRE
B39E	BASIC-function POS
B3A6	check on direct-mode
B3AB	output of 'illegal direct'
B3AE	output of 'undef'd function'
B3B3	BASIC-command DEF
B3E1	check FN-syntax
B3F4	BASIC-function FN
B465	BASIC-function STR$
B475	string administration, calculate pointer on string
B487	establish string
B526	garbage collection, remove unused strings
B63D	string connection '+'
B6A3	string administration FRESTR
B6EC	BASIC-function CHR$
B700	BASIC-function LEFT$
B72C	BASIC-function RIGHT$
B737	BASIC-function MID$
B77C	BASIC-function LEN
B782	get string parameter
B78B	BASIC-function ASC
B79B	gets byte-term (0 to 255)
B7AD	BASIC-function VAL
B7EB	gets address (0 to 65535) and byte-value (0 to 255)
B7F7	change FAC to address-format (range 0 to 65535)
B80D	BASIC-function PEEK
B824	BASIC-command POKE
B82D	BASIC-command WAIT
B849	FAC = FAC + 0.5
B850	minus FAC = constant (A/Y) - FAC
B853	minus FAC = ARG - FAC
B867	plus FAC = constant (A/Y) - FAC
B86A	plus FAC = ARG + FAC
B97E	output 'overflow'
B9BC	floating point constant for LOG
B9EA	BASIC-function LOG
BA28	multiplication FAC = constant (A/Y) * FAC
BA2B	multiplication FAC = ARG * FAC
BA8C	ARG = constant (A/Y)

BAE2	FAC = FAC * 10
BAF9	floating-point constant 10
BAFE	FAC = FAC/10
BB0F	FAC = constant (A/Y) / FAC
BB12	FAC = ARG/FAC
BB8A	output of 'division by zero'
BBA2	FAC = constant (A/Y)
BBC4	accu#4 = FAC
BBCA	accu#3 = FAC
BBD0	variable = FAC
BBFC	FAC = ARG
BC0C	ARG = FAC
BC1B	round FAC
BC2B	get signs of FAC
BC39	BASIC-function SGN
BC58	BASIC-function ABS
BC5B	compare constant (A/Y) with FAC
BC9B	change from FAC to integer
BCCC	BASIC-function INT
BCF3	change ASCII to floating-point
BDB3	floating-point constants for floating-point to A
BDC2	output of line-number at error message
BDCD	output of positive integer-number (0 to 65535)
BDDD	change FAC to ASCII-format
BF11	floating-point constant 0.5
BF16	binary numbers for change of FAC to ASCII
BF71	BASIC-function SQR
BF78	FAC = constant (A/Y) to the power of FAC
BF7B	FAC = ARG to the power of FAC
BFBF	floating point constant for EXP
BFED	BASIC-function EXP
E043	series 1 polynomial calculation
E059	series 2 polynomial calculation
E08D	floating point constant for RND
E097	BASIC-function RND
E107	output of 'break'
E10C	BSOUT output of a character
E112	BASIN receive a character
E118	CKOUT establish output-device
E11E	CHKIN establish input-device
E124	GETIN get a character
E12A	BASIC-comand SYS
E156	BASIC-command SAVE
E165	BASIC-command VERIFY
E168	BASIC-command LOAD
E1BE	BASIC-command OPEN
E1C7	BASIC-command CLOSE
E1D4	get parameters for LOAD and SAVE
E219	get parameter for OPEN
E264	BASIC-function COS
E26B	BASIC-function SIN
E2B4	BASIC-function TAN
E2E0	floating-point constants for SIN and COS
E30E	BASIC-function ATN
E33E	floating-point constants for ATN

E37B	BASIC NMI jump-in
E394	BASIC cold-start
E3A2	copy of the CHRGET-routine
E3BA	start-value for the RND-function
E3BF	initialize RAM for BASIC
E447	table of BASIC-vectors
E453	load BASIC-vectors

6.5 Low Memory Usage

Hex-address	Decimal	Description
00	0	data-direction register for processor por
01	1	processor register
02	2	unused
03 - 04	3 - 4	vector floating point to fixed
05 - 06	5 - 6	vector fixed to floating point
07	7	search character
08	8	quote flag
09	9	memory for column at TAB command
0A	10	load=0, verify=1, interpreter-flag
0B	11	pointer input-buffer, # of dimensions
0C	12	flag for DIM
0D	13	type-flag $00=numeric, $FF = string
0E	14	flag for integer=$80, floating = $00
0F	15	high-comma flag at LIST
10	16	flag for FN
11	17	flag for INPUT $00, GET $40, READ $98
12	18	flag for TAN
13	19	active I/O-device
14-15	20-21	integer-address, i.e. line number
16	22	pointer to string stack
17-18	23-24	pointer to string used last
19-21	25-33	string stack
22-25	34-37	pointer for various uses
26-2A	38-42	register for func eval. and arith.
2B-2C	43-44	pointer BASIC program-start
2D-2E	45-46	pointer to start of the variables
2F-30	47-48	pointer to start of the arrays
31-32	49-50	pointer to end of the arrays
33-34	51-52	pointer to begin of the strings
35-36	53-54	aid-pointer for strings
37-38	55-56	pointer to BASIC-RAM end
39-3A	57-58	present BASIC-linenumber
3B-3C	59-60	previous BASIC-linenumber
3D-3E	61-62	pointer to next BASIC stmt for CONT
3F-40	63-64	present linenumber for DATA
41-42	65-66	pointer to next DATA-element
43-44	67-68	pointer to origin of input
45-46	69-70	variable name
47-48	71-72	variable address
49-4A	73-74	variable-pointer for FOR/NEXT
4B-4C	75-76	intermediate memory for program ptr
4D	77	mask for comparison operations
4E-4F	78-79	pointer for FN
50-53	80-83	string descriptor
54	84	constant $4C JMP for functions
55-56	85-86	jump vector for functions
57-5B	87-91	register for arithmetic, accum#3
5C-60	92-96	register for arithmetic, accum#4
61-65	97-101	floating-point accum#1, FAC
66	102	sign of FAC
67	103	counter for polynomial evaluation
68	104	round-off byte for FAC

Hexaddress	Decimal	Description
69-6D	105-109	floating-point accum#2,ARG
6E	110	sign of ARG
6F	111	comparison of signs of FAC and ARG
70	112	round-off byte for FAC
71-72	113-114	pointer for cassette buffer
73-8A	115-138	CHRGET gets char. from BASIC text
7A-7B	122-123	program pointer
8B-8F	139-143	last RND-value
90	144	status word ST
91	145	flag for stop-key
92	146	time-constant for tape
93	147	flag for LOAD $00 or VERIFY $01
94	148	flag at IEC-output
95	149	output-buffer for IEC-bus
96	150	receive flag for EOT from tape
97	151	intermediate-memory for register
98	152	number of open files
99	153	active input-device
9A	154	active output-device
9B	155	parity for tape
9C	156	receive flag for byte
9D	157	flag direct-mode $80, program $00
9E	158	tape-pass 1 check-sum
9F	159	tape-pass 2 error-correction
A0-A2	160-162	time
A3	163	bit-counter for serial output
A4	164	counter for tape
A5	165	write counter for tape
A6	166	pointer in tape buffer
A7-AB	167-171	work-memory for tape in-/output
AC-AD	172-173	ptr for tape-buffer and scrolling
AE-AF	174-175	ptr on program end at LOAD/SAVE
B0-B1	176-177	time-constants for tape-timing
B2-B3	178-179	pointer on tape-buffer
B4	180	bit-counter for tape
B5	181	next bit for RS 232
B6	182	buffer for byte to be output
B7	183	length of file name
B8	184	logical file number
B9	185	secondary address
BA	186	device number
BB-BC	187-188	pointer to file name
BD	189	work-memory serial I/O
BE	190	pass counter for tape
BF	191	buffer for serial output
C0	192	flag for tape-drive
C1-C2	193-194	start address for I/O
C3-C4	195-196	end address for I/O
C5	197	key pressed last
C6	198	number of pressed keys
C7	199	flag for RVS-mode
C8	200	line end for input
C9	201	cursor line for input
CA	202	cursor column for input

Hexaddress	Decimal	Description
CB	203	pressed key, no key = 64
CC	204	flag for blinking cursor
CD	205	counter for cursor-blinking
CE	206	character under the cursor
CF	207	flag for cursor-blinking
D0	208	flag for input of keyboard or screen
D1-D2	209-210	ptr to start of actual screen line
D3	211	cursor column
D4	212	flag for cursor
D5	213	length of screen line
D6	214	cursor line
D7	215	various purposes
D8	216	number of inserts
D9-F2	217-242	MSB of screen-line beginnings
F3-F4	243-244	pointer to color-RAM
F5-F6	245-246	pointer to keyboard decoding table
F7-F8	247-248	pointer to RS-232 input buffer
F9-FA	249-250	pointer to RS-232 output buffer

****

00FF-010A	255-266	buffer floating point to ASCII
0100-013E	256-318	memory for correction at tape-input
0100-01FF	256-511	processor stack
0200-0258	512-600	BASIC input-buffer
0259-0262	601-610	table of logical file-numbers
0263-026C	611-620	table of device-numbers
026D-0276	621-630	table of secondary address
0277-0280	631-640	key-board buffer
0281-0282	641-642	start of BASIC-RAM
0283-0284	643-644	end of BASIC-RAM
0285	645	time-out flag for serial IEC-bus
0286	646	present color
0287	647	color under cursor
0288	648	high-byte video-RAM
0289	649	length of key-board buffer
028A	650	flag for 'repeat function' for all keys
028B	651	counter for repeat-speed
028C	652	counter for repeat-delay
028D	653	flag for shift and CTRL
028E	654	shift flag
028F-0290	655-656	pointer for key-board decoding
0291	657	flag for shift/Commodore blocked
0292	658	flag for scrolling
0293	659	RS-232 control-word
0294	660	RS-232 command-word
0295-0296	661-662	bit-timing
0297	663	RS-232 status
0298	664	number of data bits for RS-232
0299-029A	665-666	RS-232 baud-rate
029B	667	pointer to received byte RS-232
029C	668	pointer to input of RS-232
029D	669	pointer to byte RS-232 to be transferred

Hexaddress	Decimal	Description
029E	670	pointer to output on RS-232
029F-02A0	671-672	memory for IRQ during tape-operation
02A1	673	CIA 2 NMI flag
02A2	674	CIA 1 timer A
02A3	675	CIA 1 interrupt flag
02A4	676	CIA 1 flag for timer A
02A5	677	screen line
02C0-02FE	704-766	sprite 11
0300-0301	768-769	vector for error message
0302-0303	770-771	vector for BASIC warm-start
0304-0305	772-773	vector for change to interpreter-code
0306-0307	774-775	vector for change to clear text (LIST)
0308-0309	776-777	get vector for BASIC-command address
030A-030B	778-779	evaluate vector for term
030C	780	accu for SYS-command
030D	781	X-reg for SYS-command
030E	782	Y-reg for SYS-command
0310	784	$4C JMP-command for USR-function
0311-0312	785-786	$B248 USR-vector
0314-0315	788-789	$EA31 IRQ-vector
0316-0317	790-791	$FE66 BRK-vector
0318-0319	792-793	$FE47 NMI-vector
031A-031B	794-795	$F34A OPEN-vector
031C-031D	796-797	$F291 CLOSE-vector
031E-031F	798-799	$F20E CHKIN-vector
0320-0321	800-801	$F250 CKOUT-vector
0322-0323	802-803	$F333 CLRCH-vector
0324-0325	804-805	$F157 INPUT-vector
0326-0327	806-807	$F1CA OUTPUT-vector
0328-0329	808-809	$F6ED STOP-vector
032A-032B	810-811	$F13E GET-vector
032C-032D	812-813	$F32F CLALL-vector
032E-032F	814-815	$FE66 warm-start vector
0330-0331	816-817	$F4A5 LOAD-vector
0332-0333	818-819	$F5ED SAVE-vector
033C-03FB	828-1019	tape buffer
0340-037E	832-894	sprite 13
0380-03BE	896-958	sprite 14
03C0-03FE	960-1022	sprite 15

7.1 Comparison table of the ROM addresses

C64	VIC	Description
E45F	E429	messages of the operating system
E4E0	-	waits for Commodore key
E4EC	-	constants for RS-232 timing
E500	E500	gets BASIC-address of the CIA or the VIA
E505	E505	gets screen format line/column
E50A	E50A	set cursor or get cursor position
E518	E518	screen reset
E544	E55F	clear screen
E566	E581	cursor home
E5A0	E5BB	initialize video-controller
E5B4	E5CF	get character from keyboard buffer
E5CA	E5E5	waiting-loop for keyboard input
E632	E64F	get a character from the screen
E684	E6B8	checks for quote
E6B6	E6EA	calculate MSB for line starts
E8DA	E921	table of color-codes
E8EA	E975	scroll screen
E9C8	EA56	shift line up
E9FF	EA8D	clear screen-line
EA1C	EAA1	set character and color on screen
EA24	EAB2	calculate pointer on color-RAM
EA31	EABF	interrupt routine
EA87	EB1E	keyboard prompt
EB48	EBDC	checking on shift, CTRL and Commodore key
EB79	EC46	pointer on keyboard decoding tables
EB81	EC5E	decoding-tables
EC44	ED21	checking on control-character
EC78	ED69	decoding-tables
ECB9	EDE4	constants for video-controller
ECE7	EDF3	'load (cr) run (cr)'
ECF0	EDFE	LSB-tables of screen starts
ED09	EE14	send TALK
ED0C	EE17	send LISTEN
ED40	EEE4	output of byte on IEC-bus
EDB9	EEC0	send secondary address for LISTEN
EDC7	EECE	send secondary address for TALK
EDEF	EEF6	send UNTALK
EDFE	EF04	send UNLISTEN
EE13	EF19	get a byte from the IEC-bus
EEB3	EF96	one millisecond delay
EEBB	EFA3	output RS-232
EF4A	F027	calculate number of RS-232 data-bits
F014	F0ED	output in RS-232 buffer
F086	F14F	GET of RS-232
F0A4	F160	set timer for IEC time-out
F0BD	F174	error messages of the operating system
F12B	F1E0	put out messages

C64	VIC	Description
F157	F20E	BASIN get a character
F1CA	F27A	BSOUT putout a character
F20E	F2C7	CHKIN fixing of the input-device
F250	F309	CKOUT fixing of the output-device
F291	F34A	CLOSE
F30F	F3CF	look for logical file number
F31F	F3DF	set file parameter
F32F	F3EF	CLALL closes all I/O-channels
F34A	F40A	OPEN
F49E	F542	LOAD
F5AF	F647	output 'searching for file name'
F5D2	F66A	output 'loading/verifying'
F5DD	F675	SAVE
F68F	F728	output 'saving file name'
F69B	F734	UDTIM increase running time
F6DD	F760	get time
F6E4	F767	set time
F6ED	F770	ask stop -key
F6FB	F77E	put out error messages of the operating system
F72C	F7AF	read program header of tape
F76A	F7E7	write header on tape
F7D0	F84D	get start address of the tape buffer
F7D7	F854	set start and end address of the tape buffer
F7EA	F867	tape-header look for name
F80D	F88A	increase tape-buffer pointer
F817	F894	waits for tape-key for reading
F82E	F8AB	asks tape-key
F838	F8B7	waits for tape-key for writing
F841	F8C0	read block of tape
F84A	F8C9	load program of tape
F864	F8EA	write tape buffer on tape
F86B	F8EA	write block or program on tape
F8BE	F92F	wait for I/O-end
F8E1	F94B	checks on stop key
F92C	F98E	read interrupt routine for tape
FB97	F8DB	set bit-counter for serial output
FBA6	FBEA	write one bit on tape
FBCD	FC0B	write interrupt routine for tape
FCB8	FCF6	set IRQ-vector
FCCA	FD08	switch off tape drive
FCD1	FD11	checks on reaching of end address
FCDB	FD1B	increase address pointer
FCE2	FD22	RESET
FD02	FD3F	checks on ROM in $8000 or $A000
FD10	FD4D	ROM-module identification
FD15	FD52	set or get hardware and I/O-vectors
FD30	FD6D	table of hardware and I/O-vectors
FD50	FD8D	initialize work-memory
FD9B	FD6D	table of IRQ-vectors
FDF9	FE49	set parameter for file names
FE00	FE50	set parameter for active file
FE07	FE57	get status
FE18	FE66	set flag for messages of the operating system

C64	VIC	Description
FE1C	FE6A	set status
FE21	FEF6	set timeout-flag for IEC-bus
FE25	FE73	set or get RAM-upper limit
FE34	FE82	set or get RAM-lower limit
FE43	FEA9	NMI-routine
FEC2	FF5C	constants for RS 232 baud rate
FF48	FF72	interrupt handler
FF81	FF8A	jump table of the operating-system routines

7.2. Changing VIC-20 programs to the Commodore 64

Although outwardly, the Commodore 64 looks similar to the VIC-20, the '64 contains much more than its smaller brother. The with high-resolution color graphics, sprites and fabulous sound synthesizer - all this makes the Commodore 64 different from the VIC-20. Nevertheless, we don't want to do without VIC-20's software. Unfortunately it is nct possible to interchange the plug in cartridges. But there are enough program listings for you to transfer onto the Commodore 64.

One has to differentiate between two kinds of programs:

1. The machine language programs

With this program the adaption is not really difficult but yet more complicated than with BASIC programs. In order to be able to adapt these programs, you have to refer to the comparison table in chapter 7.1. For example, if you come to a jump-address that points to an address in ROM, you have to find to find this address in the comparison table of the Commodore 64 and change it with the address of the VIC-20 in the program. Generally it can be said that you can calculate the difference between the single addresses yourself. For instance, the start-address of the BASIC-GET routine at the VIC-20 is $CB7B. At the Commodore 64 it is exactly $2000 lower - $AB7B. Starting at $E000, the value 3 has to be subtracted from the Commodore 64 address in order to get the VIC-20 address.

2. The BASIC programs

With the BASIC programs, the adaption is not that complicated. The first thing to mention, of course, is the different screen format. Here you have to observe that you either have to rewrite the screen-format of the VIC-20 program completely or use a return after 22 characters so that the other characters don't slip into the same line. The only things that constitute a problem are the POKE commands. Here, too, you have to differentiate between two kinds:

1. POKE-commands into the screen memory
   Here you have to change all the addresses. Please compare the tables of the character-generator and the screen-page.

2. POKE-commands into the operating system
   The same procedure that applies to the changing of the machine programs is used.

7.3 Changing CBM/PET programs to the Commodore 64

Many people haven't even noticed yet that there is much similarity between the Commodore 64 and its big "colleagues". It is entirely possible to make use of programs of the legendary PET. The screen formats are the same - 25 lines of 40 characters each. All Commodores of this category (BASIC 2 and BASIC 3) have one advantage: their built in BASIC interpreter is fully compatible. That means that you don't have to make any changes in the BASIC-programs, unless they are POKE commands.

For POKEs you have to know the corresponding addresses of PET memory are different from the ones of the Commodore 64. There is a great amount of literature available for the PET/CBM devices. You will find the appropiate books in our bibliography.

In general one can say: BASIC and machine language are not different for these two devices. The 6510 is fully compatible with the 6502. Thus the only changes refer to the vector addresses to the different routines in the operating system or the different addresses of the screen memory and the vectors of the zero-page.

If you observe all this, you can use all the programs of the PET/ CBM or VIC-20 devices on your Commodore 64. All it takes is a little practice. And remember: by extending these programs you can even take advantage of the graphics, tone, and color of the Commodore 64. Which PET can offer you that? Besides, you have a 64K work-memory available on the Commodore 64 - enough to make the changed programs even better!

Have fun with adapting your software!

CHAPTER 8: INPUT-/OUTPUT CONTROL - CIA 6526

8.1 General notes about the 6526

The complex interface adapter (CIA) 6526 is a new peripheral element of the 65xx family. It is equipped with:

* 16 separately programmable in-output lines
* 8 or 16-bit handshake at input as well as output
* 2 independent, cascadeable 16-bit interval-timer
* 24-hour clock (am/pm) with programmable alarm
* 8-bit shift-register for the serial in-output

You'll find the block-schematic of the CIA 6526 in Diagram 8-1.

Pin-overlay of the 40-pin housing:

1	mass
2 - 9	I/O-port A; 8-bit bidirectional
10-17	I/O-port B; 8-bit bidirectional. Bits 6 and 7 can be programmed to indicate the lower course of both timers.
18	-PC (port control); exit only; signals the availability of data at port B or at both ports.
19	TOD (time of day); only 50/60 Hz entrance; triggers the real-time clock.
20	+5V; operating voltage
21	-IRQ (interrupt request); exit only; becomes 0 at the concurrence of a set bit in ICR with the happening of the appropiate event.
22	R/W (read/write); entrance only; 0= taking over of data bus, 1=output to data bus.
23	-CS (chip select); entrance only; 0=data bus valid, 1=data bus tri-state (high-ohm).
24	-FLAG; entrance only; meaning like -PC.
25	02 (system frequency 2); entrance only; all data-bus actions only take place at 02=1.
26-33	DB7-DB0(data bus); bi-directional; interface for the processor.
34	-RES(reset); entrance only; 0=setting back the CIA to original state.
35-38	RS3-RS0(register select); entrance only; serves for selecting one of the 16 registers of the CIA; only valid with -CS=0.
39	SP(serial port); bi-directional; serves as entrance/exit of the shift register.
40	CNT(count); bi-directional; entrance/exit of the shift-register frequency or trigger-entrance for the interval-timer.

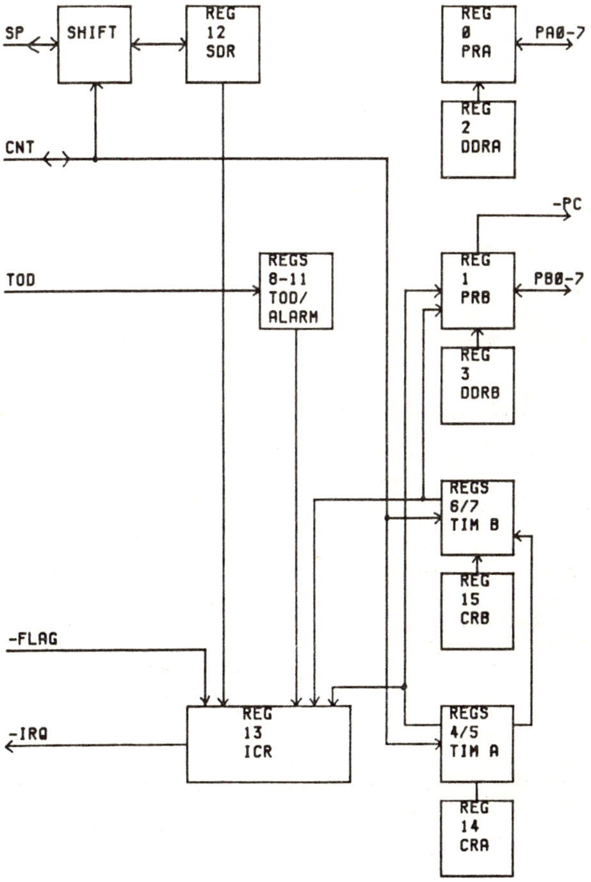

DIAGRAM 8-1 The CIA

8.2 Register Usage

REG 0 PRA (port register A)
access; READ/WRITE
bit 0-7 This register corresponds to the state of pins PA0-7

REG 1 PRB (port register B)
access: READ/WRITE
bit 0-7 This register corresponds to the state of pins PB0-7

REG 2 DDRA (data direction register A)
access: READ/WRITE
bit 0-7 These bits determine the data-direction of the corresponding data-bits of port A. 0=entrance, 1=exit.

REG 3 DDRB (data direction register B)
access: READ/WRITE
bit 0-7 These bits determine the data-direction of the corresponding data-bits of port B. 0=entrance, 1=exit.

REG 4 TA LO (timer A LO-byte)
access: READ
bit 0-7 This register represents the present state of the low-byte of timer A.
access: WRITE
bit 0-7 Into this register we load the low-byte of the value from which the timer shall count on zero.

REG 5 TA HI (timer A HI-byte)
access: READ
bit 0-7 This register represents the present state of the hi-byte of timer A.
access: WRITE
bit 0-7 Into this register we load the hi-byte of the value from which the timer shall count on zero.

REG 6 TB LO (timer B LO-byte)
access and overlay is the same as in REG 4.

REG 7 TB HI (timer B HI-byte)
access and overlay is the same as in REG 5.

REG 8 TOD 10THS (clock 1/10 sec)
access: READ
bit 0-3 tenth seconds of the real-time clock in BCD format
bit 4-7 always 0
access: WRITE and CRB bit 7=0
bit 0-3 tenth seconds in BCD format
bit 4-7 must be 0
access: WRITE and CRB bit 7=1

bit 0-3 preselection of the tenth seconds of the alarm-time in BCD format
bit 4-7 must be 0

REG 9 TOD SEC (clock sec)
access: READ
bit 0-3 single-seconds of the clock in BCD format
bit 4-6 decimal-seconds of the clock in BCD format
bit 7 always 0
Further types of access are analogous to REG 8.

REG 10 TOD MIN (clock min)
access: READ
bit 0-3 single-minutes of the clock in BCD format
bit 4-6 decimal-minutes of the clock in BCD format
bit 7 always 0
Further types of access are analogous to REG 8.

REG 11 TOD HR (clock hour)
access: READ
bit 0-3 single-hours of the clock in BCD format
bit 4 decimal-hours of the clock
bit 5-6 always 0
bit 7 0= am, 1= pm
Further types of access are analogous to REG 8.

REG 12 SDR (serial data register)
access: READ/WRITE
bit 0-7 From this register, the data is pushed out bit by bit to pin SP or pushed into this register by pin SP respectively.

REG 13 ICR (interrupt control register)
access: READ (INT DATA)
bit 0 1=lower course timer A
bit 1 1=lower course timer B
bit 2 1=parity of time and chosen alarm-time
bit 3 1=SDR full/empty, depending on the way of operation
bit 4 1=signal occured at pin FLAG
bit 5-6 always 0
bit 7 correspondence of at least one bit of INT MASK and INT DATA occured
ATTENTION: When reading this register, all bits are cleared!
access:WRITE (INT MASK)
Meaning of the bits as above, except bit 7:
bit 7 1=every 1-bit sets the corresponding mask-bit. The others remain untouched.
0=every 1-bit clears the corresponding mask-bit.
The others remain untouched.

REG 14 CRA (control register A)
access: READ/WRITE
bit 0 1=timer A start, 0=stop
bit 1 1=lower course of timer A is signaled to pin PB6.
bit 2 1=each lower course of timer A tilts PB6 into the respective position,0=each lower course of timer A creates a HI-pulse at the PB6 with the length of one system-frequency.
bit 3 1=timer A only counts once from the start-value to zero and stops then, 0=timer A continuosly counts from the start-value to zero.
bit 4 1=absolute loading of a new start-value into timer A. This bit functions as strobe. It has to be set anew at every absolute loading.
bit 5 This bit determines the source of the time_trigger. 1=timer counts increasing CNT-flanks, 0=timer counts system-frequency pulses.
bit 6 1=SP is entrance, 0=SP is exit
bit 7 1=realtime-clock trigger is 50Hz, 0=trigger is 60Hz

REG 15 CRB (control register B)
access: READ/WRITE
bit 0-4 These bits have the same meaning as in REG 14, but related to timer B and pin PB7 bit 5-6 These bits determine the source of the trigger for timer B. 00=timer counts system-frequencies, 10=timer counts increasing CNT-flanks, 01=timer B counts lower courses of timer A, 11=timer B counts lower courses of timer A if CNT=1
bit 7 1=set alarm, 0=set time.

8.3 I/O Ports

Ports A and B each consist of an 8-bit data register (PR) and an 8-bit data-direction register (DDR). If a bit is set in DDR, the corresponding bit in PR functions as an output. If a bit in DDR =0, the corresponding bit in PR is defined as input. During a READ-access, the PR represents the present state of the corresponding pin (PA0-7,PB0-7), for the entrance as well as for the exit bits. Beyond this, PB6 and PB7 can take over exit functions for both timers.

The data-transfer between the CIA and the "outside world" connected to PA/PB can be achieved by a discharge-operation. For this serve PC and FLAG. PC becomes 0 for the duration of a frequency if it was preceded by a READ or WRITE access to PRB. Thus the signal can indicate the availability of data to PB or the acceptance of data by PB. FLAG is a negatively edge-triggered input that could be connected to a PC of another CIA. A falling-edge at FLAG also sets the FLAG interrupt-bit.

The serial data port SDR is a synchronous 8-bit shift-register. CRA bit6 determines input or output mode. In the input mode, the data to SP with the increasing flank of a signal at CNT are transferred into a shift-register. After 8 CNT-pulses, the content of the shift-register is transferred to SDR and the SP-bit is set in ICR.

In the output mode, timer A functions as a baud-rate generator. The data from SDR is pushed out to SP with half the lower-course frequency of timer A. The theoretically highest baud-rate is thus 1/4 of the system frequency.

The transfer starts after the data has been written into SDR, provided that timer A is running and in continuous mode (CRA bit 0=1 and bit 3=0).

The cycle derived from timer A appears at CNT. The data from SDR are loaded into the shift-register and then pushed out of SP with every falling flank at CNT.

After 8 CNT-pulses the SP-interrupt is created. But if SDR is loaded with new data before this event, these are loaded automatically into the shift-register and pushed out. In this case no interrupt appears. The data from SDR are pushed out with the HI-byte first. Incoming data should have the same format.

8.4 The Timer

Each of the two interval-timers consists of a 16-bit counter (read only) and a 16-bit intermediate memory (write only). Data that is written into the timer ends out in the intermediate memory while the reading-data represents the present state of the counter.

Both timers can be used independently as well as together. The different ways of operation allow the creation of long time delays, variable pulse-lengths, and impulse-strings. When using th CNT-entrance, the timers can count external impulses or measure frequencies.

Every timer has a control-register assigned to it which allows it the following functions:

START/STOP (bit 0)
This bit can start or stop the timer at any time.

PB ON/OFF (bit 1)
Here, the lower course of the timer is directed to PB (PB6 for timer A, PB7 for timer B). This function has priority before the data-direction determined in DDRB.

TOGGLE/PULSE
This bit determines the kind of lower-course pulse that appears at PB. Either PB is tilted to the respective other position, or a positive pulse with the duration of one cycle is created.

ONE-SHOT/CONTINUOUS (bit 3)
In the one-shot operation the timer counts from the intermediate memory value to zero, sets the IRC-bit, loads the counter again with intermediate-memory value and stops then. In the continuous-mode the event described above happens cyclic.

FORCE LOAD (bit 4)
This bit allows the timer to load any time, no matter whether it is presently running or not.

INPUT MODE (bit 5 CRA, bit 5-6 CRB)
These allow a choice of the cycle with which the timer is counted down. Timer A can be supplied by either the system-cycle or with a cycle that was given to CNT. In addition to that, timer B can be fed with the lower-course pulses of timer A, either absolute or independent of CNT=1.

8.5 Real-Time Clock

The real-time clock (TOD) is a 24-hour clock (am/pm) with a resolution of 1/10sec.

It consists of four registers: 1/10sec, sec, min, hr. The am/pm-bit is the one with the highest value of the hour register. Every register is organized in the BCD-format so that the read values can be used without big calculation operations.

A cycle serves a 50/60Hz-signal (programmable, CRA-bit 7) at pin TOD. Furthermore, there is an alarm-register with which one can create an interrupt at any time. The alarm-register overlays the same address as the TOD-register. That is why the access is controlled with bit 7. The alarm-register is write only. Every read-access represents the state of the TOD-register, independent of CRB bit 7.

In order to set and read the time correctly, a certain order has to be kept:

If the hour-register is being written on, the clock stops automatically. It is not until a write-access to the 1/10 sec-register took place that the clock will continue to run. By this the clock starts indeed at the right time. Since a transfer into an already read register can occur during the reading of the complete time, the complete time will be buffered into an intermediate-memory at the reading of the hour-register. The intermediate-memory is not set free until the 1/10 has been read.

If only one register shall be read, this can happen easily of course; but if this register is the hour-register, the 1/10sec-register has to be read afterwards in order to set the intermediate-memory free again.

8.5.1 With a small trick, the right time

The long-time accuracy of the clock TI$, supplied by the operating system, leaves something to be desired as far as the system is concerned. You have to count on a maximum deviation of 1/2 hr. per day.

For those who insist on the correct time, the real-time clock in the CIAs offer a solution. It gets its cycle frcm the main frequency which shows an amazing long-time constancy.

In order to simplify the handling of the real-time clock for you, we worked out two small basic-programs. One serves for setting the clock, the other for reading it. First the program for setting it. The value for 1/10sec is always set on 0 here.

```
10    C=56328: REM basis address of the clock in CIA 1
20    REM C=56584 for the clock in CIA 2
30    POKE C+7,PEEK(C+7)AND127
35    POKE C+6,PEEK(C+6)OR128
40    INPUT"PUT IN TIME IN FORMAT HHMMSS";A$
50    IF LEN(A$)<>6 THEN 40
60    H=VAL(LEFT$(A$,2))
70    M=VAL(MID$(A$,3,2))
80    S=VAL(RIGHT$(A$,2))
90    IF H>23 THEN 40
100   IF H>11 THEN H=H+68
110   POKE C+3,16*INT(H/10)+H-INT(H/10)*10
120   IF M>59 THEN 40
130   POKE C+2,16*INT(M/10)+M-INT(M/10)*10
140   IF S>59 THEN 40
150   POKE C+1,16*INT(S/10)+S-INT(S/10)*10
160   POKE C,0
```

The following program enables you to read the time:

```
10    C=56328: REM basis address of the clock in CIA 1
20    PRINT "(shft/clr)":REM C=56584 for clock in CIA 2
30    H=PEEK(C+3):M=PEEK(C+2):S=PEEK(C+1):T=PEEK(C)
40    FL=1
50    IF H>32 THEN H=H-128:FL=0
60    H=INT(H/16)*10+H-INT(H/16)*16:ON FL GOTO 80
65    IF H=12 THEN 85
```

```
70    H=H+12
80    IF H=12 THEN H=0
85    M=INT(M/16)*10+M-INT(M/16)*16
90    S=INT(S/16)*10+S-INT(S/16)*16
100   T$=STR$(T)
110   H$=STR$(H):IF LEN(H$)=2 THEN H$=" 0"+RIGHT$(H$,1)
120   M$=STR$(M):IF LEN(M$)=2 THEN M$=" 0"+RIGHT$(M$,1)
130   S$=STR4(S):IF LEN(S$)=2 THEN S$=" 0"+RIGHT$(S$,1)
140   PRINT "(home)";
150   PRINT "RIGHT$(H$,2)":"RIGHT$(M$,2)":"RIGHT$(S$,2)":0";
160   PRINT RIGHT$(T$,1)
170   GOTO 30
```

After pressing STOP/RESTORE, you have to set the time again since the operating system sets all registers back to the start-value. Unfortunately, the bit for the 50/60Hz selection is affected by this as well. Your clock would be far behind.

8.6 The CIAs in the Commodore 64

If you want to use the CIAs in the CBM64 for your own purposes, please note that they were assigned special tasks in the computer. This applies especially for the usage of interrupts because they cause the operating-system to run through certain routines. So please avoid changing the mask in ICR.

The assignments for the CIAs from within CBM64 are:

CIA 1 Base address $DC00(56320)

REG 0 (PRA)

Bit 0-7 During normal operation the sequence-selection of the keyboard-matrix is determined here. Yet some bits are connected with control-port 1 outside the computer. It serves for connecting joy-sticks or paddles:

Bit 0-4 Joy-stick 0, order: up, down, left, right, key

Bit 6-7 Selection paddle-set A/B. Only one of the two bits may be 0.

REG 1 (PRB)

Bit 0-7 During normal operation occurs a column-back-report of the keyboard-matrix if a key was pressed.

Bit 0-4 The same function as REG 0, but for control-port 2 (joy-stick 1).

REG 13 (ICR)

Bit 4 Input-data from the cassette-port

CIA 2 Basis-address $DD00(56576)

REG 0 (PRA)
Bit 0-1 VA 14-15 (address bits of the highest value of the video-ram).
Bit 2 TXD (only in connection with with an RS 232 cartridge, otherwise free).
Bit 3 ATN (exit serial bus)
Bit 4 CLOCK (exit serial bus)
Bit 5 DATA (exit serial bus)
Bit 6 CLOCK (entrance serial bus)
Bit 7 DATA (entrance serial bus)

REG 1 (PRB)
Bit 0-7 Usually free. When putting on an RS 232 cartridge they get the following meaning:
Bit 0 RXD (receive data)
Bit 1 RTS (request to send)
Bit 2 DTR (data terminal ready)
Bit 3 RI (ring indicator)
Bit 4 DCD (data carrier detect)
Bit 6 CTS (clear to send)
Bit 7 DSR (data set ready)

REG 13 (ICR)
Bit 4 RXD (only at RS 232 operation, otherwise free).

8.7 Using the Joysticks

When using the joysticks you ought to know that they overlay the same CIA-bits that are used for asking the keyboard at normal operation.

In order to work with the joysticks anyway, the keyboard-input has to be eliminated for that particular time. This can only happen within a program that does not use the keyboard and thus does not contain an INPUT or the like.

The following program shows the joystick functions in a reliable manner:

```
10  POKE56322,224
20  J=PEEK(56320)
30  IF(JAND1)=0 THEN PRINT "UP"
40  IF(JAND2)=0 THEN PRINT "DOWN"
50  IF(JAND4)=0 THEN PRINT "LEFT"
60  IF((JAND8=0 THEN PRINT "RIGHT"
70  IF(JAND16)=0 THEN PRINT "BUTTON"
80  GOTO20
```

This program expects the joystick at control port 2. If the joystick is operated at control port 1, the address in line

20 has to be changed to 56321.

The only thing that'll get you out of the above program is STOP/RESTORE. The last line in a "serious" program should be:

```
100 POKE 56322,255
```

With this you unlock the keyboard again. Of course you can put this line before any keyboard action if your program needs the keyboard and the joy-sticks. But then a command like the one in line 10 has to come before every reading of the joystick.

APPENDIX A
Commodore 64 Rom Listings

```
                                          Start-Vector  $E394
A000 94 E3                                NMI-Vector    $E37b
A002 7B E3                                cbmbasic
A004 43 42

******************************            Addresses of BASIC
A00C 30 A8 41 A7 1D AD F7 A8               commands  (minus 1)
A014 A4 AB BE AB 80 B0 05 AC
A01C A4 A9 9F A8 70 A8 27 A9
A024 1C A8 82 A8 D1 A8 3A A9
A02C 2E A8 4A A9 2C B8 67 E1
A034 55 E1 64 E1 B2 B3 23 B8
A03C 7F AA 9F AA 56 A8 9B A6
A044 5D A6 85 AA 29 E1 BD E1
A04C C6 E1 7A AB 41 A6

******************************            Addresses of BASIC
A052 39 BC CC BC 58 BC 10 03               functions
A05A 7D B3 9E B3 71 BF 97 E0
A062 EA B9 ED BF 64 E2 6B E2
A06A B4 E2 0E E3 0D B8 7C B7
A072 65 B4 AD B7 8B B7 EC B6
A07A 00 B7 2C B7 37 B7 79 69

******************************            Priority codes and
A080 79 69 B8 79 52 B8 7B 2A               addresses for BASIC
A088 BA 7B 11 BB 7F 7A BF 50               opperators
A090 E8 AF 46 E5 AF 7D B3 BF
A098 5A D3 AE 64 15 B0

******************************            BASIC command words
A09E 45 4E C4 46 4F D2 4E 45              end       for
A0A6 58 D4 44 41 54 C1 49 4E              next      data
A0AE 50 55 54 A3 49 4E 50 55              input#    input
A0B6 D4 44 49 CD 52 45 41 C4              dim       read
A0BE 4C 45 D4 47 4F 54 CF 52              let       goto
A0C6 55 CE 49 C6 52 45 53 54              run       if
A0CE 4F 52 C5 47 4F 53 55 C2              restore gosub
A0D6 52 45 54 55 52 CE 52 45              return    rem
A0DE CD 53 54 4F D0 4F CE 57              stop      on
A0E6 41 49 D4 4C 4F 41 C4 53              wait      load
A0EE 41 56 C5 56 45 52 49 46              save      verify
A0F6 D9 44 45 C6 50 4F 4B C5              def       poke
A0FE 50 52 49 4E 54 A3 50 52              print#    print
A106 49 4E D4 43 4F 4E D4 4C
A10E 49 53 D4 43 4C D2 43 4D              cont      list
A116 C4 53 59 D3 4F 50 45 CE              clr       cmd       sys
A11E 43 4C 4F 53 C5 47 45 D4              open      close
A126 4E 45 D7 54 41 42 A8 54              get       new
A12E CF 46 CE 53 50 43 A8 54              tab(      to
A136 48 45 CE 4E 4F D4 53 54              spc(      then
A13E 45 D0 AB AD AA AF DE 41              not       stop
A146 4E C4 4F D2 BE BD BC 53              + - * / ^           and
```

```
A14E 47 CE 49 4E D4 41 42 D3     or   =    sgn
A156 55 53 D2 46 52 C5 50 4F     int       abs       usr
A15E D3 53 51 D2 52 4E C4 4C     fre       pos       sqr
A166 4F C7 45 58 D0 43 4F D3     rnd       log
A16E 53 49 CE 54 41 CE 41 54     exp       cos       sin
A176 CE 50 45 45 CB 4C 45 CE     tan       atn       peek
A17E 53 54 52 A4 56 41 CC 41     len       str$
A186 53 C3 43 48 52 A4 4C 45     val       asc
A18E 46 54 A4 52 49 47 48 54     chr$      left$
A196 A4 4D 49 44 A4 47 CF 00     right$    mid$      go

*****************************   BASIC error messages
A19E 54 4F 4F 20 4D 41 4E 59     1.  too many files
A1A6 20 46 49 4C 45 D3 46 49
A1AE 4C 45 20 4F 50 45 CE 46     2.  file open
A1B6 49 4C 45 20 4E 4F 54 20     3.  file not open
A1BE 4F 50 45 CE 46 49 4C 45
A1C6 20 4E 4F 54 20 46 4F 55     4.  file not found
A1CE 4E C4 44 45 56 49 43 45     5.  device not present
A1D6 20 4E 4F 54 20 50 52 45
A1DE 53 45 4E D4 4E 4F 54 20
A1E6 49 4E 50 55 54 20 46 49     6.  not input file
A1EE 4C C5 4E 4F 54 20 4F 55
A1F6 54 50 55 54 20 46 49 4C     7.  not output file
A1FE C5 4D 49 53 53 49 4E 47
A206 20 46 49 4C 45 20 4E 41     8.  missing filename
A20E 4D C5 49 4C 4C 45 47 41
A216 4C 20 44 45 56 49 43 45     9.  illegal device number
A21E 20 4E 55 4D 42 45 D2 4E
A226 45 58 54 20 57 49 54 48     10. next without for
A22E 4F 55 54 20 46 4F D2 53
A236 59 4E 54 41 D8 52 45 54     11. syntax
A23E 55 52 4E 20 57 49 54 48     12. return without gosub
A246 4F 55 54 20 47 4F 53 55
A24E C2 4F 55 54 20 4F 46 20     13. out of data
A256 44 41 54 C1 49 4C 4C 45
A25E 47 41 4C 20 51 55 41 4E     14. illegal quantity
A266 54 49 54 D9 4F 56 45 52
A26E 46 4C 4F D7 4F 55 54 20     15. overflow
A276 4F 46 20 4D 45 4D 4F 52     16. out of memory
A27E D9 55 4E 44 45 46 27 44     17. undef'd statement
A286 20 53 54 41 54 45 4D 45
A28E 4E D4 42 41 44 20 53 55
A296 42 53 43 52 49 50 D4 52     18. bad subscript
A29E 45 44 49 4D 27 44 20 41     19. redim'd array
A2A6 52 52 41 D9 44 49 56 49
A2AE 53 49 4F 4E 20 42 59 20     20. division by zero
A2B6 5A 45 52 CF 49 4C 4C 45
A2BE 47 41 4C 20 44 49 52 45     21. illegal direct
A2C6 43 D4 54 59 50 45 20 4D
A2CE 49 53 4D 41 54 43 C8 53     22. type mismatch
A2D6 54 52 49 4E 47 20 54 4F     23. string too long
A2DE 4F 20 4C 4F 4E C7 46 49
A2E6 4C 45 20 44 41 54 C1 46
A2EE 4F 52 4D 55 4C 41 20 54     24. file data
```

```
A2F6 4F 4F 20 43 4F 4D 50 4C       25. formula too complex
A2FE 45 D8 43 41 4E 27 54 20
A306 43 4F 4E 54 49 4E 55 C5       26. can't continue
A30E 55 4E 44 45 46 27 44 20       27. undef'd function
A316 46 55 4E 43 54 49 4F CE
A31E 56 45 52 49 46 D9 4C 4F       28. verify
A326 41 C4                         29. load

*****************************      Addresses of error messages
A328 9E A1 AC A1 B5 A1 C2 A1
A330 D0 A1 E2 A1 F0 A1 FF A1
A338 10 A2 25 A2 35 A2 3B A2
A340 4F A2 5A A2 6A A2 72 A2
A348 7F A2 90 A2 9D A2 AA A2
A350 BA A2 C8 A2 D5 A2 E4 A2
A358 ED A2 00 A3 0E A3 1E A3
A360 24 A3 83 A3

*****************************      BASIC interpreter messages
A364 0D 4F 4B 0D 00 20 20 45        ok
A36C 52 52 4F 52 00 20 49 4E        error
A374 20 00 0D 0A 52 45 41 44        in
A37C 59 2E 0D 0A 00 0D 0A 42        ready.
A384 52 45 41 4B 00 A0              break


*****************************      Stack routine for "GOSUB"
A38A  BA        TSX                 and "FOR-NEXT"
A38B  E8        INX
A38C  E8        INX
A38D  E8        INX
A38E  E8        INX
A38F  BD 01 01  LDA $0101,X
A392  C9 81     CMP #$81           FOR code
A394  D0 21     BNE $A3B7
A396  A5 4A     LDA $4A            Compare variable name
A398  D0 0A     BNE $A3A4
A39A  BD 02 01  LDA $0102,X
A39D  85 49     STA $49
A39F  BD 03 01  LDA $0103,X
A3A2  85 4A     STA $4A
A3A4  DD 03 01  CMP $0103,X
A3A7  D0 07     BNE $A3B0
A3A9  A5 49     LDA $49
A3AB  DD 02 01  CMP $0102,X
A3AE  F0 07     BEQ $A3B7
A3B0  8A        TXA
A3B1  18        CLC
A3B2  69 12     ADC #$12           Increase stack pointer by
A3B4  AA        TAX                 decimal 18
A3B5  D0 D8     BNE $A38F          Check next loop
A3B7  60        RTS

*****************************      Block-shift routine
A3B8  20 08 A4 JSR $A408           checks on free memory
```

```
A3BB  85 31    STA $31
A3BD  84 32    STY $32
A3BF  38       SEC          SEt Carry
A3C0  A5 5A    LDA $5A      $5F/$60   old block-start
A3C2  E5 5F    SBC $5F      $5A/$5B   old block-start+1
A3C4  85 22    STA $22      $58/$59   new block-end
A3C6  A8       TAY
A3C7  A5 5B    LDA $5B
A3C9  E5 60    SBC $60
A3CB  AA       TAX
A3CC  E8       INX
A3CD  98       TYA
A3CE  F0 23    BEQ $A3F3
A3D0  A5 5A    LDA $5A
A3D2  38       SEC
A3D3  E5 22    SBC $22
A3D5  85 5A    STA $5A
A3D7  B0 03    BCS $A3DC
A3D9  C6 5B    DEC $5B
A3DB  38       SEC
A3DC  A5 58    LDA $58
A3DE  E5 22    SBC $22
A3E0  85 58    STA $58
A3E2  B0 08    BCS $A3EC
A3E4  C6 59    DEC $59
A3E6  90 04    BCC $A3EC
A3E8  B1 5A    LDA ($5A),Y
A3EA  91 58    STA ($58),Y
A3EC  88       DEY
A3ED  D0 F9    BNE $A3E8
A3EF  B1 5A    LDA ($5A),Y
A3F1  91 58    STA ($58),Y
A3F3  C6 5B    DEC $5B
A3F5  C6 59    DEC $59
A3F7  CA       DEX
A3F8  D0 F2    BNE $A3EC
A3FA  60       RTS

******************************   Check on stack-space
A3FB  0A       ASL             accumulator must get half
A3FC  69 3E    ADC #$3E         the amount of needed space
A3FE  B0 35    BCS $A435       display "out of memory"
A400  85 22    STA $22
A402  BA       TSX
A403  E4 22    CPX $22
A405  90 2E    BCC $A435       display "out of memory"
A407  60       RTS

******************************   Creats space in memory for
A408  C4 34    CPY $34          inserted lines and
A40A  90 28    BCC $A434        variables
A40C  D0 04    BNE $A412       sets A & Y to location in
A40E  C5 33    CMP $33          memory.
```

```
A410   90 22      BCC $A434
A412   48         PHA
A413   A2 09      LDX #$09
A415   98         TYA
A416   48         PHA
A417   B5 57      LDA $57,X        save registers for
A419   CA         DEX               arithmetic
A41A   10 FA      BPL $A416
A41C   20 26 B5   JSR $B526        garbage collection
A41F   A2 F7      LDX #$F7
A421   68         PLA
A422   95 61      STA $61,X        get back register
A424   E8         INX
A425   30 FA      BMI $A421
A427   68         PLA
A428   A8         TAY
A429   68         PLA
A42A   C4 34      CPY $34
A42C   90 06      BCC $A434        O.K. ready
A42E   D0 05      BNE $A435        no space, "out of memory"
A430   C5 33      CMP $33
A432   B0 01      BCS $A435
A434   60         RTS
A435   A2 10      LDX #$10         error # for "out of memory"

****************************      Out-put error messages
A437   6C 00 03   JMP ($0300)       JMP $A43A
A43A   8A         TXA               error in x-register; 1 - 30
A43B   0A         ASL
A43C   AA         TAX
A43D   BD 26 A3   LDA $A326,X
A440   85 22      STA $22
A442   BD 27 A3   LDA $A327,X       get address of message
A445   85 23      STA $23
A447   20 CC FF   JSR $FFCC         set back active I/O
A44A   A9 00      LDA #$00           channels
A44C   85 13      STA $13           set back I/O flag
A44E   20 D7 AA   JSR $AAD7         out-put (CR) & (LF)
A451   20 45 AB   JSR $AB45         out-put "?"
A454   A0 00      LDY #$00
A456   B1 22      LDA ($22),Y       text of error message
A458   48         PHA
A459   29 7F      AND #$7F
A45B   20 47 AB   JSR $AB47         out-put error message
A45E   C8         INY
A45F   68         PLA
A460   10 F4      BPL $A456
A462   20 7A A6   JSR $A67A         initialize BASIC-pointers,
A465   A9 69      LDA #$69           block CONT
A467   A0 A3      LDY #$A3          pointer A/Y to error
A469   20 1E AB   JSR $AB1E         out-put string
A46C   A4 3A      LDY $3A           program mode?
A46E   C8         INY
A46F   F0 03      BEQ $A474         no
A471   20 C2 BD   JSR $BDC2         out-put "in (line number)"
A474   A9 76      LDA #$76          set pointer "READY."
A476   A0 A3      LDY #$A3
```

```
A478   20 1E AB JSR $AB1E           out-put string
A47B   A9 80    LDA #$80
A47D   20 90 FF JSR $FF90           set direct-mode flag

****************************        INPUT waiting loop
A480   6C 02 03 JMP ($0302)          JMP $A483
A483   20 60 A5 JSR $A560            get BASIC line into input
A486   86 7A    STX $7A               buffer
A488   84 7B    STY $7B              CHRGET pointer to buffer
A48A   20 73 00 JSR $0073            CHRGET get next character
A48D   AA       TAX
A48E   F0 F0    BEQ $A480            buffer empty, keep waiting
A490   A2 FF    LDX #$FF
A492   86 3A    STX $3A              sign for direct mode
A494   90 06    BCC $A49C            digit, then insert as line
A496   20 79 A5 JSR $A579            change line to interpreter
A499   4C E1 A7 JMP $A7E1            execute command        code

****************************        Clr & insrt of program lines
A49C   20 6B A9 JSR $A96B            change line # to addr form
A49F   20 79 A5 JSR $A579            change line to intrpr code
A4A2   84 0B    STY $0B              pointer to input buffer
A4A4   20 13 A6 JSR $A613            calculate address of line
A4A7   90 44    BCC $A4ED
****************************        Erase program line
A4A9   A0 01    LDY #$01
A4AB   B1 5F    LDA ($5F),Y
A4AD   85 23    STA $23
A4AF   A5 2D    LDA $2D
A4B1   85 22    STA $22
A4B3   A5 60    LDA $60
A4B5   85 25    STA $25
A4B7   A5 5F    LDA $5F
A4B9   88       DEY
A4BA   F1 5F    SBC ($5F),Y
A4BC   18       CLC
A4BD   65 2D    ADC $2D
A4BF   85 2D    STA $2D
A4C1   85 24    STA $24
A4C3   A5 2E    LDA $2E
A4C5   69 FF    ADC #$FF
A4C7   85 2E    STA $2E
A4C9   E5 60    SBC $60
A4CB   AA       TAX
A4CC   38       SEC
A4CD   A5 5F    LDA $5F
A4CF   E5 2D    SBC $2D
A4D1   A8       TAY
A4D2   B0 03    BCS $A4D7
A4D4   E8       INX
A4D5   C6 25    DEC $25
A4D7   18       CLC
A4D8   65 22    ADC $22
A4DA   90 03    BCC $A4DF
```

```
A4DC  C6 23     DEC $23
A4DE  18        CLC
A4DF  B1 22     LDA ($22),Y       shift-loop
A4E1  91 24     STA ($24),Y
A4E3  C8        INY
A4E4  D0 F9     BNE $A4DF
A4E6  E6 23     INC $23
A4E8  E6 25     INC $25
A4EA  CA        DEX
A4EB  D0 F2     BNE $A4DF

****************************     Insert program line
A4ED  20 59 A6 JSR $A659          CLR command
A4F0  20 33 A5 JSR $A533          tie new program line
A4F3  AD 00 02 LDA $0200          characters in buffer?
A4F6  F0 88    BEQ $A480          no, then go to waiting-loop
A4F8  18       CLC
A4F9  A5 2D    LDA $2D
A4FB  85 5A    STA $5A
A4FD  65 0B    ADC $0B
A4FF  85 58    STA $58
A501  A4 2E    LDY $2E
A503  84 5B    STY $5B
A505  90 01    BCC $A508
A507  C8       INY
A508  84 59    STY $59
A50A  20 B8 A3 JSR $A3B8          shift BASIC lines
A50D  A5 14    LDA $14
A50F  A4 15    LDY $15
A511  8D FE 01 STA $01FE
A514  8C FF 01 STY $01FF
A517  A5 31    LDA $31
A519  A4 32    LDY $32
A51B  85 2D    STA $2D
A51D  84 2E    STY $2E
A51F  A4 0B    LDY $0B
A521  88       DEY
A522  B9 FC 01 LDA $01FC,Y
A525  91 5F    STA ($5F),Y
A527  88       DEY
A528  10 F8    BPL $A522
A52A  20 59 A6 JSR $A659          CLR command
A52D  20 33 A5 JSR $A533          tie new program line
A530  4C 80 A4 JMP $A480          jump to waiting-loop

****************************     Tie new BASIC program-line
A533  A5 2B    LDA $2B
A535  A4 2C    LDY $2C
A537  85 22    STA $22
A539  84 23    STY $23
A53B  18       CLC
A53C  A0 01    LDY #$01
A53E  B1 22    LDA ($22),Y
A540  F0 1D    BEQ $A55F
```

```
A542  A0 04     LDY #$04
A544  C8        INY
A545  B1 22     LDA ($22),Y
A547  D0 FB     BNE $A544
A549  C8        INY
A54A  98        TYA
A54B  65 22     ADC $22
A54D  AA        TAX
A54E  A0 00     LDY #$00
A550  91 22     STA ($22),Y
A552  A5 23     LDA $23
A554  69 00     ADC #$00
A556  C8        INY
A557  91 22     STA ($22),Y
A559  86 22     STX $22
A55B  85 23     STA $23
A55D  90 DD     BCC $A53C
A55F  60        RTS

******************************   Input a new line
A560  A2 00     LDX #$00
A562  20 12 E1  JSR $E112         get a character
A565  C9 0D     CMP #$0D          RETURN key?
A567  F0 0D     BEQ $A576         yes, end input
A569  9D 00 02  STA $0200,X       store character in buffer
A56C  E8        INX               89'th character?
A56D  E0 59     CPX #$59          no, get next character
A56F  90 F1     BCC $A562         # for "string too long"
A571  A2 17     LDX #$17          out-put error message
A573  4C 37 A4  JMP $A437         finish buffer with $00,
A576  4C CA AA  JMP $AACA            out-put carriage return
******************************   Change line to interpreter
A579  6C 04 03  JMP ($0304)       JMP $A57C              code
A57C  A6 7A     LDX $7A
A57E  A0 04     LDY #$04
A580  84 0F     STY $0F           flag for interpreted comma
A582  BD 00 02  LDA $0200,X       get character from buffer
A585  10 07     BPL $A58E         no basic code?
A587  C9 FF     CMP #$FF          check for Pi code ?
A589  F0 3E     BEQ $A5C9
A58B  E8        INX
A58C  D0 F4     BNE $A582
A58E  C9 20     CMP #$20          empty character     " "
A590  F0 37     BEQ $A5C9
A592  85 08     STA $08
A594  C9 22     CMP #$22          interpreted comma   ","
A596  F0 56     BEQ $A5EE
A598  24 0F     BIT $0F
A59A  70 2D     BVS $A5C9
A59C  C9 3F     CMP #$3F          question mark       "?"
A59E  D0 04     BNE $A5A4
A5A0  A9 99     LDA #$99          substitute with code for
A5A2  D0 25     BNE $A5C9                            PRINT
A5A4  C9 30     CMP #$30          check for zero      "0"
A5A6  90 04     BCC $A5AC         smaller?
```

```
A5A8   C9 3C     CMP #$3C
A5AA   90 1D     BCC $A5C9
A5AC   84 71     STY $71
A5AE   A0 00     LDY #$00
A5B0   84 0B     STY $0B
A5B2   88        DEY
A5B3   86 7A     STX $7A
A5B5   CA        DEX
A5B6   C8        INY
A5B7   E8        INX
A5B8   BD 00 02  LDA $0200,X       character in buffer
A5BB   38        SEC
A5BC   F9 9E A0  SBC $A09E,Y       compare with BASIC-word
A5BF   F0 F5     BEQ $A5B6                             list
A5C1   C9 80     CMP #$80
A5C3   D0 30     BNE $A5F5
A5C5   05 0B     ORA $0B           found, code is even
A5C7   A4 71     LDY $71            counter +$80
A5C9   E8        INX
A5CA   C8        INY
A5CB   99 FB 01  STA $01FB,Y       save BASIC-code
A5CE   B9 FB 01  LDA $01FB,Y       and get status register
A5D1   F0 36     BEQ $A609         finish, then done
A5D3   38        SEC
A5D4   E9 3A     SBC #$3A          check for color    ":"
A5D6   F0 04     BEQ $A5DC         division marks?
A5D8   C9 49     CMP #$49          DATA code?
A5DA   D0 02     BNE $A5DE
A5DC   85 0F     STA $0F
A5DE   38        SEC
A5DF   E9 55     SBC #$55          REM code?
A5E1   D0 9F     BNE $A582
A5E3   85 08     STA $08
A5E5   BD 00 02  LDA $0200,X
A5E8   F0 DF     BEQ $A5C9
A5EA   C5 08     CMP $08
A5EC   F0 DB     BEQ $A5C9
A5EE   C8        INY
A5EF   99 FB 01  STA $01FB,Y
A5F2   E8        INX
A5F3   D0 F0     BNE $A5E5
A5F5   A6 7A     LDX $7A
A5F7   E6 0B     INC $0B
A5F9   C8        INY
A5FA   B9 9D A0  LDA $A09D,Y
A5FD   10 FA     BPL $A5F9         compare with listing
A5FF   B9 9E A0  LDA $A09E,Y
A602   D0 B4     BNE $A5B8
A604   BD 00 02  LDA $0200,X
A607   10 BE     BPL $A5C7
A609   99 FD 01  STA $01FD,Y
A60C   C6 7B     DEC $7B
A60E   A9 FF     LDA #$FF          set buffer pointer to -1
A610   85 7A     STA $7A
A612   60        RTS
```

```
******************************   Calculate start address of
A613  A5 2B     LDA $2B                                  line
A615  A6 2C     LDX $2C           pointer to start of program
A617  A0 01     LDY #$01
A619  85 5F     STA $5F
A61B  86 60     STX $60
A61D  B1 5F     LDA ($5F),Y       link-address high
A61F  F0 1F     BEQ $A640         even 0, then finish,
A621  C8        INY                        not found
A622  C8        INY
A623  A5 15     LDA $15           seeked line-number high
A625  D1 5F     CMP ($5F),Y       compare with present one
A627  90 18     BCC $A641         smaller then not found
A629  F0 03     BEQ $A62E         even then check number low
A62B  88        DEY
A62C  D0 09     BNE $A637         inevitable jump
A62E  A5 14     LDA $14
A630  88        DEY
A631  D1 5F     CMP ($5F),Y       compare line-number low
A633  90 0C     BCC $A641         smaller
A635  F0 0A     BEQ $A641         or even C=1
A637  88        DEY
A638  B1 5F     LDA ($5F),Y
A63A  AA        TAX
A63B  88        DEY               address of next line
A63C  B1 5F     LDA ($5F),Y
A63E  B0 D7     BCS $A617         keep searching
A640  18        CLC
A641  60        RTS

******************************   BASIC-NEW comman
A642  D0 FD     BNE $A641
A644  A9 00     LDA #$00
A646  A8        TAY
A647  91 2B     STA ($2B),Y
A649  C8        INY               $00 twice at program start
A64A  91 2B     STA ($2B),Y
A64C  A5 2B     LDA $2B
A64E  18        CLC
A64F  69 02     ADC #$02
A651  85 2D     STA $2D           variable-start = program-
A653  A5 2C     LDA $2C                          start + 2
A655  69 00     ADC #$00
A657  85 2E     STA $2E
A659  20 8E A6  JSR $A68E         CHRGET pointer to program
A65C  A9 00     LDA #$00                            start

******************************   BASIC-CLR command
A65E  D0 2D     BNE $A68D
A660  20 E7 FF  JSR $FFE7        CLALL close all I/O channels
A663  A5 37     LDA $37
A665  A4 38     LDY $38
A667  85 33     STA $33           string start to BASIC-RAM
A669  84 34     STY $34                             finish
```

```
A66B   A5 2D      LDA $2D
A66D   A4 2E      LDY $2E
A66F   85 2F      STA $2F          variable finish = variable
A671   84 30      STY $30                                start
A673   85 31      STA $31
A675   84 32      STY $32
A677   20 1D A8   JSR $A81D        RESTORE command
A67A   A2 19      LDX #$19
A67C   86 16      STX $16          set back string descriptor
A67E   68         PLA                                indexes
A67F   A8         TAY
A680   68         PLA
A681   A2 FA      LDX #$FA
A683   9A         TXS              initialize stack pointer
A684   48         PHA
A685   98         TYA
A686   48         PHA
A687   A9 00      LDA #$00
A689   85 3E      STA $3E          block CONT
A68B   85 10      STA $10
A68D   60         RTS

*****************************   Program pointer to BASIC-
A68E   18         CLC                                start
A68F   A5 2B      LDA $2B
A691   69 FF      ADC #$FF         BASIC-start
A693   85 7A      STA $7A
A695   A5 2C      LDA $2C
A697   69 FF      ADC #$FF         minus 1
A699   85 7B      STA $7B
A69B   60         RTS

*****************************   BASIC-LIST command
A69C   90 06      BCC $A6A4        sign? (line number)
A69E   F0 04      BEQ $A6A4        only list?
A6A0   C9 AB      CMP #$AB         code for "-" (through)
A6A2   D0 E9      BNE $A68D        diff. code, SYNTAX ERROR
A6A4   20 6B A9   JSR $A96B        get line number
A6A7   20 13 A6   JSR $A613        calculate start address of
A6AA   20 79 00   JSR $0079        get last symbol        line
A6AD   F0 0C      BEQ $A6BB        no line number?
A6AF   C9 AB      CMP #$AB         code for "-" (through)
A6B1   D0 8E      BNE $A641        no, SYNTAX ERROR
A6B3   20 73 00   JSR $0073        get next symbol
A6B6   20 6B A9   JSR $A96B        get line number
A6B9   D0 86      BNE $A641
A6BB   68         PLA
A6BC   68         PLA
A6BD   A5 14      LDA $14
A6BF   05 15      ORA $15          is second line-number = 0?
A6C1   D0 06      BNE $A6C9        no
A6C3   A9 FF      LDA #$FF
A6C5   85 14      STA $14
A6C7   85 15      STA $15          list to the end
A6C9   A0 01      LDY #$01
A6CB   84 0F      STY $0F
```

```
A6CD  B1 5F     LDA ($5F),Y     link address high
A6CF  F0 43     BEQ $A714       yes, ready
A6D1  20 2C A8  JSR $A82C       check on stop key
A6D4  20 D7 AA  JSR $AAD7       out-put (CR), new line
A6D7  C8        INY
A6D8  B1 5F     LDA ($5F),Y
A6DA  AA        TAX
A6DB  C8        INY             get line-number
A6DC  B1 5F     LDA ($5F),Y
A6DE  C5 15     CMP $15
A6E0  D0 04     BNE $A6E6       compare with end number
A6E2  E4 14     CPX $14
A6E4  F0 02     BEQ $A6E8
A6E6  B0 2C     BCS $A714       bigger, then finish
A6E8  84 49     STY $49
A6EA  20 CD BD  JSR $BDCD       out-put line number
A6ED  A9 20     LDA #$20        out-put " " (space)
A6EF  A4 49     LDY $49
A6F1  29 7F     AND #$7F
A6F3  20 47 AB  JSR $AB47       out-put character
A6F6  C9 22     CMP #$22        "(")"  inverted quote?
A6F8  D0 06     BNE $A700
A6FA  A5 0F     LDA $0F
A6FC  49 FF     EOR #$FF        turn inverted-comma flag
A6FE  85 0F     STA $0F
A700  C8        INY             no line-end after 255
A701  F0 11     BEQ $A714        symbols, then stop
A703  B1 5F     LDA ($5F),Y     get character
A705  D0 10     BNE $A717       no line-end, then list
A707  A8        TAY
A708  B1 5F     LDA ($5F),Y
A70A  AA        TAX             start address of next line
A70B  C8        INY
A70C  B1 5F     LDA ($5F),Y
A70E  86 5F     STX $5F
A710  85 60     STA $60         save as pointer
A712  D0 B5     BNE $A6C9       continue to BASIC
A714  4C 86 E3  JMP $E386              WARM-START

*****************************  Change BASIC-CODE into clear
A717  6C 06 03  JMP ($0306)                              text
A71A  10 D7     BPL $A6F3       no interpreter code, just
A71C  C9 FF     CMP #$FF        code for Pi          out-put
A71E  F0 D3     BEQ $A6F3       just out-put
A720  24 0F     BIT $0F         inverted comma mode?
A722  30 CF     BMI $A6F3       then just out-put symbol
A724  38        SEC
A725  E9 7F     SBC #$7F        null off off-set code to X
A727  AA        TAX
A728  84 49     STY $49         renumber character pointer
A72A  A0 FF     LDY #$FF
A72C  CA        DEX             first command word?
A72D  F0 08     BEQ $A737
A72F  C8        INY
A730  B9 9E A0  LDA $A09E,Y     find off-set for command
```

```
A733   10 FA     BPL $A72F                           word
A735   30 F5     BMI $A72C         bit/set, next word
A737   C8        INY
A738   B9 9E A0  LDA $A09E,Y       get command word from list
A73B   30 B2     BMI $A6EF         last letter, then finished
A73D   20 47 AB  JSR $AB47         out-put character
A740   D0 F5     BNE $A737         out-put next letter

****************************      BASIC-FOR command
A742   A9 80     LDA #$80          block integer
A744   85 10     STA $10
A746   20 A5 A9  JSR $A9A5         LET sets FOR variable
A749   20 8A A3  JSR $A38A         searches for loop name the
A74C   D0 05     BNE $A753         not found        same name
A74E   8A        TXA
A74F   69 0F     ADC #$0F          increase stack-pointer
A751   AA        TAX
A752   9A        TXS
A753   68        PLA               get return address from
A754   68        PLA                                  stack
A755   A9 09     LDA #$09
A757   20 FB A3  JSR $A3FB         checks on space in stack
A75A   20 06 A9  JSR $A906         searches for next BASIC-
A75D   18        CLC                              statement
A75E   98        TYA               program pointer to next
A75F   65 7A     ADC $7A                          command
A761   48        PHA               and save on stack
A762   A5 7B     LDA $7B
A764   69 00     ADC #$00
A766   48        PHA
A767   A5 3A     LDA $3A
A769   48        PHA               running line number on
A76A   A5 39     LDA $39                            stack
A76C   48        PHA
A76D   A9 A4     LDA #$A4          "TO" code
A76F   20 FF AE  JSR $AEFF         checks on code
A772   20 8D AD  JSR $AD8D         numeric variable?
A775   20 8A AD  JSR $AD8A         gets number from FAC
A778   A5 66     LDA $66
A77A   09 7F     ORA #$7F
A77C   25 62     AND $62
A77E   85 62     STA $62
A780   A9 8B     LDA #$8B
A782   A0 A7     LDY #$A7          save return address
A784   85 22     STA $22
A786   84 23     STY $23
A788   4C 43 AE  JMP $AE43         put loop-end variable on
A78B   A9 BC     LDA #$BC                             stack
A78D   A0 B9     LDY #$B9          points to constant as
A78F   20 A2 BB  JSR $BBA2         default-STEP value in FAC
A792   20 79 00  JSR $0079         get last character
A795   C9 A9     CMP #$A9          "STEP" code
A797   D0 06     BNE $A79F         no step value
A799   20 73 00  JSR $0073         get next character
A79C   20 8A AD  JSR $AD8A         gets number from FAC
```

```
A79F   20 2B BC JSR $BC2B        get signs
A7A2   20 38 AE JSR $AE38        put signs and STEP value
                                                on stack
A7A5   A5 4A    LDA $4A
A7A7   48       PHA              variable-name
A7A8   A5 49    LDA $49
A7AA   48       PHA
A7AB   A9 81    LDA #$81         and FOR code on stack
A7AD   48       PHA

*******************************  Intpreter loop
A7AE   20 2C A8 JSR $A82C        checks on stop key
A7B1   A5 7A    LDA $7A
A7B3   A4 7B    LDY $7B          program pointer
A7B5   C0 02    CPY #$02         direct mode?
A7B7   EA       NOP
A7B8   F0 04    BEQ $A7BE        yes
A7BA   85 3D    STA $3D          save pointer for CONT
A7BC   84 3E    STY $3E
A7BE   A0 00    LDY #$00
A7C0   B1 7A    LDA ($7A),Y      running character
A7C2   D0 43    BNE $A807        ? not end of line?
A7C4   A0 02    LDY #$02
A7C6   B1 7A    LDA ($7A),Y      end of program
A7C8   18       CLC              set flag for END
A7C9   D0 03    BNE $A7CE
A7CB   4C 4B A8 JMP $A84B        yes, then execute END
A7CE   C8       INY
A7CF   B1 7A    LDA ($7A),Y
A7D1   85 39    STA $39
A7D3   C8       INY              save running line #
A7D4   B1 7A    LDA ($7A),Y
A7D6   85 3A    STA $3A
A7D8   98       TYA
A7D9   65 7A    ADC $7A          set program pointer to line
A7DB   85 7A    STA $7A
A7DD   90 02    BCC $A7E1
A7DF   E6 7B    INC $7B
A7E1   6C 08 03 JMP ($0308)      execute BASIC statement
A7E4   20 73 00 JSR $0073        get next character
A7E7   20 ED A7 JSR $A7ED        execute statement
A7EA   4C AE A7 JMP $A7AE        back to interpreter loop

*******************************  Execute BASIC statement
A7ED   F0 3C    BEQ $A82B        end of line, then end
A7EF   E9 80    SBC #$80         token?
A7F1   90 11    BCC $A804        no, goto LET command
A7F3   C9 23    CMP #$23
A7F5   B0 17    BCS $A80E        function token or GOTO
A7F7   0A       ASL              BASIC-command code times 2
A7F8   A8       TAY
A7F9   B9 0D A0 LDA $A00D,Y
A7FC   48       PHA              get command address from
A7FD   B9 0C A0 LDA $A00C,Y                        listing

A800   48       PHA              as return address on stack
```

```
A801   4C 73 00 JMP $0073          next character and execute
A804   4C A5 A9 JMP $A9A5          to LET command      command


*****************************
A807   C9 3A    CMP #$3A            ":"
A809   F0 D6    BEQ $A7E1
A80B   4C 08 AF JMP $AF08           "syntax error"
*****************************      Checks on "GO" "TO" code
A80E   C9 4B    CMP #$4B            "GO"  (nimus $80)
A810   D0 F9    BNE $A80B
A812   20 73 00 JSR $0073           gets next character
A815   A9 A4    LDA #$A4            "TO"
A817   20 FF AE JSR $AEFF           checks on code
A81A   4C A0 A8 JMP $A8A0           to GOTO command

*****************************      BASIC-RESTORE command
A81D   38       SEC
A81E   A5 2B    LDA $2B
A820   E9 01    SBC #$01            program start -1
A822   A4 2C    LDY $2C
A824   B0 01    BCS $A827
A826   88       DEY
A827   85 41    STA $41
A829   84 42    STY $42             current DATA address
A82B   60       RTS

*****************************      Checks on stop-key
A82C   20 E1 FF JSR $FFE1           checks stop-key

*****************************      BASIC-STOP command
A82F   B0 01    BCS $A832           set STOP flag to 1 (C=1)

*****************************      BASIC-END command
A831   18       CLC                 set END flag to 0 (C=0)
A832   D0 3C    BNE $A870
A834   A5 7A    LDA $7A
A836   A4 7B    LDY $7B             program pointer
A838   A6 3A    LDX $3A             direct mode?
A83A   E8       INX
A83B   F0 0C    BEQ $A849           yes
A83D   85 3D    STA $3D
A83F   84 3E    STY $3E             set pointer for CONT
A841   A5 39    LDA $39
A843   A4 3A    LDY $3A             curent line number
A845   85 3B    STA $3B
A847   84 3C    STY $3C             store for CONT
A849   68       PLA
A84A   68       PLA                 get return address from
A84B   A9 81    LDA #$81                                stack
A84D   A0 A3    LDY #$A3            set pointer to "BREAK"
A84F   90 03    BCC $A854           "END" flag?
A851   4C 69 A4 JMP $A469           no, out-put "BREAK IN XXX"
A854   4C 86 E3 JMP $E386           to BASIC warm-start
```

```
******************************   BASIC-CONT command
A857  D0 17     BNE $A870
A859  A2 1A     LDX #$1A         error # for "CAN'T CONT."
A85B  A4 3E     LDY $3E          CONT blocked?
A85D  D0 03     BNE $A862        no
A85F  4C 37 A4  JMP $A437        out-put error message
A862  A5 3D     LDA $3D
A864  85 7A     STA $7A          program pointer
A866  84 7B     STY $7B
A868  A5 3B     LDA $3B          and
A86A  A4 3C     LDY $3C
A86C  85 39     STA $39          set line number
A86E  84 3A     STY $3A
A870  60        RTS

******************************   BASIC-RUN command
A871  08        PHP
A872  A9 00     LDA #$00
A874  20 90 FF  JSR $FF90        set flag for program mode
A877  28        PLP
A878  D0 03     BNE $A87D        find line number
A87A  4C 59 A6  JMP $A659        program pointer to start,
A87D  20 60 A6  JSR $A660        CLR command          CLR
A880  4C 97 A8  JMP $A897        GOTO command

******************************   BASIC-GOSUB command
A883  A9 03     LDA #$03
A885  20 FB A3  JSR $A3FB        check on stack space
A888  A5 7B     LDA $7B
A88A  48        PHA              save program pointer
A88B  A5 7A     LDA $7A
A88D  48        PHA
A88E  A5 3A     LDA $3A
A890  48        PHA              and line number
A891  A5 39     LDA $39
A893  48        PHA
A894  A9 8D     LDA #$8D         "GOSUB" code on stack
A896  48        PHA
A897  20 79 00  JSR $0079        CHRGOT get last character
A89A  20 A0 A8  JSR $A8A0        GOTO command
A89D  4C AE A7  JMP $A7AE        to interpreter loop

******************************   BASIC-GOTO command
A8A0  20 6B A9  JSR $A96B        get line number in $14/$15
A8A3  20 09 A9  JSR $A909        look for next line-start
A8A6  38        SEC
A8A7  A5 39     LDA $39
A8A9  E5 14     SBC $14          is new line # smaller than
A8AB  A5 3A     LDA $3A                   current line #?
A8AD  E5 15     SBC $15
A8AF  B0 0B     BCS $A8BC        no
A8B1  98        TYA
A8B2  38        SEC
A8B3  65 7A     ADC $7A
A8B5  A6 7B     LDX $7B          searches, stating from
```

```
A8B7  90 07     BCC $A8C0        current line #
A8B9  E8        INX
A8BA  B0 04     BCS $A8C0
A8BC  A5 2B     LDA $2B       searches from program
A8BE  A6 2C     LDX $2C                     start
A8C0  20 17 A6  JSR $A617     searches program line
A8C3  90 1E     BCC $A8E3     not found, then "UNDEF'D"
A8C5  A5 5F     LDA $5F                    statement
A8C7  E9 01     SBC #$01
A8C9  85 7A     STA $7A       set program pointer to new
A8CB  A5 60     LDA $60                         line
A8CD  E9 00     SBC #$00
A8CF  85 7B     STA $7B
A8D1  60        RTS

****************************  BASIC-RETURN command
A8D2  D0 FD     BNE $A8D1
A8D4  A9 FF     LDA #$FF
A8D6  85 4A     STA $4A
A8D8  20 8A A3  JSR $A38A     find next GOSUB data set
A8DB  9A        TXS                         in stack
A8DC  C9 8D     CMP #$8D      GOSUB code
A8DE  F0 0B     BEQ $A8EB     found?
A8E0  A2 0C     LDX #$0C      #for "RETURN WITHOUT GOSUB"
A8E2  2C A2 11  BIT $11A2
A8E5  4C 37 A4  JMP $A437     # for "UNDEF'D STATEMENT"
A8E8  4C 08 AF  JMP $AF08     out-put error message
A8EB  68        PLA           out-put "SYNTAX ERROR"
A8EC  68        PLA
A8ED  85 39     STA $39
A8EF  68        PLA
A8F0  85 3A     STA $3A       get line number from stack
A8F2  68        PLA
A8F3  85 7A     STA $7A
A8F5  68        PLA
A8F6  85 7B     STA $7B       get program pointer from
                                                 stack

****************************  BASIC-DATA and REM commands
A8F8  20 06 A9  JSR $A906     search for next statement
A8FB  98        TYA           offset
A8FC  18        CLC
A8FD  65 7A     ADC $7A
A8FF  85 7A     STA $7A
A901  90 02     BCC $A905     add to program pointer
A903  E6 7B     INC $7B
A905  60        RTS

****************************  Find offset of next "="
A906  A2 3A     LDX #$3A      ":" color
A908  2C A2 00  BIT $00A2
A90B  86 07     STX $07       end of line
A90D  A0 00     LDY #$00
A90F  84 08     STY $08       y contains offset
```

```
A911  A5 08     LDA $08
A913  A6 07     LDX $07          desired character
A915  85 07     STA $07
A917  86 08     STX $08
A919  B1 7A     LDA ($7A),Y      get character
A91B  F0 E8     BEQ $A905        end of line, then done
A91D  C5 08     CMP $08
A91F  F0 E4     BEQ $A905
A921  C8        INY              increase pointer
A922  C9 22     CMP #$22         inverted comma
A924  D0 F3     BNE $A919
A926  F0 E9     BEQ $A911

******************************  BASIC-IF command
A928  20 9E AD JSR $AD9E         calculate expression
A92B  20 79 00 JSR $0079         last character
A92E  C9 89     CMP #$89         "GOTO" code
A930  F0 05     BEQ $A937        yes
A932  A9 A7     LDA #$A7         "THEN" code
A934  20 FF AE JSR $AEFF         result of IF-term
A937  A5 61     LDA $61          expression true?
A939  D0 05     BNE $A940        no, look for next new line
A93B  20 09 A9 JSR $A909         program pointer to next new
A93E  F0 BB     BEQ $A8FB        get last character      line
A940  20 79 00 JSR $0079         no digit?
A943  B0 03     BCS $A948        to GOTO command
A945  4C A0 A8 JMP $A8A0         decode next command and
A948  4C ED A7 JMP $A7ED                          execute
******************************  BASIC-ON command
A94B  20 9E B7 JSR $B79E         get byte values (0-255)
A94E  48        PHA              save code
A94F  C9 8D     CMP #$8D         "GOSUB" code
A951  F0 04     BEQ $A957        yes
A953  C9 89     CMP #$89         "GOTO" code
A955  D0 91     BNE $A8E8        no then "SYNTAX ERROR"
A957  C6 65     DEC $65          decrease pointer
A959  D0 04     BNE $A95F        not zero yet?
A95B  68        PLA              yes, get back code and
A95C  4C EF A7 JMP $A7EF         execute command
A95F  20 73 00 JSR $0073         get next character
A962  20 6B A9 JSR $A96B         get line number
A965  C9 2C     CMP #$2C         "," comma?
A967  F0 EE     BEQ $A957        yes, then continue
A969  68        PLA              no, get return code, done
A96A  60        RTS
```

```
******************************   Gets line # and converts
A96B  A2 00     LDX #$00           it to address format
A96D  86 14     STX $14
A96F  86 15     STX $15           pre-filling of line # = 0
A971  B0 F7     BCS $A96A         resulting address of the
A973  E9 2F     SBC #$2F          line is in $16/$15
A975  85 07     STA $07
A977  A5 15     LDA $15
A979  85 22     STA $22
A97B  C9 19     CMP #$19
A97D  B0 D4     BCS $A953
A97F  A5 14     LDA $14
A981  0A        ASL
A982  26 22     ROL $22
A984  0A        ASL
A985  26 22     ROL $22
A987  65 14     ADC $14
A989  85 14     STA $14
A98B  A5 22     LDA $22
A98D  65 15     ADC $15
A98F  85 15     STA $15
A991  06 14     ASL $14
A993  26 15     ROL $15
A995  A5 14     LDA $14
A997  65 07     ADC $07
A999  85 14     STA $14
A99B  90 02     BCC $A99F
A99D  E6 15     INC $15
A99F  20 73 00  JSR $0073         CHRGET get next character
A9A2  4C 71 A9  JMP $A971                    for evaluation

******************************   BASIC-LET statement
A9A5  20 8B B0  JSR $B08B         looks for variable
A9A8  85 49     STA $49
A9AA  84 4A     STY $4A           save variable address
A9AC  A9 B2     LDA #$B2          "=" code
A9AE  20 FF AE  JSR $AEFF         checks on code
A9B1  A5 0E     LDA $0E           save integer flag
A9B3  48        PHA
A9B4  A5 0D     LDA $0D           and type flag (1=string)
A9B6  48        PHA
A9B7  20 9E AD  JSR $AD9E         get term
A9BA  68        PLA
A9BB  2A        ROL               get back type flag
A9BC  20 90 AD  JSR $AD90         and check on correct type
A9BF  D0 18     BNE $A9D9
A9C1  68        PLA
A9C2  10 12     BPL $A9D6         read?

******************************   Value assignment INTEGER
A9C4  20 1B BC  JSR $BC1B         round FAC
A9C7  20 BF B1  JSR $B1BF         and change to integer
A9CA  A0 00     LDY #$00
A9CC  A5 64     LDA $64
A9CE  91 49     STA ($49),Y       bring value into variable
```

```
A9D0   C8          INY
A9D1   A5 65       LDA $65
A9D3   91 49       STA ($49),Y
A9D5   60          RTS
*****************************        VAlue assignment REAL
A9D6   4C D0 BB JMP $BBD0             bring FAC to variable
*****************************        Value assignment string
A9D9   68          PLA
A9DA   A4 4A       LDY $4A            variable address high
A9DC   C0 BF       CPY #$BF           is variable TI$?
A9DE   D0 4C       BNE $AA2C          no
A9E0   20 A6 B6 JSR $B6A6             FRESTR
A9E3   C9 06       CMP #$06           string length = 6
A9E5   D0 3D       BNE $AA24          no, "illegal quality"
A9E7   A0 00       LDY #$00
A9E9   84 61       STY $61
A9EB   84 66       STY $66
A9ED   84 71       STY $71
A9EF   20 1D AA JSR $AA1D             checks next number
A9F2   20 E2 BA JSR $BAE2             FAC = FAC * 10
A9F5   E6 71       INC $71            increase digit counter
A9F7   A4 71       LDY $71
A9F9   20 1D AA JSR $AA1D             checks next number
A9FC   20 0C BC JSR $BC0C             copy FAC to ARG
A9FF   AA          TAX
AA00   F0 05       BEQ $AA07          FAC = 0?
AA02   E8          INX
AA03   8A          TXA
AA04   20 ED BA JSR $BAED             FAC = FAC + ARG
AA07   A4 71       LDY $71            increase digit counter
AA09   C8          INY
AA0A   C0 06       CPY #$06           6 digits yet?
AA0C   D0 DF       BNE $A9ED
AA0E   20 E2 BA JSR $BAE2             FAC = FAC * 10
AA11   20 9B BC JSR $BC9B             make FAC right-binding
AA14   A6 64       LDX $64
AA16   A4 63       LDY $63            time that was put in
AA18   A5 65       LDA $65
AA1A   4C DB FF JMP $FFDB             set time

*****************************        Check number
AA1D   B1 22       LDA ($22),Y        check number
AA1F   20 80 00 JSR $0080
AA22   90 03       BCC $AA27
AA24   4C 48 B2 JMP $B248             "ILLEGAL QUANTITY"
AA27   E9 2F       SBC #$2F           change from ASCII to hex
AA29   4C 7E BD JMP $BD7E             transfer into FAC and ARG
*****************************        Value assignment to normal
AA2C   A0 02       LDY #$02                                 string
AA2E   B1 64       LDA ($64),Y        string address high
AA30   C5 34       CMP $34            compare with string start
AA32   90 17       BCC $AA4B          smaller, string is stored
AA34   D0 07       BNE $AA3D           within the program space
AA36   88          DEY
AA37   B1 64       LDA ($64),Y        string address low
AA39   C5 33       CMP $33            compare
```

```
                                  string is in the program
AA3B  90 0E     BCC $AA4B                            space
AA3D  A4 65     LDY $65
AA3F  C4 2E     CPY $2E
AA41  90 08     BCC $AA4B
AA43  D0 0D     BNE $AA52
AA45  A5 64     LDA $64
AA47  C5 2D     CMP $2D
AA49  B0 07     BCS $AA52
AA4B  A5 64     LDA $64
AA4D  A4 65     LDY $65
AA4F  4C 68 AA  JMP $AA68
AA52  A0 00     LDY #$00
AA54  B1 64     LDA ($64),Y       length of string
AA56  20 75 B4  JSR $B475         checks memory space, sets
AA59  A5 50     LDA $50                     string pointer
AA5B  A4 51     LDY $51
AA5D  85 6F     STA $6F
AA5F  84 70     STY $70
AA61  20 7A B6  JSR $B67A         transfer string into
AA64  A9 61     LDA #$61                    string range
AA66  A0 00     LDY #$00
AA68  85 50     STA $50
AA6A  84 51     STY $51
AA6C  20 DB B6  JSR $B6DB         clear descriptor from
AA6F  A0 00     LDY #$00                    string stack
AA71  B1 50     LDA ($50),Y       length
AA73  91 49     STA ($49),Y
AA75  C8        INY
AA76  B1 50     LDA ($50),Y       address low
AA78  91 49     STA ($49),Y
AA7A  C8        INY
AA7B  B1 50     LDA ($50),Y       and address high
AA7D  91 49     STA ($49),Y       bring into variable
AA7F  60        RTS

*****************************    BASIC-PRINT# command
AA80  20 86 AA  JSR $AA86         CMD command
AA83  4C B5 AB  JMP $ABB5         to PRINT command

*****************************    BASIC-CMD command
AA86  20 9E B7  JSR $B79E         gets byte expression
AA89  F0 05     BEQ $AA90
AA8B  A9 2C     LDA #$2C          ","
AA8D  20 FF AE  JSR $AEFF         checks on comma
AA90  08        PHP
AA91  86 13     STX $13           save out-put devices #
AA93  20 18 E1  JSR $E118         set out-put device
AA96  28        PLP
AA97  4C A0 AA  JMP $AAA0
AA9A  20 21 AB  JSR $AB21         print string
AA9D  20 79 00  JSR $0079         last character
*****************************    BASIC-PRINT command
AAA0  F0 35     BEQ $AAD7
```

```
AAA2  F0 43     BEQ $AAE7
AAA4  C9 A3     CMP #$A3          "TAB(" code
AAA6  F0 50     BEQ $AAF8
AAA8  C9 A6     CMP #$A6          "SPC(" code
AAAA  18        CLC
AAAB  F0 4B     BEQ $AAF8
AAAD  C9 2C     CMP #$2C          ","
AAAF  F0 37     BEQ $AAE8
AAB1  C9 3B     CMP #$3B          ";"
AAB3  F0 5E     BEQ $AB13
AAB5  20 9E AD JSR $AD9E          get term
AAB8  24 0D     BIT $0D           type flag
AABA  30 DE     BMI $AA9A         string?
AABC  20 DD BD JSR $BDDD          change FAC to ASCII string
AABF  20 87 B4 JSR $B487          get string parameters
AAC2  20 21 AB JSR $AB21          point string
AAC5  20 3B AB JSR $AB3B          out-put space
AAC8  D0 D3     BNE $AA9D         continue
AACA  A9 00     LDA #$00          input buffer
AACC  9D 00 02 STA $0200,X        finish with $0
AACF  A2 FF     LDX #$FF
AAD1  A0 01     LDY #$01          set pointer to input buffer
AAD3  A5 13     LDA $13           number of out-put devices
AAD5  D0 10     BNE $AAE7
AAD7  A9 0D     LDA #$0D          (CR) carriage return
AAD9  20 47 AB JSR $AB47          out-put
AADC  24 13     BIT $13           logical file-number
AADE  10 05     BPL $AAE5         smaller than 128?
AAE0  A9 0A     LDA #$0A          (LF) line feed
AAE2  20 47 AB JSR $AB47          out-put
AAE5  49 FF     EOR #$FF
AAE7  60        RTS
AAE8  38        SEC
AAE9  20 F0 FF JSR $FFF0          decimal tabulator w/comma
AAEC  98        TYA               get cursor position
AAED  38        SEC
AAEE  E9 0A     SBC #$0A
AAF0  B0 FC     BCS $AAEE         subtract 10
AAF2  49 FF     EOR #$FF          not negative
AAF4  69 01     ADC #$01          invert
AAF6  D0 16     BNE $AB0E         add one

******************************   TAB(  (C=1) and SPC(  (C=0)
AAF8  08        PHP               save flag
AAF9  38        SEC
AAFA  20 F0 FF JSR $FFF0          get cursor position
AAFD  84 09     STY $09           and save it
AAFF  20 9B B7 JSR $B79B          get byte value
AB02  C9 29     CMP #$29          ")" closing ?
AB04  D0 59     BNE $AB5F         no, "SYNTAX ERROR"
AB06  28        PLP
AB07  90 06     BCC $AB0F         to SPC(
AB09  8A        TXA               TAB value in ASCII
AB0A  E5 09     SBC $09           compare w/ cursor position
AB0C  90 05     BCC $AB13         value less than position,
AB0E  AA        TAX                then ready
```

```
AB0F  E8          INX
AB10  CA          DEX
AB11  D0 06       BNE $AB19
AB13  20 73 00 JSR $0073      CHRGET get next character
AB16  4C A2 AA JMP $AAA2      and continue
AB19  20 3B AB JSR $AB3B      out-put space
AB1C  D0 F2       BNE $AB10   to loop start

****************************  Out-put string
AB1E  20 87 B4 JSR $B487      get string paremeter
AB21  20 A6 B6 JSR $B6A6      FRESTR
AB24  AA          TAX         string length
AB25  A0 00       LDY #$00
AB27  E8          INX
AB28  CA          DEX
AB29  F0 BC       BEQ $AAE7   string end?
AB2B  B1 22       LDA ($22),Y string character
AB2D  20 47 AB JSR $AB47      output
AB30  C8          INY
AB31  C9 0D       CMP #$0D    "CR" carriage return
AB33  D0 F3       BNE $AB28   no, continue
AB35  20 E5 AA JSR $AAE5      invert code
AB38  4C 28 AB JMP $AB28      and continue

****************************  Out-put an empty character
AB3B  A5 13       LDA $13
AB3D  F0 03       BEQ $AB42
AB3F  A9 20       LDA #$20    " " sqace
AB47  2C          .BYTE $2C
AB48  A9 1D       LDA #$1D    cursor right
AB4A  2C          .BYTE $2C
AB4B  A9 3F       LDA #$3F    "?" question mark
AB47  20 0C E1 JSR $E10C      out-put
AB4A  29 FF       AND #$FF    set flags
AB4C  60          RTS

****************************  Error treatment at input
AB4D  A5 11       LDA $11     flag for INPUT/GET/READ
AB4F  F0 11       BEQ $AB62   INPUT
AB51  30 04       BMI $AB57   READ
AB53  A0 FF       LDY #$FF
AB55  D0 04       BNE $AB5B   GET
****************************  Error at READ
AB57  A5 3F       LDA $3F     data line-number
AB59  A4 40       LDY $40

****************************  Error at GET
AB5B  85 39       STA $39
AB5D  84 3A       STY $3A     is line number of mistake
AB5F  4C 08 AF JMP $AF08      "SYNTAX ERROR"

****************************  Error at INPUT
AB62  A5 13       LDA $13     number of input device
AB64  F0 05       BEQ $AB6B   keyboard?
AB66  A2 18       LDX #$18    number for "FILE DATA"
```

```
AB68  4C 37 A4 JMP $A437       out-put error message
AB6B  A9 0C    LDA #$0C
AB6D  A0 AD    LDY #$AD        pointer to "?REDO FROM
AB6F  20 1E AB JSR $AB1E      out-put string   START
AB72  A5 3D    LDA $3D
AB74  A4 3E    LDY $3E         program pointer back
AB76  85 7A    STA $7A
AB78  84 7B    STY $7B         to INPUT command
AB7A  60       RTS

****************************** BASIC-GET command
AB7B  20 A6 B3 JSR $B3A6       checks on direct mode
AB7E  C9 23    CMP #$23        "#"
AB80  D0 10    BNE $AB92       no?
AB82  20 73 00 JSR $0073       get next character
AB85  20 9E B7 JSR $B79E       get byte value
AB88  A9 2C    LDA #$2C        "," comma
AB8A  20 FF AE JSR $AEFF       checks on code
AB8D  86 13    STX $13
AB8F  20 1E E1 JSR $E11E       GET gets a a character
AB92  A2 01    LDX #$01
AB94  A0 02    LDY #$02        pointer to buffer end= $201
AB96  A9 00    LDA #$00        buffer ends with $201 and$0
AB98  8D 01 02 STA $0201
AB9B  A9 40    LDA #$40        GET flag
AB9D  20 0F AC JSR $AC0F       value asignment to variable
ABA0  A6 13    LDX $13         input device
ABA2  D0 13    BNE $ABB7       not keyboard, then CLRCH
ABA4  60       RTS

****************************** BASIC-INPUT# command
ABA5  20 9E B7 JSR $B79E       gets bute va:ie
ABA8  A9 2C    LDA #$2C        ","
ABAA  20 FF AE JSR $AEFF       checks on comma
ABAD  86 13    STX $13         input device
ABAF  20 1E E1 JSR $E11E       get a character
ABB2  20 CE AB JSR $ABCE       INPUT w/o dialog string
ABB5  A5 13    LDA $13
ABB7  20 CC FF JSR $FFCC       sets back input device
ABBA  A2 00    LDX #$00
ABBC  86 13    STX $13         input device is keyboard
ABBE  60       RTS

****************************** BASIC-INPUT command
ABBF  C9 22    CMP #$22        " (") "  inverted comma
ABC1  D0 0B    BNE $ABCE       no
ABC3  20 BD AE JSR $AEBD       get dialog string
ABC6  A9 3B    LDA #$3B        semicolon
ABC8  20 FF AE JSR $AEFF       checks on code
ABCB  20 21 AB JSR $AB21       out-put string
ABCE  20 A6 B3 JSR $B3A6       checks on direct mode
ABD1  A9 2C    LDA #$2C        "," comma
ABD3  8D FF 01 STA $01FF       to buffer start
ABD6  20 F9 AB JSR $ABF9       out-put question mark
ABD9  A5 13    LDA $13         number of input device
```

```
ABDB   F0 0D      BEQ $ABEA
ABDD   20 B7 FF  JSR $FFB7
ABE0   29 02      AND #$02
ABE2   F0 06      BEQ $ABEA          keyboard?
ABE4   20 B5 AB  JSR $ABB5          get status
ABE7   4C F8 A8  JMP $A8F8
ABEA   AD 00 02  LDA $0200          Time-out?
ABED   D0 1E      BNE $AC0D          yes, CLRCH, reset keyboard
ABEF   A5 13      LDA $13            execute next statement
ABF1   D0 E3      BNE $ABD6
ABF3   20 06 A9  JSR $A906          get first character
ABF6   4C FB A8  JMP $A8FB          end?
ABF9   A5 13      LDA $13            yes, input device
ABFB   D0 06      BNE $AC03          not keyboard?
ABFD   20 45 AB  JSR $AB45          out-put "?"
AC00   20 3B AB  JSR $AB3B          out-put space
AC03   4C 60 A5  JMP $A560          get input line

****************************       BASIC-READ command
AC06   A6 41      LDX $41
AC08   A4 42      LDY $42            get DATA pointer
AC0A   A9 98      LDA #$98           READ flag
AC0C   2C A9 00  BIT $00A9
AC0F   85 11      STA $11
AC11   86 43      STX $43            set
AC13   84 44      STY $44
AC15   20 8B B0  JSR $B08B          INPUT pointer to input
AC18   85 49      STA $49            looks for variable
AC1A   84 4A      STY $4A
AC1C   A5 7A      LDA $7A            save variable address
AC1E   A4 7B      LDY $7B
AC20   85 4B      STA $4B
AC22   84 4C      STY $4C            under-save program pointer
AC24   A6 43      LDX $43                              in $4b/$4c
AC26   A4 44      LDY $44
AC28   86 7A      STX $7A            INPUT pointer
AC2A   84 7B      STY $7B            equals program pointer
AC2C   20 79 00  JSR $0079
AC2F   D0 20      BNE $AC51          CHRGOT gets last character
AC31   24 11      BIT $11
AC33   50 0C      BVC $AC41          input flag
AC35   20 24 E1  JSR $E124
AC38   8D 00 02  STA $0200
AC3B   A2 FF      LDX #$FF           write character into buffer
AC3D   A0 01      LDY #$01
AC3F   D0 0C      BNE $AC4D
AC41   30 75      BMI $ACB8
AC43   A5 13      LDA $13
AC45   D0 03      BNE $AC4A          input device
AC47   20 45 AB  JSR $AB45          not keyboard?
AC4A   20 F9 AB  JSR $ABF9          out-put "?"
AC4D   86 7A      STX $7A            out-put second "?"
AC4F   84 7B      STY $7B            set program pointer
AC51   20 73 00  JSR $0073
AC54   24 0D      BIT $0D            get next character
AC56   10 31      BPL $AC89          type flag
AC58   24 11      BIT $11
```

```
AC5A   50 09      BVC $AC65
AC5C   E8         INX
AC5D   86 7A      STX $7A
AC5F   A9 00      LDA #$00
AC61   85 07      STA $07
AC63   F0 0C      BEQ $AC71
AC65   85 07      STA $07
AC67   C9 22      CMP #$22            " (") " inverted comma
AC69   F0 07      BEQ $AC72
AC6B   A9 3A      LDA #$3A            ":"
AC6D   85 07      STA $07
AC6F   A9 2C      LDA #$2C            ","
AC71   18         CLC
AC72   85 08      STA $08
AC74   A5 7A      LDA $7A
AC76   A4 7B      LDY $7B
AC78   69 00      ADC #$00
AC7A   90 01      BCC $AC7D
AC7C   C8         INY
AC7D   20 8D B4 JSR $B48D             take over string
AC80   20 E2 B7 JSR $B7E2             program pointer behnd strng
AC83   20 DA A9 JSR $A9DA             assign string to variable
AC86   4C 91 AC JMP $AC91             continue
AC89   20 F3 BC JSR $BCF3             get digit string in FAC
AC8C   A5 0E      LDA $0E             INTEGER/REAL flag
AC8E   20 C2 A9 JSR $A9C2             assign FAC to # variable
AC91   20 79 00 JSR $0079             get last character
AC94   F0 07      BEQ $AC9D           end?
AC96   C9 2C      CMP #$2C            ","
AC98   F0 03      BEQ $AC9D
AC9A   4C 4D AB JMP $AB4D             to error treatnebt
AC9D   A5 7A      LDA $7A
AC9F   A4 7B      LDY $7B             program pointer
ACA1   85 43      STA $43
ACA3   84 44      STY $44             equals DATA pointer
ACA5   A5 4B      LDA $4B
ACA7   A4 4C      LDY $4C             get back program pointer
ACA9   85 7A      STA $7A
ACAB   84 7B      STY $7B
ACAD   20 79 00 JSR $0079             get last character
ACB0   F0 2D      BEQ $ACDF
ACB2   20 FD AE JSR $AEFD             checks on comma
ACB5   4C 15 AC JMP $AC15             continue
ACB8   20 06 A9 JSR $A906             look for next statement
ACBB   C8         INY
ACBC   AA         TAX                 line end?
ACBD   D0 12      BNE $ACD1           no
ACBF   A2 0D      LDX #$0D
ACC1   C8         INY
ACC2   B1 7A      LDA ($7A),Y
ACC4   F0 6C      BEQ $AD32           end of program?
ACC6   C8         INY                  "OUT OF DATA" X=0
ACC7   B1 7A      LDA ($7A),Y
ACC9   85 3F      STA $3F
ACCB   C8         INY
```

```
ACCC  B1 7A     LDA ($7A),Y
ACCE  C8        INY
ACCF  85 40     STA $40
ACD1  20 FB A8  JSR $A8FB      program pointer to next st-
ACD4  20 79 00  JSR $0079      get last character  atement
ACD7  AA        TAX
ACD8  E0 83     CPX #$83       "DATA"
ACDA  D0 DC     BNE $ACB8      no, keep looking
ACDC  4C 51 AC  JMP $AC51      read data
ACDF  A5 43     LDA $43
ACE1  A4 44     LDY $44        input pointer
ACE3  A6 11     LDX $11        input flag
ACE5  10 03     BPL $ACEA      no DATA?
ACE7  4C 27 A8  JMP $A827      at DATA pointer
ACEA  A0 00     LDY #$00
ACEC  B1 43     LDA ($43),Y
ACEE  F0 0B     BEQ $ACFB
ACF0  A5 13     LDA $13
ACF2  D0 07     BNE $ACFB
ACF4  A9 FC     LDA #$FC
ACF6  A0 AC     LDY #$AC       pointer to "EXTRA IGNORED"
ACF8  4C 1E AB  JMP $AB1E      out-put string
ACFB  60        RTS

ACFC 3F 45 58 54 52 41 20 49   "?EXTRA IGNORED"
AD04 47 4E 4F 52 45 44 0D 00
AD0C 3F 52 45 44 4F 20 46 52   "?REDO FROM START"
AD14 4F 4D 20 53 54 41 52 54
AD1C 0D

*****************************  BASIC-NEXT command
AD1E  D0 04     BNE $AD24       does variable name follow?
AD20  A0 00     LDY #$00
AD22  F0 03     BEQ $AD27
AD24  20 8B B0  JSR $B08B       looks for variable
AD27  85 49     STA $49
AD29  84 4A     STY $4A         variable address
AD2B  20 8A A3  JSR $A38A       looks for FOR-NEXT loop
AD2E  F0 05     BEQ $AD35       found it         in stack
AD30  A2 0A     LDX #$0A        number for "NEXT W/O FOR"
AD32  4C 37 A4  JMP $A437       out-put error message
AD35  9A        TXS
AD36  8A        TXA
AD37  18        CLC
AD38  69 04     ADC #$04
AD3A  48        PHA
AD3B  69 06     ADC #$06
AD3D  85 24     STA $24
AD3F  68        PLA
AD40  A0 01     LDY #$01
AD42  20 A2 BB  JSR $BBA2       get variable from stack,
AD45  BA        TSX                             put in FAC
AD46  BD 09 01  LDA $0109,X
AD49  85 66     STA $66
AD4B  A5 49     LDA $49         variable address
```

```
AD4D   A4 4A     LDY $4A
AD4F   20 67 B8 JSR $B867         adds STEP value to FAC
AD52   20 D0 BB JSR $BBD0         bring FAC to variable
AD55   A0 01     LDY #$01
AD57   20 5D BC JSR $BC5D         compare FAC with end value
AD5A   BA        TSX                                of loop
AD5B   38        SEC
AD5C   FD 09 01 SBC $0109,X
AD5F   F0 17     BEQ $AD78
AD61   BD 0F 01 LDA $010F,X
AD64   85 39     STA $39
AD66   BD 10 01 LDA $0110,X       get line number
AD69   85 3A     STA $3A
AD6B   BD 12 01 LDA $0112,X
AD6E   85 7A     STA $7A
AD70   BD 11 01 LDA $0111,X       get program pointer
AD73   85 7B     STA $7B
AD75   4C AE A7 JMP $A7AE         to interpreter loop
AD78   8A        TXA
AD79   69 11     ADC #$11
AD7B   AA        TAX
AD7C   9A        TXS
AD7D   20 79 00 JSR $0079         CHRGOT get last character
AD80   C9 2C     CMP #$2C         "," comma
AD82   D0 F1     BNE $AD75        no, then done
AD84   20 73 00 JSR $0073         get next character
AD87   20 24 AD JSR $AD24         next NEXT-variable

****************************** Get term and check numberic
AD8A   20 9E AD JSR $AD9E         get term

****************************** Checks on numeric
AD8D   18        CLC
AD8E 24

****************************** Checks on string
AD8F   38        SEC
AD90   24 0D     BIT $0D          check type flag
AD92   30 03     BMI $AD97
AD94   B0 03     BCS $AD99
AD96   60        RTS
AD97   B0 FD     BCS $AD96
AD99   A2 16     LDX #$16         # for "TYPE MISMATCH"
AD9B   4C 37 A4 JMP $A437         out-put error message

****************************** FRMEVL evaluation of a term
AD9E   A6 7A     LDX $7A
ADA0   D0 02     BNE $ADA4        decrease program pointer 1
ADA2   C6 7B     DEC $7B
ADA4   C6 7A     DEC $7A
ADA6   A2 00     LDX #$00
ADA8   24        .BYTE $24
ADA9   48        PHA
ADAA   8A        TXA
ADAB   48        PHA
```

```
ADAC   A9 01      LDA #$01        2 bytes
ADAE   20 FB A3   JSR $A3FB       checks on fre stack space
ADB1   20 83 AE   JSR $AE83       get next character
ADB4   A9 00      LDA #$00
ADB6   85 4D      STA $4D         mask for compare operator
ADB8   20 79 00   JSR $0079       get last character
ADBB   38         SEC
ADBC   E9 B1      SBC #$B1
ADBE   90 17      BCC $ADD7
ADC0   C9 03      CMP #$03
ADC2   B0 13      BCS $ADD7
ADC4   C9 01      CMP #$01
ADC6   2A         ROL             mask for <, =, or >
ADC7   49 01      EOR #$01
ADC9   45 4D      EOR $4D
ADCB   C5 4D      CMP $4D
ADCD   90 61      BCC $AE30
ADCF   85 4D      STA $4D
ADD1   20 73 00   JSR $0073       CHRGET get next character
ADD4   4C BB AD   JMP $ADBB       back
ADD7   A6 4D      LDX $4D
ADD9   D0 2C      BNE $AE07
ADDB   B0 7B      BCS $AE58
ADDD   69 07      ADC #$07
ADDF   90 77      BCC $AE58
ADE1   65 0D      ADC $0D
ADE3   D0 03      BNE $ADE8
ADE5   4C 3D B6   JMP $B63D       string linkage
ADE8   69 FF      ADC #$FF        code $AA
ADEA   85 22      STA $22
ADEC   0A         ASL
ADED   65 22      ADC $22         times three
ADEF   A8         TAY
ADF0   68         PLA
ADF1   D9 80 A0   CMP $A080,Y     compare with order flag
ADF4   B0 67      BCS $AE5D
ADF6   20 8D AD   JSR $AD8D       checks on numeric
ADF9   48         PHA
ADFA   20 20 AE   JSR $AE20       operator address and
ADFD   68         PLA                operands on stack
ADFE   A4 4B      LDY $4B
AE00   10 17      BPL $AE19
AE02   AA         TAX
AE03   F0 56      BEQ $AE5B
AE05   D0 5F      BNE $AE66
AE07   46 0D      LSR $0D         clear string flag
AE09   8A         TXA
AE0A   2A         ROL
AE0B   A6 7A      LDX $7A
AE0D   D0 02      BNE $AE11       decrease program pointer 1
AE0F   C6 7B      DEC $7B
AE11   C6 7A      DEC $7A
AE13   A0 1B      LDY #$1B        offset of order flag
AE15   85 4D      STA $4D         set flag
```

```
AE17  D0 D7     BNE $ADF0
AE19  D9 80 A0  CMP $A080,Y      compare with order flag
AE1C  B0 48     BCS $AE66
AE1E  90 D9     BCC $ADF9
AE20  B9 82 A0  LDA $A082,Y
AE23  48        PHA              operation address on stack
AE24  B9 81 A0  LDA $A081,Y
AE27  48        PHA
AE28  20 33 AE  JSR $AE33        operands on stack
AE2B  A5 4D     LDA $4D
AE2D  4C A9 AD  JMP $ADA9        to start of loop
AE30  4C 08 AF  JMP $AF08        gives "SYNTAX ERROR"
AE33  A5 66     LDA $66          signs
AE35  BE 80 A0  LDX $A080,Y      order flag
AE38  A8        TAY
AE39  68        PLA
AE3A  85 22     STA $22
AE3C  E6 22     INC $22          save return address
AE3E  68        PLA
AE3F  85 23     STA $23
AE41  98        TYA              sign
AE42  48        PHA
AE43  20 1B BC  JSR $BC1B        round FAC
AE46  A5 65     LDA $65
AE48  48        PHA
AE49  A5 64     LDA $64
AE4B  48        PHA
AE4C  A5 63     LDA $63
AE4E  48        PHA              FAC on stack
AE4F  A5 62     LDA $62
AE51  48        PHA
AE52  A5 61     LDA $61
AE54  48        PHA
AE55  6C 22 00  JMP ($0022)      jump to operation
AE58  A0 FF     LDY #$FF
AE5A  68        PLA
AE5B  F0 23     BEQ $AE80
AE5D  C9 64     CMP #$64
AE5F  F0 03     BEQ $AE64
AE61  20 8D AD  JSR $AD8D        checks on numeric
AE64  84 4B     STY $4B
AE66  68        PLA
AE67  4A        LSR
AE68  85 12     STA $12
AE6A  68        PLA
AE6B  85 69     STA $69
AE6D  68        PLA
AE6E  85 6A     STA $6A
AE70  68        PLA              get ARG from stack
AE71  85 6B     STA $6B
AE73  68        PLA
AE74  85 6C     STA $6C
AE76  68        PLA
AE77  85 6D     STA $6D
AE79  68        PLA
```

```
AE7A   85 6E     STA $6E
AE7C   45 66     EOR $66
AE7E   85 6F     STA $6F
AE80   A5 61     LDA $61
AE82   60        RTS

******************************       Get arithmetic term
AE83   6C 0A 03 JMP ($030A)           JMP $AE86
AE86   A9 00     LDA #$00
AE88   85 0D     STA $0D              type flag on numeric
AE8A   20 73 00 JSR $0073             get next character
AE8D   B0 03     BCS $AE92            digit?
AE8F   4C F3 BC JMP $BCF3             get variable to FAC
AE92   20 13 B1 JSR $B113             letter?
AE95   90 03     BCC $AE9A            no
AE97   4C 28 AF JMP $AF28             get variable
AE9A   C9 FF     CMP #$FF             BASIC code for Pi?
AE9C   D0 0F     BNE $AEAD
AE9E   A9 A8     LDA #$A8             pointer to Pi constant
AEA0   A0 AE     LDY #$AE
AEA2   20 A2 BB JSR $BBA2             get cpmstamt tp FAC
AEA5   4C 73 00 JMP $0073

******************************
AEA8 82 49 0F DA A1                   Constant Pi 3.14159265
AEAD   C9 2E     CMP #$2E             "."
AEAF   F0 DE     BEQ $AE8F
AEB1   C9 AB     CMP #$AB             "+"
AEB3   F0 58     BEQ $AF0D
AEB5   C9 AA     CMP #$AA             "*"
AEB7   F0 D1     BEQ $AE8A
AEB9   C9 22     CMP #$22             " (") "
AEBB   D0 0F     BNE $AECC
AEBD   A5 7A     LDA $7A
AEBF   A4 7B     LDY $7B              get program pointer
AEC1   69 00     ADC #$00
AEC3   90 01     BCC $AEC6
AEC5   C8        INY
AEC6   20 87 B4 JSR $B487             transfer string
AEC9   4C E2 B7 JMP $B7E2             program pointer to string
AECC   C9 A8     CMP #$A8             "NOT" code        end + 1
AECE   D0 13     BNE $AEE3
AED0   A0 18     LDY #$18             offset of order flag in
AED2   D0 3B     BNE $AF0F                                 list

******************************       BASIC-NOT command
AED4   20 BF B1 JSR $B1BF             change FAC to integer
AED7   A5 65     LDA $65
AED9   49 FF     EOR #$FF             turn around all bits
AEDB   A8        TAY
AEDC   A5 64     LDA $64
AEDE   49 FF     EOR #$FF
AEE0   4C 91 B3 JMP $B391             return to running comma

******************************
AEE3   C9 A5     CMP #$A5             "FN" code
```

```
AEE5  D0 03     BNE $AEEA
AEE7  4C F4 B3  JMP $B3F4      execute IN

*****************************
AEEA  C9 B4     CMP #$B4       "SGN code
AEEC  90 03     BCC $AEF1      smaller (no function)?
AEEE  4C A7 AF  JMP $AFA7      for calculation of function

*****************************  Gets term in parenthesis
AEF1  20 FA AE  JSR $AEFA      checks on parenthesis open
AEF4  20 9E AD  JSR $AD9E      FRMEVL gets term

*****************************  Checks on character in text
AEF7  A9 29     LDA #$29       ")" closeing parenthesis
AEF9  2C        .BYTE $2C
AEFA  A9 28     LDA #$28       "(" opening parenthesis
AEFC  2C        .BYTE $2C
AEFD  A9 2C     LDA #$2C       "," comma
AEFF  A0 00     LDY #$00
AF01  D1 7A     CMP ($7A),Y    compare with curent number
AF03  D0 03     BNE $AF08      no concurrence?
AF05  4C 73 00  JMP $0073      get next character
AF08  A2 0B     LDX #$0B       # for "SYNTAX ERROR"
AF0A  4C 37 A4  JMP $A437      out-put error message
AF0D  A0 15     LDY #$15       offset order code for
AF0F  68        PLA                  change of sign
AF10  68        PLA
AF11  4C FA AD  JMP $ADFA      for evaluation
AF14  38        SEC
AF15  A5 64     LDA $64
AF17  E9 00     SBC #$00
AF19  A5 65     LDA $65
AF1B  E9 A0     SBC #$A0
AF1D  90 08     BCC $AF27
AF1F  A9 A2     LDA #$A2
AF21  E5 64     SBC $64
AF23  A9 E3     LDA #$E3
AF25  E5 65     SBC $65
AF27  60        RTS

*****************************  Get variable
AF28  20 8B B0  JSR $B08B      look for variable
AF2B  85 64     STA $64
AF2D  84 65     STY $65        points to variable or
                                   string descriptor
AF2F  A6 45     LDX $45        variable name
AF31  A4 46     LDY $46
AF33  A5 0D     LDA $0D        type flag
AF35  F0 26     BEQ $AF5D      numeric?
AF37  A9 00     LDA #$00
AF39  85 70     STA $70
AF3B  20 14 AF  JSR $AF14
AF3E  90 1C     BCC $AF5C
AF40  E0 54     CPX #$54       "T"
AF42  D0 18     BNE $AF5C
AF44  C0 C9     CPY #$C9       "I$"
```

```
AF46  D0 14     BNE $AF5C
AF48  20 84 AF  JSR $AF84        get time
AF4B  84 5E     STY $5E
AF4D  88        DEY
AF4E  84 71     STY $71
AF50  A0 06     LDY #$06
AF52  84 5D     STY $5D
AF54  A0 24     LDY #$24
AF56  20 68 BE  JSR $BE68        produces string
AF59  4C 6F B4  JMP $B46F
AF5C  60        RTS
AF5D  24 0E     BIT $0E          INTEGER/REAL flag
AF5F  10 0D     BPL $AF6E        REAL?
AF61  A0 00     LDY #$00
AF63  B1 64     LDA ($64),Y      get integer number
AF65  AA        TAX
AF66  C8        INY
AF67  B1 64     LDA ($64),Y
AF69  A8        TAY
AF6A  8A        TXA
AF6B  4C 91 B3  JMP $B391        and change to running point
AF6E  20 14 AF  JSR $AF14
AF71  90 2D     BCC $AFA0
AF73  E0 54     CPX #$54         "T"
AF75  D0 1B     BNE $AF92
AF77  C0 49     CPY #$49         "I"
AF79  D0 25     BNE $AFA0
AF7B  20 84 AF  JSR $AF84        get TIME to FAC
AF7E  98        TYA
AF7F  A2 A0     LDX #$A0
AF81  4C 4F BC  JMP $BC4F
******************************  Get time
AF84  20 DE FF  JSR $FFDE        get TIME
AF87  86 64     STX $64
AF89  84 63     STY $63
AF8B  85 65     STA $65
AF8D  A0 00     LDY #$00         and into floating point
AF8F  84 62     STY $62                   accumulator
AF91  60        RTS
AF92  E0 53     CPX #$53         "S"
AF94  D0 0A     BNE $AFA0
AF96  C0 54     CPY #$54         "T"
AF98  D0 06     BNE $AFA0
AF9A  20 B7 FF  JSR $FFB7        get status
AF9D  4C 3C BC  JMP $BC3C        change byte in accum. to
                                    floating point format
AFA0  A5 64     LDA $64
AFA2  A4 65     LDY $65          variable address
AFA4  4C A2 BB  JMP $BBA2        get variable in FAC
AFA7  0A        ASL              code times 2
AFA8  48        PHA
AFA9  AA        TAX
AFAA  20 73 00  JSR $0073        next character
AFAD  E0 8F     CPX #$8F
AFAF  90 20     BCC $AFD1        function code?
AFB1  20 FA AE  JSR $AEFA        checks on parentheses open
```

```
AFB4  20 9E AD JSR $AD9E       gets any term
AFB7  20 FD AE JSR $AEFD       checks on parentheses close
AFBA  20 8F AD JSR $AD8F       checks on string
AFBD  68       PLA
AFBE  AA       TAX
AFBF  A5 65    LDA $65
AFC1  48       PHA             string descriptor address
AFC2  A5 64    LDA $64
AFC4  48       PHA
AFC5  8A       TXA
AFC6  48       PHA
AFC7  20 9E B7 JSR $B79E       get byte value to X
AFCA  68       PLA
AFCB  A8       TAY
AFCC  8A       TXA
AFCD  48       PHA
AFCE  4C D6 AF JMP $AFD6       execute routine
AFD1  20 F1 AE JSR $AEF1       gets term in parentheses
AFD4  68       PLA             BASIC code for function
AFD5  A8       TAY
AFD6  B9 EA 9F LDA $9FEA,Y
AFD9  85 55    STA $55         gets vector to calculate
AFDB  B9 EB 9F LDA $9FEB,Y               the function
AFDE  85 56    STA $56
AFE0  20 54 00 JSR $0054       execute function
AFE3  4C 8D AD JMP $AD8D       checks on numeric

*****************************  BASIC-OR command
AFE6  A0 FF    LDY #$FF        flag for OR
AFE8  2C       .BYTE $2C

*****************************  BASIC-AND command
AFE9  A0 00    LDY #$00        flag for AND
AFEB  84 0B    STY $0B         set flag
AFED  20 BF B1 JSR $B1BF       change FAC to integer
AFF0  A5 64    LDA $64
AFF2  45 0B    EOR $0B
AFF4  85 07    STA $07
AFF6  A5 65    LDA $65         connect with flag and $7/$8
AFF8  45 0B    EOR $0B
AFFA  85 08    STA $08
AFFC  20 FC BB JSR $BBFC       ARG to FAC
AFFF  20 BF B1 JSR $B1BF       FAC to integer
B002  A5 65    LDA $65
B004  45 0B    EOR $0B
B006  25 08    AND $08         logical connection
B008  45 0B    EOR $0B
B00A  A8       TAY
B00B  A5 64    LDA $64
B00D  45 0B    EOR $0B
B00F  25 07    AND $07
B011  45 0B    EOR $0B
B013  4C 91 B3 JMP $B391       change to floating point

*****************************  Comparison
```

```
B016   20 90 AD JSR $AD90        check on same variable type
B019   B0 13    BCS $B02E        strint? then continue
B01B   A5 6E    LDA $6E
B01D   09 7F    ORA #$7F         ARG in memory format
B01F   25 6A    AND $6A
B021   85 6A    STA $6A
B023   A9 69    LDA #$69         address of ARG
B025   A0 00    LDY #$00
B027   20 5B BC JSR $BC5B        compare ARG with FAC
B02A   AA       TAX
B02B   4C 61 B0 JMP $B061        get result to FAC

*****************************   String comparison
B02E   A9 00    LDA #$00
B030   85 0D    STA $0D          clear string flag
B032   C6 4D    DEC $4D
B034   20 A6 B6 JSR $B6A6        FRESTR
B037   85 61    STA $61          string length
B039   86 62    STX $62
B03B   84 63    STY $63          string address
B03D   A5 6C    LDA $6C
B03F   A4 6D    LDY $6D          pointer to second string
B041   20 AA B6 JSR $B6AA        FRESTR
B044   86 6C    STX $6C
B046   84 6D    STY $6D          address of second string
B048   AA       TAX
B049   38       SEC
B04A   E5 61    SBC $61          compare lengths
B04C   F0 08    BEQ $B056        equal?
B04E   A9 01    LDA #$01
B050   90 04    BCC $B056        second string shorter
B052   A6 61    LDX $61
B054   A9 FF    LDA #$FF
B056   85 66    STA $66
B058   A0 FF    LDY #$FF
B05A   E8       INX
B05B   C8       INY
B05C   CA       DEX
B05D   D0 07    BNE $B066
B05F   A6 66    LDX $66
B061   30 0F    BMI $B072
B063   18       CLC
B064   90 0C    BCC $B072        comparison of strings
B066   B1 6C    LDA ($6C),Y               characterwise
B068   D1 62    CMP ($62),Y
B06A   F0 EF    BEQ $B05B
B06C   A2 FF    LDX #$FF
B06E   B0 02    BCS $B072
B070   A2 01    LDX #$01
B072   E8       INX
B073   8A       TXA
B074   2A       ROL
B075   25 12    AND $12
B077   F0 02    BEQ $B07B
B079   A9 FF    LDA #$FF         get result to FAC
```

```
B07B  4C 3C BC JMP $BC3C
B07E  20 FD AE JSR $AEFD        checks on comma

****************************    BASIC-DIM command
B081  AA       TAX
B082  20 90 B0 JSR $B090        dimension variable
B085  20 79 00 JSR $0079        get last character
B088  D0 F4    BNE $B07E        not end, next variable
B08A  60       RTS
B08B  A2 00    LDX #$00         flag for non-dimensioning
B08D  20 79 00 JSR $0079        get last character
B090  86 0C    STX $0C          set DIM-flag
B092  85 45    STA $45          variable name
B094  20 79 00 JSR $0079        CHRGOT get last character
B097  20 13 B1 JSR $B113        checks on letter
B09A  B0 03    BCS $B09F        yes
B09C  4C 08 AF JMP $AF08        "SYNTAX ERROR"
B09F  A2 00    LDX #$00
B0A1  86 0D    STX $0D          clear string flag
B0A3  86 0E    STX $0E          clear integer flag
B0A5  20 73 00 JSR $0073        get next character
B0A8  90 05    BCC $B0AF        digit?
B0AA  20 13 B1 JSR $B113        chhecks on letter
B0AD  90 0B    BCC $B0BA        no
B0AF  AA       TAX              second letter of name
B0B0  20 73 00 JSR $0073        CHRGET get next character
B0B3  90 FB    BCC $B0B0        digit?
B0B5  20 13 B1 JSR $B113        checks on letter
B0B8  B0 F6    BCS $B0B0        yes, read more characters
B0BA  C9 24    CMP #$24         "$"
B0BC  D0 06    BNE $B0C4        no
B0BE  A9 FF    LDA #$FF
B0C0  85 0D    STA $0D          set string flag
B0C2  D0 10    BNE $B0D4        jump
B0C4  C9 25    CMP #$25         "%"
B0C6  D0 13    BNE $B0DB        no
B0C8  A5 10    LDA $10          integer permitted?
B0CA  D0 D0    BNE $B09C        no, "SYNTAX ERROR"
B0CC  A9 80    LDA #$80
B0CE  85 0E    STA $0E          set integer flag
B0D0  05 45    ORA $45          set bit 7 in name
B0D2  85 45    STA $45
B0D4  8A       TXA
B0D5  09 80    ORA #$80         second leter of name
B0D7  AA       TAX
B0D8  20 73 00 JSR $0073        CHRGET get next character
B0DB  86 46    STX $46          save second letter
B0DD  38       SEC
B0DE  05 10    ORA $10
B0E0  E9 28    SBC #$28         "("
B0E2  D0 03    BNE $B0E7        not parentheses open?
B0E4  4C D1 B1 JMP $B1D1        process dimensioned
                                          variable
B0E7  A0 00    LDY #$00
B0E9  84 10    STY $10
B0EB  A5 2D    LDA $2D          pointer to variable start
```

```
B0ED   A6 2E     LDX $2E
B0EF   86 60     STX $60
B0F1   85 5F     STA $5F          save for searching
B0F3   E4 30     CPX $30
B0F5   D0 04     BNE $B0FB
B0F7   C5 2F     CMP $2F          end of variables already?
B0F9   F0 22     BEQ $B11D        yes, not found
B0FB   A5 45     LDA $45          first letter of name
B0FD   D1 5F     CMP ($5F),Y      compare with variable list
B0FF   D0 08     BNE $B109        no, keep looking
B101   A5 46     LDA $46          second letter
B103   C8        INY
B104   D1 5F     CMP ($5F),Y      compare
B106   F0 7D     BEQ $B185
B108   88        DEY
B109   18        CLC
B10A   A5 5F     LDA $5F
B10C   69 07     ADC #$07         increase pointer by 7 (2+5
B10E   90 E1     BCC $B0F1              byte REAL variable)
B110   E8        INX

B111   D0 DC     BNE $B0EF        keep looking

*****************************   Checks on letter
B113   C9 41     CMP #$41
B115   90 05     BCC $B11C
B117   E9 5B     SBC #$5B
B119   38        SEC              yes, then C=1
B11A   E9 A5     SBC #$A5         no, then C=0
B11C   60        RTS

*****************************
B11D   68        PLA
B11E   48        PHA              check calling address
B11F   C9 2A     CMP #$2A         calling from FREMEVL?
B121   D0 05     BNE $B128        no
B123   A9 13     LDA #$13         pointer on constant 0
B125   A0 BF     LDY #$BF
B127   60        RTS
B128   A5 45     LDA $45
B12A   A4 46     LDY $46          variable name
B12C   C9 54     CMP #$54         "T"
B12E   D0 0B     BNE $B13B
B130   C0 C9     CPY #$C9         "I$"
B132   F0 EF     BEQ $B123        yes, TI$
B134   C0 49     CPY #$49         "I"
B136   D0 03     BNE $B13B        no
B138   4C 08 AF  JMP $AF08        "SYNTAX ERROR"
B13B   C9 53     CMP #$53         "S"
B13D   D0 04     BNE $B143
B13F   C0 54     CPY #$54         "T"
B141   F0 F5     BEQ $B138        ST, then "SYNTAX ERROR
B143   A5 2F     LDA $2F
B145   A4 30     LDY $30          pointer to array listing
B147   85 5F     STA $5F
B149   84 60     STY $60          save
B14B   A5 31     LDA $31
B14D   A4 32     LDY $32
```

```
B14F   85 5A      STA $5A
B151   84 5B      STY $5B
B153   18         CLC
B154   69 07      ADC #$07         shift by 7 in order to
B156   90 01      BCC $B159           find a new variable
B158   C8         INY
B159   85 58      STA $58
B15B   84 59      STY $59          new block end
B15D   20 B8 A3   JSR $A3B8        shift block
B160   A5 58      LDA $58
B162   A4 59      LDY $59
B164   C8         INY
B165   85 2F      STA $2F          set pointer to new array
B167   84 30      STY $30                          listing
B169   A0 00      LDY #$00
B16B   A5 45      LDA $45          first letter of name
B16D   91 5F      STA ($5F),Y
B16F   C8         INY
B170   A5 46      LDA $46          second letter of name
B172   91 5F      STA ($5F),Y
B174   A9 00      LDA #$00
B176   C8         INY
B177   91 5F      STA ($5F),Y
B179   C8         INY
B17A   91 5F      STA ($5F),Y
B17C   C8         INY              five times zero for value
B17D   91 5F      STA ($5F),Y
B17F   C8         INY
B180   91 5F      STA ($5F),Y
B182   C8         INY
B183   91 5F      STA ($5F),Y
B185   A5 5F      LDA $5F
B187   18         CLC
B188   69 02      ADC #$02
B18A   A4 60      LDY $60
B18C   90 01      BCC $B18F
B18E   C8         INY
B18F   85 47      STA $47
B191   84 48      STY $48
B193   60         RTS

******************************   Calculates pointer to first
B194   A5 0B      LDA $0B           number of DIM's    element
B196   0A         ASL               times 2
B197   69 05      ADC #$05          plus 5
B199   65 5F      ADC $5F
B19B   A4 60      LDY $60           add to $5F/$60
B19D   90 01      BCC $B1A0
B19F   C8         INY
B1A0   85 58      STA $58           result-pointer
B1A2   84 59      STY $59
B1A4   60         RTS

B1A5 90 80 00 00 00                 constant-32768

B1AA   20 BF B1   JSR $B1BF         change FAC to integer
B1AD   A5 64      LDA $64
```

```
B1AF  A4 65     LDY $65
B1B1  60        RTS

****************************** Change floating to integer
B1B2  20 73 00 JSR $0073        get next character
B1B5  20 9E AD JSR $AD9E        evaluate term
B1B8  20 8D AD JSR $AD8D        checks on numeric
B1BB  A5 66     LDA $66         sign
B1BD  30 0D     BMI $B1CC       negative, then "ILLEGAL
B1BF  A5 61     LDA $61         exponent         QUANTITY"
B1C1  C9 90     CMP #$90        sign bigger than 32768?
B1C3  90 09     BCC $B1CE       no
B1C5  A9 A5     LDA #$A5
B1C7  A0 B1     LDY #$B1        pointer to constant
B1C9  20 5B BC JSR $BC5B        compare FAC with constant
B1CC  D0 7A     BNE $B248       uneven "ILLEGAL QUANTITY"
B1CE  4C 9B BC JMP $BC9B        changes floating point to
                                                  integer

****************************** Dimension variable
B1D1  A5 0C     LDA $0C         DIM-flag
B1D3  05 0E     ORA $0E         integer flag
B1D5  48        PHA
B1D6  A5 0D     LDA $0D         string flag
B1D8  48        PHA
B1D9  A0 00     LDY #$00
B1DB  98        TYA
B1DC  48        PHA
B1DD  A5 46     LDA $46         second letter of the name
B1DF  48        PHA
B1E0  A5 45     LDA $45         first letter of the name
B1E2  48        PHA
B1E3  20 B2 B1 JSR $B1B2        get index and goto integer
B1E6  68        PLA
B1E7  85 45     STA $45
B1E9  68        PLA             get back variable name
B1EA  85 46     STA $46
B1EC  68        PLA
B1ED  A8        TAY
B1EE  BA        TSX
B1EF  BD 02 01 LDA $0102,X
B1F2  48        PHA             get flags from stack
B1F3  BD 01 01 LDA $0101,X
B1F6  48        PHA
B1F7  A5 64     LDA $64
B1F9  9D 02 01 STA $0102,X
B1FC  A5 65     LDA $65         index low and high on stack
B1FE  9D 01 01 STA $0101,X
B201  C8        INY
B202  20 79 00 JSR $0079        get last character
B205  C9 2C     CMP #$2C        "," comma?
B207  F0 D2     BEQ $B1DB       yes, then next index
B209  84 0B     STY $0B         number of indications
B20B  20 F7 AE JSR $AEF7        check on parenthesis close
B20E  68        PLA
B20F  85 0D     STA $0D
```

```
B211  68        PLA              get back flags
B212  85 0E     STA $0E
B214  29 7F     AND #$7F
B216  85 0C     STA $0C
B218  A6 2F     LDX $2F
B21A  A5 30     LDA $30          pointer to array listing
B21C  86 5F     STX $5F
B21E  85 60     STA $60          save pointer
B220  C5 32     CMP $32
B222  D0 04     BNE $B228
B224  E4 31     CPX $31          compare with end of listing
B226  F0 39     BEQ $B261        yes, not found
B228  A0 00     LDY #$00
B22A  B1 5F     LDA ($5F),Y      names from listing
B22C  C8        INY
B22D  C5 45     CMP $45          compare with hunted name
B22F  D0 06     BNE $B237
B231  A5 46     LDA $46
B233  D1 5F     CMP ($5F),Y      second letter
B235  F0 16     BEQ $B24D        found
B237  C8        INY
B238  B1 5F     LDA ($5F),Y
B23A  18        CLC              add field length
B23B  65 5F     ADC $5F
B23D  AA        TAX
B23E  C8        INY
B23F  B1 5F     LDA ($5F),Y
B241  65 60     ADC $60
B243  90 D7     BCC $B21C        and continue searching
B245  A2 12     LDX #$12         number for "BAD SUBSCRIPT"
B247  2C        .BYTE $2C
B248  A2 0E     LDX #$0E         # for "ILLEGAL QUANTITY"
B24A  4C 37 A4  JMP $A437        out-put error message
B24D  A2 13     LDX #$13         # for "REDIM'D ARRAY"
B24F  A5 0C     LDA $0C          DIM flag zero?
B251  D0 F7     BNE $B24A        no, then error message
B253  20 94 B1  JSR $B194        pointer to first element
B256  A5 0B     LDA $0B          number of found dimensions
B258  A0 04     LDY #$04
B25A  D1 5F     CMP ($5F),Y      compare with DIM number
B25C  D0 E7     BNE $B245        uneven,then "BAD SUBSCRIPT"
B25E  4C EA B2  JMP $B2EA        searches for wanted element

*****************************   Apply array variable
B261  20 94 B1  JSR $B194        length of array head
B264  20 08 A4  JSR $A408        checks on free memory
B267  A0 00     LDY #$00
B269  84 72     STY $72
B26B  A2 05     LDX #$05         default value for length
B26D  A5 45     LDA $45          first letter of the name
B26F  91 5F     STA ($5F),Y      in array listing
B271  10 01     BPL $B274        no integer?
B273  CA        DEX
B274  C8        INY
B275  A5 46     LDA $46          second leter
```

```
B277  91 5F     STA ($5F),Y     write into listing
B279  10 02     BPL $B27D       no string of integer?
B27B  CA        DEX
B27C  CA        DEX
B27D  86 71     STX $71         final variable length 2,3,5
B27F  A5 0B     LDA $0B         number of dimensions
B281  C8        INY
B282  C8        INY
B283  C8        INY
B284  91 5F     STA ($5F),Y     save
B286  A2 0B     LDX #$0B        11, default value for DIM's
B288  A9 00     LDA #$00        call by DIM command?
B28A  24 0C     BIT $0C         no
B28C  50 08     BVC $B296       get dimension from stack
B28E  68        PLA
B28F  18        CLC             add 1
B290  69 01     ADC #$01
B292  AA        TAX
B293  68        PLA
B294  69 00     ADC #$00
B296  C8        INY             and save
B297  91 5F     STA ($5F),Y
B299  C8        INY
B29A  8A        TXA
B29B  91 5F     STA ($5F),Y     calculate free memory
B29D  20 4C B3  JSR $B34C
B2A0  86 71     STX $71         save variable-end pointer
B2A2  85 72     STA $72
B2A4  A4 22     LDY $22         further dimensions?
B2A6  C6 0B     DEC $0B         yes
B2A8  D0 DC     BNE $B286
B2AA  65 59     ADC $59         field length plus start-
B2AC  B0 5D     BCS $B30B                           address
B2AE  85 59     STA $59
B2B0  A8        TAY
B2B1  8A        TXA
B2B2  65 58     ADC $58
B2B4  90 03     BCC $B2B9
B2B6  C8        INY
B2B7  F0 52     BEQ $B30B       checks on free memory
B2B9  20 08 A4  JSR $A408
B2BC  85 31     STA $31         pointer to end of listing
B2BE  84 32     STY $32         fill array with 0's
B2C0  A9 00     LDA #$00
B2C2  E6 72     INC $72
B2C4  A4 71     LDY $71
B2C6  F0 05     BEQ $B2CD
B2C8  88        DEY
B2C9  91 58     STA ($58),Y
B2CB  D0 FB     BNE $B2C8
B2CD  C6 59     DEC $59
B2CF  C6 72     DEC $72
B2D1  D0 F5     BNE $B2C8
B2D3  E6 59     INC $59
B2D5  38        SEC
B2D6  A5 31     LDA $31
```

```
B2D8  E5 5F     SBC $5F
B2DA  A0 02     LDY #$02
B2DC  91 5F     STA ($5F),Y       array length low
B2DE  A5 32     LDA $32
B2E0  C8        INY
B2E1  E5 60     SBC $60
B2E3  91 5F     STA ($5F),Y       array length high
B2E5  A5 0C     LDA $0C           call from DIM-command?
B2E7  D0 62     BNE $B34B         yes, RTS

*****************************    Search for element
B2E9  C8        INY
B2EA  B1 5F     LDA ($5F),Y       number of dimensions
B2EC  85 0B     STA $0B           save
B2EE  A9 00     LDA #$00
B2F0  85 71     STA $71
B2F2  85 72     STA $72
B2F4  C8        INY
B2F5  68        PLA
B2F6  AA        TAX
B2F7  85 64     STA $64           get index from stack
B2F9  68        PLA
B2FA  85 65     STA $65
B2FC  D1 5F     CMP ($5F),Y       compare with value in array
B2FE  90 0E     BCC $B30E         smaller?
B300  D0 06     BNE $B308         bigger,then "BAD SUBSCRIPT"
B302  C8        INY
B303  8A        TXA
B304  D1 5F     CMP ($5F),Y       when even, compare low byte
B306  90 07     BCC $B30F         smaller, then continue
B308  4C 45 B2  JMP $B245         "BAD SUBSCRIPT"
B30B  4C 35 A4  JMP $A435         "OUT OF MEMORY"

*****************************    Calculates address of array
                                                  element
B30E  C8        INY
B30F  A5 72     LDA $72
B311  05 71     ORA $71
B313  18        CLC
B314  F0 0A     BEQ $B320
B316  20 4C B3  JSR $B34C         multiplication
B319  8A        TXA
B31A  65 64     ADC $64
B31C  AA        TAX
B31D  98        TYA
B31E  A4 22     LDY $22
B320  65 65     ADC $65
B322  86 71     STX $71
B324  C6 0B     DEC $0B           number of dimensions
B326  D0 CA     BNE $B2F2         continue with next index
B328  85 72     STA $72
B32A  A2 05     LDX #$05          default for variable length
B32C  A5 45     LDA $45           first letter of name
B32E  10 01     BPL $B331
B330  CA        DEX
B331  A5 46     LDA $46           second letter of name
```

```
B333   10 02     BPL $B337
B335   CA        DEX
B336   CA        DEX
B337   86 28     STX $28           length of variables 2,3,5
B339   A9 00     LDA #$00
B33B   20 55 B3  JSR $B355         calculate offset in array
B33E   8A        TXA
B33F   65 58     ADC $58
B341   85 47     STA $47
B343   98        TYA
B344   65 59     ADC $59
B346   85 48     STA $48
B348   A8        TAY
B349   A5 47     LDA $47
B34B   60        RTS

******************************    Helper for array calculation
B34C   84 22     STY $22
B34E   B1 5F     LDA ($5F),Y
B350   85 28     STA $28
B352   88        DEY
B353   B1 5F     LDA ($5F),Y
B355   85 29     STA $29
B357   A9 10     LDA #$10
B359   85 5D     STA $5D
B35B   A2 00     LDX #$00
B35D   A0 00     LDY #$00
B35F   8A        TXA
B360   0A        ASL
B361   AA        TAX
B362   98        TYA
B363   2A        ROL
B364   A8        TAY
B365   B0 A4     BCS $B30B
B367   06 71     ASL $71
B369   26 72     ROL $72
B36B   90 0B     BCC $B378
B36D   18        CLC
B36E   8A        TXA
B36F   65 28     ADC $28
B371   AA        TAX
B372   98        TYA
B373   65 29     ADC $29
B375   A8        TAY
B376   B0 93     BCS $B30B
B378   C6 5D     DEC $5D
B37A   D0 E3     BNE $B35F
B37C   60        RTS

******************************    BASIC-FRE function
B37D   A5 0D     LDA $0D            type flag
B37F   F0 03     BEQ $B384          no string
B381   20 A6 B6  JSR $B6A6          FRESTR
B384   20 26 B5  JSR $B526          garbage collection
B387   38        SEC
```

```
B388  A5 33     LDA $33
B38A  E5 31     SBC $31          string start
B38C  A8        TAY
B38D  A5 34     LDA $34
B38F  E5 32     SBC $32          minus variable end
B391  A2 00     LDX #$00
B393  86 0D     STX $0D          set flag to numeric
B395  85 62     STA $62
B397  84 63     STY $63          save result
B399  A2 90     LDX #$90
B39B  4C 44 BC  JMP $BC44        and change to floating
                                                 point
*****************************   BASIC-POS function
B39E  38        SEC              C=1 get cursor position
B39F  20 F0 FF  JSR $FFF0        get cursor position
B3A2  A9 00     LDA #$00
B3A4  F0 EB     BEQ $B391        continue as above

*****************************   Test on direct mode
B3A6  A6 3A     LDX $3A
B3A8  E8        INX
B3A9  D0 A0     BNE $B34B        no, then RTS
B3AB  A2 15     LDX #$15         # for "ILLEGAL QUANTIY"
B3AD  2C        .BYTE $2C
B3AE  A2 1B     LDX #$1B         # for "UNDEF'D FUNCTION"
B3B0  4C 37 A4  JMP $A437        output error message

*****************************   BASIC-DEF FN  command
B3B3  20 E1 B3  JSR $B3E1        checks FN syntax
B3B6  20 A6 B3  JSR $B3A6        checks on direct mode
B3B9  20 FA AE  JSR $AEFA        checks on parenthesis open
B3BC  A9 80     LDA #$80
B3BE  85 10     STA $10          blocks integer variable
B3C0  20 8B B0  JSR $B08B        looks for variable
B3C3  20 8D AD  JSR $AD8D        checks on numeric
B3C6  20 F7 AE  JSR $AEF7        checks on parenthesis close
B3C9  A9 B2     LDA #$B2         "=" BASIC code
B3CB  20 FF AE  JSR $AEFF        checks on "="
B3CE  48        PHA
B3CF  A5 48     LDA $48
B3D1  48        PHA              FN variables on stack
B3D2  A5 47     LDA $47
B3D4  48        PHA
B3D5  A5 7B     LDA $7B
B3D7  48        PHA              program pointer on stack
B3D8  A5 7A     LDA $7A
B3DA  48        PHA
B3DB  20 F8 A8  JSR $A8F8        pointer on next statement
B3DE  4C 4F B4  JMP $B44F        get FN variable from stack

*****************************   Checks on FN syntax
B3E1  A9 A5     LDA #$A5         FN code
B3E3  20 FF AE  JSR $AEFF        checks on FN code
B3E6  09 80     ORA #$80
B3E8  85 10     STA $10          blocks integer variables
```

```
B3EA   20 92 B0 JSR $B092          looks for variable
B3ED   85 4E    STA $4E
B3EF   84 4F    STY $4F            set FN-variable pointer
B3F1   4C 8D AD JMP $AD8D          checks on numeric

*****************************     BASIC-FN function
B3F4   20 E1 B3 JSR $B3E1          checks FN syntax
B3F7   A5 4F    LDA $4F
B3F9   48       PHA                FN variable pointer on
B3FA   A5 4E    LDA $4E                                stack
B3FC   48       PHA
B3FD   20 F1 AE JSR $AEF1          gets term in parenthesis
B400   20 8D AD JSR $AD8D          checks on numeric
B403   68       PLA
B404   85 4E    STA $4E            get back FNvariable pointer
B406   68       PLA
B407   85 4F    STA $4F
B409   A0 02    LDY #$02
B40B   B1 4E    LDA ($4E),Y
B40D   85 47    STA $47
B40F   AA       TAX
B410   C8       INY
B411   B1 4E    LDA ($4E),Y        gives "UNDEF'D FUNCTION"
B413   F0 99    BEQ $B3AE
B415   85 48    STA $48
B417   C8       INY
B418   B1 47    LDA ($47),Y
B41A   48       PHA
B41B   88       DEY
B41C   10 FA    BPL $B418
B41E   A4 48    LDY $48            transfer FAC to FN variable
B420   20 D4 BB JSR $BBD4
B423   A5 7B    LDA $7B
B425   48       PHA
B426   A5 7A    LDA $7A
B428   48       PHA
B429   B1 4E    LDA ($4E),Y
B42B   85 7A    STA $7A            program pointer on FN term
B42D   C8       INY
B42E   B1 4E    LDA ($4E),Y
B430   85 7B    STA $7B
B432   A5 48    LDA $48
B434   48       PHA
B435   A5 47    LDA $47
B437   48       PHA                FRMNUM get numeric term
B438   20 8A AD JSR $AD8A
B43B   68       PLA
B43C   85 4E    STA $4E
B43E   68       PLA
B43F   85 4F    STA $4F            get last character
B441   20 79 00 JSR $0079          no more characters?
B444   F0 03    BEQ $B449          give "SYNTAX ERROR"
B446   4C 08 AF JMP $AF08
B449   68       PLA
B44A   85 7A    STA $7A            program pointer
B44C   68       PLA
```

```
B44D  85 7B     STA $7B
B44F  A0 00     LDY #$00
B451  68        PLA
B452  91 4E     STA ($4E),Y
B454  68        PLA
B455  C8        INY
B456  91 4E     STA ($4E),Y
B458  68        PLA
B459  C8        INY              and get FN variable from
B45A  91 4E     STA ($4E),Y                         stack
B45C  68        PLA
B45D  C8        INY
B45E  91 4E     STA ($4E),Y
B460  68        PLA
B461  C8        INY
B462  91 4E     STA ($4E),Y
B464  60        RTS

******************************  BASIC-STR$ function
B465  20 8D AD JSR $AD8D         checks on numeric
B468  A0 00     LDY #$00
B46A  20 DF BD JSR $BDDF         change FAC to ASCII
B46D  68        PLA
B46E  68        PLA
B46F  A9 FF     LDA #$FF
B471  A0 00     LDY #$00         start address of string =
B473  F0 12     BEQ $B487                               $FF

******************************  String administration
B475  A6 64     LDX $64
B477  A4 65     LDY $65
B479  86 50     STX $50          pointer to string descriptor
B47B  84 51     STY $51
B47D  20 F4 B4 JSR $B4F4         checks free memory, sets
B480  86 62     STX $62                    string pointer
B482  84 63     STY $63
B484  85 61     STA $61
B486  60        RTS
B487  A2 22     LDX #$22         "
B489  86 07     STX $07
B48B  86 08     STX $08
B48D  85 6F     STA $6F          start address of string
B48F  84 70     STY $70
B491  85 62     STA $62
B493  84 63     STY $63
B495  A0 FF     LDY #$FF
B497  C8        INY              increase pointer
B498  B1 6F     LDA ($6F),Y      next character of string
B49A  F0 0C     BEQ $B4A8        end symbol?
B49C  C5 07     CMP $07
B49E  F0 04     BEQ $B4A4
B4A0  C5 08     CMP $08
B4A2  D0 F3     BNE $B497
B4A4  C9 22     CMP #$22         "
B4A6  F0 01     BEQ $B4A9
B4A8  18        CLC
```

```
B4A9   84 61     STY $61       length of string
B4AB   98        TYA
B4AC   65 6F     ADC $6F
B4AE   85 71     STA $71       end address low +1
B4B0   A6 70     LDX $70
B4B2   90 01     BCC $B4B5
B4B4   E8        INX
B4B5   86 72     STX $72       end address high +1
B4B7   A5 70     LDA $70       start address high
B4B9   F0 04     BEQ $B4BF     zero?
B4BB   C9 02     CMP #$02      two?
B4BD   D0 0B     BNE $B4CA     no
B4BF   98        TYA
B4C0   20 75 B4  JSR $B475     string descriptor gets
B4C3   A6 6F     LDX $6F         length in A,address X/Y
B4C5   A4 70     LDY $70       gets start address
B4C7   20 88 B6  JSR $B688     copy string into $ range
B4CA   A6 16     LDX $16       string descriptor pointer
B4CC   E0 22     CPX #$22      string stack full?
B4CE   D0 05     BNE $B4D5     no
B4D0   A2 19     LDX #$19      # for "FORMULA TO COMPLEX"
B4D2   4C 37 A4  JMP $A437     out-put error messages
B4D5   A5 61     LDA $61
B4D7   95 00     STA $00,X     bring string length
B4D9   A5 62     LDA $62
B4DB   95 01     STA $01,X     and address
B4DD   A5 63     LDA $63
B4DF   95 02     STA $02,X     into string stack
B4E1   A0 00     LDY #$00
B4E3   86 64     STX $64
B4E5   84 65     STY $65       pointer now on descriptor
B4E7   84 70     STY $70
B4E9   88        DEY
B4EA   84 0D     STY $0D       set string flag $FF
B4EC   86 17     STX $17       index of last string descr.
B4EE   E8        INX
B4EF   E8        INX           increase by 3
B4F0   E8        INX
B4F1   86 16     STX $16       save as new index
B4F3   60        RTS
B4F4   46 0F     LSR $0F       set back flag for garbage-
B4F6   48        PHA           string length   collection
B4F7   49 FF     EOR #$FF
B4F9   38        SEC
B4FA   65 33     ADC $33
B4FC   A4 34     LDY $34
B4FE   B0 01     BCS $B501
B500   88        DEY
B501   C4 32     CPY $32
B503   90 11     BCC $B516
B505   D0 04     BNE $B50B
B507   C5 31     CMP $31
B509   90 0B     BCC $B516
B50B   85 33     STA $33
```

```
B50D  84 34     STY $34
B50F  85 35     STA $35
B511  84 36     STY $36
B513  AA        TAX
B514  68        PLA              get back string length
B515  60        RTS
B516  A2 10     LDX #$10         # for "OUT OF MEMORY"
B518  A5 0F     LDA $0F          flag for garbage collection
B51A  30 B6     BMI $B4D2        done, then "OUT OF MEMORY"
B51C  20 26 B5  JSR $B526        garbage collection
B51F  A9 80     LDA #$80         set flag
B521  85 0F     STA $0F
B523  68        PLA              string length
B524  D0 D0     BNE $B4F6

*****************************   Garbage collection
B526  A6 37     LDX $37           get rid of invalid strings
B528  A5 38     LDA $38
B52A  86 33     STX $33
B52C  85 34     STA $34
B52E  A0 00     LDY #$00
B530  84 4F     STY $4F
B532  84 4E     STY $4E
B534  A5 31     LDA $31
B536  A6 32     LDX $32
B538  85 5F     STA $5F
B53A  86 60     STX $60
B53C  A9 19     LDA #$19
B53E  A2 00     LDX #$00
B540  85 22     STA $22
B542  86 23     STX $23
B544  C5 16     CMP $16
B546  F0 05     BEQ $B54D
B548  20 C7 B5  JSR $B5C7
B54B  F0 F7     BEQ $B544
B54D  A9 07     LDA #$07
B54F  85 53     STA $53
B551  A5 2D     LDA $2D
B553  A6 2E     LDX $2E
B555  85 22     STA $22
B557  86 23     STX $23
B559  E4 30     CPX $30
B55B  D0 04     BNE $B561
B55D  C5 2F     CMP $2F
B55F  F0 05     BEQ $B566
B561  20 BD B5  JSR $B5BD
B564  F0 F3     BEQ $B559
B566  85 58     STA $58
B568  86 59     STX $59
B56A  A9 03     LDA #$03
B56C  85 53     STA $53
B56E  A5 58     LDA $58
B570  A6 59     LDX $59
B572  E4 32     CPX $32
B574  D0 07     BNE $B57D
```

```
B576  C5 31     CMP $31
B578  D0 03     BNE $B57D
B57A  4C 06 B6  JMP $B606
B57D  85 22     STA $22
B57F  86 23     STX $23
B581  A0 00     LDY #$00
B583  B1 22     LDA ($22),Y
B585  AA        TAX
B586  C8        INY
B587  B1 22     LDA ($22),Y
B589  08        PHP
B58A  C8        INY
B58B  B1 22     LDA ($22),Y
B58D  65 58     ADC $58
B58F  85 58     STA $58
B591  C8        INY
B592  B1 22     LDA ($22),Y
B594  65 59     ADC $59
B596  85 59     STA $59
B598  28        PLP
B599  10 D3     BPL $B56E
B59B  8A        TXA
B59C  30 D0     BMI $B56E
B59E  C8        INY
B59F  B1 22     LDA ($22),Y
B5A1  A0 00     LDY #$00
B5A3  0A        ASL
B5A4  69 05     ADC #$05
B5A6  65 22     ADC $22
B5A8  85 22     STA $22
B5AA  90 02     BCC $B5AE
B5AC  E6 23     INC $23
B5AE  A6 23     LDX $23
B5B0  E4 59     CPX $59
B5B2  D0 04     BNE $B5B8
B5B4  C5 58     CMP $58
B5B6  F0 BA     BEQ $B572
B5B8  20 C7 B5  JSR $B5C7
B5BB  F0 F3     BEQ $B5B0
B5BD  B1 22     LDA ($22),Y
B5BF  30 35     BMI $B5F6
B5C1  C8        INY
B5C2  B1 22     LDA ($22),Y
B5C4  10 30     BPL $B5F6
B5C6  C8        INY
B5C7  B1 22     LDA ($22),Y
B5C9  F0 2B     BEQ $B5F6
B5CB  C8        INY
B5CC  B1 22     LDA ($22),Y
B5CE  AA        TAX
B5CF  C8        INY
B5D0  B1 22     LDA ($22),Y
B5D2  C5 34     CMP $34
B5D4  90 06     BCC $B5DC
B5D6  D0 1E     BNE $B5F6
B5D8  E4 33     CPX $33
```

```
B5DA  B0 1A     BCS $B5F6
B5DC  C5 60     CMP $60
B5DE  90 16     BCC $B5F6
B5E0  D0 04     BNE $B5E6
B5E2  E4 5F     CPX $5F
B5E4  90 10     BCC $B5F6
B5E6  86 5F     STX $5F
B5E8  85 60     STA $60
B5EA  A5 22     LDA $22
B5EC  A6 23     LDX $23
B5EE  85 4E     STA $4E
B5F0  86 4F     STX $4F
B5F2  A5 53     LDA $53
B5F4  85 55     STA $55
B5F6  A5 53     LDA $53
B5F8  18        CLC
B5F9  65 22     ADC $22
B5FB  85 22     STA $22
B5FD  90 02     BCC $B601
B5FF  E6 23     INC $23
B601  A6 23     LDX $23
B603  A0 00     LDY #$00
B605  60        RTS
B606  A5 4F     LDA $4F
B608  05 4E     ORA $4E
B60A  F0 F5     BEQ $B601
B60C  A5 55     LDA $55
B60E  29 04     AND #$04
B610  4A        LSR
B611  A8        TAY
B612  85 55     STA $55
B614  B1 4E     LDA ($4E),Y
B616  65 5F     ADC $5F
B618  85 5A     STA $5A
B61A  A5 60     LDA $60
B61C  69 00     ADC #$00
B61E  85 5B     STA $5B
B620  A5 33     LDA $33
B622  A6 34     LDX $34
B624  85 58     STA $58
B626  86 59     STX $59
B628  20 BF A3  JSR $A3BF
B62B  A4 55     LDY $55
B62D  C8        INY
B62E  A5 58     LDA $58
B630  91 4E     STA ($4E),Y
B632  AA        TAX
B633  E6 59     INC $59
B635  A5 59     LDA $59
B637  C8        INY
B638  91 4E     STA ($4E),Y
B63A  4C 2A B5  JMP $B52A

******************************    String connection "+"
B63D  A5 65     LDA $65
```

```
B63F  48        PHA            save descriptor of first
B640  A5 64     LDA $64                        string
B642  48        PHA                             ↗desc.
B643  20 83 AE  JSR $AE83      get address of 2nd strings
B646  20 8F AD  JSR $AD8F      checks on string variable
B649  68        PLA
B64A  85 6F     STA $6F
B64C  68        PLA            get back descriptor
B64D  85 70     STA $70
B64F  A0 00     LDY #$00
B651  B1 6F     LDA ($6F),Y    length of first string
B653  18        CLC
B654  71 64     ADC ($64),Y    plus length of 2nd string
B656  90 05     BCC $B65D      smaller than 256
B658  A2 17     LDX #$17       # for "STRING TOO LONG"
B65A  4C 37 A4  JMP $A437      out-put error messages
B65D  20 75 B4  JSR $B475      save place for new string
B660  20 7A B6  JSR $B67A      transfer first string there
B663  A5 50     LDA $50
B665  A4 51     LDY $51        pointer to second string
B667  20 AA B6  JSR $B6AA      FRESTR        descriptor
B66A  20 8C B6  JSR $B68C      connect second string with
B66D  A5 6F     LDA $6F                 the first string
B66F  A4 70     LDY $70
B671  20 AA B6  JSR $B6AA      FRESTR
B674  20 CA B4  JSR $B4CA      descriptor in string stack
B677  4C B8 AD  JMP $ADB8      back to formula evaluation

B67A  A0 00     LDY #$00
B67C  B1 6F     LDA ($6F),Y    save string length
B67E  48        PHA
B67F  C8        INY
B680  B1 6F     LDA ($6F),Y    string address low
B682  AA        TAX
B683  C8        INY
B684  B1 6F     LDA ($6F),Y    string address high
B686  A8        TAY
B687  68        PLA            string length
B688  86 22     STX $22
B68A  84 23     STY $23        pointer to string
B68C  A8        TAY
B68D  F0 0A     BEQ $B699      length zero, then ready
B68F  48        PHA
B690  88        DEY
B691  B1 22     LDA ($22),Y    transfer string
B693  91 35     STA ($35),Y
B695  98        TYA
B696  D0 F8     BNE $B690
B698  68        PLA
B699  18        CLC
B69A  65 35     ADC $35
B69C  85 35     STA $35        pointer plus string length
B69E  90 02     BCC $B6A2
B6A0  E6 36     INC $36
B6A2  60        RTS
```

```
*****************************    String administration FRESTR
B6A3   20 8F AD JSR $AD8F         checks on string variable
B6A6   A5 64       LDA $64
B6A8   A4 65       LDY $65        pointr to string descriptor
B6AA   85 22       STA $22
B6AC   84 23       STY $23
B6AE   20 DB B6 JSR $B6DB         eliminate descriptor from
B6B1   08          PHP                          string stack
B6B2   A0 00       LDY #$00
B6B4   B1 22       LDA ($22),Y
B6B6   48          PHA
B6B7   C8          INY
B6B8   B1 22       LDA ($22),Y
B6BA   AA          TAX
B6BB   C8          INY
B6BC   B1 22       LDA ($22),Y
B6BE   A8          TAY
B6BF   68          PLA
B6C0   28          PLP
B6C1   D0 13       BNE $B6D6      string wasn't in string
B6C3   C4 34       CPY $34                         stack
B6C5   D0 0F       BNE $B6D6
B6C7   E4 33       CPX $33
B6C9   D0 0B       BNE $B6D6
B6CB   48          PHA
B6CC   18          CLC
B6CD   65 33       ADC $33
B6CF   85 33       STA $33        $33/$34 now point to string
B6D1   90 02       BCC $B6D5                          stack
B6D3   E6 34       INC $34
B6D5   68          PLA
B6D6   86 22       STX $22
B6D8   84 23       STY $23
B6DA   60          RTS
B6DB   C4 18       CPY $18
B6DD   D0 0C       BNE $B6EB
B6DF   C5 17       CMP $17        is string descriptor in
B6E1   D0 08       BNE $B6EB                string stack
B6E3   85 16       STA $16
B6E5   E9 03       SBC #$03       yes, eliminate input
B6E7   85 17       STA $17
B6E9   A0 00       LDY #$00
B6EB   60          RTS

*****************************    BASIC-CHR$ function
B6EC   20 A1 B7 JSR $B7A1         gets byte value (0 to 255)
B6EF   8A          TXA            code in accumulator
B6F0   48          PHA
B6F1   A9 01       LDA #$01       length of string = 1
B6F3   20 7D B4 JSR $B47D         reserve place for string
B6F6   68          PLA            get back ASCII code
B6F7   A0 00       LDY #$00
B6F9   91 62       STA ($62),Y    save all string characters
```

```
B6FB  68        PLA
B6FC  68        PLA
B6FD  4C CA B4  JMP $B4CA         bring descriptor to string
                                                      stack

******************************    BASIC-LEFT$ function
B700  20 61 B7  JSR $B761         string parameter from stack
B703  D1 50     CMP ($50),Y       compare length with LEFT$
                                                 parameter
B705  98        TYA
B706  90 04     BCC $B70C         is LEFT value less than
B708  B1 50     LDA ($50),Y       string length/string length
B70A  AA        TAX
B70B  98        TYA
B70C  48        PHA
B70D  8A        TXA
B70E  48        PHA
B70F  20 7D B4  JSR $B47D         save place for new string
B712  A5 50     LDA $50
B714  A4 51     LDY $51           pointer to descriptor
B716  20 AA B6  JSR $B6AA         FRESTR
B719  68        PLA
B71A  A8        TAY
B71B  68        PLA               length of new string
B71C  18        CLC
B71D  65 22     ADC $22           plus address of old string
B71F  85 22     STA $22
B721  90 02     BCC $B725
B723  E6 23     INC $23
B725  98        TYA
B726  20 8C B6  JSR $B68C         transfer newstring to range
B729  4C CA B4  JMP $B4CA         bring descriptor to string
                                                      stack

******************************    BASIC-RIGHT$ function
B72C  20 61 B7  JSR $B761         get string parameter from
B72F  18        CLC                                   stack
B730  F1 50     SBC ($50),Y
B732  49 FF     EOR #$FF          first element's # in old
B734  4C 06 B7  JMP $B706         continue as in LEFT$/string

******************************    BASIC-MID$ function
B737  A9 FF     LDA #$FF
B739  85 65     STA $65
B73B  20 79 00  JSR $0079         CHRGOT get last character
B73E  C9 29     CMP #$29          ")" closed parenthesis
B740  F0 06     BEQ $B748
B742  20 FD AE  JSR $AEFD         checks on comma
B745  20 9E B7  JSR $B79E         gets byte #, 2nd parameter
B748  20 61 B7  JSR $B761         get string address, 1st "
B74B  F0 4B     BEQ $B798         first parameter zero,
                                          "ILLEGAL QUANTITY"
B74D  CA        DEX
B74E  8A        TXA
B74F  48        PHA               # of first element in old
B750  18        CLC                                  string
B751  A2 00     LDX #$00
B753  F1 50     SBC ($50),Y       length of old string
B755  B0 B6     BCS $B70D         small, first MID parameter
B757  49 FF     EOR #$FF          new string length
```

```
B759  C5 65     CMP $65
B75B  90 B1     BCC $B70E
B75D  A5 65     LDA $65
B75F  B0 AD     BCS $B70E          absolute jump
B761  20 F7 AE  JSR $AEF7          checks on close parethesis
B764  68        PLA
B765  A8        TAY                get call address
B766  68        PLA
B767  85 55     STA $55
B769  68        PLA
B76A  68        PLA
B76B  68        PLA                first parameter
B76C  AA        TAX
B76D  68        PLA
B76E  85 50     STA $50
B770  68        PLA
B771  85 51     STA $51            address low/high of string
B773  A5 55     LDA $55                            descriptor
B775  48        PHA
B776  98        TYA
B777  48        PHA                last address back on stack
B778  A0 00     LDY #$00
B77A  8A        TXA
B77B  60        RTS


*****************************     BASIC-LEN function
B77C   20 82 B7 JSR $B782          FRESTR get string length
B77F   4C A2 B3 JMP $B3A2          change byte to floating
                                                point format
*****************************     Get string parameter
B782   20 A3 B6 JSR $B6A3          get string length in A
B785   A2 00    LDX #$00
B787   86 0D    STX $0D            set type flag on numeric
B789   A8       TAY                length in Y
B78A   60       RTS

*****************************     BASIC-ASC function
B78B   20 82 B7 JSR $B782          get $ pointer in $22/$23
B78E   F0 08    BEQ $B798          length = 0, "ILLEGAL
B790   A0 00    LDY #$00                          QUANTITY"
B792   B1 22    LDA ($22),Y        get first character
B794   A8       TAY                ASCII code
B795   4C A2 B3 JMP $B3A2          change to floating point
B798   4C 48 B2 JMP $B248          "ILLEGAL QUANTITY"

*****************************     Gets byt value to X
B79B   20 73 00 JSR $0073          CHRGET get next character
B79E   20 8A AD JSR $AD8A          FRMNUM get # value to FAC
B7A1   20 B8 B1 JSR $B1D0          checks on range and changes
B7A4   A6 64    LDX $64            high byte        to integer
B7A6   D0 F0    BNE $B798          not 0, "ILLEGAL QUANTITY"
B7A8   A6 65    LDX $65
B7AA   4C 79 00 JMP $0079          CHRGOT get last character
```

```
*****************************    BASIC-VAL function
B7AD   20 82 B7 JSR $B782         get string address and
B7B0   D0 03    BNE $B7B5         length not 0?    length
B7B2   4C F7 B8 JMP $B8F7         zero in FAC
B7B5   A6 7A    LDX $7A
B7B7   A4 7B    LDY $7B           save program pointer
B7B9   86 71    STX $71
B7BB   84 72    STY $72
B7BD   A6 22    LDX $22
B7BF   86 7A    STX $7A           bring string start-address
B7C1   18       CLC                      into string-pointer
B7C2   65 22    ADC $22
B7C4   85 24    STA $24
B7C6   A6 23    LDX $23           string end+1
B7C8   86 7B    STX $7B
B7CA   90 01    BCC $B7CD
B7CC   E8       INX
B7CD   86 25    STX $25
B7CF   A0 00    LDY #$00
B7D1   B1 24    LDA ($24),Y       first byte to string
B7D3   48       PHA               save
B7D4   98       TYA
B7D5   91 24    STA ($24),Y       and substitute with zero
B7D7   20 79 00 JSR $0079         CHRGOT get last character
B7DA   20 F3 BC JSR $BCF3         change string to floating
B7DD   68       PLA               character to string/point
B7DE   A0 00    LDY #$00
B7E0   91 24    STA ($24),Y       set back again
B7E2   A6 71    LDX $71
B7E4   A4 72    LDY $72
B7E6   86 7A    STX $7A           get back program pointer
B7E8   84 7B    STY $7B
B7EA   60       RTS
*****************************    GETADR and GETBYT 16 + 8 bit
B7EB   20 8A AD JSR $AD8A         FRMNUM gets numeric value
B7EE   20 F7 B7 JSR $B7F7         change FAC to address frmat
B7F1   20 FD AE JSR $AEFD         CHKCOM checks on camma
B7F4   4C 9E B7 JMP $B79E         gets byte value to X

*****************************    GETADR change FAC to a + 16
B7F7   A5 66    LDA $66           sign              bit number
B7F9   30 9D    BMI $B798         - then "ILLEGAL QUANTITY"
B7FB   A5 61    LDA $61           exponent
B7FD   C9 91    CMP #$91          compare # to 65536
B7FF   B0 97    BCS $B798         bigger,"ILLEGAL QUANTITY"
B801   20 9B BC JSR $BC9B         change FAC to address frmat
B804   A5 64    LDA $64
B806   A4 65    LDY $65           get value
B808   84 14    STY $14           and to $14/$15
B80A   85 15    STA $15
B80C   60       RTS

*****************************    BASIC-PEEK function
B80D   A5 15    LDA $15
B80F   48       PHA               save address $14/$15
B810   A5 14    LDA $14
```

```
B812  48        PHA
B813  20 F7 B7  JSR $B7F7       change FAC to address frmat
B816  A0 00     LDY #$00
B818  B1 14     LDA ($14),Y     get PEEK value
B81A  A8        TAY             to Y
B81B  68        PLA
B81C  85 14     STA $14
B81E  68        PLA             get back address
B81F  85 15     STA $15
B821  4C A2 B3  JMP $B3A2       Y to floating point format

****************************   BASIC-POKE command
B824  20 EB B7  JSR $B7EB       get POKE address and value
B827  8A        TXA             write POKE value into accu
B828  A0 00     LDY #$00
B82A  91 14     STA ($14),Y     and memory
B82C  60        RTS

****************************   BASIC-WAIT command
B82D  20 EB B7  JSR $B7EB       get address and value
B830  86 49     STX $49
B832  A2 00     LDX #$00        default for third parameter
B834  20 79 00  JSR $0079       CHRGOT get last character
B837  F0 03     BEQ $B83C       no third parameter?
B839  20 F1 B7  JSR $B7F1       checks on comma and gets
B83C  86 4A     STX $4A                     parameter
B83E  A0 00     LDY #$00
B840  B1 14     LDA ($14),Y     wait address
B842  45 4A     EOR $4A
B844  25 49     AND $49         connect logically
B846  F0 F8     BEQ $B840       keep waiting
B848  60        RTS

****************************   Arithmetic routines

****************************   FAC = FAC + 0.5
B849  A9 11     LDA #$11
B84B  A0 BF     LDY #$BF        pointer on constant 0.5
B84D  4C 67 B8  JMP $B867       FAC = FAC + constant (A/Y)

****************************   Minus FAC=constant (A/Y)-FAC
B850  20 8C BA  JSR $BA8C       constant (A/Y) to ARG

****************************   Minus FAC = ARG-FAC
B853  A5 66     LDA $66
B855  49 FF     EOR #$FF        change of sign
B857  85 66     STA $66
B859  45 6E     EOR $6E
B85B  85 6F     STA $6F
B85D  A5 61     LDA $61
B85F  4C 6A B8  JMP $B86A       FAC = FAC + ARG

****************************
B862  20 99 B9  JSR $B999       adjust exponent of FAC + ARG
B865  90 3C     BCC $B8A3
```

```
*****************************   Plus FAC = constant(A/Y)+FAC
B867  20 8C BA JSR $BA8C         constant (A/Y) to ARG

*****************************   Plus FAC = FAC + ARG
B86A  D0 03     BNE $B86F        FAC inverse zero?
B86C  4C FC BB  JMP $BBFC        no, the FAC = ARG
B86F  A6 70     LDX $70
B871  86 56     STX $56
B873  A2 69     LDX #$69
B875  A5 69     LDA $69
B877  A8        TAY
B878  F0 CE     BEQ $B848
B87A  38        SEC
B87B  E5 61     SBC $61
B87D  F0 24     BEQ $B8A3
B87F  90 12     BCC $B893
B881  84 61     STY $61
B883  A4 6E     LDY $6E
B885  84 66     STY $66
B887  49 FF     EOR #$FF
B889  69 00     ADC #$00
B88B  A0 00     LDY #$00
B88D  84 56     STY $56
B88F  A2 61     LDX #$61
B891  D0 04     BNE $B897
B893  A0 00     LDY #$00
B895  84 70     STY $70
B897  C9 F9     CMP #$F9
B899  30 C7     BMI $B862
B89B  A8        TAY
B89C  A5 70     LDA $70
B89E  56 01     LSR $01,X
B8A0  20 B0 B9  JSR $B9B0
B8A3  24 6F     BIT $6F
B8A5  10 57     BPL $B8FE
B8A7  A0 61     LDY #$61
B8A9  E0 69     CPX #$69
B8AB  F0 02     BEQ $B8AF
B8AD  A0 69     LDY #$69
B8AF  38        SEC
B8B0  49 FF     EOR #$FF
B8B2  65 56     ADC $56
B8B4  85 70     STA $70
B8B6  B9 04 00  LDA $0004,Y
B8B9  F5 04     SBC $04,X
B8BB  85 65     STA $65
B8BD  B9 03 00  LDA $0003,Y
B8C0  F5 03     SBC $03,X
B8C2  85 64     STA $64
B8C4  B9 02 00  LDA $0002,Y
B8C7  F5 02     SBC $02,X
B8C9  85 63     STA $63
B8CB  B9 01 00  LDA $0001,Y
B8CE  F5 01     SBC $01,X
```

```
B8D0  85 62     STA $62
B8D2  B0 03     BCS $B8D7
B8D4  20 47 B9  JSR $B947         invert mantisse from FAC
B8D7  A0 00     LDY #$00
B8D9  98        TYA
B8DA  18        CLC
B8DB  A6 62     LDX $62
B8DD  D0 4A     BNE $B929
B8DF  A6 63     LDX $63
B8E1  86 62     STX $62
B8E3  A6 64     LDX $64
B8E5  86 63     STX $63
B8E7  A6 65     LDX $65
B8E9  86 64     STX $64
B8EB  A6 70     LDX $70
B8ED  86 65     STX $65
B8EF  84 70     STY $70
B8F1  69 08     ADC #$08
B8F3  C9 20     CMP #$20
B8F5  D0 E4     BNE $B8DB
B8F7  A9 00     LDA #$00
B8F9  85 61     STA $61
B8FB  85 66     STA $66
B8FD  60        RTS
B8FE  65 56     ADC $56
B900  85 70     STA $70
B902  A5 65     LDA $65
B904  65 6D     ADC $6D
B906  85 65     STA $65
B908  A5 64     LDA $64
B90A  65 6C     ADC $6C
B90C  85 64     STA $64
B90E  A5 63     LDA $63
B910  65 6B     ADC $6B
B912  85 63     STA $63
B914  A5 62     LDA $62
B916  65 6A     ADC $6A
B918  85 62     STA $62
B91A  4C 36 B9  JMP $B936
B91D  69 01     ADC #$01
B91F  06 70     ASL $70
B921  26 65     ROL $65
B923  26 64     ROL $64
B925  26 63     ROL $63
B927  26 62     ROL $62
B929  10 F2     BPL $B91D
B92B  38        SEC
B92C  E5 61     SBC $61
B92E  B0 C7     BCS $B8F7
B930  49 FF     EOR #$FF
B932  69 01     ADC #$01
B934  85 61     STA $61
B936  90 0E     BCC $B946
B938  E6 61     INC $61
B93A  F0 42     BEQ $B97E
```

```
B93C   66 62      ROR $62
B93E   66 63      ROR $63
B940   66 64      ROR $64
B942   66 65      ROR $65
B944   66 70      ROR $70
B946   60         RTS

*****************************   Invert mantisse from FAC
B947   A5 66      LDA $66
B949   49 FF      EOR #$FF
B94B   85 66      STA $66
B94D   A5 62      LDA $62
B94F   49 FF      EOR #$FF
B951   85 62      STA $62
B953   A5 63      LDA $63
B955   49 FF      EOR #$FF
B957   85 63      STA $63
B959   A5 64      LDA $64
B95B   49 FF      EOR #$FF
B95D   85 64      STA $64
B95F   A5 65      LDA $65
B961   49 FF      EOR #$FF
B963   85 65      STA $65
B965   A5 70      LDA $70
B967   49 FF      EOR #$FF
B969   85 70      STA $70
B96B   E6 70      INC $70
B96D   D0 0E      BNE $B97D
B96F   E6 65      INC $65
B971   D0 0A      BNE $B97D
B973   E6 64      INC $64
B975   D0 06      BNE $B97D
B977   E6 63      INC $63
B979   D0 02      BNE $B97D
B97B   E6 62      INC $62
B97D   60         RTS
B97E   A2 0F      LDX #$0F           # for "OVERFLOW"
B980   4C 37 A4 JMP $A437            out-put error message

*****************************   Right-shifting of a register
B983   A2 25      LDX #$25           offset pointer on register
B985   B4 04      LDY $04,X
B987   84 70      STY $70
B989   B4 03      LDY $03,X
B98B   94 04      STY $04,X
B98D   B4 02      LDY $02,X
B98F   94 03      STY $03,X
B991   B4 01      LDY $01,X
B993   94 02      STY $02,X
B995   A4 68      LDY $68
B997   94 01      STY $01,X
B999   69 08      ADC #$08
B99B   30 E8      BMI $B985
B99D   F0 E6      BEQ $B985
B99F   E9 08      SBC #$08
```

```
B9A1   A8         TAY
B9A2   A5 70      LDA $70
B9A4   B0 14      BCS $B9BA
B9A6   16 01      ASL $01,X
B9A8   90 02      BCC $B9AC
B9AA   F6 01      INC $01,X
B9AC   76 01      ROR $01,X
B9AE   76 01      ROR $01,X
B9B0   76 02      ROR $02,X
B9B2   76 03      ROR $03,X
B9B4   76 04      ROR $04,X
B9B6   6A         ROR
B9B7   C8         INY
B9B8   D0 EC      BNE $B9A6
B9BA   18         CLC
B9BB   60         RTS

******************************   Constants for LOG
B9BC 81 00 00 00 00               1
B9C1 03                           3=polynomial degree then 4
B9C2 7F 5E 56 CB 79               .434255942   /coefficients
B9C7 80 13 9B 0B 64               .576584541
B9CC 80 76 38 93 16               .961800759
B9D1 82 38 AA 3B 20               2.88539007
B9D5 20 80 35 04 F3               .707106781 = 1/SQR(2)
B9DB 81 35 04 F3 34               1.41421356 = SQR(2)
B9E0 80 80 00 00 00               -.5
B9E5 80 31 72 17 F8               .693147181 = LOG(2)

******************************   BASIC-LOG function
B9EA   20 2B BC JSR $BC2B         get signs
B9ED   F0 02    BEQ $B9F1         zero, then ready
B9EF   10 03    BPL $B9F4         positive, then ok
B9F1   4C 48 B2 JMP $B248         "ILLEGAL QUANTITY"
B9F4   A5 61    LDA $61           exponent
B9F6   E9 7F    SBC #$7F          normalize
B9F8   48       PHA               and save
B9F9   A9 80    LDA #$80          bring number in range
B9FB   85 61    STA $61           from 0.5 to 1
B9FD   A9 D6    LDA #$D6
B9FF   A0 B9    LDY #$B9          pointer to constant1/SQR(2)
BA01   20 67 B8 JSR $B867         add to FAC
BA04   A9 DB    LDA #$DB
BA06   A0 B9    LDY #$B9          pointer to constant SQR(2)
BA08   20 0F BB JSR $BB0F         divide SQR(2) by FAC
BA0B   A9 BC    LDA #$BC
BA0D   A0 B9    LDY #$B9          pointer to constant 1
BA0F   20 50 B8 JSR $B850         1 minus FAC
BA12   A9 C1    LDA #$C1
BA14   A0 B9    LDY #$B9         pntr - polynome coefficients
BA16   20 43 E0 JSR $E043         polynome calculations
BA19   A9 E0    LDA #$E0
BA1B   A0 B9    LDY #$B9          pointer to constant -0.5
BA1D   20 67 B8 JSR $B867         add to FAC
```

```
BA20   68          PLA            get back exponent
BA21   20 7E BD JSR $BD7E         FAC=FAC+FAC
BA24   A9 E5       LDA #$E5
BA26   A0 B9       LDY #$B9       pointer to constant LOG(2)

*****************************     *  FAC = constant(A/Y) * FAC
BA28   20 8C BA JSR $BA8C         constant to ARG

*****************************     *  FAC = ARG * FAC
BA2B   D0 03       BNE $BA30      not zero?
BA2D   4C 8B BA JMP $BA8B         RTS
BA30   20 B7 BA JSR $BAB7         calculate exponent
BA33   A9 00       LDA #$00
BA35   85 26       STA $26
BA37   85 27       STA $27
BA39   85 28       STA $28        clear function register
BA3B   85 29       STA $29
BA3D   A5 70       LDA $70
BA3F   20 59 BA JSR $BA59         bitwise multiplication
BA42   A5 65       LDA $65
BA44   20 59 BA JSR $BA59         bitwise multiplication
BA47   A5 64       LDA $64
BA49   20 59 BA JSR $BA59         bitwise multiplication
BA4C   A5 63       LDA $63
BA4E   20 59 BA JSR $BA59         bitwise multiplication
BA51   A5 62       LDA $62
BA53   20 5E BA JSR $BA5E         bitwise multiplication
BA56   4C 8F BB JMP $BB8F         register to FAC, make left-
                                                     binding
*****************************     Bitwise multiplication
BA59   D0 03       BNE $BA5E
BA5B   4C 83 B9 JMP $B983         right-shifts the register
BA5E   4A          LSR
BA5F   09 80       ORA #$80
BA61   A8          TAY
BA62   90 19       BCC $BA7D
BA64   18          CLC
BA65   A5 29       LDA $29
BA67   65 6D       ADC $6D
BA69   85 29       STA $29
BA6B   A5 28       LDA $28
BA6D   65 6C       ADC $6C
BA6F   85 28       STA $28
BA71   A5 27       LDA $27
BA73   65 6B       ADC $6B
BA75   85 27       STA $27
BA77   A5 26       LDA $26
BA79   65 6A       ADC $6A
BA7B   85 26       STA $26
BA7D   66 26       ROR $26
BA7F   66 27       ROR $27
BA81   66 28       ROR $28
BA83   66 29       ROR $29
BA85   66 70       ROR $70
BA87   98          TYA
```

```
BA88  4A        LSR
BA89  D0 D6     BNE $BA61
BA8B  60        RTS

******************************   ARG = constant (A/Y)
BA8C  85 22     STA $22
BA8E  84 23     STY $23           pointer
BA90  A0 04     LDY #$04
BA92  B1 22     LDA ($22),Y
BA94  85 6D     STA $6D
BA96  88        DEY
BA97  B1 22     LDA ($22),Y
BA99  85 6C     STA $6C
BA9B  88        DEY               constant to ARG
BA9C  B1 22     LDA ($22),Y
BA9E  85 6B     STA $6B
BAA0  88        DEY
BAA1  B1 22     LDA ($22),Y
BAA3  85 6E     STA $6E
BAA5  45 66     EOR $66
BAA7  85 6F     STA $6F
BAA9  A5 6E     LDA $6E
BAAB  09 80     ORA #$80          sign
BAAD  85 6A     STA $6A
BAAF  88        DEY
BAB0  B1 22     LDA ($22),Y
BAB2  85 69     STA $69           exponent
BAB4  A5 61     LDA $61
BAB6  60        RTS
BAB7  A5 69     LDA $69
BAB9  F0 1F     BEQ $BADA
BABB  18        CLC
BABC  65 61     ADC $61
BABE  90 04     BCC $BAC4
BAC0  30 1D     BMI $BADF
BAC2  18        CLC
BAC3  2C        .BYTE $2C
BAC4  10 14     BPL $BADA
BAC6  69 80     ADC #$80
BAC8  85 61     STA $61
BACA  D0 03     BNE $BACF
BACC  4C FB B8  JMP $B8FB         FAC=0
BACF  A5 6F     LDA $6F
BAD1  85 66     STA $66
BAD3  60        RTS
BAD4  A5 66     LDA $66
BAD6  49 FF     EOR #$FF
BAD8  30 05     BMI $BADF
BADA  68        PLA
BADB  68        PLA
BADC  4C F7 B8  JMP $B8F7         FAC=0
BADF  4C 7E B9  JMP $B97E         "OVERFLOW ERROR"

******************************   FAC = FAC * 10
BAE2  20 0C BC  JSR $BC0C         round FAC and put in ARG
```

```
BAE5   AA          TAX
BAE6   F0 10       BEQ $BAF8          if FAC=0,then ready
BAE8   18          CLC
BAE9   69 02       ADC #$02           exponent +2 = exponent *4
BAEB   B0 F2       BCS $BADF          balance?
BAED   A2 00       LDX #$00
BAEF   86 6F       STX $6F
BAF1   20 77 B8    JSR $B877          FAC=FAC+ARG, = *5
BAF4   E6 61       INC $61            increase exponent, = *2
BAF6   F0 E7       BEQ $BADF          balance, then "OVERFLOW"
BAF8   60          RTS

******************************
BAF9 84 20 00 00 00                   floating point constant 10

******************************       FAC = FAC / 10
BAFE   20 0C BC    JSR $BC0C          round FAC and put in ARG
BB01   A9 F9       LDA #$F9
BB03   A0 BA       LDY #$BA           pointer to constant 10
BB05   A2 00       LDX #$00
BB07   86 6F       STX $6F
BB09   20 A2 BB    JSR $BBA2          constant 10 in FAC
BB0C   4C 12 BB    JMP $BB12          FAC = ARG / FAC

******************************       FAC = constant (A/Y) / FAC
BB0F   20 8C BA    JSR $BA8C          constant (A/Y) to ARG

******************************       FAC = ARG / FAC
BB12   F0 76       BEQ $BB8A          FAC=0, "DIVISION BY ZERO"
BB14   20 1B BC    JSR $BC1B          round FAC
BB17   A9 00       LDA #$00
BB19   38          SEC
BB1A   E5 61       SBC $61
BB1C   85 61       STA $61
BB1E   20 B7 BA    JSR $BAB7          determine exponent of result
BB21   E6 61       INC $61
BB23   F0 BA       BEQ $BADF          exponent overflow
BB25   A2 FC       LDX #$FC           pointer to function register
BB27   A9 01       LDA #$01
BB29   A4 6A       LDY $6A
BB2B   C4 62       CPY $62
BB2D   D0 10       BNE $BB3F
BB2F   A4 6B       LDY $6B
BB31   C4 63       CPY $63            compare ARG to FAC bitwise
BB33   D0 0A       BNE $BB3F
BB35   A4 6C       LDY $6C
BB37   C4 64       CPY $64
BB39   D0 04       BNE $BB3F
BB3B   A4 6D       LDY $6D
BB3D   C4 65       CPY $65
BB3F   08          PHP                save status
BB40   2A          ROL
BB41   90 09       BCC $BB4C
BB43   E8          INX
BB44   95 29       STA $29,X
BB46   F0 32       BEQ $BB7A
```

```
BB48  10 34     BPL $BB7E
BB4A  A9 01     LDA #$01
BB4C  28        PLP
BB4D  B0 0E     BCS $BB5D
BB4F  06 6D     ASL $6D
BB51  26 6C     ROL $6C
BB53  26 6B     ROL $6B
BB55  26 6A     ROL $6A
BB57  B0 E6     BCS $BB3F
BB59  30 CE     BMI $BB29
BB5B  10 E2     BPL $BB3F
BB5D  A8        TAY
BB5E  A5 6D     LDA $6D
BB60  E5 65     SBC $65
BB62  85 6D     STA $6D
BB64  A5 6C     LDA $6C
BB66  E5 64     SBC $64
BB68  85 6C     STA $6C
BB6A  A5 6B     LDA $6B
BB6C  E5 63     SBC $63
BB6E  85 6B     STA $6B
BB70  A5 6A     LDA $6A
BB72  E5 62     SBC $62
BB74  85 6A     STA $6A
BB76  98        TYA
BB77  4C 4F BB  JMP $BB4F
BB7A  A9 40     LDA #$40
BB7C  D0 CE     BNE $BB4C
BB7E  0A        ASL
BB7F  0A        ASL
BB80  0A        ASL                  accumulator * 64
BB81  0A        ASL
BB82  0A        ASL
BB83  0A        ASL
BB84  85 70     STA $70
BB86  28        PLP
BB87  4C 8F BB  JMP $BB8F            help register to FAC

*****************************
BB8A  A2 14     LDX #$14             # for "DIVISION BY ZERO"
BB8C  4C 37 A4  JMP $A437            out-put error message

*****************************        Transfer help register ($26-
BB8F  A5 26     LDA $26                                  $29) to FAC
BB91  85 62     STA $62
BB93  A5 27     LDA $27
BB95  85 63     STA $63
BB97  A5 28     LDA $28
BB99  85 64     STA $64
BB9B  A5 29     LDA $29
BB9D  85 65     STA $65
BB9F  4C D7 B8  JMP $B8D7            make FAC left-binding

*****************************        Transfer constant(A/Y) to FAC
BBA2  85 22     STA $22
```

```
BBA4   84 23     STY $23            set pointer
BBA6   A0 04     LDY #$04
BBA8   B1 22     LDA ($22),Y
BBAA   85 65     STA $65
BBAC   88        DEY
BBAD   B1 22     LDA ($22),Y
BBAF   85 64     STA $64
BBB1   88        DEY                mantisse
BBB2   B1 22     LDA ($22),Y
BBB4   85 63     STA $63
BBB6   88        DEY
BBB7   B1 22     LDA ($22),Y
BBB9   85 66     STA $66
BBBB   09 80     ORA #$80           sign for mantisse
BBBD   85 62     STA $62
BBBF   88        DEY
BBC0   B1 22     LDA ($22),Y
BBC2   85 61     STA $61            exponent
BBC4   84 70     STY $70
BBC6   60        RTS

*****************************      Transfer FAC to accum. #4
BBC7   A2 5C     LDX #$5C           address low of accum. #4
BBC9   2C        .BYTE #$2C

*****************************      Transfer FAC to accum. #3
BBCA   A2 57     LDX #$57           address low of accum. #3
BBCC   A0 00     LDY #$00           address high
BBCE   F0 04     BEQ $BBD4          absolute jump

*****************************      Transfer FAC to variable
BBD0   A6 49     LDX $49
BBD2   A4 4A     LDY $4A            variable address
BBD4   20 1B BC  JSR $BC1B          round FAC
BBD7   86 22     STX $22
BBD9   84 23     STY $23            pointer to target address
BBDB   A0 04     LDY #$04
BBDD   A5 65     LDA $65
BBDF   91 22     STA ($22),Y
BBE1   88        DEY
BBE2   A5 64     LDA $64
BBE4   91 22     STA ($22),Y
BBE6   88        DEY
BBE7   A5 63     LDA $63
BBE9   91 22     STA ($22),Y
BBEB   88        DEY
BBEC   A5 66     LDA $66
BBEE   09 7F     ORA #$7F
BBF0   25 62     AND $62            get signs on memory format
BBF2   91 22     STA ($22),Y
BBF4   88        DEY
BBF5   A5 61     LDA $61
BBF7   91 22     STA ($22),Y
BBF9   84 70     STY $70
BBFB   60        RTS
```

```
********************************   Transfer ARG to FAC
BBFC  A5 6E     LDA $6E
BBFE  85 66     STA $66
BC00  A2 05     LDX #$05              5 bytes
BC02  B5 68     LDA $68,X
BC04  95 60     STA $60,X
BC06  CA        DEX
BC07  D0 F9     BNE $BC02
BC09  86 70     STX $70
BC0B  60        RTS

********************************   Transfer FAC to ARG
BC0C  20 1B BC  JSR $BC1B             round FAC
BC0F  A2 06     LDX #$06
BC11  B5 60     LDA $60,X
BC13  95 68     STA $68,X
BC15  CA        DEX
BC16  D0 F9     BNE $BC11
BC18  86 70     STX $70
BC1A  60        RTS

********************************   Round FAC
BC1B  A5 61     LDA $61               exponent zero, then ready
BC1D  F0 FB     BEQ $BC1A
BC1F  06 70     ASL $70               rounding place bigger $7F?
BC21  90 F7     BCC $BC1A             no, then ready
BC23  20 6F B9  JSR $B96F             increase mantisse by one
BC26  D0 F2     BNE $BC1A             now zero?
BC28  4C 38 B9  JMP $B938             shift right; increase
                                                exponent
********************************   Get sign of FAC
BC2B  A5 61     LDA $61               zero?
BC2D  F0 09     BEQ $BC38
BC2F  A5 66     LDA $66
BC31  2A        ROL
BC32  A9 FF     LDA #$FF              negative?
BC34  B0 02     BCS $BC38
BC36  A9 01     LDA #$01              positive?
BC38  60        RTS

********************************   BASIC-SGN function
BC39  20 2B BC  JSR $BC2B             get sign
BC3C  85 62     STA $62
BC3E  A9 00     LDA #$00
BC40  85 63     STA $63
BC42  A2 88     LDX #$88
BC44  A5 62     LDA $62
BC46  49 FF     EOR #$FF
BC48  2A        ROL
BC49  A9 00     LDA #$00
BC4B  85 65     STA $65
BC4D  85 64     STA $64
BC4F  86 61     STX $61
```

```
BC51   85 70     STA $70
BC53   85 66     STA $66
BC55   4C D2 B8  JMP $B8D2

*****************************   BASIC-ABS function
BC58   46 66     LSR $66         clear sign bit
BC5A   60        RTS

*****************************   Compare constant(A/Y) with
BC5B   85 24     STA $24                                 FAC
BC5D   84 25     STY $25         pointer to constant
BC5F   A0 00     LDY #$00
BC61   B1 24     LDA ($24),Y     exponent
BC63   C8        INY
BC64   AA        TAX
BC65   F0 C4     BEQ $BC2B       zero, then get sign of FAC
BC67   B1 24     LDA ($24),Y
BC69   45 66     EOR $66
BC6B   30 C2     BMI $BC2F       differen signs
BC6D   E4 61     CPX $61
BC6F   D0 21     BNE $BC92
BC71   B1 24     LDA ($24),Y     compare 1. byte
BC73   09 80     ORA #$80
BC75   C5 62     CMP $62
BC77   D0 19     BNE $BC92
BC79   C8        INY
BC7A   B1 24     LDA ($24),Y     compare 2. byte
BC7C   C5 63     CMP $63
BC7E   D0 12     BNE $BC92
BC80   C8        INY
BC81   B1 24     LDA ($24),Y     compare 3. byte
BC83   C5 64     CMP $64
BC85   D0 0B     BNE $BC92
BC87   C8        INY
BC88   A9 7F     LDA #$7F
BC8A   C5 70     CMP $70
BC8C   B1 24     LDA ($24),Y     compare 4. byte
BC8E   E5 65     SBC $65
BC90   F0 28     BEQ $BCBA
BC92   A5 66     LDA $66
BC94   90 02     BCC $BC98
BC96   49 FF     EOR #$FF        result smaller, then invert
BC98   4C 31 BC  JMP $BC31       set flag for result

*****************************   Change floating-point to
BC9B   A5 61     LDA $61         exponent           integer
BC9D   F0 4A     BEQ $BCE9       zero?
BC9F   38        SEC
BCA0   E9 A0     SBC #$A0
BCA2   24 66     BIT $66
BCA4   10 09     BPL $BCAF
BCA6   AA        TAX
BCA7   A9 FF     LDA #$FF
BCA9   85 68     STA $68
BCAB   20 4D B9  JSR $B94D       invert mantisse of FAC
BCAE   8A        TXA
```

```
BCAF   A2 61      LDX ##$61
BCB1   C9 F9      CMP ##$F9
BCB3   10 06      BPL $BCBB
BCB5   20 99 B9   JSR $B999          shift FAC right
BCB8   84 68      STY $68
BCBA   60         RTS
BCBB   A8         TAY
BCBC   A5 66      LDA $66
BCBE   29 80      AND ##$80
BCC0   46 62      LSR $62
BCC2   05 62      ORA $62
BCC4   85 62      STA $62
BCC6   20 B0 B9   JSR $B9B0          shift FAC right bitwise
BCC9   84 68      STY $68
BCCB   60         RTS

*****************************       BASIC-INT function
BCCC   A5 61      LDA $61            exponent
BCCE   C9 A0      CMP ##$A0          whole number?
BCD0   B0 20      BCS $BCF2          yes, then ready
BCD2   20 9B BC   JSR $BC9B          change FAC to integer
BCD5   84 70      STY $70
BCD7   A5 66      LDA $66
BCD9   84 66      STY $66
BCDB   49 80      EOR ##$80
BCDD   2A         ROL
BCDE   A9 A0      LDA ##$A0
BCE0   85 61      STA $61
BCE2   A5 65      LDA $65
BCE4   85 07      STA $07
BCE6   4C D2 B8   JMP $B8D2          make FAC left-binding
BCE9   85 62      STA $62            fill mantise with zeros
BCEB   85 63      STA $63
BCED   85 64      STA $64
BCEF   85 65      STA $65
BCF1   A8         TAY
BCF2   60         RTS

*****************************       Change ASCII to Floating
BCF3   A0 00      LDY ##$00          point format
BCF5   A2 0A      LDX ##$0A          clear range $5D to $66
BCF7   94 5D      STY $5D,X
BCF9   CA         DEX
BCFA   10 FB      BPL $BCF7
BCFC   90 0F      BCC $BD0D
BCFE   C9 2D      CMP ##$2D          "-"
BD00   D0 04      BNE $BD06
BD02   86 67      STX $67            flag for negative
BD04   F0 04      BEQ $BD0A
BD06   C9 2B      CMP ##$2B          "+"
BD08   D0 05      BNE $BD0F
BD0A   20 73 00   JSR $0073          CHRGET get next character
BD0D   90 5B      BCC $BD6A
BD0F   C9 2E      CMP ##$2E          "."
BD11   F0 2E      BEQ $BD41
```

```
BD13  C9 45     CMP #$45      "E"
BD15  D0 30     BNE $BD47
BD17  20 73 00  JSR $0073     CHRGET get next character
BD1A  90 17     BCC $BD33
BD1C  C9 AB     CMP #$AB      "-" BASIC code
BD1E  F0 0E     BEQ $BD2E
BD20  C9 2D     CMP #$2D      "-"
BD22  F0 0A     BEQ $BD2E
BD24  C9 AA     CMP #$AA      "+" BASIC code
BD26  F0 08     BEQ $BD30
BD28  C9 2B     CMP #$2B      "+"
BD2A  F0 04     BEQ $BD30
BD2C  D0 07     BNE $BD35
BD2E  66 60     ROR $60       set bit 7
BD30  20 73 00  JSR $0073     CHRGET get next character
BD33  90 5C     BCC $BD91
BD35  24 60     BIT $60       bit 7 set?
BD37  10 0E     BPL $BD47     no
BD39  A9 00     LDA #$00
BD3B  38        SEC
BD3C  E5 5E     SBC $5E
BD3E  4C 49 BD  JMP $BD49
BD41  66 5F     ROR $5F       call by decimal point
BD43  24 5F     BIT $5F
BD45  50 C3     BVC $BD0A
BD47  A5 5E     LDA $5E
BD49  38        SEC
BD4A  E5 5D     SBC $5D
BD4C  85 5E     STA $5E
BD4E  F0 12     BEQ $BD62
BD50  10 09     BPL $BD5B
BD52  20 FE BA  JSR $BAFE     FAC = FAC / 10
BD55  E6 5E     INC $5E
BD57  D0 F9     BNE $BD52
BD59  F0 07     BEQ $BD62
BD5B  20 E2 BA  JSR $BAE2     FAC = FAC * 10
BD5E  C6 5E     DEC $5E
BD60  D0 F9     BNE $BD5B
BD62  A5 67     LDA $67
BD64  30 01     BMI $BD67
BD66  60        RTS
BD67  4C B4 BF  JMP $BFB4     change of sign FAC = -FAC

BD6A  48        PHA
BD6B  24 5F     BIT $5F
BD6D  10 02     BPL $BD71
BD6F  E6 5D     INC $5D
BD71  20 E2 BA  JSR $BAE2     FAC = FAC * 10
BD74  68        PLA
BD75  38        SEC
BD76  E9 30     SBC #$30      ASCII - $30 Hex
BD78  20 7E BD  JSR $BD7E     add next digit to FAC
BD7B  4C 0A BD  JMP $BD0A     next character
BD7E  48        PHA
BD7F  20 0C BC  JSR $BC0C     FAC to ARG
BD82  68        PLA
```

```
BD83   20 3C BC JSR $BC3C
BD86   A5 6E    LDA $6E
BD88   45 66    EOR $66
BD8A   85 6F    STA $6F
BD8C   A6 61    LDX $61
BD8E   4C 6A B8 JMP $B86A        FAC = FAC + ARG
BD91   A5 5E    LDA $5E          call by "E"
BD93   C9 0A    CMP #$0A
BD95   90 09    BCC $BDA0
BD97   A9 64    LDA #$64
BD99   24 60    BIT $60
BD9B   30 11    BMI $BDAE
BD9D   4C 7E B9 JMP $B97E        "OVERFLOW ERROR"
BDA0   0A       ASL
BDA1   0A       ASL
BDA2   18       CLC
BDA3   65 5E    ADC $5E
BDA5   0A       ASL
BDA6   18       CLC
BDA7   A0 00    LDY #$00
BDA9   71 7A    ADC ($7A),Y
BDAB   38       SEC
BDAC   E9 30    SBC #$30
BDAE   85 5E    STA $5E
BDB0   4C 30 BD JMP $BD30        get next character

*****************************   Constants for floating point
BDB3   9B 3E BC 1F FD            99999999.9
BDB8   9E 6E 6B 27 FD            999999999
BDBD   9E 6E 6B 28 00            1E9

*****************************   Out-put line # at error mesg
BDC2   A9 71    LDA #$71
BDC4   A0 A3    LDY #$A3         pointer to "IN"
BDC6   20 DA BD JSR $BDDA        output string
BDC9   A5 3A    LDA $3A
BDCB   A6 39    LDX $39          get current line number

*****************************   Out-put positive integer #
                                                  in A/X
BDCD   85 62    STA $62
BDCF   86 63    STX $63          write for change in FAC
BDD1   A2 90    LDX #$90
BDD3   38       SEC
BDD4   20 49 BC JSR $BC49        change integer to floating
BDD7   20 DF BD JSR $BDDF        change FAC to ASCII   point
BDDA   4C 1E AB JMP $AB1E        out-put string

*****************************   Change FAC to ASCII and put
                                                  in $100
BDDD   A0 01    LDY #$01
BDDF   A9 20    LDA #$20         " " space for positive #
BDE1   24 66    BIT $66          sign
BDE3   10 02    BPL $BDE7        positive?
BDE5   A9 2D    LDA #$2D         "-" minus for negative #
BDE7   99 FF 00 STA $00FF,Y      write in buffer range
BDEA   85 66    STA $66
BDEC   84 71    STY $71
```

```
BDEE  C8        INY
BDEF  A9 30     LDA #$30          "0"
BDF1  A6 61     LDX $61           exponent
BDF3  D0 03     BNE $BDF8         number not zero?
BDF5  4C 04 BF  JMP $BF04         yes, ready
BDF8  A9 00     LDA #$00
BDFA  E0 80     CPX #$80          compare FAC with 1
BDFC  F0 02     BEQ $BE00
BDFE  B0 09     BCS $BE09         FAC bigger than 1
BE00  A9 BD     LDA #$BD
BE02  A0 BD     LDY #$BD          pointer to constant 1E9
BE04  20 28 BA  JSR $BA28         constant (pointer A/Y) *FAC
BE07  A9 F7     LDA #$F7
BE09  85 5D     STA $5D
BE0B  A9 B8     LDA #$B8
BE0D  A0 BD     LDY #$BD          pntr to constant 999999999
BE0F  20 5B BC  JSR $BC5B         compare constant (pointer
BE12  F0 1E     BEQ $BE32         equal            A/Y with FAC
BE14  10 12     BPL $BE28
BE16  A9 B3     LDA #$B3
BE18  A0 BD     LDY #$BD          pntr to constant 99999999.9
BE1A  20 5B BC  JSR $BC5B         compare constant (pointer
BE1D  F0 02     BEQ $BE21                          A/Y with FAC
BE1F  10 0E     BPL $BE2F
BE21  20 E2 BA  JSR $BAE2
BE24  C6 5D     DEC $5D           FAC = FAC * 10
BE26  D0 EE     BNE $BE16
BE28  20 FE BA  JSR $BAFE
BE2B  E6 5D     INC $5D           FAC = FAC / 10
BE2D  D0 DC     BNE $BE0B
BE2F  20 49 B8  JSR $B849
BE32  20 9B BC  JSR $BC9B         FAC = FAC + .5, round
BE35  A2 01     LDX #$01          FAC to integer
BE37  A5 5D     LDA $5D
BE39  18        CLC
BE3A  69 0A     ADC #$0A
BE3C  30 09     BMI $BE47
BE3E  C9 0B     CMP #$0B          amount smaller 0.1?
BE40  B0 06     BCS $BE48
BE42  69 FF     ADC #$FF          amount greater 1E9?

BE44  AA        TAX
BE45  A9 02     LDA #$02
BE47  38        SEC
BE48  E9 02     SBC #$02
BE4A  85 5E     STA $5E
BE4C  86 5D     STX $5D
BE4E  8A        TXA
BE4F  F0 02     BEQ $BE53
BE51  10 13     BPL $BE66
BE53  A4 71     LDY $71
BE55  A9 2E     LDA #$2E          "."
BE57  C8        INY
BE58  99 FF 00  STA $00FF,Y
BE5B  8A        TXA
```

```
BE5C  F0 06     BEQ $BE64
BE5E  A9 30     LDA #$30           "0"
BE60  C8        INY
BE61  99 FF 00  STA $00FF,Y
BE64  84 71     STY $71
BE66  A0 00     LDY #$00
BE68  A2 80     LDX #$80           calculation of the seperate
BE6A  A5 65     LDA $65                                 digits
BE6C  18        CLC
BE6D  79 19 BF  ADC $BF19,Y
BE70  85 65     STA $65
BE72  A5 64     LDA $64
BE74  79 18 BF  ADC $BF18,Y
BE77  85 64     STA $64
BE79  A5 63     LDA $63
BE7B  79 17 BF  ADC $BF17,Y
BE7E  85 63     STA $63
BE80  A5 62     LDA $62
BE82  79 16 BF  ADC $BF16,Y
BE85  85 62     STA $62
BE87  E8        INX
BE88  B0 04     BCS $BE8E
BE8A  10 DE     BPL $BE6A
BE8C  30 02     BMI $BE90
BE8E  30 DA     BMI $BE6A
BE90  8A        TXA
BE91  90 04     BCC $BE97
BE93  49 FF     EOR #$FF
BE95  69 0A     ADC #$0A
BE97  69 2F     ADC #$2F
BE99  C8        INY
BE9A  C8        INY
BE9B  C8        INY
BE9C  C8        INY
BE9D  84 47     STY $47
BE9F  A4 71     LDY $71
BEA1  C8        INY
BEA2  AA        TAX
BEA3  29 7F     AND #$7F
BEA5  99 FF 00  STA $00FF,Y
BEA8  C6 5D     DEC $5D
BEAA  D0 06     BNE $BEB2
BEAC  A9 2E     LDA #$2E           "."
BEAE  C8        INY
BEAF  99 FF 00  STA $00FF,Y
BEB2  84 71     STY $71
BEB4  A4 47     LDY $47
BEB6  8A        TXA
BEB7  49 FF     EOR #$FF
BEB9  29 80     AND #$80
BEBB  AA        TAX
BEBC  C0 24     CPY #$24           table-end at FAC-change
BEBE  F0 04     BEQ $BEC4
BEC0  C0 3C     CPY #$3C           table-end at TI$ calculation
BEC2  D0 A6     BNE $BE6A
```

```
BEC4  A4 71     LDY $71
BEC6  B9 FF 00  LDA $00FF,Y
BEC9  88        DEY
BECA  C9 30     CMP #$30            "0"
BECC  F0 F8     BEQ $BEC6
BECE  C9 2E     CMP #$2E            "."
BED0  F0 01     BEQ $BED3
BED2  C8        INY
BED3  A9 2B     LDA #$2B            "+"
BED5  A6 5E     LDX $5E
BED7  F0 2E     BEQ $BF07
BED9  10 08     BPL $BEE3
BEDB  A9 00     LDA #$00
BEDD  38        SEC
BEDE  E5 5E     SBC $5E
BEE0  AA        TAX
BEE1  A9 2D     LDA #$2D            "-"
BEE3  99 01 01  STA $0101,Y
BEE6  A9 45     LDA #$45            "E"
BEE8  99 00 01  STA $0100,Y
BEEB  8A        TXA
BEEC  A2 2F     LDX #$2F
BEEE  38        SEC
BEEF  E8        INX
BEF0  E9 0A     SBC #$0A
BEF2  B0 FB     BCS $BEEF
BEF4  69 3A     ADC #$3A
BEF6  99 03 01  STA $0103,Y
BEF9  8A        TXA
BEFA  99 02 01  STA $0102,Y
BEFD  A9 00     LDA #$00            end buffer with $00
BEFF  99 04 01  STA $0104,Y
BF02  F0 08     BEQ $BF0C
BF04  99 FF 00  STA $00FF,Y
BF07  A9 00     LDA #$00            end buffer with $00
BF09  99 00 01  STA $0100,Y
BF0C  A9 00     LDA #$00
BF0E  A0 01     LDY #$01            pointer to buffer $100
BF10  60        RTS

******************************
BF11  80 00 00 00 00                constant 0.5 for SQR

******************************      Constants for Floating-point
                                     32 bit #s with signs
BF16  FA 0A 1F 00                    100 000 000
BF1A  00 98 96 80                     10 000 000
BF1E  FF F0 BD C0                      1 000 000
BF22  00 01 86 A0                        100 000
BF26  FF FF D8 F0                         10 000
BF2A  00 00 03 E8                          1 000
BF2E  FF FF FF 9C                            100
BF32  00 00 00 0A                             10
BF36  FF FF FF FF                              1
```

```
*******************************    Constants for change from TI
BF3A  FF DF 0A 80                   2 160 000              to TI$
BF3E  00 03 4B C0                     216 000
BF42  FF FF 73 60                      36 000
BF46  00 00 0E 10                       3 600
BF4A  FF FF FD A8                         600
BF4E  00 00 00 3C                          60
BF52  EC

BF53  AA ...
BF70  ... AA

*******************************    BASIC-SQR function
BF71  20 0C BC JSR $BC0C            round FAC and put in ARG
BF74  A9 11    LDA #$11
BF76  A0 BF    LDY #$BF             pointer to constant 0.5

*******************************    FAC=ARG ^ constant (A/Y)
BF78  20 A2 BB JSR $BBA2            constant to FAC

*******************************    FAC=ARG ^ FAC
BF7B  F0 70    BEQ $BFED
BF7D  A5 69    LDA $69              exponent ARG = basis?
BF7F  D0 03    BNE $BF84            not zero?
BF81  4C F9 B8 JMP $B8F9            ready
BF84  A2 4E    LDX #$4E
BF86  A0 00    LDY #$00             pointer to helping accum.
BF88  20 D4 BB JSR $BBD4            FAC to helping accumulator
BF8B  A5 6E    LDA $6E             exponent FAC= power exponent
BF8D  10 0F    BPL $BF9E            smaller one?
BF8F  20 CC BC JSR $BCCC            INT function
BF92  A9 4E    LDA #$4E
BF94  A0 00    LDY #$00             pointer to helping accum.
BF96  20 5B BC JSR $BC5B            compare with FAC
BF99  D0 03    BNE $BF9E
BF9B  98       TYA
BF9C  A4 07    LDY $07
BF9E  20 FE BB JSR $BBFE            ARG to FAC
BFA1  98       TYA
BFA2  48       PHA
BFA3  20 EA B9 JSR $B9EA            LOG function
BFA6  A9 4E    LDA #$4E
BFA8  A0 00    LDY #$00             pointer to helping accum.
BFAA  20 28 BA JSR $BA28            multiply with FAC
BFAD  20 ED BF JSR $BFED            EXP function
BFB0  68       PLA
BFB1  4A       LSR
BFB2  90 0A    BCC $BFBE
BFB4  A5 61    LDA $61              exponent
BFB6  F0 06    BEQ $BFBE
BFB8  A5 66    LDA $66
BFBA  49 FF    EOR #$FF             invert
BFBC  85 66    STA $66
BFBE  60       RTS
```

```
******************************   Constants for EXP
BFBF   81 38 AA 3B 29             1.44269504 = 1/LOG(2)
BFC4   07                         7 = polynome degree
BFC5   71 34 58 3E 56             2.14987637E-5
BFCA   74 16 7E B3 1B             1.4352314E-4
BFCF   77 2F EE E3 85             1.34226348E-3
BFD4   7A 1D 84 1C 2A             9.614011701E-3
BFD9   7C 63 59 58 9A             .055051269
BFDE   7E 75 FD E7 C6             .240226385
BFE3   80 31 72 18 10             .693147186
BFE8   81 00 00 00 00             1

******************************   BASIC-EXP function
BFED   A9 BF      LDA #$BF
BFEF   A0 BF      LDY #$BF       pointer to constant 1/LOG(2)
BFF1   20 28 BA JSR $BA28         multiply with FAC
BFF4   A5 70      LDA $70
BFF6   69 50      ADC #$50
BFF8   90 03      BCC $BFFD
BFFA   20 23 BC JSR $BC23         increase mantissa of FAC by
                                                          one
BFFD   4C 00 E0 JMP $E000
E000   85 56      STA $56
E002   20 0F BC JSR $BC0F         get FAC to ARG
E005   A5 61      LDA $61         exponent
E007   C9 88      CMP #$88        number larger than 128?
E009   90 03      BCC $E00E
E00B   20 D4 BA JSR $BAD4         in positive, "OVERFLOW"
E00E   20 CC BC JSR $BCCC         INT function
E011   A5 07      LDA $07
E013   18         CLC
E014   69 81      ADC #$81
E016   F0 F3      BEQ $E00B       eaual to 127?
E018   38         SEC
E019   E9 01      SBC #$01
E01B   48         PHA
E01C   A2 05      LDX #$05
E01E   B5 69      LDA $69,X
E020   B4 61      LDY $61,X       switch FAC and ARG
E022   95 61      STA $61,X
E024   94 69      STY $69,X
E026   CA         DEX
E027   10 F5      BPL $E01E
E029   A5 56      LDA $56
E02B   85 70      STA $70
E02D   20 53 B8 JSR $B853         ARG-FAC
E030   20 B4 BF JSR $BFB4         change of sign
E033   A9 C4      LDA #$C4
E035   A0 BF      LDY #$BF        pointer to polynome coef.
E037   20 59 E0 JSR $E059         calculate polynome
E03A   A9 00      LDA #$00
E03C   85 6F      STA $6F
E03E   68         PLA
E03F   20 B9 BA JSR $BAB9         + exponents of FAC and ARG
E042   60         RTS
```

```
*****************************   Polynome calculations y=a1*x
                                          +a1*x^3+a3*x^5
E043  85 71     STA $71          pointer to polynome degree
E045  84 72     STY $72
E047  20 CA BB  JSR $BBCA        bring FAC ot accum. #3
E04A  A9 57     LDA #$57         pointer to accum. #3
E04C  20 28 BA  JSR $BA28        FAC * accum. #3 (square)
E04F  20 5D E0  JSR $E05D        polynome calculation
E052  A9 57     LDA #$57
E054  A0 00     LDY #$00         pointer to accum. #3
E056  4C 28 BA  JMP $BA28        FAC = FAC * accum. #3

*****************************   Polynome calc. y=a0+a1*x+a2*
                                          x^2+a3*x^3
E059  85 71     STA $71          pointer to polynome degree
E05B  84 72     STY $72
E05D  20 C7 BB  JSR $BBC7        bring FAC to accum #4
E060  B1 71     LDA ($71),Y      polynome degree
E062  85 67     STA $67          as counter
E064  A4 71     LDY $71
E066  C8        INY
E067  98        TYA              increase pointer, shows
E068  D0 02     BNE $E06C          then on first coefficient
E06A  E6 72     INC $72
E06C  85 71     STA $71
E06E  A4 72     LDY $72
E070  20 28 BA  JSR $BA28        FAC = FAC * constant (A/Y)
E073  A5 71     LDA $71
E075  A4 72     LDY $72
E077  18        CLC
E078  69 05     ADC #$05         add 5 to pointer, next #
E07A  90 01     BCC $E07D
E07C  C8        INY
E07D  85 71     STA $71
E07F  84 72     STY $72
E081  20 67 B8  JSR $B867        FAC = FAC + constant (A/Y)
E084  A9 5C     LDA #$5C
E086  A0 00     LDY #$00         pointer to accum. #4
E088  C6 67     DEC $67          decrease counter
E08A  D0 E4     BNE $E070
E08C  60        RTS

*****************************   Constant for RND
E08D  98 35 44 7A 00             11879546
E092  68 28 B1 46 00             3.92767774E-4

*****************************   BASIC-RND function
E097  20 2B BC  JSR $BC2B        get sign
E09A  30 37     BMI $E0D3        negative?
E09C  D0 20     BNE $E0BE
E09E  20 F3 FF  JSR $FFF3        get basic address CIA
E0A1  86 22     STX $22
E0A3  84 23     STY $23          save as pointer
E0A5  A0 04     LDY #$04
E0A7  B1 22     LDA ($22),Y      timer 1 low
E0A9  85 62     STA $62
```

```
E0AB   C8          INY
E0AC   B1 22       LDA ($22),Y        timer 1 high
E0AE   85 64       STA $64
E0B0   A0 08       LDY #$08
E0B2   B1 22       LDA ($22),Y        timer 2 low
E0B4   85 63       STA $63
E0B6   C8          INY
E0B7   B1 22       LDA ($22),Y        timer 2 high
E0B9   85 65       STA $65
E0BB   4C E3 E0 JMP $E0E3
E0BE   A9 8B       LDA #$8B
E0C0   A0 00       LDY #$00           pointer to last RND value
E0C2   20 A2 BB JSR $BBA2           put in FAC
E0C5   A9 8D       LDA #$8D
E0C7   A0 E0       LDY #$E0           pointer to constant
E0C9   20 28 BA JSR $BA28           FAC = FAC * constant
E0CC   A9 92       LDA #$92
E0CE   A0 E0       LDY #$E0           pointer to constant
E0D0   20 67 B8 JSR $B867           FAC = FAC + constant
E0D3   A6 65       LDX $65
E0D5   A5 62       LDA $62
E0D7   85 65       STA $65
E0D9   86 62       STX $62            switch digits in FAC
E0DB   A6 63       LDX $63
E0DD   A5 64       LDA $64
E0DF   85 63       STA $63
E0E1   86 64       STX $64
E0E3   A9 00       LDA #$00
E0E5   85 66       STA $66
E0E7   A5 61       LDA $61
E0E9   85 70       STA $70
E0EB   A9 80       LDA #$80           exponent
E0ED   85 61       STA $61
E0EF   20 D7 B8 JSR $B8D7           make FAC left binding
E0F2   A2 8B       LDX #$8B
E0F4   A0 00       LDY #$00
E0F6   4C D4 BB JMP $BBD4           round FAC and save
E0F9   C9 F0       CMP #$F0
E0FB   D0 07       BNE $E104
E0FD   84 38       STY $38            set BASIC-RAM end
E0FF   86 37       STX $37
E101   4C 63 A6 JMP $A663           to CLR command
E104   AA          TAX
E105   D0 02       BNE $E109
E107   A2 1E       LDX #$1E           number for "BREAK"
E109   4C 37 A4 JMP $A437           out-put error message

*****************************        BASIC BSOUT
E10C   20 D2 FF JSR $FFD2           out-put a character
E10F   B0 E8       BCS $E0F9
E111   60          RTS

*****************************        BASIC BASIN
E112   20 CF FF JSR $FFCF           get a character
E115   B0 E2       BCS $E0F9
E117   60          RTS
```

```
*****************************    BASIC CKOUT
E118  20 AD E4 JSR $E4AD          set output device
E11B  B0 DC    BCS $E0F9
E11D  60       RTS

*****************************    BAISC CHKIN
E11E  20 C6 FF JSR $FFC6          set input device
E121  B0 D6    BCS $E0F9
E123  60       RTS

*****************************    BASIC GETIN
E124  20 E4 FF JSR $FFE4          get a character
E127  B0 D0    BCS $E0F9
E129  60       RTS

*****************************    SYS command
E12A  20 8A AD JSR $AD8A          FRMNVM, get numeric term
E12D  20 F7 B7 JSR $B7F7          change to address format
E130  A9 E1    LDA #$E1
E132  48       PHA                return address on stack
E133  A9 46    LDA #$46
E135  48       PHA
E136  AD 0F 03 LDA $030F          status
E139  48       PHA
E13A  AD 0C 03 LDA $030C          accumulator
E13D  AE 0D 03 LDX $030D          switch X register
E140  AC 0E 03 LDY $030E            and Y register
E143  28       PLP                  set status
E144  6C 14 00 JMP ($0014)        call routine
E147  08       PHP                save status
E148  8D 0C 03 STA $030C          accumulator
E14B  8E 0D 03 STX $030D          save X register,
E14E  8C 0E 03 STY $030E           Y register, and
E151  68       PLA
E152  8D 0F 03 STA $030F           status again
E155  60       RTS

*****************************    SAVE command
E156  20 D4 E1 JSR $E1D4          parameter (name, prim, sec)
E159  A6 2D    LDX $2D            end address= BASIC prgm end
E15B  A4 2E    LDY $2E
E15D  A9 2B    LDA #$2B           start address = pointer to
E15F  20 D8 FF JSR $FFD8          save routine      BASIC start
E162  B0 95    BCS $E0F9
E164  60       RTS

*****************************    VERIFY command
E165  A9 01    LDA #$01           verify flag
E167  2C       .BYTE $2C

*****************************    LOAD command
E168  A9 00    LDA #$00           load flag
E16A  85 0A    STA $0A            save
E16C  20 D4 E1 JSR $E1D4          get parameters
```

```
E16F   A5 0A     LDA $0A       flag
E171   A6 2B     LDX $2B       start address = BASIC-start
E173   A4 2C     LDY $2C
E175   20 D5 FF  JSR $FFD5     load routine
E178   B0 57     BCS $E1D1
E17A   A5 0A     LDA $0A       load/verify flag
E17C   F0 17     BEQ $E195
E17E   A2 1C     LDX #$1C      offset fo verify error
E180   20 B7 FF  JSR $FFB7     get status
E183   29 10     AND #$10      isolate error-bit
E185   D0 17     BNE $E19E     status-bit set, then error
E187   A5 7A     LDA $7A
E189   C9 02     CMP #$02      check on direct mode
E18B   F0 07     BEQ $E194     yes, the ready
E18D   A9 64     LDA #$64      pointer to "OK"
E18F   A0 A3     LDY #$A3
E191   4C 1E AB  JMP $AB1E     out-put
E194   60        RTS
E195   20 B7 FF  JSR $FFB7     get status
E198   29 BF     AND #$BF      clear EOF-bit
E19A   F0 05     BEQ $E1A1     no error
E19C   A2 1D     LDX #$1D      offset for "LOAD ERROR"
E19E   4C 37 A4  JMP $A437     out-put error message
E1A1   A5 7B     LDA $7B
E1A3   C9 02     CMP #$02      check direct mode
E1A5   D0 0E     BNE $E1B5     no, then continue
E1A7   86 2D     STX $2D       end address = program-end
E1A9   84 2E     STY $2E
E1AB   A9 76     LDA #$76      pointer on "READY."
E1AD   A0 A3     LDY #$A3
E1AF   20 1E AB  JSR $AB1E     out-put string
E1B2   4C 2A A5  JMP $A52A     find programs lines over,CLR
E1B5   20 8E A6  JSR $A68E     CHRGET pointer to start
E1B8   20 33 A5  JSR $A533     fin program lines again
E1BB   4C 77 A6  JMP $A677     initialize ROSTORE, BASIC

******************************     BASIC-OPEN command
E1BE   20 19 E2  JSR $E219     get parameter
E1C1   20 C0 FF  JSR $FFC0     OPEN routine
E1C4   B0 0B     BCS $E1D1
E1C6   60        RTS

******************************     BASIC-CLOSE command
E1C7   20 19 E2  JSR $E219     get parameter
E1CA   A5 49     LDA $49       file number
E1CC   20 C3 FF  JSR $FFC3     CLOSE routine
E1CF   90 C3     BCC $E194
E1D1   4C F9 E0  JMP $E0F9

******************************     Get parameter for LOAD/SAVE
E1D4   A9 00     LDA #$00      default for length of name
E1D6   20 BD FF  JSR $FFBD     set filename parameter
E1D9   A2 01     LDX #$01      default for device number
E1DB   A0 00     LDY #$00      default for second. address
E1DD   20 BA FF  JSR $FFBA     set file parameter
```

```
E1E0  20 06 E2 JSR $E206        further characters?
E1E3  20 57 E2 JSR $E257        get filename
E1E6  20 06 E2 JSR $E206        further characters?
E1E9  20 00 E2 JSR $E200        get parameter
E1EC  A0 00    LDY #$00
E1EE  86 49    STX $49
E1F0  20 BA FF JSR $FFBA        set file parameter
E1F3  20 06 E2 JSR $E206        more characters?
E1F6  20 00 E2 JSR $E200        get parameter
E1F9  8A       TXA
E1FA  A8       TAY
E1FB  A6 49    LDX $49
E1FD  4C BA FF JMP $FFBA        set file parameter

******************************
E200  20 0E E2 JSR $E20E        checks on "," and more let-
E203  4C 9E B7 JMP $B79E        get byte value to X    ters

******************************  Checks on further characters
E206  20 79 00 JSR $0079        CHRGOT get last character
E209  D0 02    BNE $E20D        more characters,then return
E20B  68       PLA              otherwise return to higher
E20C  68       PLA                                  routine
E20D  60       RTS

******************************
E20E  20 FD AE JSR $AEFD        checks on comma
E211  20 79 00 JSR $0079        CHRGOT get last character
E214  D0 F7    BNE $E20D        more characters,then return
E216  4C 08 AF JMP $AF08        "SYNTAX ERROR"

******************************  Get parameter for OPEN
E219  A9 00    LDA #$00         default for length of name
E21B  20 BD FF JSR $FFBD        set filename parameter
E21E  20 11 E2 JSR $E211        more characters?
E221  20 9E B7 JSR $B79E        gets logical file # to X
E224  86 49    STX $49
E226  8A       TXA
E227  A2 01    LDX #$01         default device address
E229  A0 00    LDY #$00         default for secondary addrs
E22B  20 BA FF JSR $FFBA        set file parameter
E22E  20 06 E2 JSR $E206        more characters?
E231  20 00 E2 JSR $E200        gets device address
E234  86 4A    STX $4A
E236  A0 00    LDY #$00
E238  A5 49    LDA $49
E23A  E0 03    CPX #$03
E23C  90 01    BCC $E23F
E23E  88       DEY
E23F  20 BA FF JSR $FFBA        set file parameter
E242  20 06 E2 JSR $E206        more characters?
E245  20 00 E2 JSR $E200        gets secondary address
E248  8A       TXA
E249  A8       TAY
E24A  A6 4A    LDX $4A
```

```
E24C  A5 49     LDA $49
E24E  20 BA FF  JSR $FFBA      set file parameter
E251  20 06 E2  JSR $E206      more characters?
E254  20 0E E2  JSR $E20E
E257  20 9E AD  JSR $AD9E      FRMEVL get term
E25A  20 A3 B6  JSR $B6A3      checks on string term
E25D  A6 22     LDX $22
E25F  A4 23     LDY $23
E261  4C BD FF  JMP $FFBD

*****************************  BASIC-COS function
E264  A9 E0     LDA #$E0
E266  A0 E2     LDY #$E2       pointer to constant Pi / 2
E268  20 67 B8  JSR $B867      add to FAC

*****************************  BASIC-SIN function
E26B  20 0C BC  JSR $BC0C      round FAC and put in ARG
E26E  A9 E5     LDA #$E5
E270  A0 E2     LDY #$E2       pointer to constant Pi * 2
E272  A6 6E     LDX $6E
E274  20 07 BB  JSR $BB07      divide FAC by 2 * Pi
E277  20 0C BC  JSR $BC0C      round FAC and put in ARG
E27A  20 CC BC  JSR $BCCC      INT function
E27D  A9 00     LDA #$00
E27F  85 6F     STA $6F
E281  20 53 B8  JSR $B853      ARG minus FAC
E284  A9 EA     LDA #$EA
E286  A0 E2     LDY #$E2       pointer to constant 0.25
E288  20 50 B8  JSR $B850      0.25 - FAC
E28B  A5 66     LDA $66
E28D  48        PHA            sign on stack
E28E  10 0D     BPL $E29D      positive?
E290  20 49 B8  JSR $B849      FAC + 0.5
E293  A5 66     LDA $66        sign
E295  30 09     BMI $E2A0      negative?
E297  A5 12     LDA $12
E299  49 FF     EOR #$FF       turn flag around
E29B  85 12     STA $12
E29D  20 B4 BF  JSR $BFB4      change of signs
E2A0  A9 EA     LDA #$EA
E2A2  A0 E2     LDY #$E2       pointer to constant 0.25
E2A4  20 67 B8  JSR $B867      FAA + 0.25
E2A7  68        PLA            get sign
E2A8  10 03     BPL $E2AD      positive?
E2AA  20 B4 BF  JSR $BFB4      change of sign
E2AD  A9 EF     LDA #$EF
E2AF  A0 E2     LDY #$E2       pointer to polynome coeff.
E2B1  4C 43 E0  JMP $E043      calculate polynomial

*****************************  BASIC-TAN function
E2B4  20 CA BB  JSR $BBCA      FAC to accum. #3
E2B7  A9 00     LDA #$00
E2B9  85 12     STA $12        set flag
E2BB  20 6B E2  JSR $E26B      calculate SIN
E2BE  A2 4E     LDX #$4E
```

```
E2C0  A0 00     LDY #$00         pointer to helping accum.
E2C2  20 F6 E0  JSR $E0F6        FAC to helping accumulator
E2C5  A9 57     LDA #$57
E2C7  A0 00     LDY #$00         pointer to accum. #3
E2C9  20 A2 BB  JSR $BBA2        accum. #3 to FAC
E2CC  A9 00     LDA #$00
E2CE  85 66     STA $66          sign
E2D0  A5 12     LDA $12          flag
E2D2  20 DC E2  JSR $E2DC        calculate COS
E2D5  A9 4E     LDA #$4E
E2D7  A0 00     LDY #$00         pointer to helping accum.
E2D9  4C 0F BB  JMP $BB0F        divide by FAC          (SIN)
E2DC  48        PHA
E2DD  4C 9D E2  JMP $E29D        calculate COS

******************************  Constants for SIN and COS
E2E0  81 49 0F DA A2             1.57079633  Pi/2
E2E5  83 49 0F DA A2             6.28318531  2*Pi
E2EA  7F 00 00 00 00             0.25
E2EF  05                         5 = polynomial degree
E2F0  84 E6 1A 2D 1B             -14.3813907
E2F5  86 28 07 FB F8             42.0077971
E2FA  87 99 68 89 01             -76.7041703
E2FF  87 23 35 DF E1             81.6052237
E304  86 A5 5D E7 28             -41.3147021
E309  83 49 0F DA A2             6.28318531  2*Pi

******************************  BASIC-ATN function
E30E  A5 66     LDA $66          sign
E310  48        PHA              save
E311  10 03     BPL $E316        positive?
E313  20 B4 BF  JSR $BFB4        change of signs
E316  A5 61     LDA $61          exponent
E318  48        PHA              save
E319  C9 81     CMP #$81         compare number with 1
E31B  90 07     BCC $E324        smaller?
E31D  A9 BC     LDA #$BC
E31F  A0 B9     LDY #$B9         pointer to constant 1
E321  20 0F BB  JSR $BB0F        divide 1 by FAC(reciprical)
E324  A9 3E     LDA #$3E
E326  A0 E3     LDY #$E3         pointer to polynome coeff.
E328  20 43 E0  JSR $E043        calculate polynome
E32B  68        PLA              get back exponent
E32C  C9 81     CMP #$81         was number smaller than 1?
E32E  90 07     BCC $E337
E330  A9 E0     LDA #$E0
E332  A0 E2     LDY #$E2         pointer to constant Pi/2
E334  20 50 B8  JSR $B850        Pi/2 minus FAC
E337  68        PLA              get sign
E338  10 03     BPL $E33D        positive?
E33A  4C B4 BF  JMP $BFB4        change of signs
E33D  60        RTS

******************************  Floating-point constants for
E33E  0B                         11=polynome degree       ATN
```

```
E33F  76 B3 83 BD D3              -6.84793912E-04
E344  79 1E F4 A6 F5              4.85094216E-03
E349  7B 83 FC B0 10              - .0161117015
E34E  7C 0C 1F 67 CA              .034209638
E353  7C DE 53 CB C1              - .054279133
E358  7D 14 64 70 4C              .0724571965
E35D  7D B7 EA 51 7A              - .0898019185
E362  7D 63 30 88 7E              .110932413
E367  7E 92 44 99 3A              - .142839808
E36C  7E 4C CC 91 C7              .19999912
E371  7F AA AA AA 13              -.333333316
E376  81 00 00 00 00               1

*****************************     BASIC NMI re-enterance
E37B  20 CC FF JSR $FFCC           CLRCH
E37E  A9 00    LDA #$00
E380  85 13    STA $13             input device = keyboard
E382  20 7A A6 JSR $A67A           initialize BASIC
E385  58       CLI
E386  A2 80    LDX #$80
E388  6C 00 03 JMP ($0300)         BASIC warm-start vector
E38B  8A       TXA                                (JMP $E38B)
E38C  30 03    BMI $E391
E38E  4C 3A A4 JMP $A43A           out-put error message
E391  4C 74 A4 JMP $A474           ready mode

*****************************     BASIC cold-start
E394  20 53 E4 JSR $E453           set BASIC vectors
E397  20 BF E3 JSR $E3BF           initialize RAM
E39A  20 22 E4 JSR $E422           out-put power-on message
E39D  A2 FB    LDX #$FB            set stack-pointer
E39F  9A       TXS
E3A0  D0 E4    BNE $E386           to warm-start

*****************************     Copy of CHRGET-routine
E3A2  E6 7A    INC $7A
E3A4  D0 02    BNE $E3A8
E3A6  E6 7B    INC $7B
E3A8  AD 60 EA LDA $EA60
E3AB  C9 3A    CMP #$3A
E3AD  B0 0A    BCS $E3B9
E3AF  C9 20    CMP #$20
E3B1  F0 EF    BEQ $E3A2
E3B3  38       SEC
E3B4  E9 30    SBC #$30
E3B6  38       SEC
E3B7  E9 D0    SBC #$D0
E3B9  60       RTS

*****************************     Start value for RND function
E3BA  80 4F C7 52 58               .811635157

*****************************     Initialize RAM for BASIC
E3BF  A9 4C    LDA #$4C            JMP
E3C1  85 54    STA $54             for functions
```

```
E3C3   8D 10 03 STA $0310       for USR-functions
E3C6   A9 48    LDA #$48       points to "ILLEGAL QUANTITY"
E3C8   A0 B2    LDY #$B2
E3CA   8D 11 03 STA $0311       save as USR-vector
E3CD   8C 12 03 STY $0312
E3D0   A9 91    LDA #$91        $B391
E3D2   A0 B3    LDY #$B3
E3D4   85 05    STA $05        vector for fixed to floating
E3D6   84 06    STY $06                  point conversion

E3D8   A9 AA    LDA #$AA        $B3AA
E3DA   A0 B1    LDY #$B1
E3DC   85 03    STA $03        vector for floating to fixed
E3DE   84 04    STY $04                  point conversion

E3E0   A2 1C    LDX #$1C
E3E2   BD A2 E3 LDA $E3A2,X     CHRGET-routine
E3E5   95 73    STA $73,X       copy into RAM
E3E7   CA       DEX
E3E8   10 F8    BPL $E3E2
E3EA   A9 03    LDA #$03
E3EC   85 53    STA $53         step-width for garbage-
E3EE   A9 00    LDA #$00                       collection
E3F0   85 68    STA $68
E3F2   85 13    STA $13         input-device = keyboard
E3F4   85 18    STA $18
E3F6   A2 01    LDX #$01
E3F8   8E FD 01 STX $01FD
E3FB   8E FC 01 STX $01FC
E3FE   A2 19    LDX #$19
E400   86 16    STX $16         pointer for string stack
E402   38       SEC
E403   20 9C FF JSR $FF9C       get RAM start
E406   86 2B    STX $2B
E408   84 2C    STY $2C         save as BASIC start
E40A   38       SEC
E40B   20 99 FF JSR $FF99       get RAM end
E40E   86 37    STX $37
E410   84 38    STY $38         save as BASIC end
E412   86 33    STX $33
E414   84 34    STY $34
E416   A0 00    LDY #$00
E418   98       TYA
E419   91 2B    STA ($2B),Y     $00 to BASIC start
E41B   E6 2B    INC $2B
E41D   D0 02    BNE $E421       BASIC start + 1
E41F   E6 2C    INC $2C
E421   60       RTS

*****************************
E422   A5 2B    LDA $2B
E424   A4 2C    LDY $2C         pointer to BASIC-RAM start
E426   20 08 A4 JSR $A408       checks on free memory
E429   A9 73    LDA #$73        pointer to power-on message
E42B   A0 E4    LDY #$E4
```

```
E42D  20 1E AB JSR $AB1E        out-put string
E430  A5 37    LDA $37
E432  38       SEC              BASIC end
E433  E5 2B    SBC $2B
E435  AA       TAX              ninus BASIC start
E436  A5 38    LDA $38
E438  E5 2C    SBC $2C          equals bytes free
E43A  20 CD BD JSR $BDCD        out-put quantity
E43D  A9 60    LDA ##$60        pointer to "BASIC BYTES
E43F  A0 E4    LDY ##$E4                          FREE"
E441  20 1E AB JSR $AB1E        out-put string
E444  4C 44 A6 JMP $A644        to NEW command

****************************   Table of BASIC vectors
E447 8B E3 83 A4 7C A5 1A A7
E44F E4 A7 86 AE

****************************   Load BASIC vectors
E453  A2 0B    LDX ##$0B
E455  BD 47 E4 LDA $E447,X
E458  9D 00 03 STA $0300,X
E45B  CA       DEX
E45C  10 F7    BPL $E455
E45E  60       RTS

****************************   Opperating system

****************************   System messages
E45F 00 20 42 41 53 49 43 20    BASIC BYTES FREE
E467 42 59 54 45 53 20 46 52
E46F 45 45 0D 00                 (CLR) **** COMMODORE 64
E473 93 0D 20 20 20 20 2A 2A    BASIC V2 ****
E47B 2A 2A 20 43 4F 4D 4D 4F
E483 44 4F 52 45 20 36 34 20     (CR) (CR) 64K RAM SYSTEM
E48B 42 41 53 49 43 20 56 32
E493 20 2A 2A 2A 2A 0D 0D 20
E49B 36 34 4B 20 52 41 4D 20
E4A3 53 59 53 54 45 4D 20 20
E4AB 00

E4AC 5C

****************************   BASIC-CKOUT routine
E4AD  48       PHA
E4AE  20 C9 FF JSR $FFC9         CKOUT set out-put device
E4B1  AA       TAX
E4B2  68       PLA
E4B3  90 01    BCC $E4B6
E4B5  8A       TXA
E4B6  60       RTS

E4B7  AA ...
E4D9  ... AA

****************************
```

```
E4DA  AD 21 D0 LDA $D021        back-ground color
E4DD  91 F3    STA ($F3),Y
E4DF  60       RTS

****************************** Waits for Commodore-key
E4E0  69 02    ADC #$02          2*256/60 = wait 8.5 seconds
E4E2  A4 91    LDY $91           check flag
E4E4  C8       INY
E4E5  D0 04    BNE $E4EB         key pressed?
E4E7  C5 A1    CMP $A1           is time over?
E4E9  D0 F7    BNE $E4E2
E4EB  60       RTS

****************************** Timer constants for RS-232
E4EC  19 26                      $2619=9753 50baud/Baud-Rate
E4EE  44 19                      $1944 = 6468   75 baud
E4F0  1A 11                      $111A = 4378  110 baud
E4F2  E8 0D                      $0DE8 = 3560 134.5 baud
E4F4  70 0C                      $0C70 = 3184  150 baud
E4F6  06 06                      $0606 = 1542  300 baud
E4F8  D1 02                      $02D1 = 736   600 baud
E4FA  37 01                      $0137 = 311  1200 baud
E4FC  AE 00                      $00AE = 174  1800 baud
E4FE  69 00                      $0069 = 105  2400 baud

****************************** Get basic address of the CIA
E500  A2 00    LDX #$00
E502  A0 DC    LDY #$DC          $DC00
E504  60       RTS

****************************** Gets # of lines and columns
E505  A2 28    LDX #$28          40 columns
E507  A0 19    LDY #$19          25 lines
E509  60       RTS

****************************** Set cursor (C=0) /get (C=1)
E50A  B0 07    BCS $E513
E50C  86 D6    STX $D6           line
E50E  84 D3    STY $D3           column
E510  20 6C E5 JSR $E56C         set cursor
E513  A6 D6    LDX $D6
E515  A4 D3    LDY $D3
E517  60       RTS

****************************** Reset screen
E518  20 A0 E5 JSR $E5A0         initialize video-controller
E51B  A9 00    LDA #$00
E51D  8D 91 02 STA $0291         enable shift-Commodore
E520  85 CF    STA $CF           cursor not in blink-phase
E522  A9 48    LDA #$48
E524  8D 8F 02 STA $028F         ($028F) = $EB48
E527  A9 EB    LDA #$EB
E529  8D 90 02 STA $0290         pointer to addressis for
E52C  A9 0A    LDA #$0A                  key-board decoding
E52E  8D 89 02 STA $0289         counter for repeat-speed
```

```
E531  8D 8C 02 STA $028C
E534  A9 0E    LDA #$0E         light-blue
E536  8D 86 02 STA $0286        present color
E539  A9 04    LDA #$04
E53B  8D 8B 02 STA $028B        repeat-speed
E53E  A9 0C    LDA #$0C
E540  85 CD    STA $CD          cursor blink-time
E542  85 CC    STA $CC          cursor blink-flag

*****************************   Clear screen
E544  AD 88 02 LDA $0288         memory-page for screen-RAM
E547  09 80    ORA #$80
E549  A8       TAY
E54A  A9 00    LDA #$00
E54C  AA       TAX
E54D  94 D9    STY $D9,X         addresses of the screen-
E54F  18       CLC                                 lines
E550  69 28    ADC #$28          add 40 (one line)
E552  90 01    BCC $E555
E554  C8       INY
E555  E8       INX
E556  E0 1A    CPX #$1A          26, all lines?
E558  D0 F3    BNE $E54D
E55A  A9 FF    LDA #$FF
E55C  95 D9    STA $D9,X
E55E  A2 18    LDX #$18          24 number of lines minus 1
E560  20 FF E9 JSR $E9FF         clear screen-line
E563  CA       DEX
E564  10 FA    BPL $E560

*****************************   Cursor home
E566  A0 00    LDY #$00
E568  84 D3    STY $D3           cursor column
E56A  84 D6    STY $D6           cursor line

*****************************   Calc. cursor position, set
E56C  A6 D6    LDX $D6           cursor line  screen-pointer
E56E  A5 D3    LDA $D3           cursor column
E570  B4 D9    LDY $D9,X
E572  30 08    BMI $E57C
E574  18       CLC
E575  69 28    ADC #$28
E577  85 D3    STA $D3
E579  CA       DEX
E57A  10 F4    BPL $E570
E57C  B5 D9    LDA $D9,X
E57E  29 03    AND #$03
E580  0D 88 02 ORA $0288
E583  85 D2    STA $D2
E585  BD F0 EC LDA $ECF0,X
E588  85 D1    STA $D1
E58A  A9 27    LDA #$27
E58C  E8       INX
E58D  B4 D9    LDY $D9,X
E58F  30 06    BMI $E597
```

```
E591  18        CLC
E592  69 28     ADC #$28
E594  E8        INX
E595  10 F6     BPL $E58D
E597  85 D5     STA $D5
E599  60        RTS
*******************************
E59A  20 A0 E5  JSR $E5A0         initialize video-controller
E59D  4C 66 E5  JMP $E566         cursor home

*******************************   Initialize video-controler
E5A0  A9 03     LDA #$03
E5A2  85 9A     STA $9A           out-put on screen
E5A4  A9 00     LDA #$00
E5A6  85 99     STA $99           input from keyboard
E5A8  A2 2F     LDX #$2F
E5AA  BD B8 EC  LDA $ECB8,X       write constants into
E5AD  9D FF CF  STA $CFFF,X       video-controller
E5B0  CA        DEX
E5B1  D0 F7     BNE $E5AA
E5B3  60        RTS

*******************************   Get character from keyboard-
E5B4  AC 77 02  LDY $0277         get first character
E5B7  A2 00     LDX #$00
E5B9  BD 78 02  LDA $0278,X       move buffer up front
E5BC  9D 77 02  STA $0277,X
E5BF  E8        INX
E5C0  E4 C6     CPX $C6           compare with number of
E5C2  D0 F5     BNE $E5B9                        characters
E5C4  C6 C6     DEC $C6           decrease character number
E5C6  98        TYA               get character in accumulator
E5C7  58        CLI
E5C8  18        CLC
E5C9  60        RTS

*******************************   Waiting-loop for key-board
E5CA  20 16 E7  JSR $E716         out-put character     input
E5CD  A5 C6     LDA $C6           number of pressed keys
E5CF  85 CC     STA $CC
E5D1  8D 92 02  STA $0292
E5D4  F0 F7     BEQ $E5CD
E5D6  78        SEI
E5D7  A5 CF     LDA $CF           cursor in blink-phase?
E5D9  F0 0C     BEQ $E5E7
E5DB  A5 CE     LDA $CE
E5DD  AE 87 02  LDX $0287
E5E0  A0 00     LDY #$00
E5E2  84 CF     STY $CF
E5E4  20 13 EA  JSR $EA13
E5E7  20 B4 E5  JSR $E5B4
E5EA  C9 83     CMP #$83          code for "shift-run"?
E5EC  D0 10     BNE $E5FE
E5EE  A2 09     LDX #$09          9 characters
E5F0  78        SEI
```

```
E5F1   86 C6     STX $C6        save number of characters
E5F3   BD E6 EC  LDA $ECE6,X    "load (cr) run (cr) "
E5F6   9D 76 02  STA $0276,X    get in keyboard buffer
E5F9   CA        DEX
E5FA   D0 F7     BNE $E5F3
E5FC   F0 CF     BEQ $E5CD
E5FE   C9 0D     CMP #$0D       "cr"
E600   D0 C8     BNE $E5CA      no, then back to waiting-
E602   A4 D5     LDY $D5        length of screen-line/ loop
E604   84 D0     STY $D0        set cr-flag
E606   B1 D1     LDA ($D1),Y    get character from screen
E608   C9 20     CMP #$20       eliminate sqace at line-end
E60A   D0 03     BNE $E60F
E60C   88        DEY
E60D   D0 F7     BNE $E606
E60F   C8        INY
E610   84 C8     STY $C8        save position as index
E612   A0 00     LDY #$00
E614   8C 92 02  STY $0292      cursor-column = 0
E617   84 D3     STY $D3
E619   84 D4     STY $D4
E61B   A5 C9     LDA $C9
E61D   30 1B     BMI $E63A
E61F   A6 D6     LDX $D6
E621   20 ED E6  JSR $E6ED
E624   E4 C9     CPX $C9
E626   D0 12     BNE $E63A
E628   A5 CA     LDA $CA        last column
E62A   85 D3     STA $D3        bring into column-pointer
E62C   C5 C8     CMP $C8        compare with indes
E62E   90 0A     BCC $E63A
E630   B0 2B     BCS $E65D

*****************************   Get a character from screen
E632   98        TYA
E633   48        PHA
E634   8A        TXA
E635   48        PHA
E636   A5 D0     LDA $D0        CR-flag
E638   F0 93     BEQ $E5CD      no, then to waiting-loop
E63A   A4 D3     LDY $D3        column
E63C   B1 D1     LDA ($D1),Y    get character from screen
E63E   85 D7     STA $D7
E640   29 3F     AND #$3F
E642   06 D7     ASL $D7        and change to ASCII
E644   24 D7     BIT $D7
E646   10 02     BPL $E64A
E648   09 80     ORA #$80
E64A   90 04     BCC $E650
E64C   A6 D4     LDX $D4
E64E   D0 04     BNE $E654
E650   70 02     BVS $E654
E652   09 40     ORA #$40
E654   E6 D3     INC $D3        move cursor one forward
E656   20 84 E6  JSR $E684      check on high-comma
```

```
E659  C4 C8     CPY $C8        cursor in last column?
E65B  D0 17     BNE $E674
E65D  A9 00     LDA #$00
E65F  85 D0     STA $D0        "CR"-flag
E661  A9 0D     LDA #$0D
E663  A6 99     LDX $99
E665  E0 03     CPX #$03       input from screen?
E667  F0 06     BEQ $E66F      yes
E669  A6 9A     LDX $9A        out-put on screen?
E66B  E0 03     CPX #$03       yes
E66D  F0 03     BEQ $E672
E66F  20 16 E7  JSR $E716      write character on screen
E672  A9 0D     LDA #$0D
E674  85 D7     STA $D7
E676  68        PLA
E677  AA        TAX
E678  68        PLA
E679  A8        TAY
E67A  A5 D7     LDA $D7        screen-code
E67C  C9 DE     CMP #$DE       compare with code for Pi
E67E  D0 02     BNE $E682
E680  A9 FF     LDA #$FF       yes, substitute by BASIC-
E682  18        CLC                         code for Pi
E683  60        RTS

******************************  Check on high comma
E684  C9 22     CMP #$22        " (") "?
E686  D0 08     BNE $E690       no, then ready
E688  A5 D4     LDA $D4
E68A  49 01     EOR #$01        turn around high-comma flag
E68C  85 D4     STA $D4
E68E  A9 22     LDA #$22        restore high-comma code
E690  60        RTS

******************************
E691  09 40     ORA #$40
E693  A6 C7     LDX $C7
E695  F0 02     BEQ $E699
E697  09 80     ORA #$80
E699  A6 D8     LDX $D8
E69B  F0 02     BEQ $E69F
E69D  C6 D8     DEC $D8
E69F  AE 86 02  LDX $0286       color code
E6A2  20 13 EA  JSR $EA13      write character into screen-
E6A5  20 B6 E6  JSR $E6B6       update line-start table/
E6A8  68        PLA
E6A9  A8        TAY
E6AA  A5 D8     LDA $D8
E6AC  F0 02     BEQ $E6B0
E6AE  46 D4     LSR $D4
E6B0  68        PLA
E6B1  AA        TAX
E6B2  68        PLA
E6B3  18        CLC
E6B4  58        CLI
```

```
E6B5  60        RTS

*****************************   Calculate MSB for new line-
E6B6  20 B3 E8 JSR $E8B3                                 starts
E6B9  E6 D3     INC $D3
E6BB  A5 D5     LDA $D5
E6BD  C5 D3     CMP $D3
E6BF  B0 3F     BCS $E700
E6C1  C9 4F     CMP #$4F         79 chacacters ( 2 lines)?
E6C3  F0 32     BEQ $E6F7
E6C5  AD 92 02 LDA $0292
E6C8  F0 03     BEQ $E6CD
E6CA  4C 67 E9 JMP $E967
E6CD  A6 D6     LDX $D6
E6CF  E0 19     CPX #$19
E6D1  90 07     BCC $E6DA
E6D3  20 EA E8 JSR $E8EA
E6D6  C6 D6     DEC $D6
E6D8  A6 D6     LDX $D6
E6DA  16 D9     ASL $D9,X
E6DC  56 D9     LSR $D9,X
E6DE  E8        INX
E6DF  B5 D9     LDA $D9,X
E6E1  09 80     ORA #$80
E6E3  95 D9     STA $D9,X
E6E5  CA        DEX
E6E6  A5 D5     LDA $D5
E6E8  18        CLC
E6E9  69 28     ADC #$28
E6EB  85 D5     STA $D5
E6ED  B5 D9     LDA $D9,X
E6EF  30 03     BMI $E6F4
E6F1  CA        DEX
E6F2  D0 F9     BNE $E6ED
E6F4  4C F0 E9 JMP $E9F0
E6F7  C6 D6     DEC $D6
E6F9  20 7C E8 JSR $E87C
E6FC  A9 00     LDA #$00
E6FE  85 D3     STA $D3
E700  60        RTS
E701  A6 D6     LDX $D6
E703  D0 06     BNE $E70B
E705  86 D3     STX $D3
E707  68        PLA
E708  68        PLA
E709  D0 9D     BNE $E6A8
E70B  CA        DEX
E70C  86 D6     STX $D6
E70E  20 6C E5 JSR $E56C
E711  A4 D5     LDY $D5
E713  84 D3     STY $D3
E715  60        RTS
E716  48        PHA
E717  85 D7     STA $D7
E719  8A        TXA
E71A  48        PHA
```

```
E71B  98        TYA
E71C  48        PHA
E71D  A9 00     LDA #$00
E71F  85 D0     STA $D0
E721  A4 D3     LDY $D3
E723  A5 D7     LDA $D7
E725  10 03     BPL $E72A
E727  4C D4 E7  JMP $E7D4
E72A  C9 0D     CMP #$0D
E72C  D0 03     BNE $E731
E72E  4C 91 E8  JMP $E891
E731  C9 20     CMP #$20
E733  90 10     BCC $E745
E735  C9 60     CMP #$60
E737  90 04     BCC $E73D
E739  29 DF     AND #$DF
E73B  D0 02     BNE $E73F
E73D  29 3F     AND #$3F
E73F  20 84 E6  JSR $E684
E742  4C 93 E6  JMP $E693
E745  A6 D8     LDX $D8
E747  F0 03     BEQ $E74C
E749  4C 97 E6  JMP $E697
E74C  C9 14     CMP #$14
E74E  D0 2E     BNE $E77E
E750  98        TYA
E751  D0 06     BNE $E759
E753  20 01 E7  JSR $E701
E756  4C 73 E7  JMP $E773
E759  20 A1 E8  JSR $E8A1
E75C  88        DEY
E75D  84 D3     STY $D3
E75F  20 24 EA  JSR $EA24
E762  C8        INY
E763  B1 D1     LDA ($D1),Y
E765  88        DEY
E766  91 D1     STA ($D1),Y
E768  C8        INY
E769  B1 F3     LDA ($F3),Y
E76B  88        DEY
E76C  91 F3     STA ($F3),Y
E76E  C8        INY
E76F  C4 D5     CPY $D5
E771  D0 EF     BNE $E762
E773  A9 20     LDA #$20
E775  91 D1     STA ($D1),Y
E777  AD 86 02  LDA $0286
E77A  91 F3     STA ($F3),Y
E77C  10 4D     BPL $E7CB
E77E  A6 D4     LDX $D4
E780  F0 03     BEQ $E785
E782  4C 97 E6  JMP $E697
E785  C9 12     CMP #$12
E787  D0 02     BNE $E78B
E789  85 C7     STA $C7
E78B  C9 13     CMP #$13
```

```
E78D  D0 03     BNE $E792
E78F  20 66 E5  JSR $E566
E792  C9 1D     CMP #$1D
E794  D0 17     BNE $E7AD
E796  C8        INY
E797  20 B3 E8  JSR $E8B3
E79A  84 D3     STY $D3
E79C  88        DEY
E79D  C4 D5     CPY $D5
E79F  90 09     BCC $E7AA
E7A1  C6 D6     DEC $D6
E7A3  20 7C E8  JSR $E87C
E7A6  A0 00     LDY #$00
E7A8  84 D3     STY $D3
E7AA  4C A8 E6  JMP $E6A8
E7AD  C9 11     CMP #$11
E7AF  D0 1D     BNE $E7CE
E7B1  18        CLC
E7B2  98        TYA
E7B3  69 28     ADC #$28
E7B5  A8        TAY
E7B6  E6 D6     INC $D6
E7B8  C5 D5     CMP $D5
E7BA  90 EC     BCC $E7A8
E7BC  F0 EA     BEQ $E7A8
E7BE  C6 D6     DEC $D6
E7C0  E9 28     SBC #$28
E7C2  90 04     BCC $E7C8
E7C4  85 D3     STA $D3
E7C6  D0 F8     BNE $E7C0
E7C8  20 7C E8  JSR $E87C
E7CB  4C A8 E6  JMP $E6A8
E7CE  20 CB E8  JSR $E8CB
E7D1  4C 44 EC  JMP $EC44
E7D4  29 7F     AND #$7F
E7D6  C9 7F     CMP #$7F
E7D8  D0 02     BNE $E7DC
E7DA  A9 5E     LDA #$5E
E7DC  C9 20     CMP #$20
E7DE  90 03     BCC $E7E3
E7E0  4C 91 E6  JMP $E691
E7E3  C9 0D     CMP #$0D
E7E5  D0 03     BNE $E7EA
E7E7  4C 91 E8  JMP $E891
E7EA  A6 D4     LDX $D4
E7EC  D0 3F     BNE $E82D
E7EE  C9 14     CMP #$14
E7F0  D0 37     BNE $E829
E7F2  A4 D5     LDY $D5
E7F4  B1 D1     LDA ($D1),Y
E7F6  C9 20     CMP #$20
E7F8  D0 04     BNE $E7FE
E7FA  C4 D3     CPY $D3
E7FC  D0 07     BNE $E805
E7FE  C0 4F     CPY #$4F
E800  F0 24     BEQ $E826
```

```
E802  20 65 E9 JSR $E965
E805  A4 D5    LDY $D5
E807  20 24 EA JSR $EA24
E80A  88       DEY
E80B  B1 D1    LDA ($D1),Y
E80D  C8       INY
E80E  91 D1    STA ($D1),Y
E810  88       DEY
E811  B1 F3    LDA ($F3),Y
E813  C8       INY
E814  91 F3    STA ($F3),Y
E816  88       DEY
E817  C4 D3    CPY $D3
E819  D0 EF    BNE $E80A
E81B  A9 20    LDA #$20          space
E81D  91 D1    STA ($D1),Y       write to present position
E81F  AD 86 02 LDA $0286         set
E822  91 F3    STA ($F3),Y         color
E824  E6 D8    INC $D8
E826  4C A8 E6 JMP $E6A8
E829  A6 D8    LDX $D8
E82B  F0 05    BEQ $E832
E82D  09 40    ORA #$40
E82F  4C 97 E6 JMP $E697

*****************************
E832  C9 11    CMP #$11          cursor up
E834  D0 16    BNE $E84C
E836  A6 D6    LDX $D6
E838  F0 37    BEQ $E871
E83A  C6 D6    DEC $D6
E83C  A5 D3    LDA $D3
E83E  38       SEC
E83F  E9 28    SBC #$28
E841  90 04    BCC $E847
E843  85 D3    STA $D3
E845  10 2A    BPL $E871
E847  20 6C E5 JSR $E56C
E84A  D0 25    BNE $E871
E84C  C9 12    CMP #$12
E84E  D0 04    BNE $E854
E850  A9 00    LDA #$00
E852  85 C7    STA $C7
E854  C9 1D    CMP #$1D
E856  D0 12    BNE $E86A
E858  98       TYA
E859  F0 09    BEQ $E864
E85B  20 A1 E8 JSR $E8A1
E85E  88       DEY
E85F  84 D3    STY $D3
E861  4C A8 E6 JMP $E6A8
E864  20 01 E7 JSR $E701
```

```
E867  4C A8 E6 JMP $E6A8
E86A  C9 13    CMP #$13
E86C  D0 06    BNE $E874
E86E  20 44 E5 JSR $E544
E871  4C A8 E6 JMP $E6A8
E874  09 80    ORA #$80
E876  20 CB E8 JSR $E8CB
E879  4C 4F EC JMP $EC4F
E87C  46 C9    LSR $C9
E87E  A6 D6    LDX $D6
E880  E8       INX
E881  E0 19    CPX #$19
E883  D0 03    BNE $E888
E885  20 EA E8 JSR $E8EA
E888  B5 D9    LDA $D9,X
E88A  10 F4    BPL $E880
E88C  86 D6    STX $D6
E88E  4C 6C E5 JMP $E56C
E891  A2 00    LDX #$00
E893  86 D8    STX $D8
E895  86 C7    STX $C7
E897  86 D4    STX $D4
E899  86 D3    STX $D3
E89B  20 7C E8 JSR $E87C
E89E  4C A8 E6 JMP $E6A8
E8A1  A2 02    LDX #$02
E8A3  A9 00    LDA #$00
E8A5  C5 D3    CMP $D3
E8A7  F0 07    BEQ $E8B0
E8A9  18       CLC
E8AA  69 28    ADC #$28
E8AC  CA       DEX
E8AD  D0 F6    BNE $E8A5
E8AF  60       RTS
E8B0  C6 D6    DEC $D6
E8B2  60       RTS
E8B3  A2 02    LDX #$02
E8B5  A9 27    LDA #$27
E8B7  C5 D3    CMP $D3
E8B9  F0 07    BEQ $E8C2
E8BB  18       CLC
E8BC  69 28    ADC #$28
E8BE  CA       DEX
E8BF  D0 F6    BNE $E8B7
E8C1  60       RTS
E8C2  A6 D6    LDX $D6
E8C4  E0 19    CPX #$19
E8C6  F0 02    BEQ $E8CA
E8C8  E6 D6    INC $D6
E8CA  60       RTS
E8CB  A2 0F    LDX #$0F
E8CD  DD DA E8 CMP $E8DA,X        check on color-codes
E8D0  F0 04    BEQ $E8D6          found
E8D2  CA       DEX
E8D3  10 F8    BPL $E8CD
```

```
E8D5  60        RTS
E8D6  8E 86 02  STX $0286          set color-code
E8D9  60        RTS

******************************     Table of color-codes
E8DA 90 05 1C 9F 9C 1E 1F 9E
E8E2 81 95 96 97 98 99 9A 9B

******************************     Scroll screen
E8EA  A5 AC     LDA $AC
E8EC  48        PHA
E8ED  A5 AD     LDA $AD
E8EF  48        PHA
E8F0  A5 AE     LDA $AE
E8F2  48        PHA
E8F3  A5 AF     LDA $AF
E8F5  48        PHA
E8F6  A2 FF     LDX #$FF
E8F8  C6 D6     DEC $D6
E8FA  C6 C9     DEC $C9
E8FC  CE A5 02  DEC $02A5
E8FF  E8        INX
E900  20 F0 E9  JSR $E9F0
E903  E0 18     CPX #$18
E905  B0 0C     BCS $E913
E907  BD F1 EC  LDA $ECF1,X
E90A  85 AC     STA $AC
E90C  B5 DA     LDA $DA,X
E90E  20 C8 E9  JSR $E9C8          shift screen-line up
E911  30 EC     BMI $E8FF
E913  20 FF E9  JSR $E9FF          clear screen-line
E916  A2 00     LDX #$00
E918  B5 D9     LDA $D9,X
E91A  29 7F     AND #$7F
E91C  B4 DA     LDY $DA,X
E91E  10 02     BPL $E922
E920  09 80     ORA #$80
E922  95 D9     STA $D9,X
E924  E8        INX
E925  E0 18     CPX #$18
E927  D0 EF     BNE $E918
E929  A5 F1     LDA $F1
E92B  09 80     ORA #$80
E92D  85 F1     STA $F1
E92F  A5 D9     LDA $D9
E931  10 C3     BPL $E8F6
E933  E6 D6     INC $D6
E935  EE A5 02  INC $02A5
E938  A9 7F     LDA #$7F
E93A  8D 00 DC  STA $DC00
E93D  AD 01 DC  LDA $DC01
E940  C9 FB     CMP #$FB           CTRL-key pressed?
E942  08        PHP
E943  A9 7F     LDA #$7F
E945  8D 00 DC  STA $DC00
```

```
E948  28        PLP
E949  D0 0B     BNE $E956
E94B  A0 00     LDY #$00
E94D  EA        NOP
E94E  CA        DEX
E94F  D0 FC     BNE $E94D         delay-loop
E951  88        DEY
E952  D0 F9     BNE $E94D
E954  84 C6     STY $C6           number of pressed keys = 0
E956  A6 D6     LDX $D6
E958  68        PLA
E959  85 AF     STA $AF
E95B  68        PLA
E95C  85 AE     STA $AE
E95E  68        PLA
E95F  85 AD     STA $AD
E961  68        PLA
E962  85 AC     STA $AC
E964  60        RTS

*****************************     Inserting a second-line
E965  A6 D6     LDX $D6
E967  E8        INX
E968  B5 D9     LDA $D9,X
E96A  10 FB     BPL $E967
E96C  8E A5 02  STX $02A5
E96F  E0 18     CPX #$18
E971  F0 0E     BEQ $E981
E973  90 0C     BCC $E981
E975  20 EA E8  JSR $E8EA
E978  AE A5 02  LDX $02A5
E97B  CA        DEX
E97C  C6 D6     DEC $D6
E97E  4C DA E6  JMP $E6DA

*****************************
E981  A5 AC     LDA $AC
E983  48        PHA
E984  A5 AD     LDA $AD
E986  48        PHA
E987  A5 AE     LDA $AE
E989  48        PHA
E98A  A5 AF     LDA $AF
E98C  48        PHA
E98D  A2 19     LDX #$19
E98F  CA        DEX
E990  20 F0 E9  JSR $E9F0
E993  EC A5 02  CPX $02A5
E996  90 0E     BCC $E9A6
E998  F0 0C     BEQ $E9A6
E99A  BD EF EC  LDA $ECEF,X
E99D  85 AC     STA $AC
E99F  B5 D8     LDA $D8,X
E9A1  20 C8 E9  JSR $E9C8
E9A4  30 E9     BMI $E98F
```

```
E9A6   20 FF E9 JSR $E9FF
E9A9   A2 17    LDX #$17
E9AB   EC A5 02 CPX $02A5
E9AE   90 0F    BCC $E9BF
E9B0   B5 DA    LDA $DA,X
E9B2   29 7F    AND #$7F
E9B4   B4 D9    LDY $D9,X
E9B6   10 02    BPL $E9BA
E9B8   09 80    ORA #$80
E9BA   95 DA    STA $DA,X
E9BC   CA       DEX
E9BD   D0 EC    BNE $E9AB
E9BF   AE A5 02 LDX $02A5
E9C2   20 DA E6 JSR $E6DA
E9C5   4C 58 E9 JMP $E958

******************************   Shift line up
E9C8   29 03    AND #$03
E9CA   0D 88 02 ORA $0288
E9CD   85 AD    STA $AD
E9CF   20 E0 E9 JSR $E9E0
E9D2   A0 27    LDY #$27
E9D4   B1 AC    LDA ($AC),Y
E9D6   91 D1    STA ($D1),Y
E9D8   B1 AE    LDA ($AE),Y
E9DA   91 F3    STA ($F3),Y
E9DC   88       DEY
E9DD   10 F5    BPL $E9D4
E9DF   60       RTS

******************************
E9E0   20 24 EA JSR $EA24
E9E3   A5 AC    LDA $AC
E9E5   85 AE    STA $AE
E9E7   A5 AD    LDA $AD
E9E9   29 03    AND #$03
E9EB   09 D8    ORA #$D8
E9ED   85 AF    STA $AF
E9EF   60       RTS

******************************
E9F0   BD F0 EC LDA $ECF0,X
E9F3   85 D1    STA $D1
E9F5   B5 D9    LDA $D9,X
E9F7   29 03    AND #$03
E9F9   0D 88 02 ORA $0288
E9FC   85 D2    STA $D2
E9FE   60       RTS

******************************   Clear screen-line
E9FF   A0 27    LDY #$27
EA01   20 F0 E9 JSR $E9F0
EA04   20 24 EA JSR $EA24
EA07   A9 20    LDA #$20
```

```
EA09  91 D1     STA ($D1),Y
EA0B  20 DA E4  JSR $E4DA
EA0E  EA        NOP
EA0F  88        DEY
EA10  10 F5     BPL $EA07
EA12  60        RTS

****************************
EA13  A8        TAY
EA14  A9 02     LDA #$02
EA16  85 CD     STA $CD          set blink-counter at repeat
EA18  20 24 EA  JSR $EA24                             function
EA1B  98        TYA

****************************     Get character and color on
EA1C  A4 D3     LDY $D3          column position       screen
EA1E  91 D1     STA ($D1),Y      character to accumulator
EA20  8A        TXA              color-code to X
EA21  91 F3     STA ($F3),Y      write into color-RAM
EA23  60        RTS

****************************     Calc. pointer to color-RAM
EA24  A5 D1     LDA $D1          $D1/$D2 - pointer to screen
EA26  85 F3     STA $F3                          RAM position
EA28  A5 D2     LDA $D2
EA2A  29 03     AND #$03
EA2C  09 D8     ORA #$D8         high-byte = $D8
EA2E  85 F4     STA $F4          $F3/$F4 - pointer to color-
EA30  60        RTS                              RAM position

****************************     Interupt routine
EA31  20 EA FF  JSR $FFEA        stop-key, increase time
EA34  A5 CC     LDA $CC          blink-flag for cursor
EA36  D0 29     BNE $EA61        not blinking, then continue
EA38  C6 CD     DEC $CD          lower blink-count
EA3A  D0 25     BNE $EA61        not zero, then continue
EA3C  A9 14     LDA #$14         set blink counter to 20
EA3E  85 CD     STA $CD
EA40  A4 D3     LDY $D3          cursor column
EA42  46 CF     LSR $CF          blink-switch zero the C=1
EA44  AE 87 02  LDX $0287        color under cursor
EA47  B1 D1     LDA ($D1),Y      set character-code
EA49  B0 11     BCS $EA5C        blink-switch was on, then
EA4B  E6 CF     INC $CF          blink-switch on     continue
EA4D  85 CE     STA $CE          save character under cursor
EA4F  20 24 EA  JSR $EA24        calculate pointer to color-
EA52  B1 F3     LDA ($F3),Y      get color-code           RAM
EA54  8D 87 02  STA $0287        and save
EA57  AE 86 02  LDX $0286        color-code under cursor
EA5A  A5 CE     LDA $CE          character under cursor
EA5C  49 80     EOR #$80         flip RVS-bit
EA5E  20 1C EA  JSR $EA1C        set character and color
EA61  A5 01     LDA $01
EA63  29 10     AND #$10         checks tape-key
EA65  F0 0A     BEQ $EA71        pressed?
```

```
EA67  A0 00     LDY #$00
EA69  84 C0     STY $C0         set tape-flag
EA6B  A5 01     LDA $01
EA6D  09 20     ORA #$20        tape-drive off
EA6F  D0 08     BNE $EA79
EA71  A5 C0     LDA $C0
EA73  D0 06     BNE $EA7B
EA75  A5 01     LDA $01
EA77  29 1F     AND #$1F
EA79  85 01     STA $01         tape drive on
EA7B  20 87 EA  JSR $EA87       keyboard-checking
EA7E  AD 0D DC  LDA $DC0D
EA81  68        PLA
EA82  A8        TAY
EA83  68        PLA             restore register
EA84  AA        TAX
EA85  68        PLA             and return from interrupt
EA86  40        RTI

******************************  Keyboard-checking
EA87  A9 00     LDA #$00
EA89  8D 8D 02  STA $028D       set back shift/CTRL-flag
EA8C  A0 40     LDY #$40        $40 - no key pressed
EA8E  84 CB     STY $CB         code for pressed key
EA90  8D 00 DC  STA $DC00
EA93  AE 01 DC  LDX $DC01
EA96  E0 FF     CPX #$FF        no key pressed?
EA98  F0 61     BEQ $EAFB       then end
EA9A  A8        TAY
EA9B  A9 81     LDA #$81
EA9D  85 F5     STA $F5
EA9F  A9 EB     LDA #$EB
EAA1  85 F6     STA $F6         pointer to table 1 $EB81
EAA3  A9 FE     LDA #$FE
EAA5  8D 00 DC  STA $DC00
EAA8  A2 08     LDX #$08        8 matrix-lines
EAAA  48        PHA
EAAB  AD 01 DC  LDA $DC01
EAAE  CD 01 DC  CMP $DC01       keyboard, joystick, paddles
EAB1  D0 F8     BNE $EAAB                 (data port B)
EAB3  4A        LSR             put bits, in order, into
EAB4  B0 16     BCS $EACC       "1" = not pressed
EAB6  48        PHA
EAB7  B1 F5     LDA ($F5),Y     get ASCII-code from table
EAB9  C9 05     CMP #$05
EABB  B0 0C     BCS $EAC9       bigger or equal to 5?
EABD  C9 03     CMP #$03
EABF  F0 08     BEQ $EAC9       "STOP" code?
EAC1  0D 8D 02  ORA $028D
EAC4  8D 8D 02  STA $028D       set flag
EAC7  10 02     BPL $EACB
EAC9  84 CB     STY $CB         save number of key
EACB  68        PLA
EACC  C8        INY
EACD  C0 41     CPY #$41
```

```
EACF   B0 0B      BCS $EADC        bigger than $40?
EAD1   CA         DEX
EAD2   D0 DF      BNE $EAB3        next matrix-column
EAD4   38         SEC
EAD5   68         PLA
EAD6   2A         ROL
EAD7   8D 00 DC   STA $DC00
EADA   D0 CC      BNE $EAA8        next matrix-line
EADC   68         PLA
EADD   6C 8F 02   JMP ($028F)      JMP $EB48 sets pointer to
EAE0   A4 CB      LDY $CB          number of key         table
EAE2   B1 F5      LDA ($F5),Y      get ASCII-value from table
EAE4   AA         TAX
EAE5   C4 C5      CPY $C5          compare with last key
EAE7   F0 07      BEQ $EAF0
EAE9   A0 10      LDY #$10
EAEB   8C 8C 02   STY $028C        repeat-delay counter
EAEE   D0 36      BNE $EB26
EAF0   29 7F      AND #$7F         clear bit 7
EAF2   2C 8A 02   BIT $028A        repeat for all keys?
EAF5   30 16      BMI $EB0D        bit 7 set, repeat all keys
EAF7   70 49      BVS $EB42        bit 6 set, then ingnore
EAF9   C9 7F      CMP #$7F         repeat only following keys
EAFB   F0 29      BEQ $EB26
EAFD   C9 14      CMP #$14         "DEL","INST"-code
EAFF   F0 0C      BEQ $EB0D
EB01   C9 20      CMP #$20         space
EB03   F0 08      BEQ $EB0D
EB05   C9 1D      CMP #$1D         cursor right, cursor left
EB07   F0 04      BEQ $EB0D
EB09   C9 11      CMP #$11         cursor up, cursor down
EB0B   D0 35      BNE $EB42
EB0D   AC 8C 02   LDY $028C        repeat-delay counter
EB10   F0 05      BEQ $EB17
EB12   CE 8C 02   DEC $028C        count down
EB15   D0 2B      BNE $EB42
EB17   CE 8B 02   DEC $028B        repeat-speed counter
EB1A   D0 26      BNE $EB42
EB1C   A0 04      LDY #$04
EB1E   8C 8B 02   STY $028B        set counter again
EB21   A4 C6      LDY $C6          number of characters in
EB23   88         DEY                        keyboard-buffer
EB24   10 1C      BPL $EB42        more than one character in
EB26   A4 CB      LDY $CB                 buffer, then ignore
EB28   84 C5      STY $C5
EB2A   AC 8D 02   LDY $028D
EB2D   8C 8E 02   STY $028E
EB30   E0 FF      CPX #$FF         keyboard-code invalid?
EB32   F0 0E      BEQ $EB42        yes, then ignore
EB34   8A         TXA
EB35   A6 C6      LDX $C6          # of characters in keybuffer
EB37   EC 89 02   CPX $0289        compare with max. number
EB3A   B0 06      BCS $EB42        buffer full, ignore charcter
EB3C   9D 77 02   STA $0277,X      write characters into buffer
EB3F   E8         INX
```

```
EB40  86 C6     STX $C6        increase # of characters
EB42  A9 7F     LDA #$7F       keyboard-matrix, ask as
EB44  8D 00 DC  STA $DC00                       default
EB47  60        RTS

****************************** Checks SHIFT, CTRL,Commodore
EB48  AD 8D 02  LDA $028D      flag for SHIFT/CTRL
EB4B  C9 03     CMP #$03
EB4D  D0 15     BNE $EB64      calculate pointer to decode
EB4F  CD 8E 02  CMP $028E                            table
EB52  F0 EE     BEQ $EB42
EB54  AD 91 02  LDA $0291      shift-commodore permitted?
EB57  30 1D     BMI $EB76      no, back to decoding
EB59  AD 18 D0  LDA $D018      shiftcommodore
EB5C  49 02     EOR #$02       switch small/capitol case
EB5E  8D 18 D0  STA $D018
EB61  4C 76 EB  JMP $EB76      ready
EB64  0A        ASL
EB65  C9 08     CMP #$08
EB67  90 02     BCC $EB6B
EB69  A9 06     LDA #$06
EB6B  AA        TAX
EB6C  BD 79 EB  LDA $EB79,X
EB6F  85 F5     STA $F5        load pointer to keyboard-
EB71  BD 7A EB  LDA $EB7A,X                decoding table
EB74  85 F6     STA $F6
EB76  4C E0 EA  JMP $EAE0      back to decoding

****************************** Pointer to keyboard decoding
EB79 81 EB C2 EB 03 EC 78 EC                         table

****************************** Keyboard-decoding table 1,
EB81 14 0D 1D 88 85 86 87 11                    unshifted
EB89 33 57 41 34 5A 53 45 01
EB91 35 52 44 36 43 46 54 58
EB99 37 59 47 38 42 48 55 56
EBA1 39 49 4A 30 4D 4B 4F 4E
EBA9 2B 50 4C 2D 2E 3A 40 2C
EBB1 5C 2A 3B 13 01 3D 5E 2F
EBB9 31 5F 04 32 20 02 51 03
EBC1 FF

****************************** Keyboard-decoding table 2,
EBC2 94 8D 9D 8C 89 8A 8B 91                      shifted
EBCA 23 D7 C1 24 DA D3 C5 01
EBD2 25 D2 C4 26 C3 C6 D4 D8
EBDA 27 D9 C7 28 C2 C8 D5 D6
EBE2 29 C9 CA 30 CD CB CF CE
EBEA DB D0 CC DD 3E 5B BA 3C
EBF2 A9 C0 5D 93 01 3D DE 3F
EBFA 21 5F 04 22 A0 02 D1 83
EC02 FF

****************************** Keyboard-decoding table 3,
EC03 94 8D 9D 8C 89 8A 8B 91                    "C=" key
EC0B 96 B3 B0 97 AD AE B1 01
```

```
EC13 98 B2 AC 99 BC BB A3 BD
EC1B 9A B7 A5 9B BF B4 B8 BE
EC23 29 A2 B5 30 A7 A1 B9 AA
EC2B A6 AF B6 DC 3E 5B A4 3C
EC33 A8 DF 5D 93 01 3D DE 3F
EC3B 81 5F 04 95 A0 02 AB 83
EC43 FF

*****************************    Checks on control-character
EC44   C9 0E      CMP #$0E        chr$(14)
EC46   D0 07      BNE $EC4F
EC48   AD 18 D0 LDA $D018         character generator
EC4B   09 02      ORA #$02        to capital-letter mode
EC4D   D0 09      BNE $EC58
EC4F   C9 8E      CMP #$8E        chr$(142)
EC51   D0 0B      BNE $EC5E
EC53   AD 18 D0 LDA $D018
EC56   29 FD      AND #$FD        small-letter mode
EC58   8D 18 D0 STA $D018         set
EC5B   4C A8 E6 JMP $E6A8
EC5E   C9 08      CMP #$08        chr$(8)
EC60   D0 07      BNE $EC69
EC62   A9 80      LDA #$80
EC64   0D 91 02 ORA $0291         block shift/Commodore
EC67   30 09      BMI $EC72
EC69   C9 09      CMP #$09        chr$(9)
EC6B   D0 EE      BNE $EC5B
EC6D   A9 7F      LDA #$7F
EC6F   2D 91 02 AND $0291         re-enable shift/Commodore
EC72   8D 91 02 STA $0291
EC75   4C A8 E6 JMP $E6A8

*****************************    Keyboard-decoding table 4,
                                              with CTRL-key
EC78 FF FF FF FF FF FF FF FF
EC80 1C 17 01 9F 1A 13 05 FF
EC88 9C 12 04 1E 03 06 14 18
EC90 1F 19 07 9E 02 08 15 16
EC98 12 09 0A 92 0D 0B 0F 0E
ECA0 FF 10 0C FF FF 1B 00 FF
ECA8 1C FF 1D FF FF 1F 1E FF
ECB0 90 06 FF 05 FF FF 11 FF
ECB8 FF

*****************************    Video-controller constants
ECB9 00 00 00 00 00 00 00 00
ECC1 00 00 00 00 00 00 00 00
ECC9 00 9B 37 00 00 00 08 00
ECD1 14 0F 00 00 00 00 00 00
ECD9 0E 06 01 02 03 04 00 01
ECE1 02 03 04 05 06 07

*****************************    Text after SHIFT/ RUN STOP
ECE7 4C 4F 41 44 0D 52 55 4E     "LOAD (CR) RUN (CR)"
EDEA  0D
```

```
******************************    LSB-table of screenline-
ECF0 00 28 50 78 A0 C8 F0 18                          starts
ECF8 40 68 90 B8 E0 08 30 58
ED00 80 A8 D0 F8 20 48 70 98
ED08 C0

******************************    IEC-bus routines

******************************    Send TALK
ED09   09 40     ORA #$40
ED0B   2C        .BYTE $2C

******************************    Send LISTEN
ED0C   09 20     ORA #$20
ED0E   20 A4 F0 JSR $F0A4          set timer for IEC time-out
ED11   48        PHA
ED12   24 94     BIT $94
ED14   10 0A     BPL $ED20
ED16   38        SEC
ED17   66 A3     ROR $A3
ED19   20 40 ED JSR $ED40
ED1C   46 94     LSR $94
ED1E   46 A3     LSR $A3
ED20   68        PLA
ED21   85 95     STA $95           byte to be given out
ED23   78        SEI
ED24   20 97 EE JSR $EE97
ED27   C9 3F     CMP #$3F
ED29   D0 03     BNE $ED2E
ED2B   20 85 EE JSR $EE85
ED2E   AD 00 DD LDA $DD00
ED31   09 08     ORA #$08          set ATN
ED33   8D 00 DD STA $DD00
ED36   78        SEI
ED37   20 8E EE JSR $EE8E
ED3A   20 97 EE JSR $EE97
ED3D   20 B3 EE JSR $EEB3

******************************    Out-put 1 byte to IEC-bus
ED40   78        SEI
ED41   20 97 EE JSR $EE97
ED44   20 A9 EE JSR $EEA9
ED47   B0 64     BCS $EDAD
ED49   20 85 EE JSR $EE85
ED4C   24 A3     BIT $A3
ED4E   10 0A     BPL $ED5A
ED50   20 A9 EE JSR $EEA9
ED53   90 FB     BCC $ED50
ED55   20 A9 EE JSR $EEA9
ED58   B0 FB     BCS $ED55
ED5A   20 A9 EE JSR $EEA9
ED5D   90 FB     BCC $ED5A
ED5F   20 8E EE JSR $EE8E
ED62   A9 08     LDA #$08
```

```
ED64   85 A5      STA $A5         set bit-counter for serial
ED66   AD 00 DD   LDA $DD00                          out-put
ED69   CD 00 DD   CMP $DD00
ED6C   D0 F8      BNE $ED66
ED6E   0A         ASL
ED6F   90 3F      BCC $EDB0
ED71   66 95      ROR $95
ED73   B0 05      BCS $ED7A
ED75   20 A0 EE   JSR $EEA0
ED78   D0 03      BNE $ED7D
ED7A   20 97 EE   JSR $EE97
ED7D   20 85 EE   JSR $EE85
ED80   EA         NOP
ED81   EA         NOP
ED82   EA         NOP
ED83   EA         NOP
ED84   AD 00 DD   LDA $DD00
ED87   29 DF      AND #$DF
ED89   09 10      ORA #$10
ED8B   8D 00 DD   STA $DD00
ED8E   C6 A5      DEC $A5
ED90   D0 D4      BNE $ED66
ED92   A9 04      LDA #$04
ED94   8D 07 DC   STA $DC07
ED97   A9 19      LDA #$19
ED99   8D 0F DC   STA $DC0F
ED9C   AD 0D DC   LDA $DC0D
ED9F   AD 0D DC   LDA $DC0D
EDA2   29 02      AND #$02
EDA4   D0 0A      BNE $EDB0
EDA6   20 A9 EE   JSR $EEA9
EDA9   B0 F4      BCS $ED9F
EDAB   58         CLI
EDAC   60         RTS

*****************************
EDAD   A9 80      LDA #$80        "DEVICE NOT PRESENT"
EDAF   2C         .BYTE $2C
EDB0   A9 03      LDA #$03        "TIME OUT"
EDB2   20 1C FE   JSR $FE1C       set status
EDB5   58         CLI
EDB6   18         CLC
EDB7   90 4A      BCC $EE03

*****************************     Send secondary address to
EDB9   85 95      STA $95          save secndary adrs /LISTEN
EDBB   20 36 ED   JSR $ED36        out-put with ATN
EDBE   AD 00 DD   LDA $DD00
EDC1   29 F7      AND #$F7         set back ATN
EDC3   8D 00 DD   STA $DD00
EDC6   60         RTS

*****************************     Send TALK secondary address
EDC7   85 95      STA $95          save secondary address
EDC9   20 36 ED   JSR $ED36        out-put with ATN
```

```
EDCC  78        SEI
EDCD  20 A0 EE  JSR $EEA0
EDD0  20 BE ED  JSR $EDBE        set back ATN
EDD3  20 85 EE  JSR $EE85
EDD6  20 A9 EE  JSR $EEA9
EDD9  30 FB     BMI $EDD6
EDDB  58        CLI
EDDC  60        RTS

*****************************      IECOUT out-put byte one IEC-
EDDD  24 94     BIT $94                                     bus
EDDF  30 05     BMI $EDE6
EDE1  38        SEC
EDE2  66 94     ROR $94
EDE4  D0 05     BNE $EDEB
EDE6  48        PHA
EDE7  20 40 ED  JSR $ED40        send byte to bus
EDEA  68        PLA
EDEB  85 95     STA $95
EDED  18        CLC
EDEE  60        RTS

*****************************      Send UNTALK
EDEF  78        SEI
EDF0  20 8E EE  JSR $EE8E
EDF3  AD 00 DD  LDA $DD00
EDF6  09 08     ORA #$08         set ATN
EDF8  8D 00 DD  STA $DD00
EDFB  A9 5F     LDA #$5F
EDFD  2C        .BYTE $2C

*****************************      Send UNLISTEN
EDFD  2C A9 3F  BIT $3FA9
EE00  20 11 ED  JSR $ED11
EE03  20 BE ED  JSR $EDBE
EE06  8A        TXA
EE07  A2 0A     LDX #$0A
EE09  CA        DEX              wait for 40 micro-seconds
EE0A  D0 FD     BNE $EE09
EE0C  AA        TAX
EE0D  20 85 EE  JSR $EE85        frequency on
EE10  4C 97 EE  JMP $EE97

*****************************      IECIN get character from IEC
EE13  78        SEI                                        -bus
EE14  A9 00     LDA #$00
EE16  85 A5     STA $A5
EE18  20 85 EE  JSR $EE85
EE1B  20 A9 EE  JSR $EEA9
EE1E  10 FB     BPL $EE1B
EE20  A9 01     LDA #$01
EE22  8D 07 DC  STA $DC07
EE25  A9 19     LDA #$19
EE27  8D 0F DC  STA $DC0F
EE2A  20 97 EE  JSR $EE97
EE2D  AD 0D DC  LDA $DC0D
```

```
EE30   AD 0D DC LDA $DC0D          check timer
EE33   29 02    AND #$02
EE35   D0 07    BNE $EE3E
EE37   20 A9 EE JSR $EEA9
EE3A   30 F4    BMI $EE30
EE3C   10 18    BPL $EE56
EE3E   A5 A5    LDA $A5
EE40   F0 05    BEQ $EE47
EE42   A9 02    LDA #$02
EE44   4C B2 ED JMP $EDB2
EE47   20 A0 EE JSR $EEA0
EE4A   20 85 EE JSR $EE85
EE4D   A9 40    LDA #$40           "EOF"
EE4F   20 1C FE JSR $FE1C          set status
EE52   E6 A5    INC $A5
EE54   D0 CA    BNE $EE20
EE56   A9 08    LDA #$08
EE58   85 A5    STA $A5            set bit-counter
EE5A   AD 00 DD LDA $DD00
EE5D   CD 00 DD CMP $DD00
EE60   D0 F8    BNE $EE5A
EE62   0A       ASL
EE63   10 F5    BPL $EE5A
EE65   66 A4    ROR $A4
EE67   AD 00 DD LDA $DD00
EE6A   CD 00 DD CMP $DD00
EE6D   D0 F8    BNE $EE67
EE6F   0A       ASL
EE70   30 F5    BMI $EE67
EE72   C6 A5    DEC $A5
EE74   D0 E4    BNE $EE5A
EE76   20 A0 EE JSR $EEA0
EE79   24 90    BIT $90             status
EE7B   50 03    BVC $EE80           no EOF?
EE7D   20 06 EE JSR $EE06
EE80   A5 A4    LDA $A4
EE82   58       CLI
EE83   18       CLC
EE84   60       RTS

******************************     Serial frequency on
EE85   AD 00 DD LDA $DD00
EE88   29 EF    AND #$EF
EE8A   8D 00 DD STA $DD00
EE8D   60       RTS

******************************     Serial frequency off
EE8E   AD 00 DD LDA $DD00
EE91   09 10    ORA #$10
EE93   8D 00 DD STA $DD00
EE96   60       RTS

******************************     Out-put bit "1"
EE97   AD 00 DD LDA $DD00
```

```
EE9A   29 DF     AND #$DF
EE9C   8D 00 DD STA $DD00
EE9F   60       RTS

******************************   Out-put bit "0"
EEA0   AD 00 DD LDA $DD00
EEA3   09 20     ORA #$20
EEA5   8D 00 DD STA $DD00
EEA8   60       RTS

******************************
EEA9   AD 00 DD LDA $DD00
EEAC   CD 00 DD CMP $DD00
EEAF   D0 F8     BNE $EEA9
EEB1   0A       ASL
EEB2   60       RTS

******************************   One milli-second delay
EEB3   8A       TXA
EEB4   A2 B8     LDX #$B8
EEB6   CA       DEX
EEB7   D0 FD     BNE $EEB6
EEB9   AA       TAX
EEBA   60       RTS

******************************   RS-232 out-put
EEBB   A5 B4     LDA $B4
EEBD   F0 47     BEQ $EF06
EEBF   30 3F     BMI $EF00
EEC1   46 B6     LSR $B6
EEC3   A2 00     LDX #$00
EEC5   90 01     BCC $EEC8
EEC7   CA       DEX
EEC8   8A       TXA
EEC9   45 BD     EOR $BD
EECB   85 BD     STA $BD
EECD   C6 B4     DEC $B4
EECF   F0 06     BEQ $EED7
EED1   8A       TXA
EED2   29 04     AND #$04
EED4   85 B5     STA $B5
EED6   60       RTS
EED7   A9 20     LDA #$20
EED9   2C 94 02 BIT $0294
EEDC   F0 14     BEQ $EEF2
EEDE   30 1C     BMI $EEFC
EEE0   70 14     BVS $EEF6
EEE2   A5 BD     LDA $BD
EEE4   D0 01     BNE $EEE7
EEE6   CA       DEX
EEE7   C6 B4     DEC $B4
EEE9   AD 93 02 LDA $0293
EEEC   10 E3     BPL $EED1
EEEE   C6 B4     DEC $B4
```

```
EEF0  D0 DF     BNE $EED1
EEF2  E6 B4     INC $B4
EEF4  D0 F0     BNE $EEE6
EEF6  A5 BD     LDA $BD
EEF8  F0 ED     BEQ $EEE7
EEFA  D0 EA     BNE $EEE6
EEFC  70 E9     BVS $EEE7
EEFE  50 E6     BVC $EEE6
EF00  E6 B4     INC $B4
EF02  A2 FF     LDX #$FF
EF04  D0 CB     BNE $EED1
EF06  AD 94 02  LDA $0294
EF09  4A        LSR
EF0A  90 07     BCC $EF13
EF0C  2C 01 DD  BIT $DD01
EF0F  10 1D     BPL $EF2E
EF11  50 1E     BVC $EF31
EF13  A9 00     LDA #$00
EF15  85 BD     STA $BD
EF17  85 B5     STA $B5
EF19  AE 98 02  LDX $0298
EF1C  86 B4     STX $B4
EF1E  AC 9D 02  LDY $029D
EF21  CC 9E 02  CPY $029E
EF24  F0 13     BEQ $EF39
EF26  B1 F9     LDA ($F9),Y
EF28  85 B6     STA $B6
EF2A  EE 9D 02  INC $029D
EF2D  60        RTS
EF2E  A9 40     LDA #$40          DSR (data set ready)missing
EF30  2C        .BYTE $2C
EF31  A9 10     LDA #$10          CTS (clear to send) missing
EF33  0D 97 02  ORA $0297         set status
EF36  8D 97 02  STA $0297
EF39  A9 01     LDA #$01
EF3B  8D 0D DD  STA $DD0D
EF3E  4D A1 02  EOR $02A1
EF41  09 80     ORA #$80
EF43  8D A1 02  STA $02A1
EF46  8D 0D DD  STA $DD0D
EF49  60        RTS

******************************    Find # of RS-232 data-bits
EF4A  A2 09     LDX #$09
EF4C  A9 20     LDA #$20
EF4E  2C 93 02  BIT $0293         control word
EF51  F0 01     BEQ $EF54
EF53  CA        DEX
EF54  50 02     BVC $EF58
EF56  CA        DEX
EF57  CA        DEX               X=number of data-bits
EF58  60        RTS
EF59  A6 A9     LDX $A9
EF5B  D0 33     BNE $EF90
EF5D  C6 A8     DEC $A8
EF5F  F0 36     BEQ $EF97
```

```
EF61  30 0D     BMI $EF70
EF63  A5 A7     LDA $A7
EF65  45 AB     EOR $AB
EF67  85 AB     STA $AB
EF69  46 A7     LSR $A7
EF6B  66 AA     ROR $AA
EF6D  60        RTS
EF6E  C6 A8     DEC $A8
EF70  A5 A7     LDA $A7
EF72  F0 67     BEQ $EFDB
EF74  AD 93 02  LDA $0293
EF77  0A        ASL
EF78  A9 01     LDA #$01
EF7A  65 A8     ADC $A8
EF7C  D0 EF     BNE $EF6D
EF7E  A9 90     LDA #$90
EF80  8D 0D DD  STA $DD0D
EF83  0D A1 02  ORA $02A1
EF86  8D A1 02  STA $02A1
EF89  85 A9     STA $A9
EF8B  A9 02     LDA #$02
EF8D  4C 3B EF  JMP $EF3B
EF90  A5 A7     LDA $A7
EF92  D0 EA     BNE $EF7E
EF94  85 A9     STA $A9
EF96  60        RTS
EF97  AC 9B 02  LDY $029B
EF9A  C8        INY
EF9B  CC 9C 02  CPY $029C
EF9E  F0 2A     BEQ $EFCA
EFA0  8C 9B 02  STY $029B
EFA3  88        DEY
EFA4  A5 AA     LDA $AA
EFA6  AE 98 02  LDX $0298
EFA9  E0 09     CPX #$09
EFAB  F0 04     BEQ $EFB1
EFAD  4A        LSR
EFAE  E8        INX
EFAF  D0 F8     BNE $EFA9
EFB1  91 F7     STA ($F7),Y
EFB3  A9 20     LDA #$20
EFB5  2C 94 02  BIT $0294
EFB8  F0 B4     BEQ $EF6E
EFBA  30 B1     BMI $EF6D
EFBC  A5 A7     LDA $A7
EFBE  45 AB     EOR $AB
EFC0  F0 03     BEQ $EFC5
EFC2  70 A9     BVS $EF6D
EFC4  2C        .BYTE $2C
EFC5  50 A6     BVC $EF6D
EFC7  A9 01     LDA #$01              parity-error
EFC9  2C        .BYTE $2C
EFCA  A9 04     LDA #$04              receiver-buffer full
EFCC  2C        .BYTE $2C
```

```
EFCD  A9 80     LDA #$80        receiver break-command
EFCF  2C        .BYTE $2C
EFD0  A9 02     LDA #$02        frame-error
EFD2  0D 97 02  ORA $0297
EFD5  8D 97 02  STA $0297       set status
EFD8  4C 7E EF  JMP $EF7E
EFDB  A5 AA     LDA $AA
EFDD  D0 F1     BNE $EFD0
EFDF  F0 EC     BEQ $EFCD
EFE1  85 9A     STA $9A
EFE3  AD 94 02  LDA $0294
EFE6  4A        LSR
EFE7  90 29     BCC $F012
EFE9  A9 02     LDA #$02
EFEB  2C 01 DD  BIT $DD01
EFEE  10 1D     BPL $F00D
EFF0  D0 20     BNE $F012
EFF2  AD A1 02  LDA $02A1
EFF5  29 02     AND #$02
EFF7  D0 F9     BNE $EFF2
EFF9  2C 01 DD  BIT $DD01
EFFC  70 FB     BVS $EFF9
EFFE  AD 01 DD  LDA $DD01
F001  09 02     ORA #$02
F003  8D 01 DD  STA $DD01
F006  2C 01 DD  BIT $DD01
F009  70 07     BVS $F012
F00B  30 F9     BMI $F006
F00D  A9 40     LDA #$40
F00F  8D 97 02  STA $0297       DSR-signal is missing
F012  18        CLC
F013  60        RTS

******************************  Out-put to RS-232 buffer
F014  20 28 F0  JSR $F028
F017  AC 9E 02  LDY $029E
F01A  C8        INY
F01B  CC 9D 02  CPY $029D
F01E  F0 F4     BEQ $F014
F020  8C 9E 02  STY $029E
F023  88        DEY
F024  A5 9E     LDA $9E
F026  91 F9     STA ($F9),Y
F028  AD A1 02  LDA $02A1
F02B  4A        LSR
F02C  B0 1E     BCS $F04C
F02E  A9 10     LDA #$10
F030  8D 0E DD  STA $DD0E
F033  AD 99 02  LDA $0299
F036  8D 04 DD  STA $DD04
F039  AD 9A 02  LDA $029A
F03C  8D 05 DD  STA $DD05
F03F  A9 81     LDA #$81
F041  20 3B EF  JSR $EF3B
F044  20 06 EF  JSR $EF06
```

```
F047   A9 11     LDA #$11
F049   8D 0E DD  STA $DD0E
F04C   60        RTS
F04D   85 99     STA $99
F04F   AD 94 02  LDA $0294
F052   4A        LSR
F053   90 28     BCC $F07D
F055   29 08     AND #$08
F057   F0 24     BEQ $F07D
F059   A9 02     LDA #$02
F05B   2C 01 DD  BIT $DD01
F05E   10 AD     BPL $F00D
F060   F0 22     BEQ $F084
F062   AD A1 02  LDA $02A1
F065   4A        LSR
F066   B0 FA     BCS $F062
F068   AD 01 DD  LDA $DD01
F06B   29 FD     AND #$FD
F06D   8D 01 DD  STA $DD01
F070   AD 01 DD  LDA $DD01
F073   29 04     AND #$04
F075   F0 F9     BEQ $F070
F077   A9 90     LDA #$90
F079   18        CLC
F07A   4C 3B EF  JMP $EF3B
F07D   AD A1 02  LDA $02A1
F080   29 12     AND #$12
F082   F0 F3     BEQ $F077
F084   18        CLC
F085   60        RTS

*******************************    GET from RS-232
F086   AD 97 02  LDA $0297          status
F089   AC 9C 02  LDY $029C          buffer pointer
F08C   CC 9B 02  CPY $029B
F08F   F0 0B     BEQ $F09C          buffer empty?
F091   29 F7     AND #$F7
F093   8D 97 02  STA $0297          clear in status
F096   B1 F7     LDA ($F7),Y        get byte from buffer
F098   EE 9C 02  INC $029C          increment buffer-pointer
F09B   60        RTS
F09C   09 08     ORA #$08           buffer empty
F09E   8D 97 02  STA $0297          set status
F0A1   A9 00     LDA #$00           transfer zero
F0A3   60        RTS

*******************************    Set timer for IEC time-out
F0A4   48        PHA
F0A5   AD A1 02  LDA $02A1          flag set?
F0A8   F0 11     BEQ $F0BB
F0AA   AD A1 02  LDA $02A1
F0AD   29 03     AND #$03
F0AF   D0 F9     BNE $F0AA
F0B1   A9 10     LDA #$10
F0B3   8D 0D DD  STA $DD0D          set timer
```

```
F0B6  A9 00     LDA #$00
F0B8  8D A1 02  STA $02A1
F0BB  68        PLA
F0BC  60        RTS

*****************************   Operating system error lines
F0BD 0D 49 2F 4F 20 45 52 52     I/O error number
F0C5 4F 52 20 A3
F0C9 0D 53 45 41 52 43 48 49     searching
F0D1 4E 47 A0
F0D4 46 4F 52 A0                 for
F0D8 0D 50 52 45 53 53 20 50     press play on tape
F0E0 4C 41 59 20 4F 4E 20 54
F0E8 41 50 C5
F0EB 50 52 45 53 53 20 52 45     press record & play on tape
F0F3 43 4F 52 44 20 26 20 50
F0FB 4C 41 59 20 4F 4E 20 54
F103 41 50 C5
F106 0D 4C 4F 41 44 49 4E C7     loading
F10E 0D 53 41 56 49 4E 47 A0     saving
F116 0D 56 45 52 49 46 59 49     verifying
F11E 4E C7
F120 0D 46 4F 55 4E 44 A0        found
F127  0D 4F 4B 8D                ok

*****************************   Output operators error lines
F12B  24 9D     BIT $9D           direct-mode flag
F12D  10 0D     BPL $F13C         progrom, then skip
F12F  B9 BD F0  LDA $F0BD,Y      offset of error-messages inY
F132  08        PHP
F133  29 7F     AND #$7F          clear bit 7
F135  20 D2 FF  JSR $FFD2         out-put
F138  C8        INY
F139  28        PLP
F13A  10 F3     BPL $F12F         more letters?
F13C  18        CLC
F13D  60        RTS

*****************************   GETIN
F13E  A5 99     LDA $99           input-device
F140  D0 08     BNE $F14A
F142  A5 C6     LDA $C6           # of char. in keyboard buf.
F144  F0 0F     BEQ $F155         no characters?
F146  78        SEI
F147  4C B4 E5  JMP $E5B4         get character from buffer
F14A  C9 02     CMP #$02
F14C  D0 18     BNE $F166         not RS-232, then BASIN
                                                  routine
F14E  84 97     STY $97
F150  20 86 F0  JSR $F086         GET from RS-232
F153  A4 97     LDY $97
F155  18        CLC
F156  60        RTS

*****************************   BASIN-input of a character
F157  A5 99     LDA $99           device number
```

```
F159  D0 0B     BNE $F166          not keyboard
F15B  A5 D3     LDA $D3            cursor position
F15D  85 CA     STA $CA
F15F  A5 D6     LDA $D6            set for keyboard input
F161  85 C9     STA $C9
F163  4C 32 E6  JMP $E632          input from screen
F166  C9 03     CMP #$03
F168  D0 09     BNE $F173

******************************    Input from screen
F16A  85 D0     STA $D0
F16C  A5 D5     LDA $D5
F16E  85 C8     STA $C8
F170  4C 32 E6  JMP $E632
F173  B0 38     BCS $F1AD          from IEC-bus
F175  C9 02     CMP #$02
F177  F0 3F     BEQ $F1B8

******************************    Input from tape
F179  86 97     STX $97            save X-register
F17B  20 99 F1  JSR $F199          get a character from tape
F17E  B0 16     BCS $F196
F180  48        PHA
F181  20 99 F1  JSR $F199          get a character from tape
F184  B0 0D     BCS $F193
F186  D0 05     BNE $F18D          last character?
F188  A9 40     LDA #$40           EOF
F18A  20 1C FE  JSR $FE1C          set status
F18D  C6 A6     DEC $A6            decrement tape-buffer pntr.
F18F  A6 97     LDX $97            get back X-register
F191  68        PLA
F192  60        RTS
F193  AA        TAX
F194  68        PLA
F195  8A        TXA
F196  A6 97     LDX $97
F198  60        RTS

******************************    Get character from tape
F199  20 0D F8  JSR $F80D          increment tape-buffer pntr.
F19C  D0 0B     BNE $F1A9          still characters in buffer?
F19E  20 41 F8  JSR $F841          no,get next block from tape
F1A1  B0 11     BCS $F1B4
F1A3  A9 00     LDA #$00
F1A5  85 A6     STA $A6            zero buffer-pointer, get
F1A7  F0 F0     BEQ $F199                              character
F1A9  B1 B2     LDA ($B2),Y        read character from buffer
F1AB  18        CLC
F1AC  60        RTS
F1AD  A5 90     LDA $90            check status
F1AF  F0 04     BEQ $F1B5          ok
F1B1  A9 0D     LDA #$0D           out-put "CR"-code
F1B3  18        CLC
F1B4  60        RTS
```

```
*****************************   IEC-input
F1B5  4C 13 EE JMP $EE13         get a byte from IEC-bus

*****************************   RS-232 input
F1B8  20 4E F1 JSR $F14E         get a byte from RS-232
F1BB  B0 F7    BCS $F1B4
F1BD  C9 00    CMP #$00
F1BF  D0 F2    BNE $F1B3
F1C1  AD 97 02 LDA $0297         status
F1C4  29 60    AND #$60
F1C6  D0 E9    BNE $F1B1         return "CR"
F1C8  F0 EE    BEQ $F1B8

*****************************   BSOUT-output of a character
F1CA  48       PHA
F1CB  A5 9A    LDA $9A           device number for out-put
F1CD  C9 03    CMP #$03          screen?
F1CF  D0 04    BNE $F1D5         no
F1D1  68       PLA
F1D2  4C 16 E7 JMP $E716         output character on screen
F1D5  90 04    BCC $F1DB
F1D7  68       PLA
F1D8  4C DD ED JMP $EDDD         out-put a byte on IEC-bus
F1DB  4A       LSR
F1DC  68       PLA
F1DD  85 9E    STA $9E           save character to be output
F1DF  8A       TXA
F1E0  48       PHA
F1E1  98       TYA
F1E2  48       PHA
F1E3  90 23    BCC $F208         RS-232 output
F1E5  20 0D F8 JSR $F80D         increment tape-buffer pntr.
F1E8  D0 0E    BNE $F1F8         buffer full?
F1EA  20 64 F8 JSR $F864         write buffer on tape
F1ED  B0 0E    BCS $F1FD
F1EF  A9 02    LDA #$02          control-byte for data-block
F1F1  A0 00    LDY #$00
F1F3  91 B2    STA ($B2),Y       write in buffer
F1F5  C8       INY
F1F6  84 A6    STY $A6           increment buffer-pointer
F1F8  A5 9E    LDA $9E
F1FA  91 B2    STA ($B2),Y       write character in buffer
F1FC  18       CLC
F1FD  68       PLA
F1FE  A8       TAY
F1FF  68       PLA
F200  AA       TAX
F201  A5 9E    LDA $9E
F203  90 02    BCC $F207
F205  A9 00    LDA #$00
F207  60       RTS

*****************************   RS-232 out-put
F208  20 17 F0 JSR $F017         write char. in RS232 buffer
F20B  4C FC F1 JMP $F1FC
```

```
*****************************     CHRIN-set input device
F20E  20 0F F3 JSR $F30F           looks for logical file-#
F211  F0 03    BEQ $F216           found?
F213  4C 01 F7 JMP $F701           "FILE NOT OPEN"
F216  20 1F F3 JSR $F31F           sets file parameter
F219  A5 BA    LDA $BA             device number
F21B  F0 16    BEQ $F233           0, keyboard
F21D  C9 03    CMP #$03
F21F  F0 12    BEQ $F233           3, screen
F221  B0 14    BCS $F237           IEC-bus
F223  C9 02    CMP #$02            RS-232
F225  D0 03    BNE $F22A           no, then tape
F227  4C 4D F0 JMP $F04D           yes

*****************************     Set tape as input device
F22A  A6 B9    LDX $B9             secondary address
F22C  E0 60    CPX #$60            zero?
F22E  F0 03    BEQ $F233
F230  4C 0A F7 JMP $F70A           "NOT INPUT FILE"
F233  85 99    STA $99             device number for out-put
F235  18       CLC
F236  60       RTS
F237  AA       TAX
F238  20 09 ED JSR $ED09           send TALK
F23B  A5 B9    LDA $B9             secondary address
F23D  10 06    BPL $F245
F23F  20 CC ED JSR $EDCC           waits for cycle-signal
F242  4C 48 F2 JMP $F248
F245  20 C7 ED JSR $EDC7           send secondary address for
F248  8A       TXA                                       TALK
F249  24 90    BIT $90             status
F24B  10 E6    BPL $F233           ok?
F24D  4C 07 F7 JMP $F707           "DEVICE NOT PRESENT"

*****************************     CKOUT set output device
F250  20 0F F3 JSR $F30F           looks for logical file #
F253  F0 03    BEQ $F258           found?
F255  4C 01 F7 JMP $F701           "FILE NOT FOUND"
F258  20 1F F3 JSR $F31F           sets file parameters
F25B  A5 BA    LDA $BA             device number
F25D  D0 03    BNE $F262           not zero?
F25F  4C 0D F7 JMP $F70D           "ILLEGAL DEVICE NUMBER"
F262  C9 03    CMP #$03            screen?
F264  F0 0F    BEQ $F275           yes
F266  B0 11    BCS $F279           IEC-bus
F268  C9 02    CMP #$02            RS-232
F26A  D0 03    BNE $F26F
F26C  4C E1 EF JMP $EFE1           yes

*****************************     Set tape as out-put device
F26F  A6 B9    LDX $B9             secondary address
F271  E0 60    CPX #$60            zero?
F273  F0 EA    BEQ $F25F           tape file for reading,error
F275  85 9A    STA $9A             set number of output device
```

```
F277  18        CLC
F278  60        RTS

*****************************   Lay out-put on IEC-bus
F279  AA        TAX
F27A  20 0C ED JSR $ED0C         send LISTEN
F27D  A5 B9     LDA $B9          secondary address
F27F  10 05     BPL $F286
F281  20 BE ED JSR $EDBE         set back ATN
F284  D0 03     BNE $F289
F286  20 B9 ED JSR $EDB9         send secondary address for
F289  8A        TXA                                  LISTEN
F28A  24 90     BIT $90          status
F28C  10 E7     BPL $F275        ok?
F28E  4C 07 F7 JMP $F707         "DEVICE NOT PRESENT"

*****************************   CLOSE logical file # in X
F291  20 14 F3 JSR $F314        looks for logical file# in X
F294  F0 02     BEQ $F298
F296  18        CLC              fole not present,then ready
F297  60        RTS
F298  20 1F F3 JSR $F31F         set file parameter
F29B  8A        TXA
F29C  48        PHA
F29D  A5 BA     LDA $BA          device address
F29F  F0 50     BEQ $F2F1        keyboard?
F2A1  C9 03     CMP #$03
F2A3  F0 4C     BEQ $F2F1        screen?
F2A5  B0 47     BCS $F2EE        IEC-bus?
F2A7  C9 02     CMP #$02         RS-232?
F2A9  D0 1D     BNE $F2C8        tape

*****************************   Close RS-232 file
F2AB  68        PLA
F2AC  20 F2 F2 JSR $F2F2         clear file-entery in table
F2AF  20 83 F4 JSR $F483         set back CIAs for I/O
F2B2  20 27 FE JSR $FE27         set free RS-232 I/O buffer
F2B5  A5 F8     LDA $F8          input buffer
F2B7  F0 01     BEQ $F2BA
F2B9  C8        INY
F2BA  A5 FA     LDA $FA          output buffer
F2BC  F0 01     BEQ $F2BF
F2BE  C8        INY
F2BF  A9 00     LDA #$00
F2C1  85 F8     STA $F8          set buffer free
F2C3  85 FA     STA $FA
F2C5  4C 7D F4 JMP $F47D

*****************************   CLOSE tape file
F2C8  A5 B9     LDA $B9          secondary address
F2CA  29 0F     AND #$0F
F2CC  F0 23     BEQ $F2F1        file for reading?
F2CE  20 D0 F7 JSR $F7D0         get tape-buffer start adrs.
F2D1  A9 00     LDA #$00
F2D3  38        SEC
```

```
F2D4   20 DD F1 JSR $F1DD
F2D7   20 64 F8 JSR $F864         write buffer on tape
F2DA   90 04    BCC $F2E0
F2DC   68       PLA
F2DD   A9 00    LDA #$00
F2DF   60       RTS
F2E0   A5 B9    LDA $B9           secondary address
F2E2   C9 62    CMP #$62          equal 2
F2E4   D0 0B    BNE $F2F1
F2E6   A9 05    LDA #$05          control-byte for EOT-header
F2E8   20 6A F7 JSR $F76A         write block on tape
F2EB   4C F1 F2 JMP $F2F1
F2EE   20 42 F6 JSR $F642         close IEC file
F2F1   68       PLA
F2F2   AA       TAX
F2F3   C6 98    DEC $98           decrement # of open files
F2F5   E4 98    CPX $98
F2F7   F0 14    BEQ $F30D         equal zero, then ready
F2F9   A4 98    LDY $98
F2FB   B9 59 02 LDA $0259,Y
F2FE   9D 59 02 STA $0259,X
F301   B9 63 02 LDA $0263,Y       open file parameter-table
F304   9D 63 02 STA $0263,X
F307   B9 6D 02 LDA $026D,Y
F30A   9D 6D 02 STA $026D,X
F30D   18       CLC
F30E   60       RTS

*****************************    Looks for logical file# in X
F30F   A9 00    LDA #$00
F311   85 90    STA $90           clear status
F313   8A       TXA
F314   A6 98    LDX $98           number of open files
F316   CA       DEX
F317   30 15    BMI $F32E
F319   DD 59 02 CMP $0259,X       looks for entry in table
F31C   D0 F8    BNE $F316
F31E   60       RTS

*****************************    Set file parameter
F31F   BD 59 02 LDA $0259,X
F322   85 B8    STA $B8           logical file number
F324   BD 63 02 LDA $0263,X
F327   85 BA    STA $BA           device address
F329   BD 6D 02 LDA $026D,X
F32C   85 B9    STA $B9           secondary address
F32E   60       RTS

*****************************    CLALL-closes I/O channels
F32F   A9 00    LDA #$00
F331   85 98    STA $98           number of open files = 0
F333   A2 03    LDX #$03
F335   E4 9A    CPX $9A           number of out-put device
F337   B0 03    BCS $F33C         smaller than 3
F339   20 FE ED JSR $EDFE         send IEC, UNLISTEN
```

```
F33C  E4 99     CPX $99          number of input device
F33E  B0 03     BCS $F343        smaller than 3
F340  20 EF ED  JSR $EDEF        send IEC, UNTALK
F343  86 9A     STX $9A          reset out-put to screen
F345  A9 00     LDA #$00
F347  85 99     STA $99          reset input to keyboard
F349  60        RTS

*****************************    OPEN
F34A  A6 B8     LDX $B8          file number
F34C  D0 03     BNE $F351        not zero
F34E  4C 0A F7  JMP $F70A        "NOT INPUT FILE" (??)
F351  20 0F F3  JSR $F30F        looks for logical file #
F354  D0 03     BNE $F359        not found, it can be opened
F356  4C FE F6  JMP $F6FE        "FILE OPEN"
F359  A6 98     LDX $98          number of open files
F35B  E0 0A     CPX #$0A         compare with 10
F35D  90 03     BCC $F362
F35F  4C FB F6  JMP $F6FB        "TOO MANY FILES"
F362  E6 98     INC $98          increase number
F364  A5 B8     LDA $B8          logical file number
F366  9D 59 02  STA $0259,X
F369  A5 B9     LDA $B9          secondary address
F36B  09 60     ORA #$60
F36D  85 B9     STA $B9
F36F  9D 6D 02  STA $026D,X
F372  A5 BA     LDA $BA          device number
F374  9D 63 02  STA $0263,X      write in the right table
F377  F0 5A     BEQ $F3D3        keyboard?
F379  C9 03     CMP #$03
F37B  F0 56     BEQ $F3D3        screen
F37D  90 05     BCC $F384
F37F  20 D5 F3  JSR $F3D5        open file on IEC-bus
F382  90 4F     BCC $F3D3
F384  C9 02     CMP #$02         tape?
F386  D0 03     BNE $F38B        no
F388  4C 09 F4  JMP $F409        RS-232 open
F38B  20 D0 F7  JSR $F7D0        get tape-buffer start-adrs.
F38E  B0 03     BCS $F393
F390  4C 13 F7  JMP $F713        "ILLEGAL DEVICE NUMBER"
F393  A5 B9     LDA $B9          secondary address
F395  29 0F     AND #$0F
F397  D0 1F     BNE $F3B8        not zero?
F399  20 17 F8  JSR $F817        waits for PLAY key
F39C  B0 36     BCS $F3D4
F39E  20 AF F5  JSR $F5AF        out-put"SEARCHING FOR name"
F3A1  A5 B7     LDA $B7          length of file name
F3A3  F0 0A     BEQ $F3AF        no file name, then continue
F3A5  20 EA F7  JSR $F7EA        searches for desired tape-
F3A8  90 18     BCC $F3C2                                header
F3AA  F0 28     BEQ $F3D4
F3AC  4C 04 F7  JMP $F704        out-put "FILE NOT FOUND"
F3AF  20 2C F7  JSR $F72C        search for next tape-header
F3B2  F0 20     BEQ $F3D4
F3B4  90 0C     BCC $F3C2
```

```
F3B6  B0 F4     BCS $F3AC
F3B8  20 38 F8  JSR $F838        waits for RECORD & PLAY key
F3BB  B0 17     BCS $F3D4
F3BD  A9 04     LDA #$04         control-byte for dataheader
F3BF  20 6A F7  JSR $F76A        write header on tape
F3C2  A9 BF     LDA #$BF         pointer to tape-buffers end
F3C4  A4 B9     LDY $B9          secondary address
F3C6  C0 60     CPY #$60
F3C8  F0 07     BEQ $F3D1        =0, then continue
F3CA  A0 00     LDY #$00
F3CC  A9 02     LDA #$02         control-byte for data-block
F3CE  91 B2     STA ($B2),Y      write in tape buffer
F3D0  98        TYA
F3D1  85 A6     STA $A6          pointer in tape-buffer
F3D3  18        CLC
F3D4  60        RTS

*****************************    OPEN files on IEC-bus
F3D5  A5 B9     LDA $B9          secondary address
F3D7  30 FA     BMI $F3D3
F3D9  A4 B7     LDY $B7          length of file name
F3DB  F0 F6     BEQ $F3D3        =0, then error
F3DD  A9 00     LDA #$00
F3DF  85 90     STA $90          clear status
F3E1  A5 BA     LDA $BA          device address
F3E3  20 0C ED  JSR $ED0C        LISTEN
F3E6  A5 B9     LDA $B9          secondary address
F3E8  09 F0     ORA #$F0
F3EA  20 B9 ED  JSR $EDB9        send
F3ED  A5 90     LDA $90          check status
F3EF  10 05     BPL $F3F6        ok
F3F1  68        PLA
F3F2  68        PLA
F3F3  4C 07 F7  JMP $F707        "DEVICE NOT PRESENT"
F3F6  A5 B7     LDA $B7          length of file-name
F3F8  F0 0C     BEQ $F406
F3FA  A0 00     LDY #$00
F3FC  B1 BB     LDA ($BB),Y      file-name
F3FE  20 DD ED  JSR $EDDD        out-put on IEC-bus
F401  C8        INY
F402  C4 B7     CPY $B7
F404  D0 F6     BNE $F3FC
F406  4C 54 F6  JMP $F654        UNLISTEN, return

*****************************    RS-232 OPEN
F409  20 83 F4  JSR $F483        set CIAs
F40C  8C 97 02  STY $0297        clear RS-232 status
F40F  C4 B7     CPY $B7          length of file-name
F411  F0 0A     BEQ $F41D
F413  B1 BB     LDA ($BB),Y      save the first by characters
F415  99 93 02  STA $0293,Y
F418  C8        INY
F419  C0 04     CPY #$04
F41B  D0 F2     BNE $F40F
F41D  20 4A EF  JSR $EF4A        calculate # of data-bits
```

```
F420  8E 98 02 STX $0298        and save
F423  AD 93 02 LDA $0293        control register
F426  29 0F    AND #$0F         isolate bits for baud-rate
F428  F0 1C    BEQ $F446
F42A  0A       ASL              2 for table
F42B  AA       TAX
F42C  AD A6 02 LDA $02A6
F42F  D0 09    BNE $F43A
F431  BC C1 FE LDY $FEC1,X      baud-rate, High
F434  BD C0 FE LDA $FEC0,X      baud-rate, Low
F437  4C 40 F4 JMP $F440
F43A  BC EB E4 LDY $E4EB,X      baud-rate, High
F43D  BD EA E4 LDA $E4EA,X      baud-rate, Low
F440  8C 96 02 STY $0296
F443  8D 95 02 STA $0295        save
F446  AD 95 02 LDA $0295
F449  0A       ASL
F44A  20 2E FF JSR $FF2E        determine baud-rate code
F44D  AD 94 02 LDA $0294
F450  4A       LSR
F451  90 09    BCC $F45C
F453  AD 01 DD LDA $DD01
F456  0A       ASL
F457  B0 03    BCS $F45C
F459  20 0D F0 JSR $F00D        set status for DSR
F45C  AD 9B 02 LDA $029B
F45F  8D 9C 02 STA $029C        set buffer-pointer for
F462  AD 9E 02 LDA $029E                        RS-232 I/O
F465  8D 9D 02 STA $029D
F468  20 27 FE JSR $FE27        get top of memory
F46B  A5 F8    LDA $F8
F46D  D0 05    BNE $F474        input buffer used already?
F46F  88       DEY
F470  84 F8    STY $F8          pointer for RS-232 input
F472  86 F7    STX $F7                              buffer
F474  A5 FA    LDA $FA
F476  D0 05    BNE $F47D        output buffer used already?
F478  88       DEY
F479  84 FA    STY $FA          pointer for RS-232 output
F47B  86 F9    STX $F9                              buffer
F47D  38       SEC
F47E  A9 F0    LDA #$F0
F480  4C 2D FE JMP $FE2D        set new top of memory

*****************************  Set CIAs back to RS-232
F483  A9 7F    LDA #$7F
F485  8D 0D DD STA $DD0D
F488  A9 06    LDA #$06
F48A  8D 03 DD STA $DD03
F48D  8D 01 DD STA $DD01
F490  A9 04    LDA #$04
F492  0D 00 DD ORA $DD00
F495  8D 00 DD STA $DD00
F498  A0 00    LDY #$00
```

```
F49A  8C A1 02 STY $02A1
F49D  60       RTS

*****************************  LOAD routine
F49E  86 C3    STX $C3          save start address
F4A0  84 C4    STY $C4
F4A2  6C 30 03 JMP ($0330)      MMP $F4A5  LOAD vector
F4A5  85 93    STA $93          load/verify flag
F4A7  A9 00    LDA #$00
F4A9  85 90    STA $90          clear status
F4AB  A5 BA    LDA $BA          device address
F4AD  D0 03    BNE $F4B2        not zero, then continue
F4AF  4C 13 F7 JMP $F713        "ILLEGAL DEVICE NUMBER"
F4B2  C9 03    CMP #$03         screen?
F4B4  F0 F9    BEQ $F4AF        yes, error
F4B6  90 7B    BCC $F533        smaller 3, then from tape

*****************************  IEC LOAD
F4B8  A4 B7    LDY $B7          length of file-name
F4BA  D0 03    BNE $F4BF        not zero, then ok
F4BC  4C 10 F7 JMP $F710        "MISSING FILE NAME"
F4BF  A6 B9    LDX $B9          secondary address
F4C1  20 AF F5 JSR $F5AF        "SEARCHING FOR filename"
F4C4  A9 60    LDA #$60         secondary address zero
F4C6  85 B9    STA $B9
F4C8  20 D5 F3 JSR $F3D5        open file on IEC-bus
F4CB  A5 BA    LDA $BA          device number
F4CD  20 09 ED JSR $ED09        send TALK
F4D0  A5 B9    LDA $B9
F4D2  20 C7 ED JSR $EDC7        send secondary address
F4D5  20 13 EE JSR $EE13        get byte from IEC-bus
F4D8  85 AE    STA $AE          save as start address low
F4DA  A5 90    LDA $90          status
F4DC  4A       LSR
F4DD  4A       LSR
F4DE  B0 50    BCS $F530        time out, then error
F4E0  20 13 EE JSR $EE13        get start-address high
F4E3  85 AF    STA $AF
F4E5  8A       TXA
F4E6  D0 08    BNE $F4F0        secondary address not zero?
F4E8  A5 C3    LDA $C3
F4EA  85 AE    STA $AE          no, then LOAD from given
F4EC  A5 C4    LDA $C4          address
F4EE  85 AF    STA $AF
F4F0  20 D2 F5 JSR $F5D2        out-put "LOADING/VERIFYING"
F4F3  A9 FD    LDA #$FD
F4F5  25 90    AND $90          clear time-out bit
F4F7  85 90    STA $90
F4F9  20 E1 FF JSR $FFE1        scan STOP key
F4FC  D0 03    BNE $F501        not pressed, then continue
F4FE  4C 33 F6 JMP $F633        close file
F501  20 13 EE JSR $EE13        get program-byte from bus
F504  AA       TAX
F505  A5 90    LDA $90          check status
F507  4A       LSR
```

```
F508  4A        LSR
F509  B0 E8     BCS $F4F3         error, then interrupt
F50B  8A        TXA
F50C  A4 93     LDY $93           check LOAD/VERIFY flag
F50E  F0 0C     BEQ $F51C         =0, then LOAD
F510  A0 00     LDY #$00
F512  D1 AE     CMP ($AE),Y       verify, comparison
F514  F0 08     BEQ $F51E
F516  A9 10     LDA #$10          unequal, then set status
F518  20 1C FE  JSR $FE1C         set status
F51B  2C        .BYTE $2C
F51C  91 AE     STA ($AE),Y       save byte
F51E  E6 AE     INC $AE
F520  D0 02     BNE $F524         increment address
F522  E6 AF     INC $AF
F524  24 90     BIT $90           status
F526  50 CB     BVC $F4F3         no EOF yet?
F528  20 EF ED  JSR $EDEF         send UNTALK
F52B  20 42 F6  JSR $F642         close file
F52E  90 79     BCC $F5A9         no error?
F530  4C 04 F7  JMP $F704         "FILE NOT FOUND"

*****************************
F533  4A        LSR               device number
F534  B0 03     BCS $F539         one (tape), then continue
F536  4C 13 F7  JMP $F713         RS-232, "ILLEGAL DEVICE #"
F539  20 D0 F7  JSR $F7D0         get tape-buffer start-
F53C  B0 03     BCS $F541
F53E  4C 13 F7  JMP $F713
F541  20 17 F8  JSR $F817         waits for PLAY key
F544  B0 68     BCS $F5AE
F546  20 AF F5  JSR $F5AF         output "SEARCHING FOR name"
F549  A5 B7     LDA $B7           length of file name
F54B  F0 09     BEQ $F556         =0, then continue
F54D  20 EA F7  JSR $F7EA         searches for desired tape-
F550  90 0B     BCC $F55D                                header
F552  F0 5A     BEQ $F5AE
F554  B0 DA     BCS $F530
F556  20 2C F7  JSR $F72C         search for next tape-header
F559  F0 53     BEQ $F5AE
F55B  B0 D3     BCS $F530
F55D  A5 90     LDA $90           get status
F55F  29 10     AND #$10
F561  38        SEC
F562  D0 4A     BNE $F5AE
F564  E0 01     CPX #$01          header-type 1=BASIC program
F566  F0 11     BEQ $F579                      (shiftable)
F568  E0 03     CPX #$03          3= machine-program
F56A  D0 DD     BNE $F549                  (non-shiftable)
F56C  A0 01     LDY #$01
F56E  B1 B2     LDA ($B2),Y       start-address low
F570  85 C3     STA $C3
F572  C8        INY
F573  B1 B2     LDA ($B2),Y       start-address high
F575  85 C4     STA $C4
F577  B0 04     BCS $F57D
```

```
F579  A5 B9     LDA $B9          secondary address
F57B  D0 EF     BNE $F56C        not zero,then absolute load
F57D  A0 03     LDY #$03
F57F  B1 B2     LDA ($B2),Y
F581  A0 01     LDY #$01         end-address minus
F583  F1 B2     SBC ($B2),Y
F585  AA        TAX
F586  A0 04     LDY #$04
F588  B1 B2     LDA ($B2),Y
F58A  A0 02     LDY #$02         start address
F58C  F1 B2     SBC ($B2),Y
F58E  A8        TAY
F58F  18        CLC              program length
F590  8A        TXA
F591  65 C3     ADC $C3
F593  85 AE     STA $AE          program length + start adrs
F595  98        TYA
F596  65 C4     ADC $C4          end address
F598  85 AF     STA $AF
F59A  A5 C3     LDA $C3
F59C  85 C1     STA $C1          start-address to $C1/$C2
F59E  A5 C4     LDA $C4
F5A0  85 C2     STA $C2
F5A2  20 D2 F5  JSR $F5D2        output "LOADING/VERIFYING"
F5A5  20 4A F8  JSR $F84A        load program from tape
F5A8  24        .BYTE $24
F5A9  18        CLC
F5AA  A6 AE     LDX $AE          end address to X/Y
F5AC  A4 AF     LDY $AF
F5AE  60        RTS

******************************   Out-put "SEARCHING" for name
F5AF  A5 9D     LDA $9D           check direct-mode
F5B1  10 1E     BPL $F5D1         no, then skip
F5B3  A0 0C     LDY #$0C          offset for "SEARCHING"
F5B5  20 2F F1  JSR $F12F         out-put message
F5B8  A5 B7     LDA $B7           length of file name
F5BA  F0 15     BEQ $F5D1         =0, then ready
F5BC  A0 17     LDY #$17          offset for "FOR"
F5BE  20 2F F1  JSR $F12F         out-put message
F5C1  A4 B7     LDY $B7           length of file name
F5C3  F0 0C     BEQ $F5D1         =0, then ready
F5C5  A0 00     LDY #$00
F5C7  B1 BB     LDA ($BB),Y       get file name
F5C9  20 D2 FF  JSR $FFD2         and out-put it
F5CC  C8        INY
F5CD  C4 B7     CPY $B7
F5CF  D0 F6     BNE $F5C7
F5D1  60        RTS

******************************   out-put "LOADING/VERIFYING"
F5D2  A0 49     LDY #$49          offset for "LOADING"
F5D4  A5 93     LDA $93           check load/verify flag
F5D6  F0 02     BEQ $F5DA         load, then output
F5D8  A0 59     LDY #$59          offset for "VERIFYING"
```

```
F5DA  4C 2B F1 JMP $F12B         out-put message

****************************     SAVE routine
F5DD  86 AE     STX $AE           end address low
F5DF  84 AF     STY $AF           end address high
F5E1  AA        TAX
F5E2  B5 00     LDA $00,X
F5E4  85 C1     STA $C1           start address low
F5E6  B5 01     LDA $01,X
F5E8  85 C2     STA $C2           start address high
F5EA  6C 32 03 JMP ($0332)        SAVE-vector, JMP $E5ED
F5ED  A5 BA     LDA $BA           device address
F5EF  D0 03     BNE $F5F4
F5F1  4C 13 F7 JMP $F713          "ILLEGAL DEVICE NUMBER"
F5F4  C9 03     CMP #$03
F5F6  F0 F9     BEQ $F5F1         screen, error
F5F8  90 5F     BCC $F659         tape

****************************     SAVE on IEC-bus
F5FA  A9 61     LDA #$61          secondary address 1
F5FC  85 B9     STA $B9           set
F5FE  A4 B7     LDY $B7           length of file name
F600  D0 03     BNE $F605         not zero, then ok
F602  4C 10 F7 JMP $F710          missing file name
F605  20 D5 F3 JSR $F3D5          file name on IEC-bus
F608  20 8F F6 JSR $F68F          out-put "SAVING"
F60B  A5 BA     LDA $BA           device address
F60D  20 0C ED JSR $ED0C          send LISTEN
F610  A5 B9     LDA $B9           send secondary address
F612  20 B9 ED JSR $EDB9          for LISTEN
F615  A0 00     LDY #$00
F617  20 8E FB JSR $FB8E          start address to $AC/$AD
F61A  A5 AC     LDA $AC           start address low
F61C  20 DD ED JSR $EDDD          send
F61F  A5 AD     LDA $AD           and send
F621  20 DD ED JSR $EDDD          high
F624  20 D1 FC JSR $FCD1          end-address reached yet?
F627  B0 16     BCS $F63F         yes, then ready
F629  B1 AC     LDA ($AC),Y       program bytes
F62B  20 DD ED JSR $EDDD          out-put to IEC-bus
F62E  20 E1 FF JSR $FFE1          scan STOP key
F631  D0 07     BNE $F63A         not pressed, then continue
F633  20 42 F6 JSR $F642          close IEC-bus channel
F636  A9 00     LDA #$00
F638  38        SEC               set flag for "BREAK" output
F639  60        RTS
F63A  20 DB FC JSR $FCDB          increment current address
F63D  D0 E5     BNE $F624
F63F  20 FE ED JSR $EDFE          send UNLISTEN
F642  24 B9     BIT $B9
F644  30 11     BMI $F657
F646  A5 BA     LDA $BA           device address
F648  20 0C ED JSR $ED0C          send LISTEN
F64B  A5 B9     LDA $B9           secondary address
```

```
F64D  29 EF     AND ##$EF
F64F  09 E0     ORA ##$E0
F651  20 B9 ED JSR $EDB9        output of secondary address
F654  20 FE ED JSR $EDFE        send UNLISTEN
F657  18        CLC
F658  60        RTS
F659  4A        LSR             device number / 2
F65A  B0 03     BCS $F65F       tape
F65C  4C 13 F7 JMP $F713        RS-232, "ILLEGAL DEVICE #"
F65F  20 D0 F7 JSR $F7D0        get tape buffer start-adrs.
F662  90 8D     BCC $F5F1
F664  20 38 F8 JSR $F838        waits for RECORD & PLAY key
F667  B0 25     BCS $F68E
F669  20 8F F6 JSR $F68F        out-put "SAVING name"
F66C  A2 03     LDX ##$03       header-tyep 3 machine-prgm.
F66E  A5 B9     LDA $B9         secondary address
F670  29 01     AND ##$01       bit 0 is set (1 or 3)
F672  D0 02     BNE $F676       yes, then machine program
F674  A2 01     LDX ##$01       header type 1=BASIC program
F676  8A        TXA
F677  20 6A F7 JSR $F76A        write header on tape
F67A  B0 12     BCS $F68E       jump-out at stop-key
F67C  20 67 F8 JSR $F867        write program on tape
F67F  B0 0D     BCS $F68E       jump-out at stop-key
F681  A5 B9     LDA $B9         secondary address
F683  29 02     AND ##$02       bit 1 is set (2 or 3)
F685  F0 06     BEQ $F68D       no, then ready
F687  A9 05     LDA ##$05       EOT, control byte
F689  20 6A F7 JSR $F76A        write block on tape
E68C  24        .BYTE $24
F68D  18        CLC
F68E  60        RTS

******************************  Out-put "SAVING"
F68F  A5 9D     LDA $9D          direct mode?
F691  10 FB     BPL $F68E        no, then ready
F693  A0 51     LDY ##$51        offset for "SAVING"
F695  20 2F F1 JSR $F12F         out-put message
F698  4C C1 F5 JMP $F5C1         out-put file name

******************************  VDTIM increase time
F69B  A2 00     LDX ##$00
F69D  E6 A2     INC $A2
F69F  D0 06     BNE $F6A7        increase time
F6A1  E6 A1     INC $A1
F6A3  D0 02     BNE $F6A7
F6A5  E6 A0     INC $A0
F6A7  38        SEC
F6A8  A5 A2     LDA $A2
F6AA  E9 01     SBC ##$01
F6AC  A5 A1     LDA $A1          compare with value for24 Hr
F6AE  E9 1A     SBC ##$1A
F6B0  A5 A0     LDA $A0
F6B2  E9 4F     SBC ##$4F
F6B4  90 06     BCC $F6BC        smaller, then ok
```

```
F6B6   86 A0      STX $A0
F6B8   86 A1      STX $A1                 set time on zero
F6BA   86 A2      STX $A2
F6BC   AD 01 DC LDA $DC01
F6BF   CD 01 DC CMP $DC01
F6C2   D0 F8      BNE $F6BC
F6C4   AA         TAX
F6C5   30 13      BMI $F6DA
F6C7   A2 BD      LDX #$BD
F6C9   8E 00 DC STX $DC00
F6CC   AE 01 DC LDX $DC01
F6CF   EC 01 DC CPX $DC01                 check stop-key
F6D2   D0 F8      BNE $F6CC
F6D4   8D 00 DC STA $DC00
F6D7   E8         INX
F6D8   D0 02      BNE $F6DC
F6DA   85 91      STA $91                 flag for stop-key
F6DC   60         RTS

*****************************          Get time
F6DD   78         SEI
F6DE   A5 A2      LDA $A2
F6E0   A6 A1      LDX $A1
F6E2   A4 A0      LDY $A0

*****************************          Set time
F6E4   78         SEI
F6E5   85 A2      STA $A2
F6E7   86 A1      STX $A1
F6E9   84 A0      STY $A0
F6EB   58         CLI
F6EC   60         RTS

*****************************          Scan STOP-key
F6ED   A5 91      LDA $91                 flag
F6EF   C9 7F      CMP #$7F                check on code for stop
F6F1   D0 07      BNE $F6FA
F6F3   08         PHP
F6F4   20 CC FF JSR $FFCC                 CLRCH
F6F7   85 C6      STA $C6
F6F9   28         PLP
F6FA   60         RTS

*****************************          Out-put operating systems
F6FB   A9 01      LDA #$01                                     messages
F6FD   2C         .BYTE $2C
F6FE   A9 02      LDA #$02
F700   2C         .BYTE $2C
F701   A9 03      LDA #$03
5703   2C         .BYTE $2C
F704   A9 04      LDA #$04
5706   2C         .BYTE $2C
5707   A9 05      LDA #$05
5709   2C         .BYTE $2C
570A   A9 06      LDA #$06
F70C   2C         .BYTE $2C
```

```
F70D  A9 07     LDA #$07
F70F  2C        .BYTE $2C
F710  A9 08     LDA #$08
5712  2C        .BYTE $2C
5713  A9 09     LDA #$09
F715  48        PHA             save error-number
F716  20 CC FF  JSR $FFCC       CLRCH
F719  A0 00     LDY #$00
F71B  24 9D     BIT $9D         check direct-mode flag
F71D  50 0A     BVC $F729
F71F  20 2F F1  JSR $F12F       out-put "I/O ERROR #"
F722  68        PLA
F723  48        PHA             get error number
F724  09 30     ORA #$30        to ASCII
F726  20 D2 FF  JSR $FFD2       and out-put
F729  68        PLA
F72A  38        SEC
F72B  60        RTS

******************************  Read program header off tape
F72C  A5 93     LDA $93         save load/verify flag
F72E  48        PHA
F72F  20 41 F8  JSR $F841       read block off tape
F732  68        PLA
F733  85 93     STA $93         get back load/verify flag
F735  B0 32     BCS $F769       error, then end
F737  A0 00     LDY #$00
F739  B1 B2     LDA ($B2),Y     check header type
F73B  C9 05     CMP #$05        EOT?
F73D  F0 2A     BEQ $F769
F73F  C9 01     CMP #$01        BASIC-program?
F741  F0 08     BEQ $F74B
F743  C9 03     CMP #$03        machine program?
F745  F0 04     BEQ $F74B
F747  C9 04     CMP #$04        data header?
F749  D0 E1     BNE $F72C       no
F74B  AA        TAX
F74C  24 9D     BIT $9D         direct-mode?
F74E  10 17     BPL $F767       no, then continue
F750  A0 63     LDY #$63
F752  20 2F F1  JSR $F12F       out-put "FOUND"
F755  A0 05     LDY #$05        offset of file name
F757  B1 B2     LDA ($B2),Y
F759  20 D2 FF  JSR $FFD2       out-put file name
F75C  C8        INY
F75D  C0 15     CPY #$15
F75F  D0 F6     BNE $F757
F761  A5 A1     LDA $A1         middle time byte to accum.
F763  20 E0 E4  JSR $E4E0       waits for Commodore-key or
                                                 time-loop
F766  EA        NOP
F767  18        CLC
F768  88        DEY             at error, C=1
F769  60        RTS

******************************  Generate header and write to
```

```
F76A   85 9E      STA $9E          header-type
F76C   20 D0 F7   JSR $F7D0        get tape-buffer address
F76F   90 5E      BCC $F7CF
F771   A5 C2      LDA $C2
F773   48         PHA              save start-address
F774   A5 C1      LDA $C1
F776   48         PHA              and
F777   A5 AF      LDA $AF
F779   48         PHA              end-address
F77A   A5 AE      LDA $AE
F77C   48         PHA
F77D   A0 BF      LDY #$BF         buffer-length - 1
F77F   A9 20      LDA #$20
F781   91 B2      STA ($B2),Y      clear tape-buffer
F783   88         DEY
F784   D0 FB      BNE $F781
F786   A5 9E      LDA $9E
F788   91 B2      STA ($B2),Y      header-type
F78A   C8         INY
F78B   A5 C1      LDA $C1
F78D   91 B2      STA ($B2),Y      start-address
F78F   C8         INY
F790   A5 C2      LDA $C2
F792   91 B2      STA ($B2),Y
F794   C8         INY
F795   A5 AE      LDA $AE
F797   91 B2      STA ($B2),Y      end-address
F799   C8         INY
F79A   A5 AF      LDA $AF
F79C   91 B2      STA ($B2),Y
F79E   C8         INY
F79F   84 9F      STY $9F
F7A1   A0 00      LDY #$00
F7A3   84 9E      STY $9E          counter for filename-length
F7A5   A4 9E      LDY $9E
F7A7   C4 B7      CPY $B7          compare with length
F7A9   F0 0C      BEQ $F7B7        all letters, then continue
F7AB   B1 BB      LDA ($BB),Y      get filename
F7AD   A4 9F      LDY $9F
F7AF   91 B2      STA ($B2),Y      write in header
F7B1   E6 9E      INC $9E
F7B3   E6 9F      INC $9F
F7B5   D0 EE      BNE $F7A5
F7B7   20 D7 F7   JSR $F7D7        start and end-address on
                                                   tape buffer
F7BA   A9 69      LDA #$69
F7BC   85 AB      STA $AB          header checksum block = $69
F7BE   20 6B F8   JSR $F86B        write block on tape
F7C1   A8         TAY
F7C2   68         PLA
F7C3   85 AE      STA $AE
F7C5   68         PLA              get back end-address
F7C6   85 AF      STA $AF
F7C8   68         PLA              and
F7C9   85 C1      STA $C1
F7CB   68         PLA              start-address
```

```
F7CC  85 C2     STA $C2
F7CE  98        TYA
F7CF  60        RTS

******************************    Get tape-buffer start-addr.
F7D0  A6 B2     LDX $B2
F7D2  A4 B3     LDY $B3
F7D4  C0 02     CPY #$02           address smaller $200?
F7D6  60        RTS

******************************
F7D7  20 D0 F7  JSR $F7D0          get tape-buffer address
F7DA  8A        TXA
F7DB  85 C1     STA $C1            start-address = start tape-
F7DD  18        CLC                                  buffer
F7DE  69 C0     ADC #$C0
F7E0  85 AE     STA $AE
F7E2  98        TYA                end-address = start-address
F7E3  85 C2     STA $C2                        + length(192)
F7E5  69 00     ADC #$00
F7E7  85 AF     STA $AF
F7E9  60        RTS

******************************    tape header search for name
F7EA  20 2C F7  JSR $F72C          search next tape header
F7ED  B0 1D     BCS $F80C          EOT, then ready
F7EF  A0 05     LDY #$05           filename offset in header
F7F1  84 9F     STY $9F
F7F3  A0 00     LDY #$00
F7F5  84 9E     STY $9E            counter for length of name
F7F7  C4 B7     CPY $B7            compare to searched name
F7F9  F0 10     BEQ $F80B          equal, then found
F7FB  B1 BB     LDA ($BB),Y        letter of filename
F7FD  A4 9F     LDY $9F
F7FF  D1 B2     CMP ($B2),Y        compare header filename
F801  D0 E7     BNE $F7EA          not equal,check next header
F803  E6 9E     INC $9E
F805  E6 9F     INC $9F            increment counter
F807  A4 9E     LDY $9E
F809  D0 EC     BNE $F7F7          compare further letters
F80B  18        CLC
F80C  60        RTS

******************************    Increase tape-buffer pointer
F80D  20 D0 F7  JSR $F7D0          get tape-buffer address
F810  E6 A6     INC $A6            increment pointer
F812  A4 A6     LDY $A6
F814  C0 C0     CPY #$C0           compare to max. value (192)
F816  60        RTS

******************************    Waits for Tape-key
F817  20 2E F8  JSR $F82E          scans tape-keys
F81A  F0 1A     BEQ $F836          pressed, then ready
F81C  A0 1B     LDY #$1B           offset for "PRESS PLAY ON
F81E  20 2F F1  JSR $F12F          output                TAPE"
```

```
F821   20 D0 F8 JSR $F8D0
F824   20 2E F8 JSR $F82E          scans Tape-key
F827   D0 F8    BNE $F821
F829   A0 6A    LDY #$6A           offset for "OK"
F82B   4C 2F F1 JMP $F12F          out-put

*****************************      Check if tape key pressed
F82E   A9 10    LDA #$10            check bit 4
F830   24 01    BIT $01
F832   D0 02    BNE $F836
F834   24 01    BIT $01
F836   18       CLC                 yes, the Z=1, otherwis Z=0
F837   60       RTS

*****************************      Waits for tape-key for writin
F838   20 2E F8 JSR $F82E           scan tape-key
F83B   F0 F9    BEQ $F836           pressed, then ready
F83D   A0 2E    LDY #$2E            offset for "PRESS PLAY &
F83F   D0 DD    BNE $F81E           re-check   /RECORD ON TAPE"

*****************************      Read block off tape
F841   A9 00    LDA #$00
F843   85 90    STA $90             clear status
F845   85 93    STA $93             and verify-flag
F847   20 D7 F7 JSR $F7D7           get tape-buffer address

*****************************      LOAD program from tape
F84A   20 17 F8 JSR $F817           waits for PLAY-key
F84D   B0 1F    BCS $F86E
F84F   78       SEI
F850   A9 00    LDA #$00
F852   85 AA    STA $AA
F854   85 B4    STA $B4
F856   85 B0    STA $B0             clear work-memory for IRQ-
F858   85 9E    STA $9E                                 routine
F85A   85 9F    STA $9F
F85C   85 9C    STA $9C
F85E   A9 90    LDA #$90            constant for timer high
F860   A2 0E    LDX #$0E            number of IRQ vector, $F92C
F862   D0 11    BNE $F875

*****************************      Write tape buffer on tape
F864   20 D7 F7 JSR $F7D7           get tape-buffer address
F867   A9 14    LDA #$14            check-sum
F869   85 AB    STA $AB            for data block of header $14

*****************************      Write block or prgm. on tape
F86B   20 38 F8 JSR $F838           waits for REC. & PLAY
F86E   B0 6C    BCS $F8DC
F870   78       SEI
F871   A9 82    LDA #$82            constant for timer high
F873   A2 08    LDX #$08            number of IRQ-vector $FC6A
F875   A0 7F    LDY #$7F
F877   8C 0D DC STY $DC0D
F87A   8D 0D DC STA $DC0D
```

```
F87D  AD 0E DC LDA $DC0E
F880  09 19    ORA #$19
F882  8D 0F DC STA $DC0F
F885  29 91    AND #$91
F887  8D A2 02 STA $02A2          timer A control-flag
F88A  20 A4 F0 JSR $F0A4
F88D  AD 11 D0 LDA $D011
F890  29 EF    AND #$EF           key screen dark
F892  8D 11 D0 STA $D011
F895  AD 14 03 LDA $0314          IRQ-vector
F898  8D 9F 02 STA $029F
F89B  AD 15 03 LDA $0315          save to $29F/$2A0
F89E  8D A0 02 STA $02A0
F8A1  20 BD FC JSR $FCBD          set IRQ for tape I/O
F8A4  A9 02    LDA #$02
F8A6  85 BE    STA $BE            read number of blocks
F8A8  20 97 FB JSR $FB97          set bit counter for serial
                                                     out-put
F8AB  A5 01    LDA $01
F8AD  29 1F    AND #$1F           switch on tape drive
F8AF  85 01    STA $01
F8B1  85 C0    STA $C0            set flag tape-drive
F8B3  A2 FF    LDX #$FF
F8B5  A0 FF    LDY #$FF
F8B7  88       DEY
F8B8  D0 FD    BNE $F8B7          delay-loop for tape high-
F8BA  CA       DEX                                  run time
F8BB  D0 F8    BNE $F8B5
F8BD  58       CLI                set interrupt for tape I/O
                                                        free
******************************   Wait for I/O end
F8BE  AD A0 02 LDA $02A0          IRQ vector back standard #?
F8C1  CD 15 03 CMP $0315
F8C4  18       CLC
F8C5  F0 15    BEQ $F8DC          yes, then ready
F8C7  20 D0 F8 JSR $F8D0          check on stop-key
F8CA  20 BC F6 JSR $F6BC          set flag when stop-key hit
F8CD  4C BE F8 JMP $F8BE          continue waiting

******************************   Scans stop-key
F8D0  20 E1 FF JSR $FFE1          scan stop-key
F8D3  18       CLC
F8D4  D0 0B    BNE $F8E1          no, then return
F8D6  20 93 FC JSR $FC93          tape-drive off, restore IRQ
F8D9  38       SEC                symbol for interrupt
F8DA  68       PLA
F8DB  68       PLA                clear return address
F8DC  A9 00    LDA #$00
F8DE  8D A0 02 STA $02A0          symbol for normal IRQ
F8E1  60       RTS

******************************   Prepare for tape reading
F8E2  86 B1    STX $B1
F8E4  A5 B0    LDA $B0
F8E6  0A       ASL
F8E7  0A       ASL
```

```
F8E8   18          CLC
F8E9   65 B0       ADC $B0
F8EB   18          CLC
F8EC   65 B1       ADC $B1
F8EE   85 B1       STA $B1
F8F0   A9 00       LDA #$00
F8F2   24 B0       BIT $B0
F8F4   30 01       BMI $F8F7
F8F6   2A          ROL
F8F7   06 B1       ASL $B1
F8F9   2A          ROL
F8FA   06 B1       ASL $B1
F8FC   2A          ROL
F8FD   AA          TAX
F8FE   AD 06 DC    LDA $DC06
F901   C9 16       CMP #$16
F903   90 F9       BCC $F8FE
F905   65 B1       ADC $B1
F907   8D 04 DC    STA $DC04
F90A   8A          TXA
F90B   6D 07 DC    ADC $DC07
F90E   8D 05 DC    STA $DC05
F911   AD A2 02    LDA $02A2
F914   8D 0E DC    STA $DC0E
F917   8D A4 02    STA $02A4
F91A   AD 0D DC    LDA $DC0D          read input from tape
F91D   29 10       AND #$10           isolate bit
F91F   F0 09       BEQ $F92A
F921   A9 F9       LDA #$F9
F923   48          PHA                return address on stack
F924   A9 2A       LDA #$2A
F926   48          PHA
F927   4C 43 FF    JMP $FF43          to interrupt
F92A   58          CLI
F92B   60          RTS

*****************************        Tape read interrupt-routine
F92C   AE 07 DC    LDX $DC07          timer high
F92F   A0 FF       LDY #$FF
F931   98          TYA
F932   ED 06 DC    SBC $DC06
F935   EC 07 DC    CPX $DC07
F938   D0 F2       BNE $F92C
F93A   86 B1       STX $B1
F93C   AA          TAX
F93D   8C 06 DC    STY $DC06
F940   8C 07 DC    STY $DC07
F943   A9 19       LDA #$19
F945   8D 0F DC    STA $DC0F
F948   AD 0D DC    LDA $DC0D          input from tape
F94B   8D A3 02    STA $02A3
F94E   98          TYA
F94F   E5 B1       SBC $B1
F951   86 B1       STX $B1
F953   4A          LSR
```

```
F954  66 B1     ROR $B1
F956  4A        LSR
F957  66 B1     ROR $B1
F959  A5 B0     LDA $B0
F95B  18        CLC
F95C  69 3C     ADC #$3C
F95E  C5 B1     CMP $B1
F960  B0 4A     BCS $F9AC
F962  A6 9C     LDX $9C
F964  F0 03     BEQ $F969
F966  4C 60 FA  JMP $FA60
F969  A6 A3     LDX $A3
F96B  30 1B     BMI $F988
F96D  A2 00     LDX #$00
F96F  69 30     ADC #$30
F971  65 B0     ADC $B0
F973  C5 B1     CMP $B1
F975  B0 1C     BCS $F993
F977  E8        INX
F978  69 26     ADC #$26
F97A  65 B0     ADC $B0
F97C  C5 B1     CMP $B1
F97E  B0 17     BCS $F997
F980  69 2C     ADC #$2C
F982  65 B0     ADC $B0
F984  C5 B1     CMP $B1
F986  90 03     BCC $F98B
F988  4C 10 FA  JMP $FA10
F98B  A5 B4     LDA $B4
F98D  F0 1D     BEQ $F9AC
F98F  85 A8     STA $A8
F991  D0 19     BNE $F9AC
F993  E6 A9     INC $A9
F995  B0 02     BCS $F999
F997  C6 A9     DEC $A9
F999  38        SEC
F99A  E9 13     SBC #$13
F99C  E5 B1     SBC $B1
F99E  65 92     ADC $92
F9A0  85 92     STA $92
F9A2  A5 A4     LDA $A4
F9A4  49 01     EOR #$01
F9A6  85 A4     STA $A4
F9A8  F0 2B     BEQ $F9D5
F9AA  86 D7     STX $D7
F9AC  A5 B4     LDA $B4
F9AE  F0 22     BEQ $F9D2
F9B0  AD A3 02  LDA $02A3
F9B3  29 01     AND #$01
F9B5  D0 05     BNE $F9BC
F9B7  AD A4 02  LDA $02A4
F9BA  D0 16     BNE $F9D2
F9BC  A9 00     LDA #$00
F9BE  85 A4     STA $A4
F9C0  8D A4 02  STA $02A4
F9C3  A5 A3     LDA $A3
```

```
F9C5   10 30     BPL $F9F7
F9C7   30 BF     BMI $F988
F9C9   A2 A6     LDX #$A6
F9CB   20 E2 F8  JSR $F8E2
F9CE   A5 9B     LDA $9B
F9D0   D0 B9     BNE $F98B
F9D2   4C BC FE  JMP $FEBC
F9D5   A5 92     LDA $92
F9D7   F0 07     BEQ $F9E0
F9D9   30 03     BMI $F9DE
F9DB   C6 B0     DEC $B0
F9DD   2C        .BYTE $2C
F9DE   E6 B0     INC $B0
F9E0   A9 00     LDA #$00
F9E2   85 92     STA $92
F9E4   E4 D7     CPX $D7
F9E6   D0 0F     BNE $F9F7
F9E8   8A        TXA
F9E9   D0 A0     BNE $F98B
F9EB   A5 A9     LDA $A9
F9ED   30 BD     BMI $F9AC
F9EF   C9 10     CMP #$10
F9F1   90 B9     BCC $F9AC
F9F3   85 96     STA $96
F9F5   B0 B5     BCS $F9AC
F9F7   8A        TXA
F9F8   45 9B     EOR $9B
F9FA   85 9B     STA $9B
F9FC   A5 B4     LDA $B4
F9FE   F0 D2     BEQ $F9D2
FA00   C6 A3     DEC $A3
FA02   30 C5     BMI $F9C9
FA04   46 D7     LSR $D7
FA06   66 BF     ROR $BF
FA08   A2 DA     LDX #$DA
FA0A   20 E2 F8  JSR $F8E2
FA0D   4C BC FE  JMP $FEBC
FA10   A5 96     LDA $96
FA12   F0 04     BEQ $FA18
FA14   A5 B4     LDA $B4
FA16   F0 07     BEQ $FA1F
FA18   A5 A3     LDA $A3
FA1A   30 03     BMI $FA1F
FA1C   4C 97 F9  JMP $F997
FA1F   46 B1     LSR $B1
FA21   A9 93     LDA #$93
FA23   38        SEC
FA24   E5 B1     SBC $B1
FA26   65 B0     ADC $B0
FA28   0A        ASL
FA29   AA        TAX
FA2A   20 E2 F8  JSR $F8E2
FA2D   E6 9C     INC $9C
FA2F   A5 B4     LDA $B4
```

```
FA31  D0 11     BNE $FA44
FA33  A5 96     LDA $96
FA35  F0 26     BEQ $FA5D
FA37  85 A8     STA $A8
FA39  A9 00     LDA #$00
FA3B  85 96     STA $96
FA3D  A9 81     LDA #$81
FA3F  8D 0D DC  STA $DC0D
FA42  85 B4     STA $B4
FA44  A5 96     LDA $96
FA46  85 B5     STA $B5
FA48  F0 09     BEQ $FA53
FA4A  A9 00     LDA #$00
FA4C  85 B4     STA $B4
FA4E  A9 01     LDA #$01
FA50  8D 0D DC  STA $DC0D
FA53  A5 BF     LDA $BF
FA55  85 BD     STA $BD
FA57  A5 A8     LDA $A8
FA59  05 A9     ORA $A9
FA5B  85 B6     STA $B6
FA5D  4C BC FE  JMP $FEBC           return from interrupt
FA60  20 97 FB  JSR $FB97
FA63  85 9C     STA $9C
FA65  A2 DA     LDX #$DA
FA67  20 E2 F8  JSR $F8E2
FA6A  A5 BE     LDA $BE
FA6C  F0 02     BEQ $FA70
FA6E  85 A7     STA $A7
FA70  A9 0F     LDA #$0F
FA72  24 AA     BIT $AA
FA74  10 17     BPL $FA8D
FA76  A5 B5     LDA $B5
FA78  D0 0C     BNE $FA86
FA7A  A6 BE     LDX $BE
FA7C  CA        DEX
FA7D  D0 0B     BNE $FA8A
FA7F  A9 08     LDA #$08            "LONG BLOCK" error
FA81  20 1C FE  JSR $FE1C           set status
FA84  D0 04     BNE $FA8A
FA86  A9 00     LDA #$00
FA88  85 AA     STA $AA
FA8A  4C BC FE  JMP $FEBC           return from interrupt
FA8D  70 31     BVS $FAC0
FA8F  D0 18     BNE $FAA9
FA91  A5 B5     LDA $B5
FA93  D0 F5     BNE $FA8A
FA95  A5 B6     LDA $B6
FA97  D0 F1     BNE $FA8A
FA99  A5 A7     LDA $A7
FA9B  4A        LSR
FA9C  A5 BD     LDA $BD
FA9E  30 03     BMI $FAA3
FAA0  90 18     BCC $FABA
FAA2  18        CLC
```

```
FAA3   B0 15      BCS $FABA
FAA5   29 0F      AND #$0F
FAA7   85 AA      STA $AA
FAA9   C6 AA      DEC $AA
FAAB   D0 DD      BNE $FA8A
FAAD   A9 40      LDA #$40
FAAF   85 AA      STA $AA
FAB1   20 8E FB   JSR $FB8E
FAB4   A9 00      LDA #$00
FAB6   85 AB      STA $AB
FAB8   F0 D0      BEQ $FA8A
FABA   A9 80      LDA #$80
FABC   85 AA      STA $AA
FABE   D0 CA      BNE $FA8A
FAC0   A5 B5      LDA $B5
FAC2   F0 0A      BEQ $FACE
FAC4   A9 04      LDA #$04              "SHORT BLOCK" error
FAC6   20 1C FE   JSR $FE1C             set status
FAC9   A9 00      LDA #$00
FACB   4C 4A FB   JMP $FB4A
FACE   20 D1 FC   JSR $FCD1
FAD1   90 03      BCC $FAD6
FAD3   4C 48 FB   JMP $FB48
FAD6   A6 A7      LDX $A7
FAD8   CA         DEX
FAD9   F0 2D      BEQ $FB08
FADB   A5 93      LDA $93
FADD   F0 0C      BEQ $FAEB
FADF   A0 00      LDY #$00
FAE1   A5 BD      LDA $BD
FAE3   D1 AC      CMP ($AC),Y
FAE5   F0 04      BEQ $FAEB
FAE7   A9 01      LDA #$01
FAE9   85 B6      STA $B6
FAEB   A5 B6      LDA $B6
FAED   F0 4B      BEQ $FB3A
FAEF   A2 3D      LDX #$3D
FAF1   E4 9E      CPX $9E
FAF3   90 3E      BCC $FB33
FAF5   A6 9E      LDX $9E
FAF7   A5 AD      LDA $AD
FAF9   9D 01 01   STA $0101,X
FAFC   A5 AC      LDA $AC
FAFE   9D 00 01   STA $0100,X
FB01   E8         INX\
FB02   E8         INX
FB03   86 9E      STX $9E
FB05   4C 3A FB   JMP $FB3A
FB08   A6 9F      LDX $9F
FB0A   E4 9E      CPX $9E
FB0C   F0 35      BEQ $FB43
FB0E   A5 AC      LDA $AC
FB10   DD 00 01   CMP $0100,X           error-correction at pass 2
FB13   D0 2E      BNE $FB43
FB15   A5 AD      LDA $AD
```

```
FB17  DD 01 01 CMP $0101,X
FB1A  D0 27    BNE $FB43
FB1C  E6 9F    INC $9F
FB1E  E6 9F    INC $9F
FB20  A5 93    LDA $93
FB22  F0 0B    BEQ $FB2F
FB24  A5 BD    LDA $BD          read byte
FB26  A0 00    LDY #$00
FB28  D1 AC    CMP ($AC),Y      compare with memory content
FB2A  F0 17    BEQ $FB43
FB2C  C8       INY
FB2D  84 B6    STY $B6
FB2F  A5 B6    LDA $B6
FB31  F0 07    BEQ $FB3A
FB33  A9 10    LDA #$10         "SECOND PASS" error
FB35  20 1C FE JSR $FE1C        set status
FB38  D0 09    BNE $FB43
FB3A  A5 93    LDA $93          verify?
FB3C  D0 05    BNE $FB43        yes
FB3E  A8       TAY
FB3F  A5 BD    LDA $BD          read byte
FB41  91 AC    STA ($AC),Y      save
FB43  20 DB FC JSR $FCDB        increment address-pointer
FB46  D0 43    BNE $FB8B
FB48  A9 80    LDA #$80
FB4A  85 AA    STA $AA
FB4C  78       SEI
FB4D  A2 01    LDX #$01
FB4F  8E 0D DC STX $DC0D
FB52  AE 0D DC LDX $DC0D
FB55  A6 BE    LDX $BE          decrement
FB57  CA       DEX              pass-counter
FB58  30 02    BMI $FB5C
FB5A  86 BE    STX $BE
FB5C  C6 A7    DEC $A7
FB5E  F0 08    BEQ $FB68
FB60  A5 9E    LDA $9E
FB62  D0 27    BNE $FB8B
FB64  85 BE    STA $BE
FB66  F0 23    BEQ $FB8B
FB68  20 93 FC JSR $FC93        one pass ended
FB6B  20 8E FB JSR $FB8E        address back to program
FB6E  A0 00    LDY #$00                                start
FB70  84 AB    STY $AB
FB72  B1 AC    LDA ($AC),Y      calculate program check-sum
FB74  45 AB    EOR $AB
FB76  85 AB    STA $AB
FB78  20 DB FC JSR $FCDB        increment address-pointer
FB7B  20 D1 FC JSR $FCD1        end-address reached yet?
FB7E  90 F2    BCC $FB72        no, continue comparison
FB80  A5 AB    LDA $AB          calculated check-sum
FB82  45 BD    EOR $BD          compare with tapes checksum
FB84  F0 05    BEQ $FB8B        check-sum ok?
FB86  A9 20    LDA #$20         "CHECK SUM" error
FB88  20 1C FE JSR $FE1C        set status
```

```
FB8B   4C BC FE JMP $FEBC          resum from interrupt
FB8E   A5 C2    LDA $C2
FB90   85 AD    STA $AD
FB92   A5 C1    LDA $C1
FB94   85 AC    STA $AC
FB96   60       RTS

******************************     Set bit-counter for serial
                                                        out-put
FB97   A9 08    LDA #$08            8 bits
FB99   85 A3    STA $A3
FB9B   A9 00    LDA #$00
FB9D   85 A4    STA $A4
FB9F   85 A8    STA $A8
FBA1   85 9B    STA $9B
FBA3   85 A9    STA $A9
FBA5   60       RTS

******************************     Write one bit on tape
FBA6   A5 BD    LDA $BD             bit in $8D
FBA8   4A       LSR                 bit 0 in carry
FBA9   A9 60    LDA #$60            time for "1" bit
FBAB   90 02    BCC $FBAF
FBAD   A9 B0    LDA #$B0            time for "0"bit
FBAF   A2 00    LDX #$00
FBB1   8D 06 DC STA $DC06           timer B low
FBB4   8E 07 DC STX $DC07           timer B high
FBB7   AD 0D DC LDA $DC0D           clear interrupt-flag
FBBA   A9 19    LDA #$19
FBBC   8D 0F DC STA $DC0F           start timer
FBBF   A5 01    LDA $01
FBC1   49 08    EOR #$08            invert output bit for tape
FBC3   85 01    STA $01
FBC5   29 08    AND #$08
FBC7   60       RTS
FBC8   38       SEC
FBC9   66 B6    ROR $B6
FBCB   30 3C    BMI $FC09

******************************     Write interrupt routine for
                                                        tape
FBCD   A5 A8    LDA $A8
FBCF   D0 12    BNE $FBE3
FBD1   A9 10    LDA #$10
FBD3   A2 01    LDX #$01
FBD5   20 B1 FB JSR $FBB1           write cycle on tape
FBD8   D0 2F    BNE $FC09
FBDA   E6 A8    INC $A8
FBDC   A5 B6    LDA $B6
FBDE   10 29    BPL $FC09
FBE0   4C 57 FC JMP $FC57           write second block
FBE3   A5 A9    LDA $A9
FBE5   D0 09    BNE $FBF0
FBE7   20 AD FB JSR $FBAD           write "0"-bit
FBEA   D0 1D    BNE $FC09
FBEC   E6 A9    INC $A9
FBEE   D0 19    BNE $FC09
```

```
FBF0  20 A6 FB JSR $FBA6       write bit on tape
FBF3  D0 14    BNE $FC09
FBF5  A5 A4    LDA $A4
FBF7  49 01    EOR #$01
FBF9  85 A4    STA $A4
FBFB  F0 0F    BEQ $FC0C
FBFD  A5 BD    LDA $BD
FBFF  49 01    EOR #$01        invert bit for output
FC01  85 BD    STA $BD
FC03  29 01    AND #$01
FC05  45 9B    EOR $9B
FC07  85 9B    STA $9B
FC09  4C BC FE JMP $FEBC       return from interrupt
FC0C  46 BD    LSR $BD         next bit in position 0
FC0E  C6 A3    DEC $A3         decrement bit-counter
FC10  A5 A3    LDA $A3
FC12  F0 3A    BEQ $FC4E
FC14  10 F3    BPL $FC09       out-put next bit
FC16  20 97 FB JSR $FB97       set bit-counter back to 8
FC19  58       CLI
FC1A  A5 A5    LDA $A5
FC1C  F0 12    BEQ $FC30
FC1E  A2 00    LDX #$00
FC20  86 D7    STX $D7
FC22  C6 A5    DEC $A5
FC24  A6 BE    LDX $BE
FC26  E0 02    CPX #$02
FC28  D0 02    BNE $FC2C
FC2A  09 80    ORA #$80
FC2C  85 BD    STA $BD
FC2E  D0 D9    BNE $FC09
FC30  20 D1 FC JSR $FCD1       end-address reached yet?
FC33  90 0A    BCC $FC3F
FC35  D0 91    BNE $FBC8
FC37  E6 AD    INC $AD
FC39  A5 D7    LDA $D7
FC3B  85 BD    STA $BD
FC3D  B0 CA    BCS $FC09
FC3F  A0 00    LDY #$00
FC41  B1 AC    LDA ($AC),Y     byte to be written
FC43  85 BD    STA $BD
FC45  45 D7    EOR $D7
FC47  85 D7    STA $D7
FC49  20 DB FC JSR $FCDB       increment address pointer
FC4C  D0 BB    BNE $FC09
FC4E  A5 9B    LDA $9B
FC50  49 01    EOR #$01
FC52  85 BD    STA $BD
FC54  4C BC FE JMP $FEBC       return from interrupt
FC57  C6 BE    DEC $BE         decrement counter for blocks
FC59  D0 03    BNE $FC5E       another block?
FC5B  20 CA FC JSR $FCCA       no, tape-drive off
FC5E  A9 50    LDA #$50
```

```
FC60  85 A7     STA $A7
FC62  A2 08     LDX #$08
FC64  78        SEI
FC65  20 BD FC  JSR $FCBD          IRQ on $FC6A
FC68  D0 EA     BNE $FC54          return from interrupt

******************************    Write tape interrupt routine
FC6A  A9 78     LDA #$78
FC6C  20 AF FB  JSR $FBAF          write bit on tape
FC6F  D0 E3     BNE $FC54
FC71  C6 A7     DEC $A7
FC73  D0 DF     BNE $FC54          return from interrupt
FC75  20 97 FB  JSR $FB97          set bit-counter for serial
                                                   out-put
FC78  C6 AB     DEC $AB
FC7A  10 D8     BPL $FC54
FC7C  A2 0A     LDX #$0A
FC7E  20 BD FC  JSR $FCBD          IRQ on $FBCD
FC81  58        CLI
FC82  E6 AB     INC $AB
FC84  A5 BE     LDA $BE
FC86  F0 30     BEQ $FCB8
FC88  20 8E FB  JSR $FB8E          set address back to start
FC8B  A2 09     LDX #$09
FC8D  86 A5     STX $A5
FC8F  86 B6     STX $B6
FC91  D0 83     BNE $FC16
FC93  08        PHP
FC94  78        SEI
FC95  AD 11 D0  LDA $D011
FC98  09 10     ORA #$10           turn screen back on
FC9A  8D 11 D0  STA $D011
FC9D  20 CA FC  JSR $FCCA          turn off tape drive
FCA0  A9 7F     LDA #$7F
FCA2  8D 0D DC  STA $DC0D
FCA5  20 DD FD  JSR $FDDD          CIA back to standard values
FCA8  AD A0 02  LDA $02A0
FCAB  F0 09     BEQ $FCB6
FCAD  8D 15 03  STA $0315          IRQ on standard
FCB0  AD 9F 02  LDA $029F
FCB3  8D 14 03  STA $0314
FCB6  28        PLP
FCB7  60        RTS

******************************    Set IRQ vector
FCB8  20 93 FC  JSR $FC93          IRQ on standard
FCBB  F0 97     BEQ $FC54
FCBD  BD 93 FD  LDA $FD93,X
FCC0  8D 14 03  STA $0314          set IRQ vector from table
FCC3  BD 94 FD  LDA $FD94,X
FCC6  8D 15 03  STA $0315
FCC9  60        RTS

******************************
FCCA  A5 01     LDA $01
FCCC  09 20     ORA #$20           switch off tape drive
FCCE  85 01     STA $01
```

```
FCD0  60          RTS

*****************************   Checks on reaching the end-
FCD1  38          SEC                                 address
FCD2  A5 AC       LDA $AC        current address $AC/$AD
FCD4  E5 AE       SBC $AE
FCD6  A5 AD       LDA $AD        end address $AE/$AF
FCD8  E5 AF       SBC $AF
FCDA  60          RTS

*****************************   Increment address pointer
FCDB  E6 AC       INC $AC
FCDD  D0 02       BNE $FCE1
FCDF  E6 AD       INC $AD
FCE1  60          RTS

*****************************   RESET
FCE2  A2 FF       LDX #$FF
FCE4  78          SEI
FCE5  9A          TXS
FCE6  D8          CLD
FCE7  20 02 FD JSR $FD02         checks on ROM in $8000
FCEA  D0 03       BNE $FCEF
FCEC  6C 00 80 JMP ($8000)       jump to module start
FCEF  8E 16 D0 STX $D016
FCF2  20 A3 FD JSR $FDA3
FCF5  20 50 FD JSR $FD50
FCF8  20 15 FD JSR $FD15
FCFB  20 5B FF JSR $FF5B
FCFE  58          CLI
FCFF  6C 00 A0 JMP ($A000)       to BASIC cold-start

*****************************   Checks on ROM in $8000
FD02  A2 05       LDX #$05
FD04  BD 0F FD LDA $FD0F,X
FD07  DD 03 80 CMP $8003,X       compares to "CBM80"
FD0A  D0 03       BNE $FD0F
FD0C  CA          DEX
FD0D  D0 F5       BNE $FD04
FD0F  60          RTS

*****************************   ROM module identivication
FD10  C3 C2 CD 38 30             "CBM80"

*****************************   Set/get hardware and I/O
FD15  A2 30       LDX #$30                            vectors
FD17  A0 FD       LDY #$FD       pointer to table $FD30
FD19  18          CLC
FD1A  86 C3       STX $C3
FD1C  84 C4       STY $C4
FD1E  A0 1F       LDY #$1F
FD20  B9 14 03 LDA $0314,Y
FD23  B0 02       BCS $FD27      C=1 then get vectors, C=1
FD25  B1 C3       LDA ($C3),Y
FD27  91 C3       STA ($C3),Y
```

```
FD29  99 14 03 STA $0314,Y
FD2C  88       DEY
FD2D  10 F1    BPL $FD20
FD2F  60       RTS

*****************************  Table hardware & I/O vectors
FD30 31 EA 66 FE 47 FE 4A F3
FD38 91 F2 0E F2 50 F2 33 F3
FD40 57 F1 CA F1 ED F6 3E F1
FD48 2F F3 66 FE A5 F4 ED F5

*****************************  Initialize work memory
FD50  A9 00    LDA #$00
FD52  A8       TAY
FD53  99 02 00 STA $0002,Y      zero page
FD56  99 00 02 STA $0200,Y      clear page 2
FD59  99 00 03 STA $0300,Y      and page 3
FD5C  C8       INY
FD5D  D0 F4    BNE $FD53
FD5F  A2 3C    LDX #$3C
FD61  A0 03    LDY #$03
FD63  86 B2    STX $B2          tape-buffer pointer on$033C
FD65  84 B3    STY $B3
FD67  A8       TAY
FD68  A9 03    LDA #$03
FD6A  85 C2    STA $C2          check RAM from $400
FD6C  E6 C2    INC $C2
FD6E  B1 C1    LDA ($C1),Y
FD70  AA       TAX
FD71  A9 55    LDA #$55         %01010101
FD73  91 C1    STA ($C1),Y
FD75  D1 C1    CMP ($C1),Y
FD77  D0 0F    BNE $FD88
FD79  2A       ROL              %10101010
FD7A  91 C1    STA ($C1),Y
FD7C  D1 C1    CMP ($C1),Y
FD7E  D0 08    BNE $FD88
FD80  8A       TXA
FD81  91 C1    STA ($C1),Y
FD83  C8       INY
FD84  D0 E8    BNE $FD6E
FD86  F0 E4    BEQ $FD6C
FD88  98       TYA
FD89  AA       TAX
FD8A  A4 C2    LDY $C2
FD8C  18       CLC
FD8D  20 2D FE JSR $FE2D        set memory (RAM) top
FD90  A9 08    LDA #$08
FD92  8D 82 02 STA $0282        BASIC start on $800
FD95  A9 04    LDA #$04
FD97  8D 88 02 STA $0288        Video-RAM on $400
FD9A  60       RTS

*****************************  IRQ vectors
FD9B  6A FC CD FB 31 EA 2C F9   $FC6A, $FBCD, $EA31, $F92C
```

```
FDA3   A9 7F      LDA #$7F                              (CIA1)
FDA5   8D 0D DC STA $DC0D        interrupt control register
FDA8   8D 0D DD STA $DD0D            "        "        " CIA2
FDAB   8D 00 DC STA $DC00        port A CIA 1
FDAE   A9 08      LDA #$08
FDB0   8D 0E DC STA $DC0E        control register A CIA 1
FDB3   8D 0E DD STA $DD0E        control register A CIA 2
FDB6   8D 0F DC STA $DC0F        control register B CIA 1
FDB9   8D 0F DD STA $DD0F        control register B CIA 2
FDBC   A2 00      LDX #$00       entrance mode
FDBE   8E 03 DC STX $DC03        data direction register B 1
FDC1   8E 03 DD STX $DD03        data direction register B 2
FDC4   8E 18 D4 STX $D418        volume for SID on zero
FDC7   CA         DEX            out-put mode
FDC8   8E 02 DC STX $DC02        data direction register A 1
FDCB   A9 07      LDA #$07
FDCD   8D 00 DD STA $DD00        port A CIA 2
FDD0   A9 3F      LDA #$3F
FDD2   8D 02 DD STA $DD02        data direction register A 2
FDD5   A9 E7      LDA #$E7
FDD7   85 01      STA $01
FDD9   A9 2F      LDA #$2F
FDDB   85 00      STA $00
FDDD   AD A6 02 LDA $02A6
FDE0   F0 0A      BEQ $FDEC
FDE2   A9 25      LDA #$25
FDE4   8D 04 DC STA $DC04
FDE7   A9 40      LDA #$40
FDE9   4C F3 FD JMP $FDF3
FDEC   A9 95      LDA #$95
FDEE   8D 04 DC STA $DC04
FDF1   A9 42      LDA #$42
FDF3   8D 05 DC STA $DC05
FDF6   4C 6E FF JMP $FF6E

******************************   Set parameter for filename
FDF9   85 B7      STA $B7         length
FDFB   86 BB      STX $BB         address low
FDFD   84 BC      STY $BC         address high
FDFF   60         RTS

******************************   Set active files parameter
FE00   85 B8      STA $B8         logical file number
FE02   86 BA      STX $BA         device address
FE04   84 B9      STY $B9         secondary address
FE06   60         RTS
******************************   Get status
FE07   A5 BA      LDA $BA         device number
FE09   C9 02      CMP #$02        equal ??
FE0B   D0 0D      BNE $FE1A       no
FE0D   AD 97 02 LDA $0297         get RS-232 status
FE10   48         PHA
FE11   A9 00      LDA #$00        clear status
FE13   8D 97 02 STA $0297
FE16   68         PLA
```

```
FE17  60        RTS

****************************  Set operatingsystem messages
FE18  85 9D     STA $9D

****************************  Get status
FE1A  A5 90     LDA $90

****************************  Set status
FE1C  05 90     ORA $90
FE1E  85 90     STA $90
FE20  60        RTS

****************************  Set time-out flag for IEC
FE21  8D 85 02  STA $0285
FE24  60        RTS

****************************  MEMTOP get/set end of BASIC-
                                                      RAM
FE25  90 06     BCC $FE2D
FE27  AE 83 02  LDX $0283      carry is set
FE2A  AC 84 02  LDY $0284      get address to X/Y
FE2D  8E 83 02  STX $0283      carry clear
FE30  8C 84 02  STY $0284      set X/Y to address
FE33  60        RTS

****************************  MEMBOT get/set bottom of
                                                BASIC-RAM
FE34  90 06     BCC $FE3C
FE36  AE 81 02  LDX $0281      s.a.
FE39  AC 82 02  LDY $0282
FE3C  8E 81 02  STX $0281
FE3F  8C 82 02  STY $0282
FE42  60        RTS

****************************  NMI-interrupt
FE43  78        SEI
FE44  6C 18 03  JMP ($0318)    JMP $FE47
FE47  48        PHA
FE48  8A        TXA
FE49  48        PHA            save register
FE4A  98        TYA
FE4B  48        PHA
FE4C  A9 7F     LDA #$7F
FE4E  8D 0D DD  STA $DD0D
FE51  AC 0D DD  LDY $DD0D
FE54  30 1C     BMI $FE72      RS-232 active
FE56  20 02 FD  JSR $FD02      checks on ROM in $8000
FE59  D0 03     BNE $FE5E      no, then continue
FE5B  6C 02 80  JMP ($8002)    yes, jump to module-NMI
FE5E  20 BC F6  JSR $F6BC      set flag for STOP-key
FE61  20 E1 FF  JSR $FFE1      scan stop key
FE64  D0 0C     BNE $FE72      not pressed
FE66  20 15 FD  JSR $FD15      set standard I/O vectors
FE69  20 A3 FD  JSR $FDA3      initialize I/O
FE6C  20 18 E5  JSR $E518      initialize I/O&clear screen
                               to BASIC warm-start
```

```
FE6F  6C 02 A0 JMP ($A002)
FE72  98       TYA
FE73  2D A1 02 AND $02A1
FE76  AA       TAX
FE77  29 01    AND #$01
FE79  F0 28    BEQ $FEA3
FE7B  AD 00 DD LDA $DD00
FE7E  29 FB    AND #$FB
FE80  05 B5    ORA $B5
FE82  8D 00 DD STA $DD00
FE85  AD A1 02 LDA $02A1
FE88  8D 0D DD STA $DD0D
FE8B  8A       TXA
FE8C  29 12    AND #$12
FE8E  F0 0D    BEQ $FE9D
FE90  29 02    AND #$02
FE92  F0 06    BEQ $FE9A
FE94  20 D6 FE JSR $FED6           RS-232 in
FE97  4C 9D FE JMP $FE9D
FE9A  20 07 FF JSR $FF07           RS-232 out
FE9D  20 BB EE JSR $EEBB           RS-232 output
FEA0  4C B6 FE JMP $FEB6           return from interrupt
FEA3  8A       TXA
FEA4  29 02    AND #$02
FEA6  F0 06    BEQ $FEAE
FEA8  20 D6 FE JSR $FED6           RS-232 in
FEAB  4C B6 FE JMP $FEB6           return from interrupt
FEAE  8A       TXA
FEAF  29 10    AND #$10
FEB1  F0 03    BEQ $FEB6
FEB3  20 07 FF JSR $FF07           RS-232 out
FEB6  AD A1 02 LDA $02A1
FEB9  8D 0D DD STA $DD0D
FEBC  68       PLA
FEBD  A8       TAY
FEBE  68       PLA                 get back register
FEBF  AA       TAX
FEC0  68       PLA
FEC1  40       RTI

*****************************     Baud-rate timer constants
FEC2  C1 27                        $27C1 = 29377      50 baud
FEC4  3A 1A                        $1A3A = 6718       75 baud
FEC6  C5 11                        $11C5 = 4549      110 baud
FEC8  74 0E                        $0E74 = 3700    134.5 baud
FECA  ED 0C                        $0CED = 3309      150 baud
FECC  45 06                        $0645 = 1605      300 baud
FECE  F0 02                        $02F0 = 752       600 baud
FED0  46 01                        $0146 = 326      1200 baud
FED2  B8 00                        $00B8 = 184      1800 baud
FED4  71 00                        $0071 = 113      2400 baud

*****************************     NMI-routine for RS-232 input
FED6  AD 01 DD LDA $DD01
FED9  29 01    AND #$01
FEDB  85 A7    STA $A7
```

```
FEDD  AD 06 DD LDA $DD06
FEE0  E9 1C    SBC #$1C
FEE2  6D 99 02 ADC $0299
FEE5  8D 06 DD STA $DD06
FEE8  AD 07 DD LDA $DD07          RS-232 timer baud constants
FEEB  6D 9A 02 ADC $029A
FEEE  8D 07 DD STA $DD07
FEF1  A9 11    LDA #$11
FEF3  8D 0F DD STA $DD0F
FEF6  AD A1 02 LDA $02A1
FEF9  8D 0D DD STA $DD0D
FEFC  A9 FF    LDA #$FF
FEFE  8D 06 DD STA $DD06
FF01  8D 07 DD STA $DD07
FF04  4C 59 EF JMP $EF59

****************************     NMI-routine for RS232 output
FF07  AD 95 02 LDA $0295
FF0A  8D 06 DD STA $DD06
FF0D  AD 96 02 LDA $0296          RS-232 timer baud constants
FF10  8D 07 DD STA $DD07
FF13  A9 11    LDA #$11
FF15  8D 0F DD STA $DD0F
FF18  A9 12    LDA #$12
FF1A  4D A1 02 EOR $02A1
FF1D  8D A1 02 STA $02A1
FF20  A9 FF    LDA #$FF
FF22  8D 06 DD STA $DD06
FF25  8D 07 DD STA $DD07
FF28  AE 98 02 LDX $0298          number of bits to be sent
FF2B  86 A8    STX $A8
FF2D  60       RTS

****************************
FF2E  AA       TAX
FF2F  AD 96 02 LDA $0296
FF32  2A       ROL
FF33  A8       TAY
FF34  8A       TXA
FF35  69 C8    ADC #$C8
FF37  8D 99 02 STA $0299          RS-232 timing
FF3A  98       TYA
FF3B  69 00    ADC #$00
FF3D  8D 9A 02 STA $029A
FF40  60       RTS
FF41  EA       NOP
FF42  EA       NOP

****************************     Interrupt from tape-routine
FF43  08       PHP
FF44  68       PLA
FF45  29 EF    AND #$EF           clear break-flag
FF47  48       PHA

****************************     IRQ-interrupt
```

```
FF48  48        PHA
FF49  8A        TXA
FF4A  48        PHA              save register
FF4B  98        TYA
FF4C  48        PHA
FF4D  BA        TSX
FF4E  BD 04 01  LDA $0104,X      get break-flag from stack
FF51  29 10     AND #$10         anc check
FF53  F0 03     BEQ $FF58        not set
FF55  6C 16 03  JMP ($0316)      BREAK-routine
FF58  6C 14 03  JMP ($0314)      interrupt-routine

*****************************
FF5B  20 18 E5  JSR $E518        initialize video-controller
FF5E  AD 12 D0  LDA $D012
FF61  D0 FB     BNE $FF5E
FF63  AD 19 D0  LDA $D019
FF66  29 01     AND #$01
FF68  8D A6 02  STA $02A6
FF6B  4C DD FD  JMP $FDDD

*****************************
FF6E  A9 81     LDA #$81
FF70  8D 0D DC  STA $DC0D
FF73  AD 0E DC  LDA $DC0E
FF76  29 80     AND #$80
FF78  09 11     ORA #$11
FF7A  8D 0E DC  STA $DC0E
FF7D  4C 8E EE  JMP $EE8E
FF80  00        BRK

*****************************   Jump-table for operating-
                                          system routines
FF81  4C 5B FF  JMP $FF5B        initialize CIAs
FF84  4C A3 FD  JMP $FDA3        clear or check RAM
FF87  4C 50 FD  JMP $FD50        initialize I/O
FF8A  4C 15 FD  JMP $FD15        initialize I/O vectors
FF8D  4C 1A FD  JMP $FD1A        set status
FF90  4C 18 FE  JMP $FE18        send LISTEN secondary adrs.
FF93  4C B9 ED  JMP $EDB9        send TALK secondary address
FF96  4C C7 ED  JMP $EDC7        set/get RAM-end
FF99  4C 25 FE  JMP $FE25        set/get RAM-start
FF9C  4C 34 FE  JMP $FE34        scan keyboard
FF9F  4C 87 EA  JMP $EA87        set IEC-bus time-out flag
FFA2  4C 21 FE  JMP $FE21        input from IEC-bus
FFA5  4C 13 EE  JMP $EE13        output to IEC-bus
FFA8  4C DD ED  JMP $EDDD        send UNTALK
FFAB  4C EF ED  JMP $EDEF        send UNLISTEN
FFAE  4C FE ED  JMP $EDFE        send LISTEN
FFB1  4C 0C ED  JMP $ED0C        send TALK
FFB4  4C 09 ED  JMP $ED09        get status
FFB7  4C 07 FE  JMP $FE07        set file parameter
FFBA  4C 00 FE  JMP $FE00        set filename parameter
FFBD  4C F9 FD  JMP $FDF9        $F34A OPEN
FFC0  6C 1A 03  JMP ($031A)      $F291 CLOSE
FFC3  6C 1C 03  JMP ($031C)
```

```
FFC6  6C 1E 03 JMP ($031E)     $F20E CHKIN set input device
FFC9  6C 20 03 JMP ($0320)     $F250 CKOUT set output device
FFCC  6C 22 03 JMP ($0322)     $F333 CLRCH
FFCF  6C 24 03 JMP ($0324)     $F157 BASIN input character
FFD2  6C 26 03 JMP ($0326)     $F1CA BSOUT output character
FFD5  4C 9E F4 JMP $F49E       LOAD
FFD8  4C DD F5 JMP $F5DD       SAVE
FFDB  4C E4 F6 JMP $F6E4       set time
FFDE  4C DD F6 JMP $F6DD       get time
FFE1  6C 28 03 JMP ($0328)     $F6ED scan STOP-key
FFE4  6C 2A 03 JMP ($032A)     $F13E GET
FFE7  6C 2C 03 JMP ($032C)     $F32F CLALL
FFEA  4C 9B F6 JMP $F69B       increase time
FFED  4C 05 E5 JMP $E505       SCREEN get # lines & columns
FFF0  4C 0A E5 JMP $E50A       set/get cursor position
FFF3  4C 00 E5 JMP $E500       get start of I/O element
FFF6  52 52 42 59

****************************   Hardware vectors
FFFA  43 FE     $FE43           NMI-vector
FFFC  E2 FC     $FCE2           RESET-vector
FFFE  48 FF     $FF48           IRQ-vector
```

APPENDIX B

A Short Introduction to Hexadecimal Arithmetic

Computers represent data in binary format. In the binary number system, a digit may take on a value of either 0 or 1. Each digit position in the binary number system has a value that is a power of 2, just as each digit position in the decimal number system has a value that is a power of 10.

BINARY NUMBER SYSTEM

Power of 2	7	6	5	4	3	2	1	0
Value	128	64	32	16	8	4	2	1

DECIMAL NUMBER SYSTEM

Power of 10	5	4	3	2	1	0
Value	100000	10000	1000	100	10	1

If you want to represent the decimal number 17 in the binary number system, you would use the string of binary digits 10001 which stands for:

$$
\begin{aligned}
& 1 \times 2^4 + 0 \times 2^3 + 0 \times 2^2 + 0 \times 2^1 + 1 \times 2^0 \\
= & \ 16 + 0 + 0 + 0 + 1 \\
= & \ 17
\end{aligned}
$$

Representing numbers as a string of binary digits (commonly called "bits") would look as shown:

Decimal	Binary	Decimal	Binary
0	0	13	1101
1	1	14	1110
2	10	15	1111
3	11	16	10000
4	100	17	10001
5	101	18	10010
6	110	19	10011
7	111	20	10100
8	1000	21	10101
9	1001	22	10110
10	1010	23	10111
11	1011	24	11000
12	1100	25	11001

Eight bits (remember - binary digits) is called a byte. A byte is the smallest accessible unit of data in the Commodore 64. Eight bits is capable of representing a value equivalent to decimal 255.

A string of eight bits however, is not very easy to read or write. Because they are awkward to interpret, bits are often represented in the hexadecimal numbering system (base 16). Each hexadecimal digits stands for four bits.

Hexadecimal notation uses 16 symbols to represent the 16 different values. These symbols are the numerals 0 thru 9 and the letter A thru F. Below is an equivalency chart:

DECIMAL	BINARY	HEXADECIMAL
0	0	0
1	1	1
2	10	2
3	11	3
4	100	4
5	101	5
6	110	6
7	111	7
8	1000	8
9	1001	9
10	1010	A
11	1011	B
12	1100	C
13	1101	D
14	1110	E
15	1111	F

To convert binary numbers to hexadecimal notation, divide the binary number into groups of four bits, starting at the right hand side. Replace each group of four bits by the corresponding hexadecimal symbol. If the left most group of bits is not a full four bits, then fill in with zeros. The example below illustrates this:

```
     10100110101101O110       =     (binary number)
0010/1001/1010/1101/0110      =     (4-bit groups)
   2    9    A    D    6            (hexadecimal number)
```

APPENDIX C

Summary of the Commodore 64

What are the features of the Commodore 64 that other computers don't offer? What makes its capabilities so different from the others? We'll attempt to summarize at this time.

The Commodore 64 is far from being a game only machine. It has ambitions that are far beyond those computers that offer color, graphics, and sound. It can be a computer for commercial use as well. With its graphics capabilities, you can get results that were formerly available only on much larger and more expensive computers. Yet even the micros of today will have a hard time competing against the Commodore. Through the use of BASIC 2, it is suitable for most applications. The beginner will be able to use it just as well as the experienced programmer. Since it can be programmed in assembler, there are excellent possibilities for expansion with the several assemblers already on the market.

Besides BASIC and assembler, there are other languages such as PILOT, PASCAL, LOGO, and FORTH currently available. In addition, a Z-80 card is available that makes it possible to use the CP/M operating system. CP/M is the world's most popular an operating system and opens a new level of programming and software applications to the Commodore 64 user.. This Z-80 card, for which the Commodore 64 already has a built-in slot, contains, as its name already implies, a Z-80 processor. It was to complement this processor that the 6510 was developed.

In addition to this card, there are 80-column cards which enable the Commodore 64 to display 80 character lines. This card is very useful for word processing.

Obviously you won't be left without support for your Commodore 64. Every day there are new developments. Others receently announced include graphics tablets, sketch pads such as the KOALA Pad, and voice synthesizers. Software support is also rapidly expanding to fill the void felt earlier.

Since the Commodore 64 has the ability to use other Commodore machine's software, you have a wide variety of software available. Considering its capabilities, the Commodore 64 is superior to other CBM/PET computers and the VIC-20 while being one of the least expensive on the market.

BASIC for the Commodore 64 is, as mentioned before, BASIC 2.

This BASIC is a version developed by Microsoft for Commodore. It is not only very capable, but also very easy to learn. The professional will like the first point; the beginner will appreciate the second.

There are some advantages to Commodore BASIC compared to other versions. For one thing, editing programs is very fast and efficient. In order to change a line, you simply move the cursor to the proper line, clear characters or whole words, insert new text if needed, and move to the next line by pressing RETURN. On pressing RETURN, the Commodore 64 determines if there is a program-line in the next line. If there is, BASIC automatically places the cursor at the beginning of the line. In a like manner you may go through your entire program making necessary changes. When editing is completed, press the CLR key clearing the screen and returning the cursor to HOME position.

This screen-oriented editor offers yet another advantage. After an error in direct mode input which is refused by a SYNTAX ERROR message, it is possible to bring the cursor back to this line, correct it, and then RETURN. This saves a considerable amount of retyping.

The third time the editor is useful is in loading programs from diskette. You move the cursor to the line containing the chosen program title (you must have called the index previously, of course, using LOAD"$",8), type LOAD over the number indicating blocks used, cursor to the end of the title and type ',8:'. On RETURN, the program is loaded. This procedure eliminates the possibility of FILE NOT FOUND errors common with mistyped titles, and again you are spared excessive typing.

Another advantage of the 64 is the option of using abbreviations for commands and statements. On the 64, a command may normally be given by typing the first letter of the word followed by a shifted second letter and pressing RETURN. For example, 'L' followed by SHIFT'I' is the replacement for LIST.

There are, of course, differences between the various versions of BASIC. In order to use programs that run on other computers, you must know these differences. One of the first is in clearing the screen. In every system, this command is different. In some it's called HOME, in others it's CLS, and some use CHR$. The 64 has two options.

The first is the input of a control character, CHR$(147). This control character issues the command to clear the screen. The other possibility is to insert a CLR command within a print instruction. On the screen you will see an inverse heart. This command has the same effect as the CHR$(147). It is used more often in Commodore listings.

Another difference is in the output of inverse text. There are systems that use an INVERSE/NORMAL command routine. Again, the 64 has two options. The first is to use CHR$(18); the second is to place RVS-ON in a print statement. To return to normal, the command is either CHR$(146) or including RVS-OFF in a print statement. On other machines, it may be the use of the command NORMAL.

Naturally other systems have an extended BASIC as well. There are, for instance, commands for a formatted number output (PRINT USING) or automatic error branching (ON ERROR or GOSUB). As you have found out while reading this book, it is not difficult to develop these routines yourself.

Following is a list of commands used by the Commodore 64:

CONT	RUN
LIST	SAVE
LOAD	VERIFY
NEW	

and statements:

CLOSE	GOSUB	PRINT
CLR	GOTO or GO TO	PRINT#
CMD	IF..THEN	READ
DATA	INPUT	REM
DEF FN	INPUT#	RESTORE
DIM	LET	RETURN
END	NEXT	STOP
FOR..TO..STEP	ON	SYS
GET	OPEN	WAIT
GET#	POKE	

Besides these, BASIC offers a great number of efficient mathematical functions, and it also contains string functions that allow convenient working with text.

APPENDIX D - Bibliography

Fisher, E. and Jensen, CW. PET AND THE IEEE 488 BUS. Berkeley, CA: Osborne/McGraw-Hill, 1980.

Leventhal, Lance and Saville, W. 6502 ASSEMBLY LANGUAGE SUBROUTINES. Berkeley, CA: Osborne/McGraw-Hill, 1982.

Leventhal, Lance. 6502 ASSEMBLY LANGUAGE PROGRAMMING. Berkeley, CA: Osborne/McGraw-Hill, 1979.

Osborne, A.; Strasma, J.; and Strasma, E. PET PERSONAL COMPUTER GUIDE. Berkeley, CA: Osborne/McGraw-Hill, 1982.

West, Raeto Collin. PROGRAMMING THE PET/CBM. Greensboro, NC: Level Limited, 1982.

Zaks, Rodney. 6502 APPLICATIONS BOOK. Berkeley, CA: Sybex, 1979.

OTHER BOOKS AVAILABLE:

The Anatomy of the Commodore 64 - is our insider's guide to your favorite computer. This book is a must for those of you who want to delve deep into your micro. This 300+ page book is full of information covering all aspects of the '64. Includes fully commented listing of the ROMs so you can investigate the mysteries of the BASIC interpreter, kernal and operating system. It offers numerous examples of machine language programming and several samples that make your programming sessions more enjoyable and useful.

ISBN# 0-916439-00-3 Available now: $19.95

The Anatomy of the 1541 Disk Drive - unravels the mysteries of working the the Commodore 1541 disk drive. This 320+ page book starts by explaining program, sequential and relative files. It covers the direct access commands, diskette structure, DOS operation and utilties. The fully commented ROM listings are presented for the real "hackers". Includes listings for several useful utilities including BACKUP, COPY, FILE PROTECTOR, DIRECTORY. This is the authoritive source for 1541 disk drive information.

ISBN# 0-916439-01-1 Available now: $19.95

The Machine Language Book of the Commodore 64 - is aimed at the Commodore 64 owner who wants to progress beyond BASIC. If you want to write programs that run faster, use less memory or perform functions not available in BASIC, then this book will help you learn machine language. Included are listings for three full length programs: a working assembler so you can create your own machine language program; a disassembler so you can inspect other machine language programs; and a 6510 simulator so that you can "see" the operation of the processor.

ISBN# 0-916439-02-X Available now: $14.95
Optional program diskette: $14.95

Tricks & Tips for the Commodore 64 - presents a collection of easy-to-use programming techniques and hints. Chapters cover advanced graphics, easy data entry, enhancements for advanced BASIC, CP/M, connecting to the outside world and more. Other tips include sorting, variable dumps, and POKEs that do tricks. All-in-all a solid set of useful features.

ISBN# 0-916439-03-8 Available June 29th $19.95

OTHER TITLES COMING SOON!!!